W9-BLZ-613

SCHOOL LAW CASEBOOK SERIES — NO. 5

The Law Governing School Board Members and School Board Meetings

By

LEE O. GARBER

and

NEWTON EDWARDS

The Interstate
Printers and Publishers
Danville, Illinois

CONTENTS

INTRODUCTION

This publication is the first of four proposed books which, taken together, may be thought of as a second cycle of casebooks. The first cycle of four School Law Casebooks provides a complete coverage of one-half of a comprehensive course in School Law. They deal with "The Public School in Our Governmental Structure," "The Law Relating to the Creation, Alteration, and Dissolution of School Districts," "The Law Governing Teaching Personnel," and "The Law Governing Pupils."

The second cycle of four proposed casebooks will provide a complete coverage of the last half of a comprehensive course in School Law. Like those already in print, this book and those to follow will provide a welcome addition to the materials available for the teaching of School Law.

The authors of the books forming the first cycle have prepared this book and are currently engaged in the preparation of the other three in the second cycle. They need no introduction. Newton Edwards, the pioneer in the field of School Law, is the author of the leading textbook in the field—*The Courts and the Public Schools.* Lee O. Garber is the author of the *Yearbooks of School Law,* an annual publication since 1950. He has also authored other books in School Law and has served as a regular contributor to *The Nation's Schools* for over a decade, having written approximately 150 articles on School Law for that journal.

Russell L. Guin
Publisher

AUTHORS' PREFACE

This, another in the series of School Law Casebooks, follows the same general pattern as do the others. It contains two main sections—"Legal Principles" and "Court Decisions." The decisions have been carefully selected to illustrate the basic legal principles mentioned in the first section.

While this is the fifth in the series of casebooks, it is the first of a group of four that will cover the material generally included in the second half or second semester of a course in "School Law." The first four give a coverage of the first half or first semester of such a course.

It is hoped that these casebooks will serve to supplement the material currently available for students of School Law. In addition, it is hoped that they will meet a need for legal material appropriate for certain specialized courses in School Administration.

Again the authors wish to point out that the legal principles mentioned are not exhaustive. For the sake of brevity they have been carefully selected on the basis of their importance as well as their uniform acceptance by the courts. This does not mean that all courts will, necessarily, accept each principle isolated. Deviations will occur, but to mention them is impractical in a book of this sort.

To the instructor who does not have the time to consider all cases included, a selection is possible. This is because a number of cases illustrate more than one legal principle.

Lee O. Garber
Newton Edwards

I.

LEGAL PRINCIPLES

THE LAW GOVERNING SCHOOL BOARD MEMBERS AND SCHOOL BOARD MEETINGS

Status of School Board Members

The powers and duties conferred by statute upon school districts are exercised by their legally constituted officers, the boards of education. Members of a board of education represent the state. They act in the performance of a state function, and they are state officers. School board members are not municipal officers even though they may have been appointed by the mayor and/or city council. The status of an officer is not determined by the method of his appointment but by the nature of his duties. County superintendents of schools have frequently been held to be state officers, although in some instances they have been held to be county officers.

Where the statutes require that school board members or other school officers meet certain eligibility requirements, it is the general rule that these requirements do not have to be met at the time of appointment or election; it is sufficient if they are met at the time of induction into office. School offices may be incompatible with other offices because they are made so by statute, or because the performance of the duties of one interferes with the performance of the duties of the other. The common law rule is that when an officer accepts an incompatible office he *ipso facto* relinquishes the first office.

A school official may perform the duties of the office for a time even though his title to the office is defective. He may not be a *de jure* officer but under certain circumstances the courts may regard him as a *de facto* officer. A school board member who, under color of appointment or election to the office, performs its duties with the general acquiescence of the public long enough to give rise to the reasonable assumption that he is the officer he represents himself as being, will be held to be a *de facto* officer. Public policy requires that the acts of a *de facto* officer, until he is removed from office by the proper procedure, be regarded as legally binding as the acts of a *de jure* officer.

Statutes frequently provide that a school board member shall hold office until a legal successor qualifies for the office, but even in the absence of such a statute the courts commonly hold that the school board member may hold over. A school board member may resign his office but he may not do so before he is duly qualified. An unconditional resignation, one to take effect immediately, cannot be withdrawn. But a conditional resignation, one to take effect at some future time, may be withdrawn at any time before being acted upon. A temporary removal of a board member from the district does not vacate the office unless the circumstances surrounding the case clearly indicate his intent to relinquish the office. A school board member who has been appointed or elected for a fixed term may not be removed from office without a notice of the charges against him and an opportunity to be heard in his own defense.

When a school board member is in active possession of his office, public policy requires that he be accepted as the officer he represents himself as being until he is removed from the office by proper legal proceedings. A school board member cannot be enjoined from acting on the ground that his title to office is defective. The courts will never, through the issuance of injunctions, determine disputes with respect to title to office. The law provides a special action for the determination of title to office. This action is an action in the nature of *quo warranto* brought by the state through its attorney general or state's attorney. This action is a prerogative of the state. It may not be brought by a private individual who has no interest in the matter different from that of the public in general.

School boards are agencies of the state, created by it to carry out its educational policies in local communities. They possess no inherent powers nor are any powers conferred upon them by the local community. Whatever authority a school board may possess, it is authority which has been delegated to it by the state. The courts are agreed that a school board may exercise the following powers and no others: (1) those which have been expressly conferred upon it by statute, (2) those which may be fairly implied from express grants, and (3) those which are essential to the accomplishment of the purposes for which the board was created. Here again the courts apply the principle of strict construction. If there is any doubt with respect to the authority of a school board to act, the doubt will be resolved against the board, and the authority will be denied. The courts will not, by a too liberal interpretation of the statutes, confer authority on school boards; to do so would be to usurp the legislative function.

The courts are cautious in interpreting the powers of boards of education, but once authority to act has been recognized, discretion in the exercise of it will not be controlled by the courts unless clearly abused. When called upon to review the discretion of a school board, the courts will inquire whether the board acted within the scope of its authority, whether it followed the procedures prescribed by statute, and whether it had some reasonable basis for its action. The court will not reweigh the evidence to determine where the preponderance of the evidence lies; it will examine the evidence only to determine whether the board acted arbitrarily and unreasonably. And if the evidence is such that reasonable men might disagree with respect to the conclusion to be drawn from it, the action of the board will be sustained. The board's action will be overruled only when it has acted arbitrarily, unreasonably, under an erroneous theory of the law, or without any substantial basis of fact.

A board of education must itself exercise the authority imposed upon it by statute where the exercise of such authority involves judgment or discretion. A board may delegate to a committee of its own members or to the superintendent authority to make recommendations, but if the final action involves the exercise of judgment and discretion, it must be taken by the board. The board does, however, have the authority to delegate to others the performance of a purely ministerial function. A board of education does not have the authority to limit the free exercise of its judgment and discretion by prior announcement of policy, promise, or agreement. When the time comes for a board to act, public policy requires that it be untrammeled by any previous commitments. Those to whom such promises or commitments are made are presumed to know that the board is merely giving expression to its present intent and that it may later change its policy.

Conducting School Board Meetings

A school board is a legal entity and must act as such; action taken by board members acting separately is not the action of the board and is without legal force. All the members of a board of education must be given actual or constructive notice of any meeting of the board; otherwise the action taken by the board will not be legal. Where the statutes or the rules of the board provide that the board shall meet at certain designated times, the board members have constructive notice and no further notice is necessary. In case all the members of a board are present and consent to act, the necessity of notice is waived.

Under the common law a simple majority of the board is a legal quorum. A board has no authority to change the common law rule under a statute which authorizes it to establish its own rules of procedure. A quorum must be present in order for a board to take legal action. But in the absence of a statute which stipulates otherwise, the majority of the quorum is not necessary to pass a measure. Where a quorum is present, a motion is carried by a majority of those voting on it. The law assumes that those who refrain from voting are willing to be bound by those who do vote. Of course, if the statutes provide that a measure must be carried by a majority of the board or of those present, the statutes must be followed. The same general rule applies to blank ballots. It is commonly held that blank ballots are to be considered a nullity—they are not to be counted for or against a measure, nor are they to be counted in ascertaining the number of ballots cast. A board of education is free to change its policies as circumstances may dictate. It may, therefore, rescind any action it has taken before vested rights have accrued to third parties. Rules and regulations of school boards have the binding force of law and may not be changed by the board where vested rights have accrued to third parties who have relied upon them. Rules of a school board which relate merely to parliamentary procedure may be changed at any time.

A school board should, of course, keep a record of its actions, but in the absence of statute requiring that it do so, failure to keep a record of an action does not render the action void. In some instances, it has been held that a record is not necessary although the statutes require it—the statutes are regarded as directory rather than mandatory. Where a school board keeps a record, the record is *prima facie* evidence of the action taken by the board. It is, in fact, the only evidence of the action taken by the board. The rule is well established that where the records of a board are clear, oral or extrinsic evidence is inadmissible to vary, contradict, or subtract from them. But oral or extrinsic evidence is admissible to clarify the meaning of a record that is indefinite or obscure, and to supply omissions in a record; action taken at a lawful meeting will not be rendered void because no record of it is kept. A school board may amend its records to make them speak the truth, but this cannot be done to the prejudice of third parties who had relied upon them.

II.

COURT DECISIONS

COURT DECISIONS

1. "Members of a board of education . . . act in the performance of a state function, and they are state officers" (p. 3).

PEOPLE v. PELLER,
34 Ill. App. (2d) 372, 181 N. E. (2d) 376 (1962)
(Decided by the Appellate Court of Illinois)

[The facts of this case are to be found in the first paragraph of the material which follows. The lower court ruled in favor of plaintiffs, and the higher court upheld the decision of the lower court. In so holding, the court commented on the legal status of school board members.]

BURKE, Justice.

Plaintiffs are residents and taxpayers of the area comprising School District 89 and have children who attend a school of the district. Defendants are members of the Board of Education of the district and govern and administer the schools within the district. On April 4, 1960, at a designated time and place previously consented to by the defendants for the inspection of the financial records of the Board of Education of the district for the years 1955 through 1960, the plaintiffs were refused the right to make photographic reproduction thereof. They had brought a professional photographer with them to enable them to photographically reproduce the records. In their pleadings plaintiffs allege the right to photograph the records under the common law as well as pursuant to the State Records Act, Sec. 43.7, Ch. 116, Ill. Rev. Stat. 1959. The pleadings present the issue whether relators have the right to photograph the records. From the judgment that a writ of mandamus issue commanding the defendants to permit relators to examine and reproduce by photographic means the financial records of expenditures and receipts of the Board for the years 1955 to 1960, inclusive, the defendants appeal.

Defendants insist that the State Records Act does not apply to them. They concede the right of relators to inspect the records and take copies thereof when necessary to the attainment of justice. They deny the right of relators to photograph the records for the period mentioned. We are of the opinion that the State Records Act applies to members of a Board of Education and to the public records in custody of the members and the Board. A Board of Education is an agency of the state government. . . . As an agency of the state government the nature and status of the Board of Education is administrative. . . . The Board of Education executes and administers the law promulgated by the Legislature. The Board of Education is an executive administrative agency of the state. Inasmuch as it is an agency of the state government and its members public officers of the state government, Sec. 43.7 of the State Records Act applies to permit the relators to photograph the records of the Board of Education.

Guides for Class Discussion

1. Are you in agreement with the court's thinking regarding the status of school board members?
2. In addition to commenting on the status of school board members, the court commented on the corporate status of the board. What did it say in this connection?

2. *"School board members are not municipal officers, even though they may have been appointed by the mayor and/or city council"* (p. 3).

HAM v. THE MAYOR, ALDERMEN AND COMMONALTY OF THE CITY OF NEW YORK,
70 N.Y. 459 (1877)
(Decided by the Court of Appeals of New York)

[This action was brought against the City of New York to recover damages resulting from the negligence of an employee of the department of public instruction. Plaintiff operated a store where he sold carriages and harness. The department of public instruction occupied the upper part of the same building where it operated a normal school. Plaintiff alleged his stock was damaged when dirty and foul water ran down into his store due to the fact the water-closets located in the area occupied by the school were "defectively constructed, and negligently used." He contended the city was liable for damages which resulted from the negligence of the school's employees. The trial court ruled in his favor, but the Superior Court, on appeal, overruled the trial court. When this appeal was taken to the Court of Appeals, it upheld the Superior Court and ruled in favor of the city on the ground that the person whose negligence was alleged was not an employee of the city.]

MILLER, J. The liability of the defendant in this action rests upon the principle that it is responsible for the negligent act of its servants, under the doctrine of *respondeat superior,* which is based upon the right of the employer to select his servants, to discharge them if careless, unskillful or incompetent, and to direct and control them while in his employ. This rule has no application where the power referred to does not exist. . . .

The application of the rule referred to in this case depends upon the question whether the power to discharge, direct and control, existed and is the main point which is now to be determined. This of necessity involves an inquiry as to the relation which existed between the defendant and the department of public instruction, which, by virtue of chapter 574, S. L. of 1871, §7, was created a branch of the government of the city of New York "to have the same powers and discharge the same duties which are now vested in the board of education in said city."

The latter board was a corporation authorized to hold property for educational purposes, and was vested with the management of the schools, and control over the school buildings. . . .

. . . Whether it [the school corporation] was a corporate body is not material, for although formally constituted a department of the municipal government, the duties which it was required to discharge were not local or corporate, but related and belonged to an important branch of the administrative department of the State government. Although the commissioners were appointed by the mayor, they were vested with full power and authority to manage and control the educational interests of the entire municipality, and to appoint all subordinate officers and employes who were subject to their government and control exclusively, and were their servants and subordinates. The commissioners, in the discharge of their functions, were not amenable to the corporation in any respect, and those who were in their employ as servants and subordinates were subject to the commissioners, bound to obey their orders and directions, and the defendant had no authority whatever either to employ, manage, control and direct their action, or to remove or discharge them for unskillfulness or neglect of duty. Having no right either to select or to remove, as already seen, the rule of *respondeat superior* could not well be applied. To render the corporation liable for the acts of officers or agents, they must necessarily have been its agents and servants, selected or appointed, and liable to be removed by, and responsible to the corporation for the manner in which they should discharge the trust reposed in them; and even when represented or elected by the corporation, it is only when the duties relate to the exercise of corporate power, and is for the benefit of the corporation that they are servants and agents within the maxim referred to. If only elected or appointed in accordance with the mandates of the law to perform a duty which is neither local or corporate, and if they are independent of the corporation in the tenure of their office, and the mode of discharging its duties, they are not servants or agents of the corporation, but public or State officers, with such powers and duties as the statute prescribes, and no action lies against the corporation for their acts or negligence.

Guides for Class Discussion

1. On what ground can it be argued that school officers are state and not municipal officers?
2. Do you think the court today would hold as it did in 1877? Give reasons.
3. To what extent was this case governed by statute? By principles of common law?

3. *"The status of an officer is not determined by the method of his appointment but by the nature of his duties" (p. 3).*

STATE EX REL. WALKER v. BUS,
135 Mo. 325, 36 S.W. 636 (1896)
(Decided by the Supreme Court of Missouri)

[This was a proceeding in *quo warranto* to test the title of one acting as a school board member to the office he alleged belonged to him. In 1893 he was elected a director of the public schools of St. Louis for a term of four years. The territory of the school district of the city of St. Louis was coterminous with that of the city of St. Louis, and the board members were elected by the qualified voters of the city. In January, 1895, defendant was appointed a deputy sheriff of the city of St. Louis and continued to serve and hold that position until April 10, 1895, when he resigned. After his appointment, acceptance, and qualification as deputy sheriff he continued to act as a school director. One of the questions before the court was whether he had the authority to act as school director, or whether the acceptance of the office of deputy sheriff automatically acted as a relinquishment of the office of school director.

[The charter of the public school system stated that no member of the board of aldermen or board of delegates, or any other person holding an office under the city of St. Louis, could become a member of the board of school directors of the city. The state constitution also provided that, in cities or counties having more than 200,000 inhabitants, no person could, at the same time, be a state officer and an officer of any county, city, or other municipality, and that no person could at the same time fill two municipal offices either in the same or different municipalities. The court ruled that the two positions or offices with which this case was concerned were not incompatible and refused to oust defendant from the office of school director. In arriving at this decision the court found it necessary to discuss the nature of public office and, in so doing, pointed out that the status of a public officer was not determined by the method of his appointment.]

MacFarlane, J. . . .

. . . .

From what has been said, it follows that if the position of school director and deputy sheriff are incompatible public offices, or if the constitution or statute prohibits both positions to be held by the same person at the same time, then an acceptance of the office of deputy sheriff operated as a resignation of the office of school director. The subsequent resignation of the former office by respondent would not restore him to the latter. If the office of director became vacant, respondent "could not put himself back into it by his own act." State v. Goff, 15 R. I. 508, 509, 9 Atl. 226.

A public office is defined to be "the right, authority, and duty, created and conferred by law, by which, for a given period, either fixed by law or enduring at the pleasure of the creating power, an individual is invested with some portion of the sovereign functions of the government, to be exercised by him for the benefit of the public." Mechem, Pub. Off. 1. The individual who is invested with the authority, and is required to perform the duties, is a public officer. The courts have undertaken to give definitions in many cases; and while these have been controlled more or less by laws of the particular jurisdictions, and the powers conferred and duties enjoined thereunder, still all agree substantially that if an officer receives his authority from the law, and discharges some of the functions of government, he will be a public officer. . . . Deputy sheriffs are appointed by the sheriff, subject to the approval of the judge of the circuit courts. They are required to take the oath of office, which is to be indorsed upon the appointment, and filed in the office of the clerk of the circuit court. After appointment and qualification, they "shall possess all the powers and may perform any of the duties prescribed by law to be performed by the sheriff." Rev. St. 1889, § § 8181, 8182. The right, authority, and duty are thus created by statute. He is invested with some portions of the sovereign functions of the government, to be exercised for the benefit of the public, and is, consequently, a "public officer," within any definition given by the courts or text writers. *It can make no difference that the appointment is made by the sheriff,* or that it is in the nature of an employment, or that the compensation may be fixed by contract. The power of appointment comes from the state; the authority is derived from the law; and the duties are exercised for the benefit of the public. Chief Justice Marshall defines a public office to be "a public charge or employment." U. S. v. Maurice, 2 Brock, 96, Fed. Cas. No. 15, 747. Whether a public employment constitutes the employé a public officer depends upon the source of the powers and the character of the duties. [Emphasis supplied.]

Guides for Class Discussion

1. Compare this case with *Pruitt* v. *Glen Rose Independent School District, infra.*
2. How did the court define "public officer"? Are you in agreement?

4. *"County superintendents of schools have frequently been held to be state officers, although in some instances they have been held to be county officers"* (p. 3).

MATHEW V. ELLIS,
214 Ga. 665, 107 S. E. (2d) 181 (1959)
(Decided by the Supreme Court of Georgia)

[The facts of this case will be found in the first paragraph of the following quotation.]

CANDLER, Justice.
This is a mandamus proceeding, and the only question presented for decision is whether or not the Board of County Commissioners in and for Jeff Davis County are authorized to have the books and accounts of the Superintendent of Schools in and for that county audited and to compel him to produce them for such purpose. The trial judge held that the board had such authority, and ordered the defendant, as the county's superintendent of schools, to produce his records for such purpose. The exception is to that judgment. . . .

The Code (Ann.) § 23-1301, provides: "The ordinary, or commissioners of roads and revenues in the counties having such commissioners, are authorized, whenever they deem it necessary to do so, to employ an expert accountant to examine and report on the books, vouchers, and accounts of any county officer whose duty it is under the law to handle county funds. . . ." The county superintendent of schools is a *county officer* [emphasis added] who handles county funds and he is the legal custodian of all county school records. . . . The present board of commissioners for Jeff Davis County was created by an act which the legislature passed in 1958. . . . By section 10 of that act the newly created board was required to have the books and accounts of the county superintendent of schools and other specified county officers audited immediately after the act became effective and annually thereafter by a certified public accountant; and there is no merit in the defendant's contention that this section of the act offends article 1, section 4, paragraph 1 of the Constitution of 1945 which provides that laws of a general nature shall have uniform operation throughout the state, and no special law shall be enacted in any case for which provision has been made by an existing general law. The attacked section is not, as the defendant contends, in conflict with Code, § § 40-1811 and 40-1812, which require the State Auditing Department to thoroughly audit and check the books and accounts of the county superintendent of schools; but even if it were, the legislature has authority under article 6, section 17, paragraph 1 of the Constitution of 1945 . . . to create county commissioners in such counties as may require them, and define their duties. . . .

Judgment affirmed.

Guides for Class Discussion

1. See *State ex rel. Walker* v. *Bus, supra;* and *People* v. *Peller, supra.*
2. Does the fact that the court here spoke of the county superintendent as a county officer mean that, under different circumstances, it might not have held that he was a state officer?
3. From this decision, may it be concluded that the courts are in agreement that all superintendents are officers rather than employees?

5. *"Where the statutes require that school board members or other school officers meet certain eligibility requirements, it is the general rule that these requirements do not have to be met at the time of appointment or election; it is sufficient if they are met at the time of induction into office"* (p. 3).

BRADFIELD V. AVERY,
161 Idaho 769, 102 P. 687 (1909)
(Decided by the Supreme Court of Idaho)

[In this case one question before the court was whether the requirements of a particular statute that listed the qualifications for eligibility to the office of county superintendent must be met at the time one is elected to office or whether it is sufficient if one elected meets them before taking office. In ruling on this matter, the court, after canvassing the problem carefully, held that all that was required by the statute in question was that the requirements be met before one takes office.]

STEWART, J.

. . . .

. . . The only statutory provision in this state which attempts to prescribe the qualifications of a county superintendent is section 585, Rev. Codes, as follows: "Provided, that no person shall be eligible to the office of county superintendent of public instruction except a first grade practical teacher of not less than two years' experience in Idaho, one of which must have been while holding a valid first grade certificate issued by a county superintendent, and the holder of a first grade certificate at the time of his election or appointment, nor unless twenty-five years of age."

The serious question in this case is to determine whether by the language used in the above section the Legislature intended to prescribe and fix the capability or fitness of a person to be elected to the office of county superintendent, or intended to fix and determine the capability and qualification of such person to hold such office after election. The word "eligibility," as used in connection with an office or the person to be elected to fill an office, has been variously defined by the courts and various constructions given to the use of such word with reference to whether the same applies to the election to office or the induction into office. The authorities upon both sides of this question are cited in 29 Cyc. 1376, and 10 Ency. of Law, pp. 970, 971. We are satisfied that the better reason is with the proposition that where the word "eligibility" is used in connection with an office, and there are no explanatory words indicating that such word is used with reference to the time of election, it has reference to the qualification to hold the office rather than the qualification to be elected to the office. . . . It will be observed that the language of the statute above quoted is "no person shall be eligible to the office" and not "eligible to be elected to the office." "Eligible to the office" clearly implies the qualification or capacity to hold the office, and clearly indicates the intent of the Legislature to use the word "eligible" in the sense that it applies to the capacity or qualification of the person to hold the office. While it is true that the word "eligible" may mean capable of being chosen, fit to be chosen, subject to selection, and applies to the time of selection or election, yet, where such meaning is not clearly indicated by the manner in which the word is used or by the qualifications or modifications thereof, we think it naturally applies to one's fitness or qualification to hold the office. . . . Had the statute read "eligible to be elected to the office," then it would have been clear that the qualification had reference to the capability of the person to be elected, but where the language is "shall be eligible to the office," and then follow attainments, the result of experience, and education, it seems to us the Legislature was intending to deal with the fitness of a person to hold the office rather than the capability of one to be elected to such office.

Guides for Class Discussion

1. Do you think the court furthered the ends of equity, justice, and fair dealing by holding as it did? Give reasons.
2. As a result of this decision may it be concluded that all statutes relating to qualifications of public officers will be satisfied if those elected as such meet statutory requirements at the time they take over the office rather than at the time of election?

6. *"School offices may be incompatible with other offices because they are made so by statute, or because the performance of the duties of one interferes with the performance of the duties of the other"* (p. 3).

ADAMS v. COMMONWEALTH,
268 S. W. (2d) 930 (Ky.) (1954)
(Decided by the Court of Appeals of Kentucky)

[This was an action brought in the name of, and by the authority of, the Attorney General, to determine whether the office of member of the county board of education is incompatible with the office of county election commissioner. Defendant, appellant here, had been a member of the county board of education of Letcher County. Later, he was appointed to and discharged some of the duties of the office of county election commissioner. The lower court held the two offices were incompatible and that defendant, by accepting the latter, had forfeited his right to the first-mentioned office, and defendant appealed.]

CULLEN, Commissioner.

. . . .

There are two kinds of incompatibility between offices which have been recognized and applied in declaring the first office vacant upon acceptance of the latter. The first is a constitutional or statutory incompatibility, which is one so declared by the Constitution or legislative enactment. The second is a common-law or functional incompatibility, which is declared by courts without the aid of specific constitutional or statutory prohibition when the two offices are inherently inconsistent or repugnant, or when the occupancy of the two offices is detrimental to the public interest. . . . The constitutional and statutory enumerations of incompatible offices are not the exclusive instances of incompatibility. . . .

Without elaboration, we will mention that there is no constitutional or statutory incompatibility in the case before us . . . , unless the office of member of the county board of election commissioners is in law a local office as distinguished from a state office. We consider it unnecessary to pass on this question, because we think it is clear that the two offices are functionally incompatible, in that the occupancy of both offices by the same person is detrimental to the public interest.

Ordinarily, the courts look to the legislature for declarations of public policy or of the public interest. Upon examining the legislative enactments relating to boards of education, we find running through them a clear expression of policy that such board members shall be divorced from political considerations.

KRS 160.200 provides that elections for school board members shall be in the even-numbered years, the apparent purpose being to separate these elections from the regular elections for state and county offices. KRS 160.230 prohibits any party emblem on the school board ballot. KRS 160.250 forbids disclosing to the voters the political affiliation of any candidate for school board. KRS 160.180 (1) (d), in prohibiting a school board member from holding any office "under the city or county of his residence," indicates the legislative intent that school board members shall not take part as officers in local government affairs.

If a school board member would be permitted to serve as a member of the county board of election commissioners, he would be participating actively in elections as the representative of a particular political party, since he must be nominated by his party in order to serve. . . . He would be required to pass upon the election of his fellow school board members. In serving as an election commissioner, a school board member necessarily would become involved in local government affairs, contrary to the spirit of KRS 160.180 (1) (d), and would become involved in regular state and county elections. . . .

We think the lower court correctly held that the offices are incompatible.

Guides for Class Discussion

1. Do you agree with the court that the two offices were incompatible? Give reasons.
2. On what grounds did the court consider the two offices incompatible?

7. *"The common law is that when an officer accepts an incompatible office he ipso facto relinquishes the first office"* (p. 3).

Pruitt v. Glen Rose Independent School District,
126 Tex. 45, 84 S.W. (2d) 1004 (1935)
(Decided by the Commission of Appeals of Texas)

[This case involved the liability of sureties on the bond of a defaulting school district tax collector—one Perry Kugle. On November 5, 1928, Kugle was elected sheriff and tax collector for Somervell County, Texas. On October 23, 1928, the trustees of Glen Rose Independent School District appointed him as collector of taxes for the school district. On November 8, 1928—three days after having been elected as sheriff and tax collector for the county—he executed a bond guaranteeing his faithful performance of the duties as school district tax collector in the amount of $6,000. (Pruitt was one of the sureties.) On the same day he took the required oath of office and entered upon the discharge of his duties. He collected the taxes for the district from that date until April 30, 1931, during which time he defaulted in the amount of some $600. On January 1, 1929, Kugle took the oath of office and made bond as county sheriff and tax collector. In the fall of 1930, his term of office having expired, he was re-elected as sheriff and tax collector, and on January 1, 1931, he took the oath and again made bond. Following his defalcation, the district brought suit against Kugle and his sureties to collect the amount due it. In the trial court the district received a verdict in the amount of $635.25. Sureties appealed and the Court of Civil Appeals affirmed the decision of the lower court. Sureties then again appealed and the court found in their favor. It held that the two jobs being incompatible, Kugle's qualification as county sheriff and tax collector automatically acted as a relinquishment of the position as school district tax collector, the one for which he first qualified.]

RYAN, Commissioner.

. . . .

Here, we have two separate taxing bodies with two separate assessing officers and two separate tax collectors, their duties separate and distinct. . . .

The Court of Civil Appeals correctly held that the tax collector of this particular district and the tax collector of the county are therefore two separate and distinct offices, each of emolument . . . , and when Kugle qualified as county tax collector, he automatically forfeited his right to the office of collector for the school district, because the holding of both said offices at the same time by the same person is within the prohibition of article 16, § 40, of our State Constitution.

If a person holding an office is elected or appointed to another (where the two offices cannot be legally held by the same person) and he accepts and qualifies as to the second, such acceptance and qualification operate, ipso facto, as a resignation of the former office. . . .

Therefore, the term of office as district collector ended automatically on January 1, 1929, when the term as county tax collector began, and the obligation of the district collector's sureties likewise ended as to his future acts as such, unless the term as district collector continued, notwithstanding, because of article 16, § 17, of the Constitution, which states that all officers within this state shall continue to perform the duties of their offices until their successors shall be duly qualified.

It is argued that Kugle remained at least the de facto collector for the district and the liability of his sureties continued even after he became county tax collector and had therefore ceased being the de jure district collector.

In Odem v. Sinton Independent School District (Tex. Com. App.) 234 S. W. 1090, 1092, one G. L. Cellum, city assessor and collector of the city of Sinton, was selected by the school board to assess and collect taxes for the school district. He undertook to assess the taxes in the district. Proceedings were begun by certain taxpayers of the district to enjoin the collection of the school tax. Cellum never took the oath or gave bond as district assessor and collector, being doubtful whether he could hold both offices, the Attorney General in the meantime having ruled he could not hold both offices at the same time. Presiding Judge Taylor, of the Commission of Appeals, said: "It is clear that Cellum could not hold his office as city assessor and collector, and at the same time act as de facto assessor and collector of the school district. The Constitution prohibits the holding and exercise of two such offices. Section 40, art. 16, Constitution of Texas. He could not hold or exercise both offices in either a de jure or de facto capacity."

. . . .

We therefore reject the contention that liability of Kugle's sureties on the district bond continued after he qualified as county tax collector, for acts thereafter committed.

Guides for Class Discussion

1. Do you agree that Kugle, after taking office as county sheriff and tax collector, did not continue in a de facto capacity to occupy the position of school district collector? Give reasons.

2. Do you think the fact that Kugle was elected to the county position before he was appointed to the district position had or should have had any bearing on this case? Why or why not?

8. "*A school officer may perform the duties of the office for a time even though his title to the office is defective. He may not be a de jure officer but under certain circumstances the courts may regard him as a de facto officer*" (p. 3).

HAZLETON-MOFFIT SPECIAL SCHOOL DISTRICT v. WARD,
107 N. W. (2d) 636 (N.D.) (1961)
(Decided by the Supreme Court of North Dakota)

[This was an action in mandamus brought by the Hazleton-Moffit Special School District, against the board members and officers of two former school districts, to require them to turn over to petitioner all the properties and assets in their hands that belonged to the former districts. It was alleged that these districts lost their existence by virtue of having been incorporated into the petitioner district as a result of reorganization. The respondents denied the existence of petitioner district and questioned the legality of the reorganization proceedings. They based their case, in part, on the contention that the county committee, "purporting to perform pursuant to statute," was not legally constituted and that the county superintendent was not in legal possession of the office because he did not meet the statutory requirements for office.]

TEIGEN, Judge.

.   .   .   .

The second category of the respondents' answer attacks the legality of the county committee and the legality of the county superintendent of schools. They attack the legality of the county committee on the ground that certain members thereof who acted with the remaining members of the committee on the reorganization plan in question were not legally selected for their positions for the reason that they were appointed thereto by the county superintendent of schools who, it is argued, had no right to make such appointment for the reason that a vacancy did not exist, it being the contention of the appellants that the expiration of a term of a county committeeman did not create a vacancy as contemplated by [statute]. . . . The right of the county superintendent of schools elected to hold office is attacked on the ground that he did not possess the educational requirements; he did not possess a first grade professional certificate with a major or minor in education, as [required]. . . . The facts of the challenge are admitted in the stipulation. However, it is clearly established by the evidence that the county committee, including the county committeemen whose right to office is challenged, and the county superintendent of schools, did in fact carry out the respective duties of their offices as provided in the reorganization of school districts Act. These officers are not parties to this action. It is admitted they exercised the functions of public office, were in possession thereof, and discharged their duties under color of authority. They were at least de facto officers. . . .

As de facto officers, under the wise provisions of the law every act done in the capacity of the office was valid and effective. . . .

As such they were clothed with all the rights and powers that they would have enjoyed as a de jure officer possessed of every qualification.

Guides for Class Discussion

1. Compare this decision with *Green Mountain School District* v. *Durkee, infra.*
2. Compare this decision with *State* v. *Russell, infra.*
3. What criteria did the court set up for determining whether an officer was, at least, a *de facto* officer?

9. *"A school board member who, under color of appointment or election to the office, performs its duties with the general acquiescence of the public long enough to give rise to the reasonable assumption that he is the officer he represents himself as being, will be held to be a de facto officer"* (p. 3).

STATE V. RUSSELL,
162 Ohio 254, 122 N. E. (2d) 780 (1954)
(Decided by the Supreme Court of Ohio)

[In an action to oust a superintendent of schools from office, it was contended that his appointment was illegal because he received the vote of only three members of a five-man board, and one of the three was not qualified. The member in question, one Ankrim, had been appointed by the Court of Probate, when four members on the board, because of some dissension, failed to appoint a fifth member to fill a vacancy caused by resignation. It was contended that the appointment by the court was invalid because it was made under the wrong statute. The Supreme Court held that, while the board member was a *de facto* officer, the election of the superintendent was legal.]

WEYGANDT, Chief Justice.

. . . .

To . . . [the] contention of the relator the respondent offers several pertinent comments. One of these is that, irrespective of which statute determined the duration of Ankrim's service as a *de jure* board member, he was at least a *de facto* member . . . and hence entitled to vote in favor of the appointment of the respondent as superintendent on November 30.

This court concurs in that view.

The Court of Probate was acting within its authority when it appointed Ankrim a member of the county board on October 3, 1953; Ankrim accepted the appointment; under color of authority he continued to discharge the duties of the office for the unexpired term; it is alleged that two board members protested against his incumbency; there is no allegation of protest on the part of the other two board members; there is no allegation that anyone was elected or was even a candidate for the unexpired term; except for his vote in favor of the respondent, there is no allegation that any of Ankrim's official actions have been attacked; nor is there a claim that some other person was entitled to the office for the unexpired term.

It has been said that the doctrine of *de facto* officers rests on the principle of protection to the interests of the public and third parties, not to protect or vindicate the acts or rights of the particular *de facto* officer or the claims or rights of rival claimants to the particular office. The law validates the acts of *de facto* officers as to the public and third persons on the ground that, although not officers *de jure,* they are, in virtue of the particular circumstances, officers in fact whose acts public policy requires should be considered valid. . . .

The instant case provides a typical example of such a situation. For months the Board of Education of Lawrence County had failed to perform its duty to fill the existing vacancy in its membership. The appointment of Ankrim enabled the board to function again, and this resulted in the selection of the respondent for the office of superintendent.

Guides for Class Discussion

1. See *Hazleton-Moffit Special School District* v. *Ward, supra.*
2. See *Green Mountain School District* v. *Durkee, infra.*
3. How did the court justify its position that the actions of a *de facto* officer should be upheld as legal?

4. What criteria did the court mention for determining whether an officer is a *de facto* officer?

10. *"Public policy requires that the acts of a de facto officer, until he is removed from office by the proper procedure, be required as legally binding as the acts of a de jure officer"* (p. 3).

GREEN MOUNTAIN SCHOOL DISTRICT v. DURKEE,
56 Wash. 154, 351 P. (2d) 525 (1960)
(Decided by the Supreme Court of Washington)

[This was an action seeking a review of an order of a county school superintendent transferring a portion of one school district to another district. The sole question of law was whether the county committee on the organization of school districts was legally constituted at the time the transfer was initiated. The trial court ruled in favor of the legality of the county superintendent's order and plaintiff—Green Mountain School District—appealed. The higher court upheld the decision of the lower court.]

FOSTER, Judge.

. . . .

Assuming, *arguendo*, that the three challenged members of the committee were not then legally committeemen, they were, nevertheless, *de facto* members.

In State v. Britton, 27 Wash. 2d 336, 178 P. 2d 341, 346, this court quoted with approval from Hamlin v. Kassafer, 15 Or. 456, 15 P. 778, 3 Am. St. Rep. 176, as follows:

" '. . . To constitute a person an officer *de facto*, he must be in the actual possession of the office, and in the exercise of its functions, and in the discharge of its duties. . . . "*An officer de facto*," said Storrs, J., "*is one who exercises the duties of an office, under color of an appointment or election to that office.* He differs, on the one hand, from a mere usurper of an office, who undertakes to act as an officer without any color of right; and on the other hand, from an officer *de jure*, who is, in all respects, legally appointed and qualified to exercise the office. . . ." [Town of] Plymouth v. Painter, 17 Conn. 588, [44 Am. Dec. 574]. The distinction, then, which the law recognizes, is that an officer *de jure* is one who has the lawful right or title, without the possession, of the office, while an officer *de facto* has the possession, and performs the duties under the color of right, without being actually qualified in law so to act, both being distinguished from the mere usurper, who has neither lawful title nor color of right. . . .'" (Italics ours.)

The challenged members of the county committee were duly elected, and thus clearly acted under color of right. They were, therefore, *de facto* officers. Appellant admits in its brief:

". . . it follows that these members were mere *de facto* officers holding over."

In State v. Britton, supra, the appellant, who had been convicted of a crime, sought to have the judgment set aside on the ground that the trial judge had not been lawfully appointed. This court affirmed the judgment, holding that the trial judge was at least a *de facto* officer, and that:

"'An officer *de facto* must be submitted to as such until displaced by a regular direct proceeding for that purpose; . . . he is a legal officer until ousted. . . .'"

In State v. London, 194 Wash. 458, 78 P.2d 548, 553, 115 A.L.R. 1255, this court approved the statement made in 2 Cooley's Constitutional Limitations (8th ed.), 1355, as follows:

"'. . . the acts of an officer *de facto* are as valid and effectual, while he is suffered to retain the office, as though he were an officer by right, and the same legal consequences will flow from them for the protection of the public and of third parties. . . .'"

Guides for Class Discussion

1. See *Hazleton-Moffit Special School District* v. *Ward, supra.*
2. See *State* v. *Russell, supra.*
3. Under what conditions will an officer be considered to be a *de facto* officer, at least?
4. Distinguish between a *de jure* and a *de facto* officer.

11. "Statutes frequently provide that a school board member shall hold office until a legal successor qualifies for the office, but even in the absence of such a statute the courts commonly hold that the school board member may hold over" (pp. 3-4).

JONES v. ROBERTS COUNTY,
27 S.D. 519, 131 N.W. 861 (1911)
(Decided by the Supreme Court of South Dakota)

[This was an action by a county superintendent to collect salary for four months which he served following the expiration of his term in office. The statute provided that no person should be eligible to hold the office of county superintendent for more than four years in succession. Preceding the time his second two-year term expired, an election was held for county superintendent at which a Miss Gee was elected to follow plaintiff in office. An action was brought to prevent her from taking office, on the ground she was not qualified. The court found this to be true and refused to permit Miss Gee to take over the office of county superintendent. Consequently, on the date when plaintiff's term expired, there was no one eligible to succeed him as county superintendent. As a result, he continued in office for four months, during which time he was not paid. The board of county commissioners had approved his claim for $500 but the state's attorney, upon the petition of seven taxpayers, appealed the county commissioner's action. The lower court held that plaintiff (Jones) was not eligible to hold the office and was not entitled to the salary claimed, whereupon he appealed.]

CORSON, J. . . .

. . . .

The first question, therefore, presented is: Was the plaintiff entitled to hold and perform the duties of the office of county superintendent after his term of office expired, and until his successor was elected or appointed and qualified? It is contended by the appellant that under the provisions of the Constitution and the law, while not eligible to re-election, he could legally and properly remain in possession and discharge the duties of the office until his successor was elected or appointed and qualified. We are of the opinion that the appellant is right in his contention. It will be noticed that the language of the Constitution and the law is: "No person shall be eligible for more than four years in succession to any of the above named offices," except the clerk of courts. The appellant was not in terms prohibited from performing the duties of his office after his term expired, but was not eligible to re-election after four years.

It is contended by the respondent that, as it is provided that no person shall be eligible for more than four years, it was clearly intended to prohibit the party who had held the office four years from further performing the duties of his office, but we are not able to agree with respondent in this contention. The word "eligible," as used in our Constitution and law, was evidently intended to be used in the sense, legally qualified for election or appointment. . . . To hold that all county officers are prohibited from retaining their offices and performing their duties after the term for which they have been elected has fully expired and until their successors are elected or appointed and qualified might result in very serious inconvenience and loss to the public. The section of the Constitution not only includes the superintendent of schools, but all of the other county officers, including county treasurers and sheriffs, except the clerk of the court. And the general rule seems to be that, in the absence of a statute or constitutional provision in terms prohibiting an officer from holding over after the expiration of his term, such officer may continue to retain and perform the duties of his office after the expiration of his term until his successor is elected or appointed and qualified. . . .

In the case at bar it was determined by the adjudication of the court that Agnes E. Gee was ineligible to hold the office, and therefore was not an officer de jure. It necessarily follows, therefore, that the appellant was not only entitled to hold and perform the duties of the office until his successor should be elected or appointed and qualified, but that he was also entitled to the salary and emoluments of the office until the election or appointment of a successor. The court was clearly in error, therefore, in holding that the appellant was not entitled to his salary during the time in which he held and performed the duties of the office as such county superintendent of schools.

Guides for Class Discussion

1. Are you in agreement with the decision as handed down by the court? Give your reasons.
2. If in this case the plaintiff, in spite of the statute, had been a candidate for office and elected, and then had continued in office, how do you think the court would have held?

12. "*A school board member may resign his office but he may not do so before he is duly qualified*" (p. 4).

MILLER v. THE BOARD OF SUPERVISORS,
25 Cal. 93 (1864)
(Decided by the Supreme Court of California)

[In this case plaintiff, who had been elected at the general election for the year 1863 to the office of Public Administrator of Sacramento County for a term of office to commence on the first Monday of March, 1864, attempted to resign his office. On the day he was to take office, but before taking his oath and executing the proper bond, he tendered his resignation to the Judge of the County Court, who accepted it and transmitted it to the Board of Supervisors. Afterward, on the 15th of March, plaintiff wrote to the Supervisors to the effect that he withdrew his resignation and submitted proof that he had duly taken the oath required of him, and tendered to the Board his official bond. The board met on the 5th of April and accepted his resignation.

[On the following day the board met again and rejected the bond on the ground that it was no longer necessary, as the plaintiff had resigned. Immediately before the plaintiff gave the Board notice of the withdrawal of his resignation, he applied to the County Judge to be permitted to withdraw the resignation. The judge consented, and advised him to notify the Board, to whom the resignation had been transmitted, of his desire to withdraw it. The court ruled that plaintiff had the right to withdraw his resignation because the resignation was ineffective, due to the fact he had not qualified for the office.]

By the Court, CURREY, J.

.   .   .   .

The act performed by the Board of Supervisors, alleged to have been an excess of their jurisdiction, consisted in determining, in effect, that the petitioner had resigned the office to which he was elected, and in rejecting the bond for that reason, and because of a previous attempt on his part to sell the office. Whatever may have been the truth as to such attempt, and however open to animadversion, conduct of this kind may be, that was a question with which the Board had no authority to deal, and the inquiry must be narrowed down to the point whether the petitioner had resigned the office to which he was elected by the people of the county, and whether his resignation was a subsisting fact at the time the Board acted. If this inquiry be answered in the negative, then the Board, according to the case cited from 10 Cal. 344, exceeded its jurisdiction in treating the alleged resignation as effectual, and rejecting the bond tendered and filed for the reasons by them assigned.

At the time the petitioner undertook to resign the office of Public Administrator he was not in fact invested with that office. Before he could become so he was required by law to take the constitutional oath, and execute with sureties a proper bond to be approved by the Board. Had these things been done within the ten days allowed for the purpose, he would have become the Public Administrator of Sacramento County, and fully invested with the office. Having the mere naked right to the office of Public Administrator, the taking of the constitutional oath of office and executing the bond prescribed were conditions which, fully completed, were essential to the constituting of the petitioner such officer.

. . . .

There can be but one incumbent of the office of Public Administrator at the same time, and he who held the office prior to the first Monday in March remained the incumbent on that day, notwithstanding the petitioner was then entitled to the office upon taking the oath and filing the necessary bond. The petitioner's term, or the term for which he was elected, commenced on the First Monday of March; but that fact alone could not constitute him the incumbent of the office, because an incumbent is one who is in the present possession of an office. . . .

. . . .

By reference to these subdivisions of section thirty, it will be observed that the term "incumbent" refers to him alone who has become qualified and has entered into the possession of the office; and that the person who has been elected or appointed to an office, who refuses or neglects to take the oath of office, or to give a bond when required, within the time prescribed by law, is not denominated an incumbent; and nothing is said as to the resignation of any other than an incumbent of the office.

In *The People* v. *Van Horne*, 18 Wend. 518, Mr. Chief Justice Savage said: "An office cannot be said to be vacant while any person is authorized to act in it, and does so act." And in reference to a statute like the first section of our Act concerning Public Administrators, he said: "In such cases there is, in fact, no vacancy, because the officers of the preceding year hold the offices until others are chosen or appointed in their places and have qualified."

If the petitioner had not become the incumbent of the office which he was elected to fill, he had no office to resign; and though he may have supposed he had, yet that did not alter the fact, and his attempted resignation and the acceptance of it by the County Judge was abortive and ineffectual.

Guides for Class Discussion

1. Compare the decision in this case with those in *State ex rel. Williams* v. *Fitts, infra* and *Biddle* v. *Willard, infra*.
2. Are you in agreement with this decision? Give reasons.
3. Would the court have held as it did had a statute permitted an elective officer to resign before being qualified? Why or why not?
4. For what reasons do you think this case has application to a situation where a school board member resigns an office before qualifying for it?

13. *"An unconditional resignation, one to take effect immediately, cannot be withdrawn"* (p. 4).

STATE EX REL. WILLIAMS V. FITTS,
49 Ala. 402 (1873)
(Decided by the Supreme Court of Alabama)

[The facts of this case will be found in the quotation which follows and are therefore not repeated here. It should be noted, however, that the case concerns one who held the office of solicitor of a county. Because school board members are officers, the same line of reasoning would apply to them.]

B. F. SAFFOLD, J. The suit is in the nature of *quo warranto*, to try whether the right to the office of solicitor of Tuscaloosa County is in the relator or the appellee. The relator, Williams, was the solicitor; but some time between the 6th and 12th of May, 1869, he wrote an unconditional resignation, and gave it to Mr. Miller, the secretary of State, for transmission to the proper authority entitled to receive it. It came to the executive department, whence it was sent by mail, at the instance of the governor, to the judge of the circuit which includes Tuscaloosa County. The judge was absent from his home at the time, and when he returned, and before he had taken any action about it, he received also other letters from Williams, virtually withdrawing his resignation. Nevertheless, the judge appointed Mr. Fitts to the office, who qualified, and entered upon the duties thereof, and is still performing them. The question to be determined is, whether there was a resignation, and consequently a vacancy, which the judge of the circuit was authorized to fill.

The state Constitution gives the appointing power, in case of vacancy, to the judge of the circuit. In the case of *Marbury* v. *Madison* (1 Cranch, 137), it was held that when a commission for an officer, not holding his office at the will of the President, is by him signed and transmitted to the Secretary of State, to be sealed and recorded, it is irrevocable. The appointment is complete. The correctness of this proposition was argued by Chief Justice Marshall, with that conclusiveness which characterized all of his reasoning. The same rule may be well applied to the revocability of a resignation. Except in some rare instances, no person is compelled to hold office. He may retire at his mere will, upon the moment. Some point must be fixed, at which the expression of this will becomes obligatory on himself. What better period can be selected in respect to him than that which, on the other hand, would clothe him with the office beyond the authority or the appointing power to recall it? When he transmits an unconditional resignation, which he intends shall reach the officer or authority entitled to receive it, he resigns. He has given formal expression to his will, and sent away a notice of it to whom it may concern. There is nothing more for him to do. Nobody else is authorized to accept it. It needs no acceptance. *Nevada, ex rel. Nourse* v. *Clarke*, 3 Nevada, 566; *People* v. *Porter*, 6 Cal. 26. The charges given by the court were much more favorable to the relator than we conceive the law to be. The charge asked by him was properly refused.

The judgement is affirmed.

Guides for Class Discussion

1. What is meant by an "unconditional resignation"?
2. Compare the decision in this case with the one which follows—*Biddle* v. *Willard*.
3. Are you in agreement with the court's reasoning? Give reasons.

14. "*. . . a conditional resignation, one to take effect at some future time, may be withdrawn at any time before being acted upon*" (*p. 4*).

BIDDLE v. WILLARD,
10 Ind. 62 (1857)
(Decided by the Supreme Court of Indiana)

[In this case one William Z. Stuart, who had been elected to the position of Judge of the Supreme Court for the term of six years and who had qualified and entered upon the duties of the office, offered his resignation to the governor in August, 1857. By the terms of the resignation he indicated that he wished it to take effect on the first Monday of January, 1858—that is, some four months in the future. In October of 1857 a successor—Horace P. Biddle—was elected. When he demanded a commission it was refused, whereupon he brought an action against the governor of the state to require the governor to issue the commission. The court refused to grant his request on the ground that he had no right to the office because, for a vacancy to exist, there must be a complete and operative resignation, accompanied by a relinquishment of the office. Because the resignation was to take effect at a date in the future, the conditions requisite to the creation of a vacancy did not exist and the election was ineffective.]

PERKINS, J. . . .

. . . .

There was no existing vacancy. The election was in *October*. The vacancy did not occur by Judge *Stuart's* resignation till *January* following. The term of no appointee was about to expire. The term for which a judge had been elected was not about to expire.

The question, then, alone remains, was there any other case in which, under the constitution and statutes, an election was to be held for a judge of the Supreme Court, at the last *October* election, and if so, what was it? For it can scarcely be necessary to remark that an election to fill an anticipated vacancy could not be valid unless authorized by law. 3 Blackf. 158.

It is contended that there was, or may have been, such a case, viz., where a judge, before the election, had made a prospective resignation to take effect after that, and before the next succeeding election.

After patient reflection, we have not been able to come to such a conclusion.

1. The case does not fall within the letter of the constitution or statutes relative to elections; it does not embrace the material fact of the expiration of the term of office. The elective term of the judicial office is, by the constitution, as we have seen, six years; for that period the successful candidate at an election is chosen; for that period he is disqualified to hold any political office; and for that period he has a right to hold the office of judge. That term of six years cannot expire except by its own limitation. It may be abandoned by the incumbent. It may be vacated of that incumbent by the act of *God*, and by law a new term may be made to then begin; but the term itself can only legally expire by the efflux of time. If, in the case of a prospective resignation, there is an expiration of any term, it is the term attempted to be created

by the resignation itself. But such a term is not known to, or contemplated by, the constitution or statutes, and did not in law exist, in this case, if it can in any. This will appear when we consider what a resignation is.

2. To constitute a complete and operative resignation, there must be an intention to relinquish a portion of the term of the office, accompanied by the act of relinquishment. *Webster* and *Richardson* define the words *resign* and *resignation*, substantially thus: to resign, is to give back, to give up, in a formal manner, an office; and resignation is the act of giving it up. *Bouvier* says, resignation is the act of an officer by which he declines his office, and renounces the further right to use it. . . .

Hence, a prospective resignation may, in point of law, amount but to a notice of intention to resign at a future day, or a proposition to so resign; and for the reason that it is not accompanied by a giving up of the office—possession is still retained, and may not necessarily be surrendered till the expiration of the legal term of the office, because the officer may recall his resignation—may withdraw his proposition to resign. He certainly can do this at any time before it is accepted; and after it is accepted, he may make the withdrawal by the consent of the authority accepting, where no new rights have intervened. The record nowhere shows us, in this case, that the prospective resignation of Judge *Stuart* was ever accepted; and, therefore, it does not show that any special term, not known to the law, was created by it, if in any event there could have been, which might have been filled at the *October* election.

3. It will appear beyond doubt, that a prospective resignation does not create a case for an election in *October*, in contemplation of law, when we consider how a resignation is to be made, and the course that is to be afterward pursued in relation to it.

Guides for Class Discussion

1. How would you define a "conditional resignation"?
2. Are you in agreement with the court's thinking in this case? Give reasons.
3. Compare this case with *State ex rel. Williams* v. *Fitts, supra.*
4. Is the reasoning followed by the court in this case, which involved the resignation of a Judge of the Supreme Court, applicable to a case involving the resignation of a school board member? Give reasons.

15. *"A temporary removal of a board member from the district does not vacate the office unless the circumstances surrounding the case clearly indicate his intent to relinquish the office"* (p. 4).

School District v. Garrison,
90 Ark. 335 (1909)
(Decided by the Supreme Court of Arkansas)

[The facts of this case are to be found in the material quoted and for that reason are not stated here.]

Frauenthal, J. On March 16, 1907, R. H. Waggoner and John L. Cook, as directors of School District No. 54 of Howard County, Arkansas, entered into a written contract with J. T. Garrison, the plaintiff, by which they did, on behalf of said school district, employ him to teach a common school in said district for a term of six months, commencing on the 4th day of November, 1907, at a salary of $60 per month. On the date specified in the contract for the beginning of the term of school, he offered his services to teach the school in compliance with the contract; but the directors refused to permit him to do so. Thereafter, in July, 1908, he instituted this suit to recover from the said school district the entire amount of the six months' salary, less such sums as he had been able to earn during that time. The defendant made answer, claiming, among other defenses, that the contract was invalid because the two directors who signed the contract were not the sole directors of the district; and that the contract was entered into at a special meeting at which the third director of the district was not present, and of which he had no notice. Upon the trial, a verdict was returned in favor of plaintiff, from which defendant has appealed to this court.

. . . .

Under the policy of our school laws it is deemed best for the interests of the common school districts that they should have the service and counsel of three directors. It is provided that three directors shall be elected to constitute the school board; and, while it is also provided that two of them may transact the business of the school district under certain conditions, it is nevertheless required that due notice in writing must be given to each director of any special meeting called for the transaction of such business.

. . . the office does not become vacant by mere neglect of or failure to perform these duties. It is true that the incumbent of the office can abandon the office and thus create a vacancy, and such abandonment may occur through resignation or removal from the district. The authorities seem to be in accord in holding that an office cannot be abandoned without the actual intention on the part of the officer to abandon and relinquish the office. The relinquishment of the office must be well defined, and it is not produced merely by nonuser or neglect of duty. The officer must clearly intend an absolute relinquishment of the office; and a removal from the district, if only temporary, would not evince such intention. The nonuser, or neglect of duty, or removal from the district, in order to amount to a vacation of the office, must be not only total and complete, but of such a continuance as to make it permanent, and under such circumstances so clearly indicating absolute relinquishment as to preclude all future questions of fact. Otherwise there must be a judicial determination of the vacancy of the office before it can be so declared. . . .

Now, in this case the evidence tended to prove that the director, Booker Wakley, moved out of the district a distance of about a mile and one-half or two miles; but he testified that he did not intend such removal to be permanent; that it was done simply to cultivate a crop at such place, and that it was only temporary; that he still owned property in the district and returned in four or five months; that while out of the district he did not exercise any of the duties of a director or claim to be one. It also appears from the testimony that he did not state to any one that he was not a director, and no election was called to fill any alleged vacancy, and no notice given to the county court of such alleged vacancy. There is no sufficient evidence to prove that this director, Wakley, intended to abandon or relinquish the office. The most that can be said under the evidence is that this director during his absence from the district was guilty of neglect of his duty as director and of a partial nonuser of the office. Because the other directors may have claimed that the office of director Wakley was vacant, or because Wakley so thought, did not make the office vacant. A vacancy in office only exists when there is no person authorized by law to perform the duties of the office. There is such authorized person, as long as the duly elected officer does not remove permanently from the district or has not intentionally and absolutely relinquished the office.

In this connection the court instructed the jury, on behalf of plaintiff, in substance, that if the jury believed from the evidence that Wakley had moved out of the district and did not at the time act or claim to act as director, and he and the other directors considered the office vacant, then it was not necessary to give him notice of the special meeting at which the contract was made. This was instruction number two given on the part of plaintiff. It left doubtful the question as to whether the removal of Wakley from the district should be temporary or permanent; and, if the removal was not permanent, it entirely ignored the requisite of an intention on the part of Wakley to absolutely relinquish the office before it could become vacant. This instruction was therefore misleading, and its effect was prejudicial. It was therefore erroneous.

If the office of director Wakley was not vacant, then it was necessary to have given him proper notice of the special meeting at which this contract was entered into; and in event this was not done the contract was invalid. . . .

Guides for Class Discussion

1. Are you in agreement with the court on this decision? Give reasons.
2. Would the court have ruled as it did had there been a statute providing that removal from the district for any cause was to be interpreted as a vacancy in office?
3. Compare this case with *Green v. Jones, infra.*

16. "*A school board member who has been appointed or elected for a fixed term may not be removed from office without a notice of the charges against him and an opportunity to be heard in his own defense*" (p. 4).

JACQUES v. LITLE,
51 Kan. 300, 33 P. 106 (1893)
(Decided by the Supreme Court of Kansas)

[This case involved the title to office of a board member who was elected school treasurer. Defendant—Litle—was elected treasurer of the district at the annual meeting in 1891. Later, without any meeting of the district board, two of the three board members entered into an agreement with a teacher and offered him a written contract. The teacher was without a certificate, but obtained a temporary one from the county superintendent, even though no written request therefor was made by the district board, as required by the statute. Litle opposed the employment of the teacher and protested against his taking charge of the school, but to no avail. Litle then refused payment of school orders which were issued to the teacher by the other district officers, even though there was sufficient money on hand belonging to the funds upon which such orders were drawn.

[When the other members of the board complained about his refusal to pay the school orders and attend the board meetings, the county superintendent, without any notice to Litle, considered that he had forfeited his right to the office of treasurer, declared it vacant, and appointed plaintiff. Jacques qualified as treasurer and made his demand upon Litle for the books and records, but Litle refused to comply, insisting that he was still the treasurer of the district, although he was not so recognized by the county superintendent. The question before the court was whether the county superintendent could remove Litle, on the ground he had neglected or refused to perform his duty, without giving him a notice and hearing. The court held the county superintendent had no such authority.]

JOHNSTON, J. . . .

Has the plaintiff any right to the office in question, or to maintain this action? He cannot employ quo warranto for the purpose of ascertaining whether Litle has been guilty of neglect or refusal to perform any duty required of him, and to declare a forfeiture therefor. Such a proceeding can only be prosecuted in the name of the state, and at the instance of the attorney general or county attorney. The plaintiff seems to be proceeding upon the theory that the county superintendent may summarily, and without notice to the defendant or hearing, determine for himself that a school officer has neglected his duty, and, having reached that conclusion, is authorized to appoint some one in his stead. . . . Where an office is held at the pleasure of the appointing power, and also where the power of removal may be exercised at its discretion, it is well settled that the officer may be removed at any time without notice or hearing. . . . The defendant holds his office by virtue of an election, and is chosen for a definite time. Nothing in the law warrants the implication that a school-district officer who has been elected and qualified, and entered upon his duties, may be removed at the will or pleasure of any officer. The statute prescribes the causes for which a removal may be had, and fairly implies that the cause must be shown, and that the party charged with negligence and wrong is entitled to notice, and a right to be heard in his own defense. It is well established by the great weight of authority that where an officer is elected by the people for a definite term, and provision is made for his removal for cause, the power of removal cannot, in the absence of the positive mandate of statute, be exercised without notice and hearing. The mere silence of the statute with respect to notice and hearing will not justify the removal of such an officer upon a charge of misconduct and negligence, without knowledge of the charges, and an opportunity to explain his conduct, and defend his course and character. . . . The defendant was in possession of the office, holding it by as good a title as that of any other officer of the state who has been elected by the people. He was charged with negligence and misconduct, and shall he be condemned unheard? He refused to sign or recognize orders for the salary of the teacher, and it is admitted that the contract with the teacher was illegally made. It is true that a majority of the board, at a legal meeting held about three months later, tried to cure the illegal action. Whether they succeeded or not, and whether the refusal of Litle thereafter to sign the warrant can be held to be a neglect of duty which would justify removal, must be inquired into and determined by some competent tribunal or officer. Whether the grounds of forfeiture prescribed in the statute exist must be ascertained, and this cannot be done until specific charges are made, and full opportunity is given to the officer to produce proofs, and defend his rights. Without a removal made in a legal manner, no vacancy existed in the treasurer's office, and the county superintendent had no authority to appoint the plaintiff. . . .

Guides for Class Discussion

1. Compare this case with *School District* v. *Garrison, supra;* and *State ex rel. Taylor* v. *Board of Commissioners, infra.*
2. Is the ruling in this case sound? Give reasons.

17. *"When a school board member is in active possession of his office, public policy requires that he be accepted as the officer he represents himself as being until he is removed from the office by proper legal proceedings" (p. 4).*

STATE EX REL. TAYLOR V. BOARD OF COMMISSIONERS,
124 Ind. 554, 25 N.E. 10 (1890)
(Decided by the Supreme Court of Indiana)

[In this case one who had been duly elected county superintendent of schools in Warrick County by the trustees of the county brought an action against the board of commissioners of the county when it refused to accept his bond. The board of commissioners contended that before election plaintiff was a trustee of one of the townships of the county and had made a "political deal" with the county auditor whereby, after resigning as trustee, he received the appointment as county superintendent of schools. For that reason defendants refused to recognize plaintiff as the legally elected county superintendent.

[The court held that, because the county superintendent had been duly elected and qualified and was in possession of the office, he must be recognized as the holder of that office until he was removed by proper legal proceedings. The lower court held against the superintendent, who appealed. The higher court overruled the decision of the lower court. The ruling laid down in this case would in all probability be applicable to a board member as well as a county superintendent of schools, as board members are officers just as was the county superintendent in this case.]

Coffey, J. . . .

We are not favored with a brief by the appellees, and are not advised of the ground upon which the court based its judgment; but in our opinion the court erred in overruling the appellant's motion for a new trial. In all of its essential features, this case is like the case of Commissioners v. Johnson, 24 N.E. Rep. 148, (decided at last term,) except in the matter of defense set up by the appellees. The appellant, at the time he tendered his special bond to the board of commissioners of Warrick county, had been duly elected, qualified, and was acting as county superintendent of schools, was in the possession of the office, and was discharging the duties pertaining thereto. Such being the case, the appellees could not attack his title in the collateral manner attempted by their answer. The public have an interest in the discharge of the duties of the office; and until such time as the appellant shall be ousted by a proper proceeding for that purpose, every one must recognize him as the legally elected and qualified county superintendent. . . . The certificate of election issued to the appellant, and his qualification as county superintendent, bar all inquiry into his right to hold the office except in a direct proceeding for that purpose. . . . It is not denied that the appellant was selected county superintendent by the votes of a majority of the trustees of Warrick county, and that he duly qualified, and entered upon the discharge of the duties of his office. No one is contesting his election, and no proceeding is pending to oust him. It is settled . . . that he was entitled to have the bond in question approved at the time it was tendered. The appellees could not go behind his election, and inquire into his title to the office. It was their duty to approve his bond. Having refused to do so, mandate is the proper remedy to compel them to perform that duty. . . .

Guides for Class Discussion

1. Compare the decision in this case with the one in *Jacques v Litle, supra.*

2. Compare the decision in this case with the one in *In Re Board of School Directors of Carroll Township, infra.*

18. *"The law provides a special action for the determination of title to office. This action is an action in the nature of quo warranto brought by the state through its attorney general or state's attorney"* (p. 4).

In Re Board of School Directors of Carroll Township,
407 Pa. 156, 180 A. (2d) 16 (1962)
(Decided by the Supreme Court of Pennsylvania)

[The facts of the case are contained in the excerpt quoted.]

Musmanno, Justice.

On December 28, 1961, twelve taxpayers in Carroll Township, Washington County, filed a petition in the Court of Common Pleas of that county, alleging that a vacancy existed on the Board of School Directors of the Carroll Township School District because one of the directors, John L. Blangger, had removed from Carroll Township to the State of New Jersey and had failed to attend seven consecutive regular meetings of the Board. The petition requested the Court to fill the supposed vacancy. Judge Cummins granted the petition forthwith and appointed Henry Zermani in Blangger's place. The Order of Court provided that it was to become absolute if exceptions were not filed within five days after service on Blangger of the Order and copy of the petition.

On January 2, 1962, Blangger, through his attorney, filed exceptions denying that he had changed residence, that he had failed to attend seven consecutive meetings, and that a vacancy existed on the Board. Judge Cummins then, with the concurrence of Judge Roy I. Carson, vacated the order of December 2, 1961. The taxpayers filed exceptions to this new order of January 2, 1962 and in consequence a hearing was scheduled for January 12, 1962 before a Court en banc.

On that day Blangger through his attorney, presented a motion to quash the taxpayers' petition, their exceptions and appeal, averring that, as the School Board had not declared a vacancy on the Board, the only manner in which Blangger's right to continue to hold office could be tested was by an action of quo warranto.

The lower Court accepted this petition, dismissed the taxpayers' petition and the taxpayers appealed.

The action of the Court below must be affirmed. Quo warranto is the Gibraltar of stability in government tenure. Once a person is duly elected or duly appointed to public office, the continuity of his services may not be interrupted and the uniform working of the governmental machinery disorganized or disturbed by any proceeding less than a formal challenge to the office by that action which is now venerable with age, reinforced by countless precedent, and proved to be protective of all parties involved in a given controversy, namely, *quo warranto*.

The petitioners in this case attempted to declare an office vacant through ex parte proceedings, which is inimical to the whole scheme of democratic government.

The legislature may, of course, provide special procedures for vacating offices under certain conditions and when those procedures are indicated, they must be strictly followed.

Guides for Class Discussion

1. What did the court mean when it said, "Quo warranto is the Gibraltar of stability in government tenure"?
2. Can the legislature provide a different type of action, rather than *quo warranto*, for testing one's right to office?

19. *"Whatever authority a school board may possess, it is authority which has been delegated to it by the state" (p. 4).*

Barth v. School District of Philadelphia,
393 Pa. 557, 143 A. (2d) 909 (1958)
(Decided by the Supreme Court of Pennsylvania)

[This action was brought to restrain the board of education of the School District of Philadelphia from spending or contributing money, services, materials, or facilities in carrying out an agreement entered into with the City of Philadelphia to assist in the support of the Youth Conservation Commission. The Commission was to be created for the purpose of organizing, operating, formulating, and financing a program to curb juvenile delinquency in Philadelphia. Among other things, the agreement provided for the school district's cooperation with the city and authorized the payment by the district of amounts up to $125,000, for the calendar year 1958, for the support of the Commission and its program. It was to prevent the expenditure of this amount that this action was brought. Plaintiff contended that the school board was without authority to spend this amount for this purpose. The trial court ruled in plaintiff's favor, and the Supreme Court affirmed its decision.]

BELL, Justice.

. . . .

A program to study and curb juvenile delinquency is not only worthy, but highly desirable. The crime wave which is sweeping our Country, and particularly the rise and extent of juvenile delinquency, and the vandalism and the atrocious crimes committed by juveniles has astonished, troubled and appalled our entire nation. Law and order, prevention, suppression and punishment of crime, control of gangs, improvement of living conditions, rehabilitation of problem persons and persons with criminal tendencies—these are and since ancient times have been matters for the Sovereign (in our Country, local or State, and more recently, National Government), and have never heretofore been considered as a part of "Education." Furthermore a worthy objective does not justify the action of a School District or a public body, which has no fundamental or inherent powers of Government, unless that action is authorized by the Constitution or by an Act of the Legislature.

A School District is not a Constitutional body. . . .

. . . .

A School District is a creature or agency of the Legislature and has only the powers that are granted by statute, specifically or by necessary implication. . . .

In Slippery Rock Area Joint School System v. Franklin Township School District, 389 Pa. 435, at page 442, 133 A. 2d 848, at page 852, supra, the Court said: " 'First it should be remembered that our entire school system is but an agency of the State Legislature—maintained by them to carry out a constitutional duty. . . . The school system, or the school district, then, are but agencies of the state legislature to administer this constitutional duty. Wilson v. Philadelphia School District, 328 Pa. 225, 230, [195 A. 90, 113 A.L.R. 1401]. Within that school system, a school district is an agency of the State, created by law *for the purpose of promoting education, deriving all of its powers from the statute, and discharging only such duties as are imposed upon it by statute. . . .' "* [Italics supplied by the Court.]

. . . .

The Public School Code minutely details in approximately 270 pages, the powers, functions and duties of a School District. It also provides in Article VI, § 610: "The use or payment of any public school funds of any school district, *in any manner or for any purpose not provided in this act,* shall be illegal." 24 P.S. § 6-610. A study, nay a reading, of the Public School Code demonstrates that the Legislature unquestionably intended and provided that the School District could possess and exercise only those powers and functions detailed in the Code, and that public school funds could be used only in the manner and for the purposes which are expressly or by necessary implication provided for in this detailed Act.

Never heretofore have schools or school districts possessed or exercised, under the theory or name of Education, the wide basic powers, functions and duties of Municipal Government which are now claimed by the Board of Education, namely the prevention, suppression, correction, elimination and punishment of juvenile delinquency—euphemistic language to describe vandalism, misdemeanors and crimes committed by young persons—, gang control and the improvement of living conditions. It is clear that the main purposes of this Agreement is, at best, very indirectly and very remotely connected with Education. . . .

. . . .

To particularize: A program to curb juvenile delinquency, and to control gangs, and to coordinate programs of various agencies of and throughout the City for the purpose of reducing juvenile delinquency, and to organize sensitive areas in the City on a block-to-block basis in an effort to improve living conditions—these are not and never have been a part of the function, power or duty of a school or a school district. They are a very important and essential part of municipal Government: They are not and never have been a part of or embraced within "Education," as that term has always been understood. . . .

. . . .

We are therefore convinced that neither the sections relied upon by the School District and the City, nor any other section in the Public School Code authorize this Agreement.

The authorities relied upon by the City and the School District which involved, *not the power,* but the discretion of school boards are clearly inapposite. The School District was properly enjoined, not because the Agreement represented an abuse of discretion, but because, being unauthorized by statute, it was beyond the legal power of the School Board.

Guides for Class Discussion

1. Are you in agreement with the thinking of the court? Give reasons.

2. Compare this case with *McGilvra* v. *Seattle School District No. 1, infra.*

3. Compare it also with *State ex rel. School District* v. *Moore, infra.*

20. *"The courts are agreed that a school board may exercise the following powers and no others: (1) those which have been expressly conferred upon it by statute, (2) those which may be fairly implied from express grants, and (3) those which are essential to the accomplishment of the purposes for which the board was created"* (p. 4).

McGilvra v. Seattle School Dist. No. 1,
113 Wash. 619, 194 P. 817 (1921)
(Decided by the Supreme Court of Washington)

[This action was brought to test the authority of a school board to maintain a "clinic" in one of its school buildings and to spend funds therefor. As indicated by the decision, the word "clinic" might best be designated as "hospital." The clinic or hospital was set up for the purpose of providing medical, surgical, and dental treatment for the physical ailments of pupils whose parents or guardians were financially unable to provide such treatment themselves. The trial court held the board had the authority to maintain and support the clinic, but the Supreme Court reversed the decision of the lower court and enjoined the district and its officers from "furnishing or equipping upon the school premises, or elsewhere, appliances for the medical, surgical, or dental treatment of the physical ailments of the pupils of the schools at the expense of the district, and from employing physicians, dentists, or nurses for the rendering of such medical, surgical, or dental treatment. . . ."]

PARKER, J. . . .

.   .   .   .

. . . To summarize, we have the fact that the officers of the school district are maintaining in one of its buildings a so-called "clinic," equipped with appliances for rendering of medical, surgical, and dental services in the treatment of the physical ailments of pupils of the schools, at the expense of the district in substantial excess of that necessary for the rendering of such services and treatment to pupils of the district's parental schools, and that they propose continuing so to do.

The question to be here answered is: Have the school district and its officers legal authority for so furnishing the use of, and equipping rooms in its buildings and the maintenance therein of such clinic, by the expenditure of the taxpayers' funds collected and placed at their disposal, for the sole purpose of maintaining the public schools of the district? At the outset let us be reminded in the language of Judge Dillon, in his work on Municipal Corporations, quoted with approval by this court in State ex rel. Winsor v. Mayor and Council, 10 Wash. 4, 37 Pac. 761, that—

> "It is a general and undisputed proposition of law that a municipal corporation possesses and can exercise the following powers, and no others: First, those granted in express words; second, those necessarily or fairly implied in or incident to the powers expressly granted; third, those essential to the declared objects and purposes of the corporation—not simply convenient but indispensable. Any fair or reasonable doubt concerning the existence of power is resolved by the courts against the corporation, and the power is denied."

This view of the law is of added weight when applied to school districts, because they are municipal corporations with powers of a much more limited character than are cities, or towns, or even than counties. . . .

. . . .

The specific legislative enumeration of these powers which it seems could with much sounder reason be considered as implied powers in the absence of express language in the statute than the claimed powers here in question, argues, in the light of well-settled rules of statutory construction, that the Legislature has not intended that there should be an exercise of such claimed powers. We see no argument lending any substantial support, in a legal way, to the view that a school district and its officers possess the powers they are seeking to exercise and threatening to continue to exercise. There is much in the argument of counsel for the school officers which might be considered as lending support to the view that such powers ought to be possessed by the school district and its officers, and it is probable that counsel has many well meaning people upon his side of that question. The Legislature may give heed to such arguments, but the courts cannot do so.

Guides for Class Discussion

1. See *Barth* v. *School District of Philadelphia, supra.*

2. Are you in agreement with the court's thinking? Give reasons.

3. On what ground did the court base its decision?

21. *"If there is any doubt with respect to the authority of a school board to act, the doubt will be resolved against the board, and the authority will be denied"* (pp. 4-5).

STATE EX REL. SCHOOL DISTRICT V. MOORE,
45 Neb. 12, 63 N.W. 130 (1895)
(Decided by the Supreme Court of Nebraska)

[This was an action in mandamus to compel an auditor of public accounts to register bonds issued by a school district. The bonds were issued for the purpose of exchanging them for warrants in the same amount held by a bank, when the district was unable to pay the amount due on the warrants. The auditor demurred, thereby putting in issue the authority of the district to issue the bonds. At the root of the matter was the question of the meaning of a statute that authorized certain named municipal corporations, including school districts, to compromise their indebtedness and issue new bonds therefor.]

HARRISON, J. . . .

.   .   .   .

. . . the main question for our determination is, are the provisions of the act of 1887 sufficiently broad to authorize the issuance of bonds by a school district to substitute or exchange for an indebtedness of the district other than a bonded indebtedness? The other points noticed are only incidental to this, and important alone insomuch as they bear upon and affect its disposition.

In the interpretation and construction of statutes, one of the cardinal rules is that it is the intent of the law that is to be sought after, and, if possible, ascertained; and where the law is expressed in words which are clear and not ambiguous, and no doubt as to its purpose and meaning can arise from the language employed, where to understand and know its intent it is but necessary to read, then there is no call for an interpretation; but where the intention and meaning of the lawmakers, as expressed in the statute enacted, is uncertain or obscure, as in the one now under consideration, a bare reading will not suffice, and we are obliged to resort to a construction of its terms and provisions. This statute contemplates the issue of bonds by officers of certain governmental divisions and subdivisions of our state, and necessarily carries with it a resort to the power of taxation of the people to raise the funds to meet the indebtedness created by such action, in the majority of instances not accorded until the proposition involved is submitted to and approved by a vote of the electors of the particular political body or subdivision whose tax bearers are to be affected thereby, and hence, agreeably to a well-established rule, is to be strictly construed, and, *where there is any doubt, it must be resolved in favor of the public or taxpayers.* [Emphasis added.] The first section of the act under discussion enumerates the particular bodies or municipalities to which power is granted, and contains the authorization to compromise indebtedness without designation of any particular kind of indebtedness. Section 2 provides for the presentation of a petition by two-thirds of the resident taxpayers of the county, city, town, or school district, etc., asking that such a compromise be made, and empowers the proper officers to negotiate with the holders of "any such indebtedness, of whatever form, scaling, discounting, or compromising the same." The words "of whatever form," applied in explanation of the indebtedness, and making it include, as given their natural and ordinary purport they do, any and all indebtedness, seem to make the intention in relation to what claims were in contemplation and referred to by the legislature passing the act plain and certain; and, if there were no statements in other portions of the law bearing upon this same point, we might well stop here content with the determination to which it would lead us. Section 3 of the law authorizes the issuance of the bonds upon the surrender and cancellation or satisfaction of the indebtedness and presentment of a petition by two-thirds of the taxpayers requesting such action. It does not designate or indicate any particular kind of indebtedness, but refers to it in each instance by the use of the general term. In section 4, in referring to the bonds to be issued, it is stated: "They shall bear interest at a rate not exceeding seven (7) per cent., nor the rate borne by the bond surrendered;" thus, it would seem, clearly indicating that it was an indebtedness evidenced by bonds which the legislator had in mind when he framed and introduced the bill containing the act in question, and in contemplation of the legislative body when it passed the act. From a study of the body of the law, we think it must be concluded that there is a doubt whether the compromise of all kinds of indebtedness is intended to be authorized, or only those of a bonded nature. . . . [W]e have the title stating that the act is to provide for new bonds, which conveys the idea of compromising, replacing, or renewing other or old bonds; a statement in the text that the bonds issued shall not bear interest at a rate in excess of that borne by the bonds surrendered, which, to say the least, leaves us in doubt and renders it uncertain whether the law was intended by the legislature to empower the issuance of bonds in the manner stated therein for the compromise of an existing indebtedness other than in the form of bonds. Add to these the thought that there was no provision for submitting the proposition of the issuance of these bonds to a vote, it being the wise and wholesome policy of our law to so submit such questions (involving, as they necessarily do, the levying of a tax) to the decision of the voters, who must pay the tax, and, further, that such laws are the subject for strict interpretation, and, if there is a doubt as to the intention, it must be resolved in favor of the taxpayers or public, and we are constrained to say that our conclusion is that the act we are considering did not empower the issuance of the bonds to replace the indebtedness, consisting, as it did, of school warrants or orders, and the writ prayed for in this action must be denied.

Guides for Class Discussion

1. What is the rationale back of the principle that, in case of doubt regarding the authority of a school board, courts will resolve the doubt against the board?

2. Do you support this line of reasoning? Give reasons.

22. *The courts are cautious in interpreting the powers of boards of education, but once authority to act has been recognized, discretion in the exercise of it will not be controlled by the courts unless clearly abused"* (p. 5).

STATE V. MARION COUNTY BOARD OF EDUCATION,
202 Tenn. 29, 302 S.W. (2d) 57 (1957)
(Decided by the Supreme Court of Tennessee)

[This was an action in mandamus to require a school board to restore to enrollment a girl who had been suspended from school, during her senior year, because of marriage. The board had a rule that a student who married during a school term would be automatically expelled for the remainder of that term. In February, 1957, the girl in question married. She was 18 years of age and was a student in the high school at Jasper, Tennessee. Her school achievement had been excellent, and she expected to graduate in May. Following her marriage the board suspended her for the remainder of that year, whereupon her father-in-law brought this action to have her reinstated.

[The court's decision in this case really turned on the question of whether the board had the authority to enact such a rule, or whether the rule was arbitrary or unreasonable. The lower court held the board was authorized to enact the rule, and the Supreme Court upheld its decision.]

TOMLINSON, Justice.

. . . .

The case was heard on bill and on answer that was sworn to. It discloses that there are four high schools in Marion County. It is averred in the answer that for a period of years previous to the adoption of this resolution there had been a deterioration of the discipline and decorum in these schools "due to student marriages," and that the situation had become such that each of the four principals requested the Board to adopt the resolution in question. It was represented to the Board by these principals that the confusion, disorder, etc., caused by student marriages "mostly occur immediately after the marriage and during the period of readjustment, and the influence of married students on the other students is also greatest at this time." The answer avers that this is the reason the Board adopted the resolution forbidding attendance during the remainder of the school term immediately following the marriage.

Code Section 49-214(9) makes it the duty of the Board "to suspend or dismiss pupils when the progress or efficiency of the school makes it necessary." . . . [A]ny activity of students which can be said to have a reasonable bearing on his or her influence upon the students or school is within the bounds of reasonable regulation by the Board in the exercise of the statutory duty vested in it to suspend pupils "when the progress or efficiency of the school makes it necessary."

If the representations made to the County Board of Education by every high school principal in Marion County as to their respective observations and experiences on this subject is [sic] at all accurate, then married students, and by virtue of the psychological effect thereof, for a few months immediately following marriage, have a detrimental influence upon fellow students, hence, a detrimental effect upon the progress and efficiency of the school. Therefore, if these principals know whereof they speak, the attendance during such period of such married students in the schools is within the bounds of reasonable regulation by the Board.

. . . .

It is to be gathered from the statement of these teachers that some regulation is necessary. A milder one than that adopted by this resolution is not suggested. Nor does one occur to this Court. Based on this line of reasoning the conclusion must be that the regulation has a reasonable bearing on the progress and efficiency of these schools.

Boards of Education, rather than Courts, are charged with the important and difficult duty of operating the public schools. So, it is not a question of whether this or that individual judge or court considers a given regulation adopted by the Board as expedient. The Court's duty, regardless of its personal views, is to uphold the Board's regulation unless it is generally viewed as being arbitrary and unreasonable. Any other policy would result in confusion detrimental to the progress and efficiency of our public school system.

. . . .

The extreme to which a Court will go sometimes to carry out the wholesome policy of not interfering with the acts of Boards of Education, unless clearly arbitrary and unreasonable, is reflected in the case of Pugsley v. Sellmeyer, 158 Ark. 247, 250 S.W. 538, 30 A.L.R. 1212. The regulation there forbade girl students from the use of cosmetics. This rule was upheld by the majority opinion of that Court, and the eighteen year old girl deprived of the privilege of attending school because she insisted upon putting face powder on her face. Maybe it should be observed that this was back in 1923.

The decree of the Chancellor will be affirmed with costs adjudged against the relator and his sureties.

Guides for Class Discussion

1. Do you agree with the court that the board, in enacting the rule in question, did not abuse its discretion? Give reasons.
2. What is the court's responsibility or duty in matters of the sort considered here?
3. Compare this decision with the one rendered in *School District* v. *Powell, infra;* compare with *State ex rel. Ball* v. *McPhee, infra.*

23. "*When called upon to review the discretion of a school board, the courts will inquire whether the board acted within the scope of its authority, whether it followed the procedures prescribed by statute, and whether it had some reasonable basis for its action*" (p. 5).

STATE EX REL. BALL v. McPHEE,

6 Wis. (2d) 190, 94 N.W. (2d) 711 (1959)

(Decided by the Supreme Court of Wisconsin)

[While this case involved a state board of education—the Wisconsin Board of Regents of State Colleges—the principles laid down are applicable to local boards of education. This action was brought by a teacher to set aside a resolution of the defendant state board sustaining his discharge and requiring it to either reinstate plaintiff or to give him a new hearing. The trial court held for the teacher, and the board appealed. The higher court affirmed the decision of the lower court. One of the main points before the court was the conditions under which the court could review a discretionary act of the board.]

CURRIE, Justice.

.   .   .   .

The brief of the attorney general contends that when review is sought by certiorari of a decision of an administrative agency, such as the defendant board in the instant case, the sole question is whether the agency acted within its jurisdiction. We are satisfied that this is too narrow an interpretation of the scope of such review. This is borne out by the declaration of this court in State ex rel. Progreso Development Co. v. Wisconsin Real Estate Brokers Board, 1930, 202 Wis. 155, 168, 231 N.W. 628, 633, that a reviewing court in certiorari will inquire "to ascertain, not only whether the subordinate officer or board kept within its jurisdiction, but also to see whether or not he or it acted according to law."

Construing the phrase "acted according to law," we deem the word "*law*" means not only any applicable statutes but also the common law concepts of due process and fair play and avoidance of arbitrary action. As Mr. Justice Fritz well stated in State ex rel. Madison Airport Co. v. Wrabetz, 1939, 231 Wis. 147, 153, 285 N.W. 504, 507, "the cardinal and ultimate test of the presence or absence of due process of law in any administrative proceeding is the presence or absence of the 'rudiments of fair play long known to our law.'"

The Minnesota court in Oliver Iron Mining Co. v. Commissioner of Taxation, 1956, 247 Minn. 6, 10, 76 N.W. 2d 107, 111, recently stated in a certiorari case that "it is well settled that . . . this court will go no further than to determine: (1) Whether the board kept within its jurisdiction; (2) whether it proceeded on correct theory of the law; (3) whether its action was arbitrary, oppressive, or unreasonable and represented its will and not its judgment; and (4) whether the evidence was such that it might reasonably make the order or determination in question."

In School City of Elwood v. State ex rel. Griffin, 1932, 203 Ind. 626, 180 N.E. 471, 473, 81 A.L.R. 1027, the Indiana court had before it a teachers' tenure statute similar to sec. 37.31 (1), Wis. Stats., which provided that the school board's action in discharging a teacher "shall be final." Acts Ind. 1927, c. 97. In a mandamus proceeding brought in behalf of a lady teacher who had been discharged because she had married, the court ordered reinstatement on the ground that such fact of marriage was not a statutory ground for discharge. In discussing the scope of review the court stated:

"If a school board dismisses a teacher for a cause named in the statute, such action is conclusive and is not subject to review by the courts, unless the board in taking the action *acted in bad faith, arbitrarily, corruptly, fraudulently, or in gross abuse of its discretion.*" (Emphasis supplied.)

This same court later decided School City of Peru v. State ex rel. Youngblood, 1937, 212 Ind. 255, 7 N.E. 2d 176, 1002, 9 N.E. 2d 80, arising under the same tenure statute, in which a discharged teacher sought reinstatement by mandamus, and the trial court's judgment of reinstatement was reversed. The court found that the school board had complied with all the requirements of the teachers' tenure statute in making the discharge, and concluded with this statement (7 N.E. 2d at page 181):

"Under the circumstances here presented, the jurisdiction of the trial court was limited to a consideration of whether or not there was *substantial evidence* before the board to support the charges against the appellee." (Emphasis supplied.)

We deem that the foregoing quotations from the cited court decisions, which bear on the scope of court review in certiorari or mandamus of a decision of an administrative agency, merit our approval and are applicable to the instant appeal.

Guides for Class Discussion

1. Compare the decision in this case with the one rendered by the court in *School District* v. *Powell, infra,* and also with *State* v. *Marion County Board of Education, supra.*

2. Are you in agreement with the court's reasoning? Why or why not?

24. *"The board's action will be overruled [by the court] only when it has acted arbitrarily, unreasonably, under an erroneous theory of the law, or without any substantial basis of fact"* (p. 5).

SCHOOL DISTRICT v. POWELL,
203 Ore. 168, 279 P. (2d) 492 (1954)
(Decided by the Supreme Court of Oregon)

[The District School Board of School District No. 7, Sherman County, Oregon, filed a petition in circuit court to obtain judicial approval of the proceedings which authorized a bond issue in the amount of $360,000 for a new high school. A taxpayer and voter—Powell—appeared in opposition to the petition. He contended that the bond issue should not be approved because the school board had not followed the statute, relating to the issuance of bonds, precisely. The circuit court sustained the proceedings authorizing the bond issue, and Powell appealed. The Supreme Court affirmed the decree of the trial court. In arriving at its decision, the court found it necessary to comment on its authority to interfere with the actions of a school board.]

LUSK, Justice.

.   .   .   .

It is properly conceded by the contestant that a school board has a wide discretion in the exercise of the authority committed to it. Courts can interfere only when the board refuses to exercise its authority or pursues some unauthorized course. . . . The wisdom or expediency of an act, or the motive with which it was done, is not open to judicial inquiry or consideration where power to do it existed. . . . Acts in abuse of discretion may be restrained, but the presumption is that there was no abuse . . . and the burden of proving abuse of discretion is on the one asserting it, and it must be established by clear and convincing evidence. . . . It is always to be borne in mind when questions of this kind arise that it is the school board, not the courts, to which the administration of the affairs of a school district is entrusted, and that the right to obtain relief from the courts against the action of the board depends upon a clear showing that such action is illegal or arbitrary. A court is not a Super School Board. "With the exercise of discretionary powers courts rarely, and only for grave reasons, interfere. . . . Difference in opinion or judgment is never a sufficient ground for interference." Dailey v. New Haven, 60 Conn. 314, 319, 22 A. 945, 947. . . .

Much of the criticism in contestant's brief of the action of the board—and, it may be added, of the action of the people in the district themselves since they voted by a large majority in favor of the bond issue—is founded on a difference of opinion between the contestant and the board as to whether the new high school building is really needed and will be worth what it is proposed to pay for it. With these matters the court cannot concern itself. The other basis of attack is the alleged ignorance of the school directors concerning the new building and the affairs of the district. The directors were called first as witnesses by the petitioner; they were recalled by the contestant in support of the claim of abuse of discretion. One or two of them, it may be conceded, did not make very effective witnesses, and one displayed a lamentable lapse of memory as to some of the matters about which he was questioned. Whether this was due to the fact that he was in the unaccustomed role of a witness in court or to some other cause there is no way of telling. In any event the testimony does not convince us, as it did not convince the trial judge, that when the school board met more than eight months before the trial and adopted the resolution calling the bond election they did not exercise an informed judgment respecting the business in hand.

Guides for Class Discussion

1. Compare the decision in this case with the one rendered in *State* v. *Marion County Board of Education, supra.*
2. Compare this case with *State ex rel. Ball* v. *McPhee, supra.*
3. Are you in agreement with the court's thinking? Give reasons.

25. "*A board of education must itself exercise the authority imposed upon it by statute where the exercise of such authority involves judgment or discretion*" (*p. 5*).

JOHNSON v. SABINE PARISH SCHOOL BOARD,
19 La. App. 272, 140 So. 87 (1932)
(Decided by the Court of Appeal of Louisiana,
Second Circuit, Second Division)

[Plaintiff brought this action to enforce the specific performance of an alleged contract, or, in the alternative, to obtain damages. The facts of the case indicate that on the 6th of August, 1930, the defendant school board passed a motion authorizing one of its members to obtain the services of a driver for a school bus route. This board member—Cates—entered into a contract with plaintiff in the name of the board to render the services indicated. Plaintiff later purchased a bus and built a body for it. Later the board, with full knowledge of all of the facts, was alleged to have canceled the contract by employing another man to perform the same services. The board defended this action on the ground that the contract was illegal because it had no authority to delegate the powers it did to Cates. The lower court held in favor of the board, and the court here affirmed its decision.]

STEPHENS, J.

. . . .

A public board is constituted to act in the interest of the public welfare as a deliberative body with each of its members assisting the board to arrive at a conclusion which reflects the result of their united wisdom and experience. The board alone, therefore, must finally determine every subject committed to its discretion and judgment.

The general rule, succinctly stated, is that legislative and discretionary powers devolved by law on a public board or governing body politic cannot be delegated or referred to the discretion and judgment of its subordinates or any other authority. A contrary rule prevails, however, as to ministerial duties or administrative functions of such board or body.

The act of the Legislature . . . which confers the power and authority, and imposes the duty on the school board to provide for the transportation of school children, is general in its terms. The method by which the purpose of the act is to be accomplished is not specified, and is therefore impliedly committed to the discretion of the board.

Mr. A. B. Cates, acting under the authority of the resolution, as set forth in the petition, contracted with the plaintiff in the name of the defendant board, thereby exercising its power to contract, and substituting his judgment and discretion for that of the board in determining the person to be employed as driver of the transfer route, and the compensation to be paid for that service.

Clearly, the action of the defendant board in delegating its power to contract with reference to a matter in which it was necessary to exercise a discretion, and in referring the exercise of that discretion to an individual, is without statutory authority or other legal sanction.

Guides for Class Discussion

1. The rule laid down by the court was one regarding a discretionary power. How would the court have ruled had the power in question been ministerial in character rather than discretionary?

2. See *Looney* v. *Consolidated Independent School District, infra.*

3. Differentiate between ministerial and discretionary powers.

26. *"The board does, however, have the authority to delegate to others the performance of a purely ministerial function"* (p. 5).

LOONEY v. CONSOLIDATED INDEPENDENT SCHOOL DISTRICT,
201 Iowa 436, 205 N.W. 328 (1925)
(Decided by the Supreme Court of Iowa)

[This was an action in equity to require the defendant district and its officers to pay a $3,000 warrant which had been issued on March 14, 1922, in payment for a school site which the district had allegedly purchased for $3,000. Among other questions before the court in this case was the authority of the board to delegate to the president the power to enter into a contract with plaintiff-appellee. Another question concerned the election held in 1923 at which the voters rescinded and canceled bonds approved in

1920. The lower court ruled in favor of the plaintiff, and the higher court affirmed its decision.]

ALBERT, J. In the early part of 1920, certain territory lying in Union and Adams counties was regularly formed into a consolidated school district. On the 3d of May following, at an election called for that purpose, the electors of said district voted to issue $75,000 worth of bonds for the purpose of building and furnishing a schoolhouse and securing a site therefor. Shortly thereafter an action of quo warranto to test the legality of the organization of the district was brought. On the trial thereof in the district court, relators lost, and on appeal to the Supreme Court, the judgment of the district court was affirmed on February 7, 1922. See State v. Kinkade, 192 Iowa, 1362.

In the intervening time, negotiations were had between the appellant school board and the appellee looking to the purchase of a site for a schoolhouse, which resulted in appellee giving to the appellant board an option to buy 5 acres of land owned by him for the sum of $3,000, to be used as a schoolhouse site.

On the 11th day of March, 1922, appellant board of directors met, with all members present, accepted appellee's offer and voted unanimously to buy said property for $3,000. The record of the board reads:

"Director F. M. Webb offered a motion that the president of the Consolidated Independent School District of Cromwell in the counties of Union and Adams, state of Iowa, be empowered to close the option with G. T. Looney for school building site as previously agreed upon, and a warrant be drawn upon the school treasury to be paid out of the first money received from the sale of bonds, and warrant to be delivered to said G. T. Looney as soon as deed to land is delivered. Consideration to be $3,000. Director Grant Sammons seconded the motion. On roll call, the motion was unanimously carried."

Pursuant thereto a warrant was issued as follows:
"No. 278   State of Iowa, March 14, 1922.

"The Treasurer of Consolidated Independent District of Cromwell, in Union and Adams County: Pay to George T. Looney, or order, the sum of three thousand and no/100 dollars, out of schoolhouse fund deposited in Cromwell Bank, Cromwell, Iowa.

"By order of board of directors.
        "E. E. Kinkade, President.
          G. E. Sutton, Secretary."

$3,000

.   .   .   .

This warrant was presented by the president of the board to Looney, who thereupon, with his wife, made proper warranty deed to the defendant for the land in controversy. On the 20th of March, 1922, said warrant was presented to the treasurer of the district, who indorsed the same and marked it "Not paid for want of funds." On the 12th day of August, 1924, the instant action was brought.

. . . .

Appellant . . . urges that the board of directors was without authority to delegate, to the president and secretary, the power to enter into a contract with the appellee for the purchase of the land in question. "Such power rests solely with the board, and cannot be delegated."

As heretofore recited, this land was optioned by the appellee to the board for $3,000. At the meeting of the board, a motion was made and unanimously carried, to accept the offer and close the option, at $3,000, for the particular land in controversy. This was the official action of the board, and all the president of the board was instructed to do, and all he in fact did do, was to turn over to the appellee Looney, the warrant for $3,000 and receive from Looney the deed. The power, therefore, delegated to the president of the board in this instance was wholly ministerial. . . . It is our holding that the board in its official capacity, selected this site and bought this property, and what the president of the board did in procuring the deed and recording the same was purely ministerial.

Guides for Class Discussion

1. How does this case differ from *Johnson* v. *Sabine Parish School Board, supra?*
2. What general legal principles are illustrated by this case?

27. *"A board of education does not have the authority to limit the free exercise of its judgment and discretion by prior announcement of policy, promise, or agreement"* (p. 5).

State v. Trent Independent School District,
141 S.W. (2d) 438 (Tex.) (1940)
(Decided by the Court of Civil Appeals of Texas)

[Among other questions before the court was the legality of an agreement by a school district to maintain a certain elementary school even though the district became consolidated. When the board of the consolidated district of which it later became a part failed to maintain the school, this action was brought by the plaintiff. The lower court held in favor of the district, and the higher court affirmed the decision of the lower court.]

FUNDERBURK, Justice.

. . . .

. . . The relief prayed in this . . . action was to have a former consolidation of the Goodman Common School District (itself a consolidated common county line district partly in Fisher and partly in Jones Counties) with Trent Independent School District, in Taylor County, decreed to be void. An alternative purpose was that a certain pre-election agreement be held binding, and the Trent Independent School District be directed to "maintain the elementary schools at the Goodman school house according to their pre-election agreement and that said elementary schools be continuously maintained at the Goodman school house and school plant and that the trustees of the Trent Independent School District be directed by the order of this court to properly equip and maintain said school plant and the elementary school at the Goodman school house. . . ."

. . . .

. . . All of the assignments of error relate to the alternative purpose of the suit, which, as we construe the pleading, was to procure something in the nature of a mandatory injunction requiring the trustees of the Trent Independent School District to permanently maintain an elementary school at the school house in the territory comprising the former Goodman Common School District, as it existed before the consolidation with the Trent Independent School District. It was, in substance, alleged that after maintaining such elementary school for a short while following the consolidation, it had been abandoned, contrary to an alleged pre-election agreement to so maintain it.

We think the judgment rendered by the court was the only proper judgment for, perhaps, a number of different reasons. It is deemed sufficient, however, to discuss but one.

. . . .

The alleged pre-election agreement was not a contract to which the trustees of the Trent Independent School District and said individuals were respecting the parties. Persons acting upon such agreement were, as a matter of law, we think, charged with notice that the powers of the trustees were conferred by law for public purposes, and the exercise thereof, involving, as it does, a matter of future policy, properly subject to change to meet changing conditions, could not be restricted by an agreement of the nature of the one here involved.

The decisions relied upon by appellants are, we think, not at all applicable. In one of them (Black v. Strength, 112 Tex. 188, 246 S.W. 79, 80) is this significant statement: "The court was not binding itself to a certain course of action in the future." The agreement here in question, if effective as contended, did bind the board of trustees to a certain course of action in the future, namely, the perpetual maintenance of an elementary school at a particular place, even if the need therefor in the judgment of the trustees may have ceased to exist.

It is our conclusion that the judgment of the court below should be affirmed, and it is accordingly so ordered.

Guides for Class Discussion

1. What line of reasoning motivated the court in arriving at the decision it did?
2. Are you in agreement with this decision? Give reasons.
3. See *Jennings v. Clearwater School District, infra.*

28. *"Those to whom . . . promises or commitments are made are presumed to know that the board is merely giving expression to its present intent and that it may later change its policy"* (p. 5).

JENNINGS V. CLEARWATER SCHOOL DISTRICT,
65 Cal. App. 102, 223 P. 84 (1924)
(Decided by the District Court of Appeal,
Second District, Division 2, California)

[This action was brought to restrain a school board from using any part of the funds raised by the issuance of school bonds for the purchase of a school site which did not adjoin a site already used for school purposes. It was contended by plaintiff that an understanding existed between the district's trustees and the electors of the district that, if the issuance of the bonds was approved, a site would be obtained adjacent to one already used for school purposes and a building would be constructed thereon. The question before the court was whether such an understanding was binding upon the board. The lower court held it was not, and the higher court affirmed the decision of the lower court.]

CRAIG, J. . . .

. . . .

The contention which apellant urges most strongly is that prior to the election an understanding was entered into between the electors of the school district and the trustees that the proceeds of the bonds, if voted, would be used to purchase a site adjoining that of the school owned by the district. This proposition is not worthy of serious consideration. The law makes no provision for informal understandings of this character. On the contrary, the authorities cited by appellant expressly hold that the proposition submitted to the electors, and upon which bonds are voted, and which is later evidenced by the bonds themselves, constitutes a contract, and necessarily the only contract between the parties. In addition to this the electors may, if called together by the school board for the purpose of consultation, make recommendations as to the selection of the school site, which the board may not disregard. But there is no place in the entire procedure for understandings, except such as are expressed in the submission upon which the electors vote. None of the authorities cited by appellant upon this phase of the appeal sustain his position, but, as we have indicated, practically preclude the acceptance of this view. This is true of Peery v. City of Los Angeles, 187 Cal. 753, 203 Pac. 992, 19 A.L.R. 1044, and Hollywood High School Dist. et al. v. Keyes, 12 Cal. App. 172, 107 Pac. 129. In the instant case the amended complaint shows that the electors voted bonds for the purpose of "raising money for purchasing school lots," etc. It is nowhere alleged that the site to be purchased was more definitely designated, and this without doubt was a sufficient description to present the proposition to the voters.

But the law expressly authorizes the school trustees to call a meeting of the electors of the district for purposes of consultation. This they did, specifying in the notice that the subject of the consultation should be "instructing the board of trustees with respect to the purchase of a school site and the erecting thereon of a schoolhouse." This notice sufficiently designated the matter to be considered and acted upon by the electors. It informed everyone interested of the general subject to be discussed and determined. The meeting was held, and a resolution was adopted directing the board of trustees to purchase certain property, which action upon the part of the board the petitioner now seeks to enjoin. In addition to the argument based upon the claim that an understanding existed, to which we have adverted, it is further urged that neither the notice of the meeting held on January 13, 1922, nor the resolution adopted at that meeting specified that the school site to be purchased and the schoolhouse to be erected thereon were to be financed from the proceeds of the bonds which had been voted on July 12, 1921. We think this contention is devoid of merit. The records discloses that there was but one source supplying Clearwater school district with the funds needed for the purposes in question. The history of the entire proceedings as disclosed by appellant's amended complaint shows that all of the meetings which were held, of which the one held January 13th was the third, had to do with the disposition of the money derived from the sale of the bonds voted on July 12, 1921. In numerous cases cited by respondent language equally general in

character embodied in notices for similar purposes was held sufficient.
. . .

Guides for Class Discussion

1. Compare this case with *State* v. *Trent Independent School District, supra.*
2. Are you in agreement with the court? Give reasons.

29. ". . . *action taken by board members acting separately is not the action of the board and is without legal force*" (pp. 5-6).

STATE v. CONSOLIDATED SCHOOL DISTRICT,
281 S.W. (2d) 511 (Mo.) (1955)
(Decided by the Springfield Court of Appeals)

[This was an action in the nature of *quo warranto* brought by taxpayers against certain school districts which had attempted a reorganization. The taxpayers questioned the legality of the special elections which resulted in the votes that approved reorganization. One ground for questioning the legality of the elections was that the school board meeting at which the elections were approved was not a legal meeting.]

RUARK, Judge.

. . . .

The board of directors of a school district is an entity which can act and speak only as such. The separate and individual acts and decisions of the director members, even though they be in complete agreement with each other, have no effect. They must be assembled and act *as a board*. . . . This applies to meetings calling special school elections. . . . It is true that the meeting may be informal and it may be by agreement and without formal call. The keeping of written minutes is not necessarily a requisite to the validity of its actions. . . . But we think the failure to keep minutes is a fact to be considered in determining whether the coming together was in fact a discussion between individuals or was intended as a function of the board.

The board of directors of Slicer District was composed of Messrs. Moore, Sparks and Cooper, Cooper being the president. At some time (date not shown) a petition to annex to Bernie was delivered to president Cooper. He in turn delivered it to Mr. Gulledge, the clerk, and "told him to put up the notices if the other two were willing," "and I gave him my okay on it." His statement in this respect is substantially verified by the clerk. A petition to annex to Malden was presented to director Moore. Thereafter Moore took the petition by Sparks's [sic] home and asked Sparks if he saw anything wrong with it. The next day directors Sparks and Moore met at the residence of Gulledge and discussed the two petitions. . . . This get-together, if we may call it that, by the two directors was entirely informal. It was not called to order as such and there were no votes taken. Both the clerk and director Sparks testified no minutes were kept and the minute book showed none, but director Moore testified that the clerk "wrote it down that us two was favoring election." In this discussion it was agreed to hold the two elections, which are the March and April elections here in question. The two directors agreed that the Bernie election would be held in March and the Malden election was to be held on the 7th day of April at the regular annual meeting of the district.

We think the discussion between the two directors at the clerk's house cannot be dignified as one which fills the requirements of the law. While individually the parties may have been in agreement as to the necessity of an election, at least in respect to the Bernie proposal, there was no concerted action and apparently no intent to perform any act in the capacity and entity of that of a board of directors. . . . The evidence shows that there was no meeting or action of the board in respect to either the March or April election other than the discussion at the clerk's house which the appellants contend sufficed for such. While there is no question but that the motives of the directors were of the highest, we think their manner of getting together had no more dignity in law than any ordinary fence-row conference. For this reason we are forced to the conclusion that the March and April elections were not called and were therefore nullities.

Guides for Class Discussion

1. Are you in agreement with the court's decision that a school board must act as a body and that action taken by board members acting separately is without effect? Give reasons.

2. What other principles of law relating to board meetings did the court mention?

30. *"All the members of a board of education must be given actual or constructive notice of any meeting of the board"* (p. 6).

GREEN V. JONES,
144 W. Va. 276, 108 S. W. (2d) 1 (1959)
(Decided by the Supreme Court of Appeals of West Virginia)

[While this was an election contest brought by plaintiff—Green—who sought a declaration of his election as a member of the Board of Education of Mason County, one of the principal questions for decision was the legality of a board meeting. It was contended that two board members who were not present at a special meeting of the board which accepted the resignation of a board member, thereby creating the vacancy to fill which the election was held, had not received sufficient notice of the meeting. It was stipulated that these men were served with proper notice of a board meeting to be held at 7:00 o'clock, about 4:30 p.m. of that same day shortly after reporting for work some 20 miles distant from the place where the meeting was to be held. The statute provided for special meetings, but was silent on the question of notice required. The lower court upheld the legality of the meeting in question, as did also the higher court on appeal. In discussing the matter the higher court laid down certain principles of law regarding special meetings.]

HAYMOND, Judge.

. . . .

Regardless of the absence from the current statute of any requirement of a notice of a special meeting of a board of education, however, it is elementary that no authority existing in a number of persons can be rightfully exercised, in the absence of any members of such group or body, unless all have had reasonable notice and an opportunity to be present. . . . It is also fundamental that notice must be given an interested party of any proposed step which affects his rights. . . . No notice of a special meeting of a board of education is necessary, however, if all members are present and participate in the meeting; and notice of a special meeting of a board of education is for the benefit of the members of the board. . . .

Notwithstanding the lack of any specific provision in Section 4, Article 5, Chapter 18, Code, 1931, as amended, requiring notice of a special meeting of the board of education, it is clear that in the absence of any of its members, reasonable notice of the time and place of a special meeting of a board of education is essential to enable the board to take valid official action at such meeting. When a statute or rule or regulation does not prescribe the period for which notice of a meeting shall be given a notice given a reasonable time before the meeting is sufficient. . . . A reasonable time within which notice of a meeting must be given before such meeting means sufficient time to the party notified for preparation and attendance at the time and place of such meeting. . . . The burden of proving notice rests upon the party who asserts the existence of notice. . . .

It is the contention of the contestant that the written notice given to Adkins and Arnold [the two board members] and with which they were served about 4:30 o'clock of the afternoon of the day of the meeting was not a sufficient notice; that the special meeting of the board held pursuant to such notice was not a legal meeting of the board; and that the action of the board in accepting the resignation of Schultz was invalid. There is no merit in this contention.

Guides for Class Discussion

1. What principles of law relating to school board meetings were mentioned by the court?
2. Why does the law insist that adequate notice be given of school board meetings?
3. This case involved a special meeting. What is the law regarding regular meetings?
4. See *School District* v. *Garrison, supra.*

31. *"Where the statutes or the rules of the board provide that the board shall meet at certain designated times, the board members have constructive notice [of meetings] and no further notice is necessary"* (p. 6).

Marchant v. Langworthy,
6 Hill (N.Y.) 646 (1844)
(Decided by the Supreme Court, Utica, New York)

[This was an action brought by plaintiff against trustees of the district to recover a horse which had been sold to settle a tax imposed by defendants against plaintiff. The main question before the court was the validity of the annual district meeting at which the defendants were chosen, held on the first Monday of October, 1842. The clerk admitted he posted no notice of the meeting, believing it to be unnecessary, and produced the record of the annual meeting held on the first Monday of October, 1841, which indicated adjournment until the first Monday of October, 1842. The lower court decided this was sufficient notice for the meeting held in 1842 and none other was required. The higher court affirmed this decision.]

By the Court, BEARDSLEY, J. The substance of the objection to the legality of the annual meeting of 1842 was, that notice had not been posted by the clerk of the district as the statute directs. . . . The court of common pleas seems to have proceeded upon the ground that the adjournment of the annual meeting of 1841 to that of 1842 was a sufficient notice of the latter. But the power "to adjourn from time to time, as occasion may require," . . . does not apply to such a case. Meetings are required to be held in each school district annually, and each annual meeting is to fix the time and place for holding the next. . . . An annual meeting therefore, cannot be an adjourned meeting, within the meaning of the statute. The latter is one to be held between two annual meetings "as occasion may require."

It is declared by statute that "the proceedings of no district meeting, annual or special, shall be held illegal, for want of a due notice to all the persons qualified to vote thereat, unless it shall appear that the omission to give such notice, was wilful and fraudulent." . . . In the present instance, the clerk omitted to post notice, believing it to be unnecessary. It was not pretended in the court below that the omission was fraudulent, and no such question can be made here. The annual meeting of 1842 must therefore be taken to have been a legal assemblage; and as the defendants were duly chosen at the meeting, their defence is complete.

The result in this case would be the same if the statute had omitted to declare that the want of notice should not invalidate the proceedings of an annual meeting. The provision requiring the clerk to post notice of annual meetings, is merely directory to that officer. And "there is a known distinction," says Lord Mansfield, "between circumstances which are of the *essence* of a thing required to be done by an act of parliament, and clauses *merely directory*." . . . An annual meeting is required to be held in each school district; and at each annual meeting, the time and place of holding the next annual meeting is to be fixed. . . . For greater caution, and to give greater publicity to the meeting, the statute directs the clerk to post notice of it; but that is not essential to its validity. The time and place for holding it may always be ascertained by examining the clerk's records; and an objection that notice was not duly posted should never be allowed to prevail. The foundation of the meeting is the order of a previous annual meeting; not the posting of a notice by the clerk. The former is indispensable; but not the latter. . . .

The judgment of the common pleas must be affirmed.

Ordered accordingly.

Guides for Class Discussion

1. Do you think the fact that this was a meeting of the inhabitants of a school district rather than a school board made any difference?
2. Do you think the court today would hold as it did in 1844?
3. See *Green* v. *Jones, supra.*

32. "*In case all the members of a board are present and consent to act, the necessity of notice is waived*" (p. 6).

SCHOOL DISTRICT V. ALLEN,
83 Ark. 491, 104 S.W. 172 (1906)
(Decided by the Supreme Court of Arkansas)

[The facts of the case will be found in the material which follows.]

Action by Jessie Allen against school district No. 68. From a judgment for plaintiff, defendant appeals. Affirmed.

Appellee sued appellant, alleging that on the 24th of March, 1905, appellee entered into a contract with appellant through two of its directors, whereby appellee was employed by appellant to teach a school for a period of seven months at $40 per month; that services of appellee were to commence on the 10th of July, 1905; that at the time of the making of the contract all the directors of the district had notice, and all were present; that appellee was present at the time and place agreed upon, and offered to enter upon the service of appellant as teacher, but the appellant through its directors refused to permit her to enter upon such service and refused to pay her for such service. Wherefore she prayed for judgment in the sum of $280 damages. Appellant denied all material allegations of the complaint, except that it was a school district.

. . . .

Wood, J. . . .

Appellant contends that there was no notice. Conceding that this is true, it did not affect the validity of the contract under the evidence adduced, for Emerson, one of the directors, testified as follows: "We three directors met in the schoolyard and Mr. West said to me that Mr. Davidson was here, and we had better talk the matter over as to who we will employ to teach our school another year. We all three of us got together, and at this time Mr. West asked what we thought of employing Miss Allen to teach our next school. Mr. Davidson said that he thought the district wanted a man to teach, and that he thought it would be best to have a man. Mr. West said that he was in favor of Miss Allen, the plaintiff, and I said I was, too. Mr. Davidson stated that he would not be contrary, or words to that effect. I got up about this time, it being understood we would employ Miss Allen to teach our next term of school, and I notified Miss Allen later that she could consider herself employed to teach our next term of school." In School District v. Adams, 69 Ark. 159, 61 S. W. 793, we held that two directors could not bind the district by entering into a contract for the employment of a teacher at a special meeting of which the third director had no notice, though he was present, if he declined to participate in the meeting. But the above evidence tended to prove that all the directors participated in the meeting. It was sufficient for the jury to find that they did, although Davidson, one of the directors, testified to the contrary. In School District v. Adams, supra, speaking of a special or called meeting, we said: "Notice is indispensable, unless waived by the presence of all the directors, and their participation, to the legality of its action to bind the district."

Guides for Class Discussion

1. See *Green* v. *Jones, supra;* and *State* v. *Consolidated School District, supra.*
2. What is the rationale back of this decision?

33. *"Under the common law a simple majority of the board is a legal quorum"* (p. 6).

GUNNIP V. LAUTENKLOS,
33 Del. Ch. 415, 94 A. (2d) 712 (1953)
(Decided by the Court of Chancery of Delaware)

[This case was brought to compel a school-building commission to award a school-building contract to plaintiff whose bid was not the lowest but who accompanied his bid with a letter suggesting the making of certain changes in the specifications which, if they were made, would decrease his bid and make it the lowest. The building commission ignored his letter and this action was brought. The court held that, in refusing to consider the letter, the commission did not abuse its discretion.]

BRAMHALL, Vice Chancellor.

. . . .

Plaintiffs contend that the final plans, specifications and estimates of costs were never approved by the School Building Program Board and the State Board of Education, as provided by Chapter 148, of Volume 48, Laws of Delaware, 1951.

This statute provides that the School Building Program Board shall consider and determine the necessity for any school construction program and shall certify to the State Treasurer its determination, together with the total estimated costs of construction and the respective shares of such total costs to be paid by the state and the local school district. The minutes of this Board show that such approval was given with reference to the Krebs School on October 10, 1951. This act further provides that the School Building Program Board and the State Board of Education shall approve the final plans, together with estimates of cost and specifications. The minutes of the Krebs school program show that such approval was given to the Krebs school program on September 24, 1952. The minutes of the State Board of Education show that consideration and approval were given to the preliminary plans on March 20, 1952, and to the final plans and specifications on August 28, 1952. The act provides that the School Building Commission shall carry out the construction program and in doing so shall make and enter into all contracts for school construction, furniture, equipment, et cetera; there is no provision therein for the approval of the plans and specifications by the School Building Commission.

Plaintiffs contend that the construction program for the Krebs School was never formally approved because: (1) such approval was not given by all of the members of the School Program Board and the State

Board of Education, since all of the members were not present at any one meeting. . . .

The assertion of plaintiffs that the approval of the construction program was void because all of the members of these bodies were not present at each meeting is without merit. It is sufficient if all the members were duly notified of the meetings and had an opportunity to participate therein. If due notice has been given, a majority constitutes a quorum. . . . This is the common law rule. In the absence of a statute the common law rule will be applied. . . . There was therefore a quorum present at all meetings of the School Building Program Board and all meetings of the State Board of Education. The minutes of these meetings were regular and complete. In the absence of evidence to the contrary, it will be presumed that all the members thereof had due notice of these meetings. . . .

There was one meeting of the School Building Commission on February 16, 1952, at which only three of the six members were present. However, the statute does not provide that the Commission give formal approval to the plans and specifications for the construction program; its duty was to see that they were put into effect.

Guides for Class Discussion

1. Compare the decision in this case with the decision in *Endeavor-Oxford Union Free High School District* v. *Walters, infra.*

2. What legal principles relating to school board meetings did the court recognize?

34. "A board has no authority to change the common law rule [regarding a quorum] under a statute which authorizes it to establish its own rules of procedure" (p. 6).

ENDEAVOR-OXFORD UNION FREE HIGH SCHOOL DISTRICT v. WALTERS,
270 Wis. 567, 72 N. W. (2d) 535 (1955)
(Decided by the Supreme Court of Wisconsin)

[This was an action to determine the legality of a board resolution relating to reorganization which was approved by a majority of a quorum of a school board committee, but not by a majority of the entire committee. The trial court held the resolution was legal and its decision was approved by the Supreme Court, which ruled that for approving such a petition the requirement of a vote greater than that required by common law was erroneous.]

STEINLE, Justice.

.   .   .   .

At common law a majority of the membership of a board or a committee constitutes a quorum for the transaction of business, and a majority vote of the quorum is decisive.

Where the legislature confers powers upon a board to be exercised by it without providing as to the number of members necessary to act in concert to exercise the power or powers conferred on the board by the statute, then the common law rule prevails that a majority of the board constituting a quorum may lawfully act. . . .

In Seiler v. O'Maley, 190 Ky. 190, 227 S. W. 141, 142, it was held that under the common law rule, a majority of the authorized membership of a representative body consisting of a definite number of members constitutes a quorum for the purpose of transacting business, but it is competent for the statutes or the Constitution creating the body to prescribe the number of members necessary to constitute a quorum or to delegate to the creative body the authority to so prescribe.

In Ex parte Willcocks, 7 Cow., N.Y. 402, 409, 17 Am. Dec. 525, the court said that the general rule is that to make a quorum of a select and definite body of men possessing the power to elect, a majority, at least, must be present, and then a majority of the quorum may decide.

In the absence of other controlling provision, the common law rule that a majority of a whole body is necessary to constitute a quorum, applies. . . .

.   .   .   .

Under these common law principles, it is plain that since the legislature did not prescribe the number of votes required for the passage of a matter before a county school committee or joint committee, a majority of the committee constitutes a quorum, and a majority of the quorum may decide the matter. The committee has no implied power to adopt a rule that a greater or lesser number shall constitute a quorum. In the instant situation the joint committee by its action required a greater vote for approval of the petition than is provided by common law. Such requirement was erroneous. It was within the jurisdiction of the court to issue an order correcting the committee's error on the basis that such error constituted an abuse of discretion.

Guides for Class Discussion

1. Are you in agreement with the thinking of the court in this case? Why or why not?

2. How can the common-law rule to the effect that a simple majority constitutes a quorum be changed?

35. "*A quorum must be present in order for a board to take legal action*" (p. 6).

STATE V. SCHOOL DISTRICT,
116 Mont. 294, 151. P. (2d) 168 (1944)
(Decided by the Supreme Court of Montana)

[This case involved the legality of the action taken by a school board when a quorum was not present. It appears that the population of a school district declined to such a point that in 1940 the only pupils that resided in the district were the children of Nels and Florence Amundson. In 1941 the only eligible persons as trustees were these two individuals and Sophus Amundson, brother of Nels. In the school election, held in April, the three were elected as board members; Sophus for a three-year term, Nels for a two-year term, and Florence for a one-year term. The first two qualified, but Florence did not qualify as a trustee but continued to act as clerk for which she received a small salary. Other significant facts appear in the following quoted material.]

JOHNSON, C. J.

. . . .

The trustees took no action upon the employment of a teacher and in September, 1941, Florence Amundson claimed the right to teach under section 1075, Revised Codes, because she had been employed for three consecutive years and had not been notified on or before May first, 1941, that her services would not be required. But plaintiff ruled that she could not be employed as teacher because her employment would violate the Nepotism Act, sections 456.1 to 456.3, Revised Codes; she did not appeal to the state superintendent of public instruction from his ruling, but taught her children and claims pay for her services as teacher. In the summer of 1941 the trustees had one of the district's school houses moved to the Amundson ranch at an expense to the district of $112; at a special meeting of the board, held by the two trustees on March 6, 1942, according to minutes written by Florence Amundson as clerk, it was decided that an election should be held on

March 19th to authorize the sale of the school building to save the renewal of fire insurance, and the three Amundsons were appointed judges of election. Sophus Amundson moved out of the district and the county on about the 12th of March; at the election Nels and Florence Amundson were the only voters, and voted unanimously to authorize the sale; thereafter Nels Amundson, acting as sole trustee, sold the building to his wife, Florence, who was still the clerk of the district, for $75, and she tendered that sum to the county treasurer and claimed the school house as her own property.

In their briefs the defendants strenuously contended that the sale of the building was valid, but upon oral argument they abandoned that contention, and we need not therefore consider it. The first question to be considered is whether, after the departure of Sophus Amundson about March 12, 1942, Nels Amundson, as the sole remaining trustee, and Florence Amundson, as clerk, had authority to conduct the affairs of the district. Since the board of trustees of a third class school district consists of three trustees . . . and a *majority is required for a quorum* . . . it is apparent that Nels Amundson, the only trustee purporting to act as such after the departure of his brother from the district, had no power to perform any valid official action on behalf of the district, and that without reference to the Nepotism Act his wife Florence had no authority as clerk of the district to give effect to any of his actions. [Emphasis added.]

Guides for Class Discussion

1. Are you in agreement with the court's reasoning? Why or why not?
2. How would the court have held had Sophus Amundson remained in the district and continued to act as a board member —i.e. do you think that because all the members were related their action would be illegal?

36. *"Where a quorum is present, a motion is carried by a majority of those voting on it"* (p. 6).

ATTORNEY-GENERAL V. SHEPARD,
62 N. H. 383 (1882)
(Decided by the Supreme Court of New Hampshire)

[This was an action in *quo warranto* to test the validity of the election of certain aldermen of Concord. The main question before the court involved the legality of an amendment to the city's charter adopted by the board of aldermen, May 27, 1882. The board of aldermen consisted of seven members of whom six were present. Three voted in the affirmative, three refused to vote, and the chairman declared the ordinance passed. Each of the three non-voting members had been asked to vote by the chairman but each refused.]

DOE, C. J. The amendment of the city charter was a local legislative question that could be submitted by the senate and house, either to the people of Concord, or to the city council elected by the people as their representatives for the general purpose of exercising such powers of local legislation and administration as may be delegated to municipalities. . . . And the rejection of the amendment by the council would not render its subsequent adoption by the people unconstitutional.

There were seven aldermen. Four were a quorum. Six were present. Three voted for the adoption of the amendment, and the refusal of the other three to vote was inoperative. In the absence of express regulation, a proposition is carried in a town-meeting, or *other legislative assembly,* by a majority of the votes cast. [Emphasis added.] . . . The exercise of law-making power is not stopped by the mere silence and inaction of some of the law-makers who are present. An arbitrary, technical, and exclusive method of ascertaining whether a quorum is present, operating to prevent the performance of official duty and obstruct the business of government, is no part of our common law. The statute requiring the presence of four aldermen does not mean that in the presence of four a majority of the votes cast may not be enough. The journal properly shows how many members were there when the vote was taken by yeas and nays; there was no difficulty in ascertaining and recording the fact; and the requirement of a quorum at that time was not intended to furnish a means of suspending the legislative power and duty of a quorum.

No illegality appears in the adoption of the amendment.

Judgment for the defendants.

Guides for Class Discussion

1. What is the significance of the three italicized words, "other legislative assembly"?
2. See *Somers* v. *City of Bridgeport, infra.*
3. Do you think the court today would hold as it did in 1882? Give reasons.
4. Do you think this legal principle is applicable to a vote taken at a school-board meeting? Why?

37. "... *if the statutes provide that a measure must be carried by a majority of the board or of those present, the statutes must be followed*" (p. 6).

SOMERS V. CITY OF BRIDGEPORT,
60 Conn. 521 (1891)
(Decided by the Supreme Court of Connecticut)

[This was an action to restrain the defendant city from paying salaries to certain policemen. Among other things, it was claimed that the policemen were not legally appointed. The appointment was made by a non-partisan board of police commissioners, consisting of the Mayor and two representatives from each of the two major political parties. The Mayor could vote only in case of a tie. "Any action of the board required the concurrence of three members." At the time the policemen were allegedly employed, two members of the board announced they would not vote. Nevertheless, the Mayor put the question to a vote. Two members voted in favor of their appointment and two refrained from voting, whereupon the Mayor declared the resolution passed. The non-voting members protested but the vote was recorded. The question before the court was whether the patrolmen were legally appointed. In its decision the court held that failure to vote acted as an affirmative vote. In discussing this rule, it commented on the affect of a statute that required a majority vote of the whole number of the board or a majority of those present.]

Carpenter, J. . . .

. . . .

Were the patrolmen legally appointed? Action was taken at a regular meeting of the board at which all the members were present. The board had been directed four months before to appoint four additional patrolmen to supply a want caused by the annexation of West Stratford to the city. . . . An attempt to supply this need was met by two of the commissioners, not by any objection to the time or manner of making the appointment, nor by any objection to the character or competency of the men, but simply by a refusal to take any action in the matter. We are not told what their motive was; nor are we at liberty to indulge in conjecture. On the face of the record they appear as obstructionists, and as such we must treat them. As it was the duty of the board to appoint, it was their duty to act. By their refusal to vote they neglected their duty. The needs of the city demanded action. Sound policy requires that public interests should not suffer by their inaction. Had they voted against the resolution there would have been a tie, and the mayor would have given a casting vote. Had he voted in the affirmative the legality of the appointment could not have been questioned. But they did not vote although present. Their presence made a quorum. A quorum was present, and all who voted, voted in the affirmative. Why was not the mayor justified in declaring the resolution passed? The silence of the non-voting members was acquiescence, and acquiescence was concurrence. Their previous declaration and their subsequent protest avail nothing. The test is, not what was *said* before or after, but what was *done* at the time of voting.

. . . .

Upon principle two members could not, by inaction, prevent action by the board. Being present, it was their duty to vote. Had they done so, a result would have been certain. The most that they could have done would have been to make a tie; and then the mayor, by his vote, could have passed or rejected the resolution. Their presence made a quorum and made it possible for the board to act. It would be strange if by their mere neglect of duty they could accomplish more than they could by direct action. The legal effect of their silence was an affirmative vote. . . .

. . . .

The principle thus enunciated has been sanctioned and applied by some excellent authorities in this country. . . .

. . . .

Proceeding upon that theory we should come to the same result—a tie, untied by the casting vote of the mayor. He was not required to give a formal vote; the declaration of the result was sufficient. . . . But the weight of authority regards the non-voting members as assenting to the action of the majority, whether in the affirmative or negative. In some instances a statute requires a majority of the whole number; or, as in the Pennsylvania case, *(Commonwealth* v. *Wickersham, supra),* a majority of those present. In such cases those not voting are necessarily counted with the minority. But in the absence of some special provision of that nature, so counting them might result in absurd consequences or serious inconvenience. In many instances the silent vote added to the minority would change the result; and in all cases it would be necessary to ascertain the number present and not voting, which would be attended with much inconvenience. But a presumed acquiescence in the result is attended with no such consequences. Hence we think that is the better view.

Guides for Class Discussion

1. The court's comments with respect to the effect of a statute that requires a majority vote of a board or of those present may be thought of as *dictum.* As such what was its legal effect?
2. See *Attorney-General* v. *Bickford, infra.*
3. On what ground could the court justify its ruling on the principle in question?

38. *"It is commonly held that blank ballots are to be considered a nullity—they are not to be counted for or against a measure, nor are they to be counted in ascertaining the number of ballots cast"* (p. 6).

ATTORNEY GENERAL v. BICKFORD,
77 N. H. 433, 92 A. 835 (1914)
(Decided by the Supreme Court of New Hampshire

[The facts of the case are to be found in the quoted material.]

Information, in the nature of quo warranto, to determine the right of the defendant to the office of superintendent of schools in Manchester. The board of school committee is a municipal body which is authorized and required to elect biennially in the month of June a superintendent of public instruction for the city. The defendant held the office for the term ending July 1, 1914. June 5, 1914, the school board at a regular meeting voted to proceed to ballot for a superintendent. Thereupon a vote was taken, which resulted as follows: Charles W. Bickford, five votes; John Smith, two votes; John Doe, one vote; blank, three votes. The chairman declared there was no choice. Since that time the defendant has been elected from month to month acting superintendent, and has performed the duties of superintendent, claiming that he was legally elected to that office, and has refused to accept the office of acting superintendent. The question of the effect of the above vote was transferred from the September term, 1914, of the superior court by Branch, J., on an agreed statement of facts.

. . . .

WALKER, J. At the time of the attempted election of a superintendent of schools by the school board, a quorum of the board were present. It then had the necessary legal authority to proceed with the election, and if a candidate for that office had received a majority of the votes cast he would have been legally elected. It is assumed by counsel in argument that a majority vote was necessary for an election, and the case has been considered upon that assumption. But it is not necessary that the successful candidate should receive a majority of the votes of those present constituting the quorum; a majority of the votes actually cast is sufficient. Attorney General v. Shepard, 62 N. H. 383. If, therefore, the three blank ballots are omitted from the count, the defendant would be elected, having received five of the eight votes cast. This is, in effect, conceded by the plaintiff; but it is argued that the three blanks should be counted and included in the declaration of the whole number of votes cast. Upon this theory the number necessary for a choice would be six, and the defendant would fail of election. While it is admitted that the blanks could not be counted as votes for any candidate, the fact of their being cast by members of the board shows, it is claimed, that those members were unwilling to vote for the defendant, and that they adopted this method of preventing his election. In other words, it was not an affirmative vote for any one, but a negative expression of their opposition to the election of the defendant, which can only be made effective by counting their blank ballots in the total of votes cast. This reasoning is not based upon any statute or rule of law of this state, nor upon any by-law or rule governing the action of the school board, and, if sound, it can only be supported by a judicial interpretation of the meaning of the blank ballots; that is, by the exercise of judicial ingenuity in deciding that a piece of paper upon which nothing is written or printed, which is found in a ballot box among the votes cast, clearly indicates that the person who deposited it was opposed to the election of the man who might have the most votes. The claim is it should be counted as one of the votes cast, although manifestly it cannot be counted as a vote for any particular person.

This theory in the case of general elections is opposed to the statutory declaration that "blank pieces of paper shall not be counted as ballots." P. S. c. 34, §2. The purpose of the Legislature was to exclude blanks from the count because, as it would seem, they are not votes within the meaning of the Constitution (articles 26, 30, 32). In Attorney General v. Colburn, 62 N. H. 70, 72, it is said that:

"It may be a question whether a paper containing and intended to contain no evidence of a purpose to vote for some person can be considered, as a vote, or be counted as an expression of a voter's choice, and whether a statute forbidding the counting of such papers is anything more than a statement of the meaning of the Constitution."

But if the statute above quoted is not applicable to this case because it relates only to general elections, as the plaintiff contends, the result is the same. The obvious definition of a vote, as used in reference to elections, includes the expression of a choice of candidates or measures submitted to the voters.

"A ballot may be defined to be a piece of paper, or other suitable material, with the name written or printed upon it of the person to be voted for." Cush. Leg. Assem. §103; Cooley, Const. Lim. (7th Ed.) 914.

Because blank pieces of paper are not votes expressive of a choice, Cooley says (page 921) that:

"In determining upon a majority or plurality, the blank votes, if any, are not to be counted; and a candidate may therefore be chosen without receiving a plurality or majority of votes of those who actually participated in the election."

According to authority, the mere participation in an election determinable by ballot does not render a voter's blank ballot effective in determining the result of the contest.

The argument that such a ballot indicates a purpose of the voter to register his refusal to vote for the successful candidate overlooks the fact that it is just as indicative of his purpose to concur in the result which the regular ballots disclose. It is difficult to see how it has any more effect upon the result than a refusal to vote, which is regarded, so far as it is important, as an acquiescence in the result. It has no negative effect. What the voter's purpose was is not apparent. It may have been one thing or another. He has not furnished sufficient evidence to enable the court to ascertain it, and the vote cannot be counted. . . .

Guides for Class Discussion

1. On what ground did the court arrive at its decision—that is, what reasoning motivated it?
2. Are you in agreement with this decision? Give reasons.
3. See *Somers* v. *City of Bridgeport, supra.*

39. "A board of education is free to change its policies as circumstances may dictate . . . [providing it acts] before vested rights have accrued to third parties" (p. 6).

STATE v. CARROLL COUNTY BOARD OF EDUCATION,
129 Ohio St. 262, 194 N.E. 867 (1935)
(Decided by the Supreme Court of Ohio)

[This was an action in mandamus instituted by relators as taxpayers residing in the Augusta Rural School District of Carroll County, Ohio, to compel the school board of that county to appoint a board of education for a new school district which relators alleged had recently been created by, and at the instance of, respondent. The facts of the case indicate that the county board had voted to create the new school district and later, following the receipt of a remonstrance petition, it voted to rescind the action previously taken creating the district. Plaintiff contended this action was illegal. The question before the court was the authority of the school board to rescind the action it had previously taken before rights had accrued to anyone.]

WEYGANDT, Chief Justice.

. . . .

The second question involves the effect of the final resolution adopted January 8, 1935. There is no claim of bad faith or abuse of discretion. The relators contend that under the provisions of section 4736, General Code, the action of the respondent on October 8, 1934, was final inasmuch as there was no valid remonstrance on file at the end of the thirty-day period. However, it must be observed that the creation of a new school district is an administrative matter addressed to the sound discretion of the board of education. The statute employs the word "may" and contains no language indicating an intention by the Legislature to so demarcate the powers of a board of education as to prevent a bona fide reconsideration and rescission of such action within a reasonable time and before further procedure in perfecting the new plan of operation. In the instant case neither the pleadings nor the agreed statement of facts disclose that anything whatsover had been accomplished except the adoption of the original resolution of October 8, 1934. There had been no "equitable division of the funds or indebtedness" as the statute provides; however, it is of course true that none was necessary since the creation of the new district involved no division of an existing district but merely the merger of two entire ones. Nevertheless, with reference to the many remaining administrative matters necessarily incident to such a project, nothing had been done. Necessarily considering this question as one merely of power and not of policy, this court is of the opinion that under the circumstances of this case a board of education is not precluded from a reconsideration and rescission of its original action, as was done on January 8, 1935.

Consistent with the foregoing views, the motion of the relators is overruled and that of the respondent is granted. The peremptory writ is thereby denied, and the action dismissed at the costs of the relators.

Writ denied.

Guides for Class Discussion

1. Had there been any "equitable division of the funds or indebtedness" with respect to the districts involved, previously to the time the board attempted to rescind its action, how do you think the court would have held?
2. Do you think the rule enunciated by the court is sound? Give reasons.

40. *"A school board should . . . keep a record of its actions, but in the absence of statute requiring that it do so, failure to keep a record of an action does not render the action void"* (p. 6).

FLEMING v. BOARD OF TRUSTEES,
112 Cal. App. 225, 296 p. 925 (1931)
(Decided by the District Court of Appeal, Third District, California)

[This was an action by a teacher to compel a school board to permit her to teach in the public schools of the district and to pay her salary therefor. The teacher in question had been serving as a probationary teacher, and the board had refused to employ her for the following year, which would have put her on tenure. No minutes of the board meeting at which this took place were kept. Likewise, no formal motion or vote of the members was taken or registered. Evidence indicated, however, that the subject in question was discussed and that at least two of the three board members declared their objection to the teacher's reelection. Among other questions before the court was whether the action of the board members which was not recorded in the minutes was legal. The court held it was.]

Mr. Justice R. L. THOMPSON delivered the opinion of the court.

. . . .

This formal action, however, has never been held to require strict adherence to the technical procedure approved by "Roberts' Rules of Order." Nowhere has it been held that a business proposition must necessarily be decided by a school board by means of the formal vote of the members indicated by the signs aye or nay. Any other method of securing the definite decisions of the respective members is sufficient so long as it enables them to determine whether a majority of the members of the board favor or oppose the proposition. Nowhere has it been held the proceedings of a school board are invalid unless they are formally recorded. In the absence of a statute requiring this to be done, it is unnecessary. If all of the members of a school board are present, or have knowledge of the meeting and have an opportunity to attend, and a majority of the members of the board, after a formal discussion as to the advisability of employing or discharging a teacher, definitely, separately, and finally declare themselves as opposed to the election or discharge of the particular teacher under discussion, in the absence of subsequent action of the board to the contrary, their decision will amount to a valid binding determination of the board just as conclusively as though they had formally voted by means of the ordinary signs of aye or nay. The result is just as definite and certain. . . .

This is precisely what occurred at the meeting of the board regarding the matter which is here in controversy. There can be no question in the present case that a majority of the members of the board separately, deliberately, and unequivocally decided, at a meeting in which the subject was formally discussed, that they did not desire to re-elect the petitioner for the ensuing year. . . .

Guides for Class Discussion

1. What was the legal principle or principles involved in the part of the decision quoted above?
2. Are you in agreement with the court's decision? Give reasons.

41. ". . . it has been held that a record is not necessary although the statutes require it—the statutes are regarded as directory rather than mandatory" (p. 6).

School District of Soldier Township v. Moeller,
247 Iowa St. 239, 73 N. W. (2d) 43 (1955)
(Decided by the Supreme Court of Iowa)

[This action was brought to enjoin the county treasurer from paying to an independent school district funds it claimed were due it for tuition and transportation for elementary pupils, residing in a township subdistrict, who attended school in the independent district during the school year 1949-1950. The trial court dismissed plaintiff's petition and plaintiff appealed. The higher court upheld the action of the lower court. The subdistrict, which had closed its school in 1947-1948 and 1948-1949, because of inability to obtain a teacher, had filed with the county superintendent a paper purporting to designate certain elementary pupils to attend school in the independent district during the school year 1949-1950. This designation was approved by the county board of education and filed with the state department of public instruction, by whom it was approved. The pupils designated attended school in the independent district. A tuition charge of $1,003.40 was approved and ordered paid by the county board of education. To enjoin the county treasurer from paying this amount to the independent district, the subdistrict brought this action. The paper designating the pupils to attend the independent district was signed by the president and secretary of the subdistrict board and was in proper form except that "only one of four forms usually filed was signed." Likewise, there was no official record authorizing such action, although the statute required the keeping of such a record. It was on this ground, largely, that plaintiff sought to enjoin the payment of the tuition.]

Thompson, Justice.

· · · · · · · · · · · · · · · · · · · ·

It is elementary that the officers of a school board have only such authority as the board may give them; they can take no action in the name of the board unless it has, in a legal meeting, empowered them so to do. . . . But it is also long settled in Iowa that a statute directing an official record of board proceedings is directory only. . . . The actions of the board may be shown by evidence outside the official minutes. . . . We went into the question of admissibility of oral evidence to show the action taken by an administrative board at some length in Morrow v. Harrison County, 245 Iowa 725, 739, 740, 64 N. W. 2d 52, 61. The body there concerned was the county board of supervisors, but the reasoning would certainly apply to a school board also. Many authorities are cited in the opinion (Garfield, J.), and the conclusion is reached that oral evidence is clearly admissible. ("We have repeatedly held that where there is no record of action taken at a board meeting oral evidence thereof is competent.")

The evidence for the plaintiff tending to deny the execution of the designation by any official act of the board is found in the absence of any official record authorizing it; in the testimony of the president and secretary that no official action was taken; that they did not knowingly sign it; and in plaintiff's Exhibit L, consisting of five sheets of unruled paper, undated except for the year 1949, which purports to contain designations of high school and elementary pupils for the following school year. There is no designation of the defendant school for elementary pupils thereon. The board secretary, Gustav Seils, testified it is a record of the designations made by the plaintiff board at its July meeting, written by him. Why he did not make this record in the official minutes instead of upon scratch paper he does not explain.

.   .   .   .

It will be noted that the action to be taken by the board in regard to designating elementary pupils to other schools is predicated upon a closing of the school "for lack of pupils or by action of the board." It is urged by the plaintiff that there is no showing the school was closed for lack of pupils. Passing the clear showing in the record that there were only four pupils resident in the subdistrict who would attend the school, it seems undisputed that the school was closed "by action of the board." It may be there is no record evidence of any action of the board closing the school. But it does appear without contradiction that the school had been closed for two years past, and no teacher had been secured for the coming school term. The rule which we have previously stated that the actions of a board are not void because no record is made in the official minutes but may be shown by outside evidence, is a salutary one. The officers and directors of small districts such as the one involved here are citizens who serve without compensation, whose other affairs occupy most of their time, and who are generally not trained in keeping exact records of their actions in managing the affairs of their schools. It would be an unduly harsh rule, leading to endless litigation and unjust results, to hold that no action may be upheld unless it is meticulously recorded in the official minute book. It would be highly unrealistic to hold here that the school was closed for two years without some action of the board. We cannot presume the board suffered the closing of the school for the length of time through the law of inertia; that it did not in some way take proper action, unrecorded though it may have been, approving such closing.

Guides for Class Discussion

1. Compare this decision with the decision in *Lewis* v. *Board of Education of Johnson County, infra.*

2. Do you agree with this decision that a statute requiring the keeping of a record is directory only? Give reasons.

42. "... *the record is prima facie evidence of the action taken by the board. It is, in fact, the only evidence of the action taken ...*" (p. 6).

LEWIS v. BOARD OF EDUCATION OF JOHNSON COUNTY,
348 S. W. (2d) 921 (Ky.) (1961)
(Decided by the Court of Appeals of Kentucky)

[This was an action to determine the rights of a high school principal under a teachers' tenure law. The facts of the case indicate that the school board voted to change the principals in its three high schools for the school year 1953-1954. One principal, Lewis, who contended he was on tenure, received a letter from the board stating that he would not be employed for this year as principal. There was evidence that the board offered Lewis a position as Director of Transportation but that he refused it. The board contended that this refusal to accept the position offered "constituted an abandonment and a valid termination of Lewis' employment status, whatever it may have been." Lewis brought this action to have his status determined by the court. The trial court ruled against him and he appealed. The higher court reversed the decision of the lower court.]

MONTGOMERY, Judge.

•   •   •   •   •   •   •   •   •   •   •   •   •   •   •

In considering the acts and actions of the Board with reference to the employment of Lewis, the rule is that the governing body of a municipal corporation such as a board of education can speak only through its records and can confer authority to make or terminate contracts only by proper proceedings at a meeting regularly called and held when its acts are duly recorded and authenticated. . . . A member cannot act separately or individually to bind the municipality. . . . This rule applies to the governing bodies of cities and counties. . . . Such records cannot be enlarged or restricted by parol testimony. . . . The formal records of such municipal corporations constitute the only legal evidence of all that was done by any such corporation and that nothing more was done. . . .

The trial court's judgment was not based on the records of the Board's action; hence, it was erroneous. The only record of the Board's action here, Minute 678, has not been construed by the trial court. It may be difficult or impossible to determine Lewis' employment status from this record alone. There may be other Board records which would prove enlightening. This status should be determined by the trial court from all pertinent and competent records. The recent decision in *Moore* v. *Babb*, Ky., 343 S. W. 2d 373, may be of interest and assistance.

The record in this case suggests that Lewis may have become less efficient in the performance of his duties than desired by the Board; hence, the effort to assign him other duties. The means by which a tenure contract may be terminated are set forth by statute. . . . The statutory method should be used rather than the indirect means of unworthy or undesirable reassignment.

Judgment reversed for proceedings consistent herewith.

Guides for Class Discussion

1. What specific principles of law relating to school-board meetings did the court mention?
2. Compare this decision with the one rendered in *School District of Soldier Township* v. *Moeller*, *supra*.

43. "... *where the records of a board are clear, oral or extrinsic evidence is inadmissible to vary, contradict, or subtract from them*" (p. 7).

HANKENSON V. BOARD OF EDUCATION OF WAUKEGAN TOWNSHIP HIGH SCHOOL DISTRICT,
10 Ill. App. (2d) 79, 134 N.E. (2d) 356 (1956)

(Decided by the Appellate Court of Illinois)

[This action was brought to review the decision of a board of education dismissing plaintiffs as teachers. The trial court affirmed the board's decision, and the teachers—plaintiffs—appealed. The Appellate Court reversed the lower court's decision. Plaintiffs, who were on tenure, contended the board's attempted removals were contrary to the tenure law and void. On March 15, 1954, the board adopted a resolution dismissing plaintiffs, which resolution was under judicial review. On March 17, 1954, plaintiffs received letters from the school principal informing them of their dismissal. The evidence indicated that enrollment in the high school would be diminished by about 581 pupils during the school year 1954-1955. The resolution adopted by the board stated that the dismissal was because of the "separation of North Chicago territory from Waukegan Township High School District." The principal's letters to the plaintiffs gave the reason for dismissal as the reduction in the number of teachers due to the withdrawal of the North Chicago territory from the district, and the resulting decrease in enrollment. The plaintiffs, among other things, based their action on the contention that the board's resolution was void and ineffective as it did not state a statutory cause for dismissal. The statute, section 24-3, provided that tenure teachers could be dismissed if such action resulted from the board's decision to decrease the number of teachers or to discontinue some particular type of teaching service. If the dismissal was for this purpose then the board was not required to give teachers written notice and a hearing. Dismissal for any other reason necessitated a hearing. The real question before the court was whether the reason stated in the board's resolution—"the separation of North Chicago territory"—qualified as a decision to decrease the number of teachers, so as to warrant dismissal without notice and hearing.]

CROW, Justice.

. . . .

. . . under . . . [the statute], no official business shall be transacted by the directors except at a regular or a special meeting, and the clerk shall keep in a punctual, orderly, and reliable manner a record of the official acts of the board which shall be signed by the president and the clerk. Powers conferred upon a board of education can be exercised only at regular or special meetings of the board. . . . Proper minutes and records should be kept by a board of education to the end that the persons who are carrying the tax load may make reference thereto and that future boards may be advised of the manner of disposition of questions that have arisen. . . . A record is required to be kept of the essential steps in the exercise by the board of its powers; every essential proceeding in the course of its exercise of its powers must appear in some written and permanent form in the records of the body authorized to act upon them; and where public officials are required to keep a record of their proceedings such record constitutes the only lawful evidence of action taken, and cannot be contradicted, added to, or supplemented by parol, assuming the record correctly states the facts as to what occurred, and subject to the board's limited power (not applicable to the case at bar) in a proper case and under proper circumstances to amend its record to make it correctly state the facts as to what occurred. . . .

The resolution of the defendant Board of March 15, 1954, set out above is, admittedly, the only official act or decision of the defendant in this record, and this record, the defendant says, is entire, full, complete, and accurate. It must stand or fall as is. We cannot read into it by interpolation, implication, or inference, things which are not in fact in it. That resolution is not a decision of the Board to decrease the number of teachers employed by the Board. The subject of *decreasing* that *number* is not therein referred to at all. It is simply a decision honorably discharging the plaintiffs (and some others). It recites a so-called "reason" for their discharge,—"*the separation of North Chicago Territory from Waukegan Township High School District No. 119*,"—which is not a statutory reason or cause for removal or dismissal. That circumstance is not mentioned in the statute, and is, at best, only a part of some general background information. . . . Whatever else it may be as a final administrative decision honorably discharging the plaintiffs, which it is, it is not a "*decision of the board to decrease the number of teachers employed by the board*" within the meaning of that second sentence of Section 24-3. This is not a mere matter of form, but of the substantive rights, powers, and duties of the plaintiffs and defendant. The general background information recited in the resolution, if true, together with several other material facts such as reduction in pupils, etc., if true, might have furnished some good reason for the defendant Board to decide to decrease the total number of teachers employed by it, but so far as this record is concerned it either never in fact made such a decision, or, if it did, the same is not reflected in its records.

Guides for Class Discussion

1. Compare this decision with the one in *Lewis* v. *Board of Education of Johnson County, supra*. Compare it with the decision in *Spann* v. *Joint Boards of School Directors, infra*.
2. Do you agree with the court's reasoning? Give reasons.
3. What other legal principles related to board meetings and board records are mentioned by the court?

44. ". . . *oral or intrinsic evidence is admissible [however] to clarify the meaning of a record that is indefinite or obscure, and to supply omissions in a record. . .*" (p. 7).

SPANN V. JOINT BOARDS OF SCHOOL DIRECTORS,
381 Pa. 338, 113 A. (2d) 281 (1955)
(Decided by the Supreme Court of Pennsylvania)

[This was an action to restrain the school boards of districts which were members of a jointure from condemning 20 acres of farm land to be used for a school site. At issue was the authority of the boards' action. One of the principal questions before the court was the significance or meaning of the minutes of the joint board for October 6, 1952. The minutes for that date show that the solicitor outlined the prerequisite steps for the exercise of the right of eminent domain, and that a resolution was adopted authorizing the taking of possession of the land in question. Appended to the minutes of October 6, was a carbon copy of a document captioned " 'Resolution Appropriating Certain Lands Adjoining the Darlington Township—Darlington Borough Joint Consolidated Elementary School.' " On this document was a pencil notation to the effect " 'Refer to November Minutes.' " This document, which was unsigned and not referred to in the minutes proper, recited that since the joint boards were unable to agree with plaintiffs on the purchase price, it was resolved that the land in question be condemned for school purposes and the solicitor and surveyor be authorized to enter upon, take possession of, and mark boundary lines of the land.]

CHIDSEY, Justice.

. . . .

It is urged by the plaintiffs that the condemnation proceedings in the instant case were invalid because three essential conditions precedent for divesting title as set forth in the Act of 1949 had not been complied with when the petition for appointment of viewers was filed on October 9th, namely, (1) no condemnation resolution was ever adopted by the joint board; (2) the board did not offer the ultimatum of a final maximum price to plaintiffs; (3) the board did not fix the metes and bounds of the 20 acres seized. The court below found as a fact, and the finding was confirmed by the court en banc, that a resolution condemning plaintiffs' land and describing it by legal description was unanimously adopted at the meeting held on October 6, 1952 and concluded that the boards' action did comply with legal requirements. The court based its finding on the uncontradicted testimony of Helen Nicely, the recording secretary for the boards, who testified that the type-written sheet containing the condemnation resolution was referred to on the first page of the minutes authorizing taking possession of the Spann property. Appellants argue that the pencil notation on the typewritten resolution clearly shows that the documented draft did not reach the board for action until November 3rd, practically a month after the filing of petition for viewers, and therefore the latter proceeding was without warrant of law and the court was without jurisdiction to appoint viewers. We deem it of no significance that the typewritten resolution makes specific reference to the November minutes which in turn state that "The resolution to authorize taking of property was to be taken by each individual Board as of October 6th." From this notation the inference could just as readily be drawn that the board was merely clarifying any ambiguity that might, and eventually did, arise by not actually including the rather lengthy resolution in the handwritten minutes. In any event there was ample testimony by the members comprising a majority of each of the constituent boards that all were present at the meeting of the joint board held on October 6, 1952, and that all voted in favor of the condemnation resolution which was attached to the minutes of that meeting. Since this testimony was not offered to supplement or alter the minutes, but solely for the purpose of interpreting the action of the board as recorded therein, it was clearly admissible and in fact furnished the most promising avenue of inquiry as to what the board intended. . . . When the resolution is considered in this light there can be no question that it sets forth the amount and location of the condemned tract with sufficient definiteness to satisfy the statutory requirement. The property to be seized is described by courses, distances and total acreage and covers one full page of the typewritten resolution.

Guides for Class Discussion

1. Compare this decision with the ones rendered in *Lewis* v. *Board of Education of Johnson County, supra;* and *Hankenson* v. *Board of Education of Waukegan Township High School District, supra.* Can they be harmonized?
2. Do you think this decision serves the ends of equity and justice? Give reasons.

45. *"A school board may amend its records to make them speak the truth. . ." (p. 7).*

Lingle v. Slifer,
8 Ill. App. (2d) 489, 131 N.E. (2d) 822 (1956)
(Decided by the Appellate Court of Illinois)

[This was an action brought by a music teacher who sought to compel the board of education to reinstate her as a teacher in the district for the school year 1954-55. She had been continuously employed as a teacher of music from 1949 until the alleged termination of her service. The Illinois Teachers Tenure Act provided for the removal or dismissal of teachers by a board of education for the purpose of decreasing the number of teachers employed by the board or as a result of discontinuing some particular type of teaching service. In so doing it required that written notice be given to the teacher by registered mail at least 60 days before the end of the term, together with a statement of the reason therefor. In this case a letter had been sent to the plaintiff by the board advising her that the particular position which she held was to be abolished, and that there would be no place for her in the schools after the end of the current school year. Plaintiff contended that her position had not, in fact, been abolished, and that she was wrongfully so advised. Evidence in the case indicated that teaching or instruction in music had been discontinued and that music instruction was not being provided in the school district. It also indicated that no teacher of vocal music had been employed by the board to take the place of plaintiff.

[The action complained of by plaintiff had taken place on March 22, 1954. At a regular meeting of the board on March 14, 1955—almost one year later—the minutes of the earlier meeting had been amended, showing the action of the board authorizing the dismissal. Among other things, plaintiff questioned the right of the board to amend the minutes of the earlier meeting.]

CULBERTSON, Judge.

. . . .

The record of a School Board may be amended at any time to show what was in fact done at such proceeding, Phenicie v. Board of Education. . . . The Board of Education may order the clerk to amend the record of a previous meeting to show the facts, although the personnel of the Board has changed and a long period of time has elapsed. . . . Boards of Education have not been required to maintain the highest degree of formality in the conduct of proceedings on the principle that to do so would result in injury to the public . . . and formality or a high degree of accuracy on the part of School Trustees and officials is not exacted by the Courts. . . .

The Court, in the case of Phenicie v. Board of Education, supra, 326 Ill. at page 78, 157 N.E. at page 36, stated: "The general rule as established by the decisions of this court is, that a school board has the right to amend the records of its action at any time so as to make them conform to the real facts." The record shows that four former members of the Board of Education who know the facts and the two new members who heard a full disclosure and discussion of the proceedings, voted to allow the amendment to show the action and proceedings which resulted in the motion to except certain named teachers, one of whom was plaintiff, from those who were to be re-employed.

It is contended in this Court by plaintiff that allowance of the amendment was improper and that the record of the proceedings of the Board of Education, as originally kept, constituted the only lawful evidence of the action taken and could not be contradicted or supplemented by parol evidence. She sought to introduce evidence of conversations by members of the Board of Education among themselves in their official capacity, but the Court refused to admit such evidence on the ground that the record could not be contradicted by parol evidence. This was proper under the precedents in this State, Phenicie v. Board of Education, supra.

Guides for Class Discussion

1. Compare the decision in this case with the one rendered by the same court in *Hankenson* v. *Board of Education of Waukegan Township High School District, supra.*
2. Are you in agreement with the court's thinking? Give reasons.

SELECTED BIBLIOGRAPHY

1. Edwards, Newton. *The Courts and the Public Schools,* rev. ed. Chicago: University of Chicago Press, 1955.

2. Garber, Lee O. *Yearbook of School Law.* "School Districts and School Officers." Danville, Illinois: The Interstate Printers and Publishers, Inc., annually since 1950.

3. Hamilton, Robert H. and Paul R. Mort. *The Law and Public Education,* rev ed. Brooklyn: The Foundation Press, Inc., 1959.

4. Remmlein, Madaline Kinter. *School Law,* rev. ed. Danville, Illinois: The Interstate Printers and Publishers, Inc., 1962.

5. Reutter, E. Edmund, Jr. *Schools and the Law.* ("Legal Almanac Series," No. 17.) New York: Oceana Publications, Inc., 1960.

SCHOOL LAW CASEBOOK SERIES — NO. 6

Tort and Contractual Liability of School Districts and School Boards

By

LEE O. GARBER

and

NEWTON EDWARDS

The Interstate
Printers and Publishers
Danville, Illinois

Second Printing

Library of Congress
Catalog Card Number: 63-22405

CONTENTS

INTRODUCTION

This book is the second in the second cycle of casebooks which will provide, when all eight have been completed, a thorough coverage for the entire field of "School Law." The earlier books deal with "The Public School in Our Governmental Structure," "The Law Relating to the Creation, Alteration, and Dissolution of School Districts," "The Law Governing Teaching Personnel," "The Law Governing Pupils," and "The Law Governing School Board Members and School Board Meetings." Casebooks still in the process of completion will deal with "The Law Governing School Property and School Buildings," and "The Law Governing School Finance." Work on these two books has already begun, and it is expected that their publication will follow shortly.

Professors of School Law who are seeking supplementary and illustrative material, and who are desirous of using the case method of instruction, will find these books extremely helpful. It is expected that they will also be welcomed by professors teaching other aspects of school administration.

The authors need no introduction, as they have established themselves, and are recognized as, specialists in the field of "School Law." Newton Edwards, Professor Emeritus, University of Chicago, is the author of numerous School Law articles, as well as the leading text in the field—*The Courts and the Public Schools*—which originally appeared in 1933 and was revised in 1955. Lee O. Garber, Professor of Education, University of Pennsylvania, is the author of the *Yearbook of School Law*, an annual publication which first appeared in 1950. In addition, he is known for his articles relating to School Law which have been regular features of *The Nation's Schools* for the past dozen years.

Russell L. Guin
Publisher

Authors' Preface

This—the sixth in the "School Law Casebook Series"—follows the same general pattern as that used in the first five. The first section deals with "Legal Principles," and the second one deals with "Court Decisions." The cases in the second section—"Court Decisions"—have been selected to illustrate the basic principles mentioned in the first section.

It will be noted that this casebook is divided into two main parts. One deals with the tort liability of school districts and school boards, and the other deals with the contractual liability of school districts and school boards.

It is hoped that this book will prove of value in courses in "School Law." Likewise, it is hoped that it will prove of value in supplementing the material offered in other professional courses in the field of School Administration. Finally, it is hoped that this book may find a place in some undergraduate teacher education courses designed to give students a concept of the authority of school districts as administrative units.

The authors again wish to state that the legal principles are not exhaustive. Those selected for inclusion are, however, chosen on the basis of their importance to school boards, school administrators, and teachers. Again the authors wish to point out that the courts in all jurisdictions do not, and should not, necessarily, agree in all their holdings; consequently exceptions will be found to many principles. Many of these exceptions have been included as legal principles. To mention all deviations from principles, however, would be impossible and inadvisable in a treatment of this sort.

Lee O. Garber
Newton Edwards

I.

LEGAL PRINCIPLES

Tort and Contractual Liability of School Districts and School Boards

Tort Liability

Liability for Negligence.—It is a long-established principle of the common law that school districts, in the performance of their governmental functions, are not liable in tort for injuries growing out of the negligent acts of their officers, agents, or employees. This immunity applies in the case of injuries sustained either on or off the school grounds. It applies not only to injuries sustained by pupils but to injuries sustained by teachers and other employees of the school district, such as workmen engaged in constructing or repairing school buildings. The principle of immunity applies also to members of the public who use the school building as a social or civic center. The principle is applicable to cities and municipalities when engaged in the performance of any educational function which the statutes authorize them to perform.

The doctrine of nonliability of school boards for the negligent acts of their officers, agents, or employees rests primarily upon the consideration that the school board is the agent of the state in the performance of a governmental function and, like the state itself, is not liable unless made so by statute. Some courts have also pointed out, in support of the immunity doctrine, that school districts have no funds with which to pay damages, that school funds are trust funds, and cannot be diverted from the use imposed upon them. Some courts also point out that the relation of master and servant does not exist between a school board and its agents and employees.

In recent years the principle of immunity from tort liability in case of negligence has come in for a good deal of criticism as being illogical and contrary to sound public policy. Even so, the courts continue to sustain and apply the common-law principle of immunity. In 1959, however, the Supreme Court of Illinois, in a very significant case, abrogated the common-law rule and held a board of education liable in tort in the absence of a statute making it liable. Whether the Illinois decision will serve as a precedent which other courts will follow remains to be seen. In 1962, the Supreme Courts in Wisconsin and in Minnesota abrogated the nonliability rule. In cases arising in a number of other states the rule continues to be followed. It should be pointed out that the principle of nonliability is a long and well-established one. Some courts take the position that if the principle is an historical anachronism and works injustice it should be abrogated, but that the change should be made by the legislature and not by the courts.

In some states, notably California, Washington, and New York, statutes have been enacted which abrogate the common-law rule and make school districts liable for injuries sustained as a result of the negligence of school officers, agents, and employees.

The effect of a school district's carrying insurance to protect itself against loss or to protect others against the negligence of its employees has been litigated on numerous occasions. In some states where statutes have been enacted permitting school boards to carry such insurance, it has been held that they do not act to abrogate the common-law rule of immunity, and school districts will not be held liable in an amount in excess of the coverage in the insurance policy. Where there is no statute authorizing the board to carry the insurance mentioned, the situation is somewhat different. In this connection it has been held that a board may not spend its funds to purchase liability insurance to protect itself against a contingency that can never arise. In other cases it has been held that, because a school district is immune from tort liability, its purchase of liability insurance does not constitute a waiver of such immunity. In other jurisdictions, however, it has been held that where the district carried liability insurance, even though it had no statutory authority so to do, it can be held liable up to the amount of the insurance coverage.

Liability in the Performance of Proprietary Functions.—In recent years a number of cases have come into the courts in which the plaintiff has contended that the school district was in the performance of a proprietary rather than a governmental function at the time the injury was received and that in such instances the principle of immunity does not apply. Some courts have taken the position that school districts are created to operate schools, that this is a governmental function, that while acting within their scope of authority they cannot engage in a proprietary function—

that in legal contemplation there is no such thing as a school board acting in a proprietary capacity for private gain. Other courts take the position that the immunity doctrine is applicable in all cases regardless of whether the injury complained of had its origin in a proprietary or a governmental function. Other courts recognize a distinction between a governmental and proprietary function and intimate or expressly declare that a school board may be held liable in damages if the act complained of grew out of the performance of a proprietary function. In a few instances the courts have held that recovery could be had in the case of injuries growing out of the performance of a proprietary function. The courts, however, have commonly held that a function carried on by a board of education does not lose its governmental nature and become a proprietary function merely because it yields some profit or produces some revenue. Thus it has been held in a number of instances that a school board does not engage in a proprietary function where it charges admission fees to athletic contests. It has been held, too, that a school board does not lose its immunity from tort liability by engaging in a proprietary function where it leases an athletic field for playing baseball, leases an auditorium for holding a concert, sells articles made by students in a vocational high school, or charges pupils living outside the district fees for transportation to its own schools.

Liability for Trespass or the Maintenance of a Nuisance.—Some courts, in the matter of tort liability of school districts, draw a distinction between ordinary negligence and wilful, positive misconduct. In some instances the courts have held school districts liable for trespass. In some instances, too, a school district has been held liable for the maintenance of a nuisance. It is difficult to draw a distinction between negligence and a nuisance, but the courts commonly point out that in the case of nuisance there is a wrongful continuing danger to person or property.

Some courts hold that school districts are not liable in tort for trespass or the maintenance of a nuisance. These courts take the position that school districts are not liable for any kind of tort. School boards, it is said, are not authorized to commit a tort and when they do so the district is not bound.

Contractual Liability

Authority of a Board of Education to Enter Into a Binding Contract.—Boards of education, being agents of the state created for the purpose of carrying out the educational policy of the state, have no inherent authority to contract. It follows that a board of education cannot enter into a binding contract unless authorized to do so expressly or impliedly by statute. Where the statutes prescribe the mode of making a contract, as, for example, that it be reduced to written form or be made on the basis of competitive bidding, the mode of making the contract is the measure of power and a contract made in any other mode cannot be enforced against the school district. Where the statutes confer upon a board of education the performance of duties involving the exercise of judgment or discretion, the board is under obligation to perform the duties itself; it cannot delegate to others the performance of a duty involving the exercise of judgment and discretion which the law contemplates it will exercise in its corporate capacity. It follows that a board cannot delegate to its school superintendent, business manager, secretary, or to a committee of its own members, final authority to enter into a contract. A board of education has no authority to enter into contracts which are clearly violative of public policy.

Board Liability on Void Contracts.—Contracts of school boards which are prohibited or unauthorized by statute, which are made in violation of the exclusive statutory mode of making them, or which are violative of public policy are null and void; the school board will not, as a rule, be held liable on such contracts even though they have been fully performed and the school district retains the benefit of the performance. The only recourse of the other party to the contract is to abandon the contract in a court of law, throw himself on a court of equity, and seek to recover on *quantum meruit* the actual value of the services rendered or goods furnished.

Liability of School Districts for Benefits Received Under Illegal Contracts.—Where a school board has statutory authority to make a contract, but the contract is illegal because of some irregularity or invalidity in the making of it, courts of equity commonly permit recovery on *quantum meruit* or *quantum valebat* for the actual value of the services rendered or the goods delivered under the contract. As a general rule, courts of equity will not permit recovery on *quantum meruit,* however, for benefits received under a contract which a board of education had no authority to make. As a general rule, courts of equity will also not permit recovery for the value of services rendered or goods delivered under a contract which violates the statutory mode of making it. Where a board's authority to contract depends upon some prior action by another board or agency, most courts of equity hold that no recovery can be had for the actual value of goods or services which were delivered or rendered under a contract made without the necessary prior action having been taken.

In some states, courts of equity do not follow the general rule that no recovery can be had for the actual value of goods delivered or services rendered under an illegal or void contract; these courts reason that a school district should not be permitted, in justice and good conscience, to enjoy the benefits of the illegal contract without paying for the actual value of the goods or services.

Right to Recover Money or Goods Delivered Under an Illegal Contract.—Where money has been paid to a school board in the performance of an illegal contract, such as for the purchase of illegal bonds, and the money paid has not been spent or so mingled with other moneys of the board that it can no longer be identified, a court of equity will require its return to the original owner. In such cases, the courts will put the parties *in statu quo.* A court of equity will permit one who has delivered property to a school board under an illegal contract to recover it if the property can be restored without any substantial damage to the property of the district. In cases of this kind the law of fixtures does not apply; the question always is, not whether the property has become a fixture, but whether it can be restored without any substantial injury to the property of the school district.

Liability of School Board on Contracts Between the Board and One or More of Its Members.—Where the statutes prohibit a school board member from entering into a contract with the board of which he is a member, a contract entered into in violation of the statute is void and no recovery can be had on it, in a court of law, or on *quantum meruit* in a court of equity, for the actual value of the goods delivered or services rendered under the illegal contract. In the absence of statute prohibiting it, a contract between a board and one of its members is commonly held to be contrary to public policy and the district may repudiate it any time before performance. In some jurisdictions a contract between a school board and one of its members, even though not prohibited by statute, is considered so violative of public policy as to be void, and no recovery can be had for benefits received under it. According to the weight of authority, however, a contract between a school board and one of its members is not void but merely voidable and, if the board permits performance of the contract, it will be held liable for benefits received.

Ratification of Contracts.—Courts commonly apply the rule that a school board may ratify contracts which it had authority to make in the first instance. A school board cannot, of course, ratify a contract that is *ultra vires*, violative of the statutory mode of making it, or violative of public policy. Where a school board has the authority to ratify a contract, it may do so by formal resolution or by action that is incompatible with any reasonable assumption other than that it intended to ratify. Where a board has authority to ratify a contract and does so, the contract is ratified *in toto* and not in part; the whole agreement becomes binding.

Recovery of Funds Paid Out on Illegal Contracts.—The cases dealing with the recovery of money already paid out on illegal contracts cannot be harmonized. It has frequently been held that, where money has been paid out in violation of an express constitutional or statutory prohibition or for a purpose entirely outside the powers of the school district, it may be recovered from the party or parties to whom it has been paid in an action brought by taxpayers on behalf of the district. In some jurisdictions, however, it is held that money paid out on a contract made in violation of some statutory provision or of public policy cannot be recovered, where the facts show that the contract was made in good faith and the district retains and enjoys the benefits of its performance.

Authority of School Board Members to Make Contracts Extending Beyond Their Term of Office.—A school board is a continuing corporate entity, and it may make contracts extending beyond the term of office of one or more of its members.

II.

COURT DECISIONS

Court Decisions

1. *"It is a long-established principle of the common law that school districts, in the performance of their governmental functions, are not liable in tort for injuries growing out of the negligent acts of their officers, agents, or employees"* (p.3).

School District v. Rivera,
30 Ariz. 1, 243 P. 609 (1926)
(Decided by the Supreme Court of the State of Arizona)

[Because the facts of the case are included in the following quoted material, they are not presented here.]

Lockwood, J.—Eduardo Rivera, hereinafter called plaintiff, brought suit against school district No. 48 of Maricopa county, and V. C. White, Walter Dunn and J. R. Steward, as trustees of said district, and also in their individual capacity, to recover damages for the destruction of a building belonging to plaintiff which was burned while used and occupied by the district. The complaint alleged, in substance, that plaintiff was the owner of certain lots in Scottsdale, Maricopa county, with a large wooden house thereon; that about February 6, 1924, the trustees took possession of the house and established a public school therein without the knowledge or consent of plaintiff; that they placed a stove in the house, cutting a hole through the wall for the stove-pipe, and later, through the negligence of the janitor employed by the district in caring for the stove, the house was set on fire and destroyed. The damages set up were $950, part for rental and part for the value of the building.

The defendants entered a general demurrer and denial, and then set up as a special defense that the year before they had rented the building from the owner for school purposes; that in January, 1924, they again sought to rent it, but, learning that plaintiff was in California, and that the premises had been leased to one Serna, they sub-leased it from the latter, and were occupying it when the fire occurred. The demurrer was overruled as to the district and the trustees in their individual capacity, but sustained as to the trustees officially. The case went to trial before a jury, and at the close of plaintiff's case the court sustained a motion for a directed verdict in favor of the trustees individually, and a verdict was rendered against the school district in the sum of $900. Judgment was duly entered upon the verdict, and, upon the motion for a new trial being denied, this appeal was prosecuted by the district.

There are some eight assignments of error; the first being that the complaint does not state a cause of action against the school district. This is based on the theory that a school district, under the laws of Arizona, cannot be sued except when such suit is impliedly or expressly authorized by statute, and admittedly there is no act allowing it where the trustees or their employees have committed a tort.

In the case of *State* v. *Sharp*, 21 Ariz. 424, 189 Pac. 631, we said:

"The question is whether the state is liable to respond in damages for the negligent acts of its agents, servants or employees. As to this question it is well settled by the great weight of authority that the state, in consequence of its sovereignty, is immune from prosecution in the courts and from liability to respond in damages for negligence, except in those cases where it has expressly waived immunity or assumed liability by constitutional or legislative enactment,". . . .

A school district, under our system of government, is merely an agency of the state. . . .

. . . .

. . . the overwhelming weight of authority naturally is to the effect that school districts are not liable for the negligence of their officers, agents or employees, unless such liability is imposed by statute either in express terms or by implication. . . .

. . . .

That there is a difference between the ordinary school district and a municipal corporation, and that the former is purely a state agency as the latter is not, cannot be doubted. We see no distinction in principle between the liability of the district for the acts of its officers in one class of torts as against another. As was said in *Board of Education* v. *Volk*, [72 Ohio St. 469, 74 N. E. 646] . . . :

"The board is not authorized to commit a tort—to be careless or negligent—and, when it commits a wrong or tort, it does not in that respect represent the district, and for its negligence or tort in any form the board cannot make the district liable."

And, as stated in *Wiest* v. *School Dist.*, [68 Or. 474, 49 L.R.A. (N.S.) 1026, 137 Pac. 749]:

"We do not believe that it was the intent or is the policy of our law to take the fund intended for the education of the young and apply it to payment for any malicious act of its officers. . . ."

. . . .

Therefore, if the trustees of the school district committed a trespass, since the statute neither directly nor impliedly authorizes such action on their part, the act was an individual one, and the liability, if any, is theirs, and not that of the district.

For the foregoing reasons the judgment is reversed. . . .

Guides for Class Discussion

1. Compare the decision in this case with the one in *Krutili* v. *Board of Education, infra;* compare it with *Ferris* v. *Board of Education of Detroit, infra.*
2. How did the court arrive at its decision? Are you in agreement with it?

2. ". . . *[the rule of] immunity [of school districts] applies in the case of injuries sustained either on or off the school grounds*" (p. 3).

Thurman v. Consolidated School District,
94 F. Supp. 616 (1950)
(Decided by the United States District Court, D. Kansas)

[This was an action for damages for injuries against the school district. The injuries in question resulted from a collision of motor vehicles on a public highway in Kansas. One of the vehicles was a school bus owned by an Oklahoma school district, which was being used to transport seniors on a trip, apparently for the purpose of attending the automobile races in Indianapolis, Ind. In Kansas, where the accident occurred, the school bus hit an automobile registered in the state of Arizona. As a result of diverse citizenship, the action was brought in a federal court. Among other things, it was contended that, while the district might be held liable for damages resulting from injuries received in Oklahoma, it could not plead immunity where the injuries occurred in another state. As a result of holding that the district was immune from liability for accidents occurring outside the state, the court made it clear that the rule of immunity very definitely applies to injuries received off of school property.]

MELLOTT, Chief Judge.
. . . Apparently the bus had been acquired for the purpose of furnishing free transportation to pupils attending the schools in the district. Recognizing that the operation of such vehicles is "a public governmental function," that school districts are but auxiliary parts of the sovereignty and, in the absence of express statute (none has been shown) are not liable for negligence, plaintiffs seek to subject the school district and its officers to damages by this somewhat circuitous

line of reasoning: out-of-state excursions by a school bus are prohibited; when permitted by a school district, such district is not then engaging in a governmental function and cannot rely on that ground for immunity from suit; the school district is then acting in a proprietary capacity and may be sued for its torts like any municipal, or private, corporation. Inferentially judgment, when rendered, would be payable out of funds derived from taxation. It is also contended upon brief that governmental immunity of a political subdivision of Oklahoma from suit cannot be asserted outside of that state; that there is no requirement suits such as the one at bar be filed only in the courts of that state; and finally, that the fourth ground of the present motion cannot be sustained because the moving defendants "cannot rely upon the defense of *ultra vires* to defeat the ends of justice where their acts resulted in personal injuries and damages to the plaintiffs."

. . . The second ground is good under Consolidated School District No. 1 v. Wright. . . . Cases cited by plaintiffs involving municipal corporations carrying on proprietary functions in other states—e.g., operating a water works plant—are clearly inapposite. Nor is the court convinced that the Supreme Court of Oklahoma, in holding in Joint School District No. 132 v. Dabney that the corporate existence of a school district is just as complete as that of a city, town or village, intended that school districts should be subjected to actions for negligence. . . . The Dabney case is to be read in the light of the question before the court—whether the word "municipality" as used in the title to an act permitting the funding of bonds was broad enough to include a school district—; and if the court had intended to overrule the recent Wright case, it is reasonable to assume it would have done so in no uncertain terms. It would be anomalous, to say the least, if a school district which cannot be required to respond in damages when legally transporting its children to school, could be subjected to such damages because its board permitted such bus to be used in an illegal out-of-state excursion.

Guides for Class Discussion

1. Do you think the court was right in holding that the immunity of the district extended to injuries received outside of the state? Give your reasons.
2. Was the court's decision based upon the fact that the act in question was of a proprietary or of a governmental nature?
3. On what grounds did this case get into a federal rather than a state court?

3. ". . . [*The rule of immunity of school districts*] *applies not only to injuries sustained by pupils but to injuries sustained by teachers and other employees of the school district*" (p. 3).

KRUEGER V. BOARD OF EDUCATION OF CITY OF ST. LOUIS,
310 Mo. 239, 274 S.W. 811 (1925)
(Decided by the Supreme Court of Missouri)

[This was an action for damages brought by a person employed in a lunchroom and cafeteria maintained by one of the schools in the defendant district. The injury resulted when a food-chopping machine was set in motion while plaintiff was engaged in cleaning it. The lower court ruled in favor of defendant, and the higher court upheld the decision of the lower court.]

LINDSAY, C.

·   ·   ·   ·   ·   ·   ·   ·   ·   ·

Plaintiff's case is founded upon the claim that the operation of a lunchroom in the school, as a thing merely authorized or permitted by law, was in the nature of a special, voluntary, and self-imposed duty; and, not being a duty enjoined upon defendant by the law, such operation of it was not the exercise of a governmental function, and for that reason the rule of nonliability for negligence announced in the Dick, Cochran, and many other cases is not applicable.

The determination of the case, therefore, depends upon whether there is a controlling distinction to be made between the performance of an enjoined duty, and the exercise of a power expressly given by the law, whose exercise is not mandatory but rests in the discretion of such quasi corporation. . . .

·   ·   ·   ·   ·   ·   ·   ·   ·   ·

The statute under which defendant in this case acted was not designed for pecuniary profit to the defendant, and it sets up also a bar against intrenchment upon the funds of the school other than for the initial expense of providing the materials necessary for instituting the service.

There is reason as well as authority for holding that the duty undertaken in this case was the exercise of a governmental function, and that its voluntary but authorized assumption did not take from the defendant that immunity from liability which attends the performance of duties imposed.

The power given, is given for a public purpose, and to a governmental agency. It is a means, a facility, which the Legislature conceived might be an aid to efficiency and progress in the schools. The power was given to all boards of education. The exercise of the power was left to the discretion of the respective boards—a discretion to be exercised not in aid of any private interest, but only in the interest of the public. The exercise of the power of discretion in any city or school district is itself an exercise of governmental power. The actual execution of the thing thus deemed necessary and expedient is not less so.

There is no good reason why a school district should be liable to an action for damages because voluntarily, yet pursuant to a general authority, it furnishes a certain convenience in aid of its schools, when, if the furnishing of that convenience were made mandatory, there would be no liability under a like charge of negligence. In one case the necessity and expediency would be determined by the Legislature; in the other, the necessity and expediency would be left by the Legislature to be determined by the local governmental agency. In either event, it is the same power that is exercised, and for the same purpose. . . .

. . . .

The true ground of distinction to be observed is not so much that the duty is mandatory rather than self-imposed pursuant to authority of a general law, but is that the duty assumed is public in character, and not for profit, but for the public good, and is directly related to and in aid of the general and beneficent purposes of the state. . . .

Guides for Class Discussion

1. Do you think that the court would have held as it did had the plaintiff been a pupil instead of an employee of the district?
2. How do you think the court would have held had the duty mentioned been mandatory?
3. Compare this case with *Morris* v. *School District of Township of Mt. Lebanon, infra;* and *Richards* v. *School District of City of Birmingham, infra.*

4. *"The principle of immunity applies . . . to members of the public who use the school building as a social or civic center"* (p. 3).

KELLAM V. SCHOOL BOARD OF THE CITY OF NORFOLK,
202 Va. 252, 117 S.E. (2d) 96 (1960)
(Decided by the Supreme Court of Appeals of Virginia)

[When one who paid admission to attend a concert held in a junior high school auditorium was injured when she fell, she brought this action for damages. She alleged the board failed to maintain the common passageways in a reasonably safe condition and allowed them to become so slick and slippery as to be hazardous. In ruling that the plaintiff could not collect, the court commented on the matter of the district's liability to members of the public, not pupils, injured while on school property.]

MILLER, Justice.

. . . .

A demurrer was interposed to the motion for judgment, the grounds of which were that in maintaining and operating the school, the Board was acting as an agent of the State and performing governmental functions and duties imposed upon it by law, and was not liable for a negligent personal injury. The demurrer was sustained and the problem presented on this appeal is whether the School Board, in maintaining and operating the school building can be held liable for negligent injury to a member of the public lawfully upon the premises in attendance upon a concert held in the building. The demurrer admitted the truth of all well-pleaded facts, but did not admit the conclusion of law that conducting a concert was a non-governmental function.

In solving the precise questions presented, which do not seem to have been heretofore decided in Virginia, we must determine whether or not, in the absence of statute imposing liability, the doctrine of governmental immunity from liability for this character of tort applies to a school board in the maintenance of its school building, and if so, does the board forfeit or lose its immunity by maintenance of the building in so dangerous a condition and for such a time as to constitute a nuisance that results in injury to a member of the public lawfully upon the premises.

The doctrine that the State and its governmental agencies, while acting in their governmental capacities, are immune from liability for tortious personal injury negligently inflicted, has long been recognized and applied in Virginia. . . .

The basis for a school board's immunity from liability for tortious injury has been generally found in the fact that it is a governmental agency or arm of the state and acts in a governmental capacity in the performance of its duties imposed by law.

. . . .

By §§ 22-164.1 and 22-164.2, 1960 Cum. Supp., Code 1950, a county school board is expressly authorized to permit the use of school property under its control under such terms and conditions as it deems proper. . . . The School Board therefore asserts that when it rented the auditorium for a concert, it was . . . exercising powers expressly conferred upon it as a school board and for a governmental purpose. In support of this assertion it relies upon 160 A.L.R. at page 220.

"Where those in charge of a public school have authority to permit the school premises to be used for other than strictly school purposes, it has been ruled that a board of education, in permitting a third person or organization to use school premises, when not otherwise needed for school purposes, for public lectures, concerts, or other educational or social interests, is engaged in a purely governmental function . . . even though the school authorities also furnish light, heat, attendance [*sic*], and the like in connection therewith and charge a nominal sum to defray the expense thereof, and that, in the absence of statute, the school board is immune from liability for injuries sustained by a member of the public while on school premises for the occasion." We agree with the principles here expressed.

Guides for Class Discussion

1. Compare this case with *Krueger* v. *Board of Education of City of St. Louis, supra.*
2. Do you think that the members of the public should be covered by the same principles of law relating to liability as those covering pupils? Give reasons.
3. What did the court mean when it said, "A demurrer was interposed to the motion for judgment . . .?"

5. *"The principle [of immunity from tort] is applicable to cities and municipalities when engaged in the performance of any educational function which the statutes authorize them to perform"* (p. 3)

GOLD v. MAYOR AND CITY COUNCIL OF BALTIMORE,
137 Md. 335, 112 A. 588 (1921)
(Decided by the Court of Appeals of Maryland)

[This was an action to recover damages for certain injuries received by a pupil in one of the public schools in the city of Baltimore. It was alleged that the injury resulted from "the negligence of the defendant in permitting an unsafe condition to exist in the doorway in the school building." The action was brought against the mayor and city council of Baltimore on the ground that they were charged with the duty of providing a public school system for the education of the children, as well as the necessary buildings and grounds. The district demurred. The court held in favor of the district.]

BRISCOE, J. . . .

. . . .

The facts of the case are admitted by the demurrer, and the single question presented on the record is the liability vel non of the mayor and city council of Baltimore, a municipal corporation, in an action of tort, for negligence in connection with the school buildings used by it for educational purposes.

While the cases and text-writers are not in accord upon the general proposition here presented, the weight of authority is to the effect that, when a municipal corporation is charged by law with the duty of erecting and maintaining public schools for the education of the children of the municipality, it performs a public or governmental duty and function, and, in the absence of statute, is exempt from corporate liability for torts in connection with the maintenance and repairing of school buildings.

In section 2675, vol. 6, of McQuillin on Municipal Corporations, it is said:

"A municipality is not liable for the negligence or other wrongful act of school officers, since education is a governmental function. Likewise, for the same reason, it is not liable for injuries arising in connection with its ownership of school buildings or grounds. . . ."

In Shearman and Redfield on negligence, § 267, it is said:

"The duty of providing means of education, at the public expense, by building and maintaining schoolhouses, . . . is purely a public duty, in the discharge of which the local body, as the state's representative, is exempt from corporate liability for the faulty construction or want of repair of its school buildings or the torts of its servants employed therein."

. . . .

In Wixon v. Newport, 13 R.I. 458, 43 Am. Rep. 35, it was said:
"If we understand the cases aright, the ground of exemption from liability is not that the duty or service is compulsory, or that it is public, and that a municipal corporation, in performing it, is acting for the state or public in a matter in which it has no private or corporate interests, and that therefore, inasmuch as it can only act through its officers or servants, it is entitled to have them, while engaged in the performance of the duty or service, regarded as the officers or servants of the public, and to be exempt from any private responsibility for them."

. . . .

The immunity or exemption from liability in such cases rests upon the theory that the municipality is in the performance of a public or a governmental duty, and is the instrumentality of the state, exercising a governmental function. In the absence of statute expressly or by necessary implication giving the right of action, the municipality is not liable.

Guides for Class Discussion

1. On what basis did the court arrive at its decision?
2. Are you in agreement with the court's thinking? Give reasons.
3. Could the statute have made the city responsible under circumstances here narrated?

6. "*The doctrine of nonliability of school boards for the negligent acts of their officers, agents, or employees rests primarily upon the consideration that the school board is the agent of the state in the performance of a governmental function and, like the state itself, is not liable unless made so by statute*" (p. 3).

KRUTILI V. BOARD OF EDUCATION,
99 W. Va. 466, 129 S.E. 486 (1925)
(Decided by the Supreme Court of Appeals of West Virginia)

[The facts of this case will be found in the first paragraph of the following quoted material.]

Woods, J. Nick Krutili, an infant under the age of 21 years, by William Krutili, his next friend, sues in the circuit court of Hancock county the board of education of Butler district in said county in trespass on the case for damages sustained by him while he was attending and a pupil in the high school of said district situate in the town of Weirton, over which said board had charge and control, which injuries were alleged to have been caused by the negligence of the defendant. The declaration substantially states that the defendant is a body politic and corporate under the laws of the state of West Virginia, and as such has general control and supervision of the public schools and their property in said Butler district, and that it was its duty to keep this property in such condition as to be safe for the children attending the school as pupils thereof; that in maintaining said Weirton high school the said defendant used a certain planing machine for the purpose of planing and smoothing boards in connection with its manual training department of said school; that, while plaintiff was performing his duties as a student in said school, and while engaged in the work and labor in the manual training department of said school, as he was required so to do as such pupil, the defendant did negligently furnish the plaintiff a machine known as a "planer" which had a dangerous knife or knives that were not protected by a mantle or guard; that by reason thereof, while planeing a board under the direction and instruction of the principal of said school, and without fault on the part of said plaintiff, but because of the improper and insecure condition of said machine, the said plaintiff's left hand was caught and thrown against the knife or knives of said machine, by reason whereof his left hand was cut and lacerated, and certain of his fingers cut off, and for this alleged negligence in causing said injury the plaintiff brings his suit. The defendant demurred to this declaration, which demurrer was sustained. On joint application of the parties this ruling was certified to this court. But one point of law was made on the demurrer: That the defendant in maintaining its manual training department was in the exercise of a governmental function and an agent of the state, and as such is not liable to the things complained of in the declaration.

The general rule in this country is that a school district, municipal corporation, or school board is not, in the absence of a statute imposing it, subject to liability for injuries to pupils of public schools suffered in connection with their attendance thereat, since such district, corporation, or board, in maintaining schools, acts as an agent for the state, and performs a purely public or governmental duty imposed upon it by law for the benefit of the public, and for the performance of which it receives no profit or advantage. . . .

As a case involving the liability of school authorities in their official capacity for injuries to pupils, it is a case of first impression in this state. However, we have the guidance of cases wherein principles were announced that makes our course plain here. The rule announced respecting the nonliability of school districts to individuals for injuries brought about in the performance of governmental functions applies to other municipalities such as cities and towns as well. The exemption of the government from liability is based on the theory of sovereignty. The acts of the government were those of the king. In our state, instead of the king being the sovereign, the powers of government reside in all the citizens of the state. The idea was also that certain things worked for the good of the many, and the welfare of the few must be sacrificed in the public interest. . . .

. . . .

. . . this court, in holding that a municipality, unless there be a statute imposing the liability, is not liable for damages caused by its negligence in the exercise of a purely governmental function, gives its sanction to the rule announced herein at the outset by the courts generally of the land in respect to boards of education as well. But, to come within the stated rule, these duties must be governmental in character. Can they be held to be so under our law? School districts in this state are a part of the education system of the state, established in compliance with article 12, section 1, of our Constitution, which makes it the duty of the Legislature "to provide, by general law, for a thorough and efficient system of free schools." They are involuntary corporations, organized, not for the purpose of profit or gain, but solely for the public benefit, and have only such limited powers as were deemed necessary for that purpose. Such corporations are but the agents of the state for the sole purpose of administering the state system of public education. It is the duty of the boards of education of a district to take charge of the educational affairs of their respective localities, and, among other things, to build and keep in repair the public school buildings and the furniture used for school purposes therein. In performing the duties required of them it is observed they exercise merely a public function and an agency for the public good for which they receive no private or corporate benefit. . . .

. . . .

Guides for Class Discussion

1. See *Gold* v. *Mayor and City Council of Baltimore, supra;* and *School District* v. *Rivera, supra.*
2. What did the court mean when it said: "The exemption of the government from liability is based on the theory of sovereignty"?
3. What did the court mean when it said this was a case of first impression in West Virginia?

7. *"Some courts have also pointed out, in support of the immunity doctrine, that school districts have no funds with which to pay damages, that school funds are trust funds, and cannot be diverted from the use imposed upon them"* (p. 3).

FREEL v. SCHOOL CITY OF CRAWFORDSVILLE,
142 Ind. 27, 41 N.E. 312 (1895)
(Decided by the Supreme Court of Indiana)

[Plaintiff, who was employed by defendant as a laborer, was injured while making repairs on a schoolhouse. He brought this action to recover damages for the injuries. The court held the district was not liable.]

MONKS, J. Appellant brought this action to recover for personal injuries sustained by him while in the employment of appellee as a laborer, making repairs on a school house. . . .

School corporations . . . are involuntary corporations, organized, not for the purpose of profit or gain, but solely for the public benefit, and have only such limited powers as were deemed necessary for that purpose. Such corporations are but the agents of the state for the sole purpose of administering the state system of public education. . . . In performing the duties required of them they exercise merely a public function and agency for the public good, for which they receive no private or corporate benefit. School corporations, therefore, are governed by the same law, in respect to their liability to individuals for the negligence of their officers or agents as are counties or townships. It is well established that where subdivisions of the state are organized solely for a public purpose, by a general law, no action lies against them for an injury received by a person on account of the negligence of the officers of such subdivision, unless a right of action is expressly given by statute. Such subdivisions then, as counties, townships, and school corporations, are instruments of government, and exercise authority given by the state, and are no more liable for the acts or omissions of their officers than the state. . . . Besides, school corporations in this State have no fund out of which such damages can be paid, nor have they any power, express or implied, to raise a fund for such purpose, by taxation or otherwise. The law specifically states what taxes shall be levied for their benefit, and how and for what the same shall be disbursed, and no provision is made for the payment of damages for personal injuries. This fact alone would be decisive of the question against appellant. . . . Certainly, a public corporation is not liable to respond in damages in any instance, for the negligence of its officers or agents, unless it has the authority to raise the money from the taxpayers to pay the same. The officer, agent, or other person whose negligence was the proximate cause of the injury may be liable, but appellee is not. . . .

Guides for Class Discussion

1. Do you think the court's reason for refusing to hold the school district liable, namely, that there was no fund out of which to pay the damages, was a good reason? Explain.

2. Compare the reason for not holding the district liable, as given by the court in this case, with the one given by the court in *Krutili* v. *Board of Education, supra,* and with the one given by the court in *Taylor* v. *Knox County Board of Education, infra.*

8. *"Some courts . . . point out that the relation of master and servant does not exist between a school board and its agents and employees"* (p. 3).

REYNOLDS V. BOARD OF EDUCATION,
53 N.Y.S. 75 (1898)
(Decided by the Supreme Court of New York)

[This was an action in damages brought against a board of education by the parent of a child who was killed as the result of the alleged negligence of an employee of the board—an attendance officer. The child in question who was not a truant, was arrested by the attendance officer. At the time of the arrest the child was in the presence of his father and was absent from school with his father's permission. Nevertheless, he broke away from the attendance officer, who pursued him against the father's express command, and ran across a railroad track in the face of an approaching train. The train struck him, and he was killed. The court held the attendance officer was acting outside the scope of his authority and refused to hold the board liable. In its decision it found it necessary to comment on the relationship of a school board to its employees.]

WARD, J. . . .

. . . .

The theory upon which the plaintiff seeks to recover in this action is that Murray bore such a relation to the defendant as his acts were the acts of the defendant; that he was an improper person to be appointed to the position of attendance officer, and that he executed his duties in attempting to arrest the deceased in an unlawful and negligent manner, and for these acts the defendant corporation is responsible; that the statute has created the defendant a corporation, and it is subject to the liabilities of other corporations whose employes, agents, or servants are guilty of negligent acts resulting in injury to others.

The attendance officer is a creation of the statute. The board of education is required to make the appointment. Though a corporation, the board of education is only such to discharge the important duties connected with education that the statute requires. It has no private interests, and derives no special benefit or advantage from its corporate capacity, but its duties are essentially and exclusively of a public character. *The rule of respondeat superior does not apply to the relations between the board of education and the attendance officer.* [Emphasis supplied.] That rule is based upon the right which the employer has to select his servants, to discharge them if not competent or skillful or well behaved, and to direct and control them while in his employ. Maxmilian v. Mayor, etc., 62 N. Y. 163. The duties of the attendance officer are prescribed by the statute, and not by the board of education, although the board may make regulations governing his conduct to some extent as the statute provides. The cases bearing upon this subject found in the Reports relate mainly to municipal corporation [*sic*], and point out the dual relations of those corporations to the public and to private interests; and, in so far as they touch upon the public duties of the corporations, they are instructive upon the subject we are considering. These cases define two kinds of duties that are imposed upon a municipal corporation. One is that kind which arises from a grant of a special power in the exercise of which the municipality is as a legal individual; the other is that kind which arises or is implied from the use of political rights under the general law in the exercise of which it is a sovereign. The former power is private, and is used for private purposes; the latter is public, and is used for public purposes. The former is not held by the municipality as one of the political divisions of the state; the latter is. Where the power is intrusted to the corporation as one of the political divisions of the state and is conferred, not for the immediate benefit of the municipality, but as a means to the exercise of the sovereign power, for the benefit of all citizens, the corporation is not liable for nonuser nor for misuser by the public agents. Where the duties which are imposed upon the municipality are of the latter class, they are generally to be performed by officers who, though deriving their appointment from the corporation itself, through the nomination of some of its executive agents by a power devolved thereon as a convenient mode of exercising the function of government, are yet the officers, and hence the servants, of the public at large; and they are not under the control of the municipality. They are not its agents or servants, but are public officers, agents, and servants of the public at large; and the corporation is not responsible for their acts or omissions, nor for the acts or omissions of their subordinates by them appointed. . . .

. . . .

The learned counsel for the plaintiff strenuously insists that allegations in the complaint charge the defendant itself with specific negligence in appointing an incompetent person as attendance officer, and in failing to make proper regulations to govern his conduct, and this is the serious point in the case. The trend of the decisions we have cited sustain the proposition that a body corporate of the character of this defendant, whose duties are of a public character only, is not liable for negligence which results from the execution of a statutory duty, un-

less the liability is expressly created by statute. This would seem to
be the general rule. . . .

. . . .

. . . But another insuperable objection to the plaintiff's recovery in
this action appears in another feature of the case. The complaint clearly shows that the deceased was not a truant; that he was not liable to
arrest, and at the time of the arrest was in the presence of his father,
and was absent from school with his permission, to the knowledge of
the officer. His act was a bald, naked trespass. The pursuit of this child
in the face of an approaching train, at this dangerous point, across the
railroad track, against the express commands of the child's father, was
not only an unauthorized, but a criminal, act; and it cannot be claimed
that the officer, in doing the things enumerated in the complaint, was
acting within the scope of his authority; and, in this view of the case,
it is unimportant whether Murray was incompetent to fill the position
to which he was appointed.

Guides for Class Discussion

1. Do you think courts today would reason as did this court in
   1898? Give reasons.
2. Had the position of attendance officer not been created by
   statute, as stated by the court, would it have held as it did?
3. Does this case, concerned with the relationship of the board
   to an attendance officer, have application to a case involving
   the relationship of the board to a teacher or administrator?

9. *"In recent years the principle of immunity from tort liability
in case of negligence has come in for a good deal of criticism as
being illogical and contrary to sound public policy"* (p. 3).

BUCK v. McLEAN,
115 So. (2d) 764 (Fla.) (1959)
(Decided by the District Court of Appeal of Florida, First District)

[This was an action for damages against a school board. Plaintiff was injured while attending a high school baseball game as a
paying spectator, when hit by a foul ball which came through
a hole in the screen. She contended the board was negligent in per-

mitting the screen to deteriorate. The lower court ruled in favor of the board and plaintiff appealed. The higher court upheld the decision of the lower court.]

WIGGINTON, Chief Judge.

. . . .

The immunity of the State from suit is absolute and unqualified and the constitutional provision securing it is not to be so construed as to place the State within reach of the court's process. County boards of public instruction are agencies of the State and as such are clothed with the same degree of immunity from suit as is the State. They are the creatures of the Constitution, constituted as quasi corporations for the purpose of exercising under legislative authority such part of the governmental powers of the State as the law confides in them. In short, county school boards are part of the machinery of government operating at the local level as an agency of the State in the performance of public functions. The character of their functions, and the extent and duration of their powers rests exclusively in the legislative discretion. Their powers may be enlarged, diminished, modified or revoked, and their acts set aside or confirmed, at the pleasure of the legislature.

. . . .

As . . . authority for the proposition that county school boards are not immune from liability for torts committed by their agents or employees while in the performance of a corporate or proprietary function, appellant refers us to the case of Hoffman decided in 1949 by a district court in Pennsylvania, and Sawaya decided in 1955 by the Supreme Court of Arizona. To these may be added the case of Molitor decided by the Supreme Court of Illinois on May 22, 1959, which extends the rule by withdrawing from county school districts immunity from tort liability for the negligent acts of their employees even when committed in the performance of governmental functions. We have carefully studied the cited decisions and in all frankness must agree that they are solid support for the position which appellants here take. They completely discredit and repudiate the ancient doctrine of sovereign immunity and reject as unsound the several reasons relied upon by our Supreme Court for the settled rule which immunizes county school boards against liability for torts committed by their agents or employees. We are compelled to the view, however, that such conflict in judicial opinion does not in any manner alter the established law of this jurisdiction.

We share the wonderment expressed by Mr. Justice Thomas in Suwannee County Hospital as to when the entry of government into businesses as well and as readily operatable by private enterprises will cease. Courts are not blind to the many instances within the personal knowledge of their members where departments and agencies of the State, as well as counties and local school boards, are engaged in activities which by any reasonable standard must be considered corporate and proprietary in nature. In so doing they are directly competing with private business in fields which could and in most instances are better served by the latter. It is a harsh doctrine indeed which leaves one without remedy for wrong suffered by him through the negligence of a state agent or employee committed while performing a proprietary function, but under similar circumstances imposes liability on everyone else engaged in the performance of similar functions.

Regardless of our personal views, we feel that a proper administration of justice invites respect for the admonition of Alexander Hamilton, who once wrote that courts "must declare the sense of the law; and if they should be disposed to exercise *Will* instead of *Judgment,* the consequences would equally be the substitution of their pleasure to that of the legislative body." If, therefore, a change in the long established rule of immunity prevailing in this State is to be made, it must come as it did in the States of New York, Washington and California either by constitutional amendment, or by enactment of appropriate legislation, or both.

Guides for Class Discussion

1. Compare this decision with the one made by the Illinois court in *Molitor* v. *Kaneland Community Unit District, infra,* and by the Minnesota court in *Panel* v. *Mounds View School District, infra.*
2. See *McGraw* v. *Rural High School District, infra.*
3. What is the meaning of the quotation from Alexander Hamilton that appears in the last paragraph?

10. "*In 1959 . . . the Supreme Court of Illinois . . . abrogated the common-law rule and held a board of education liable in tort in the absence of a statute making it liable*" (p. 3).

MOLITOR V. KANELAND COMMUNITY UNIT DISTRICT,
18 Ill. 11, 163 N.E. (2d) 89 (1959)
(Decided by the Supreme Court of Illinois)

[The facts of this case are to be found in the material quoted below.]

KLINGBIEL, Justice.

Plaintiff, Thomas Molitor, a minor, by Peter his father and next friend, brought this action against Kaneland Community Unit School

District for personal injuries sustained by plaintiff when the school bus in which he was riding left the road, allegedly as a result of the driver's negligence, hit a culvert, exploded and burned.

The complaint alleged, in substance, the negligence of the School District, through its agent and servant, the driver of the school bus; that plaintiff was in the exercise of such ordinary care for his own safety as could be reasonably expected of a boy of his age, intelligence, mental capacity and experience; that plaintiff sustained permanent and severe burns and injuries as a proximate result of defendant's negligence, and prayed for judgment in the amount of $56,000. . . .

The complaint contained no allegation of the existence of insurance or other non-public funds out of which a judgment against defendant could be satisfied. Although plaintiff's abstract of the record shows that defendant school district did carry public liability insurance with limits of $20,000 for each person injured and $100,000 for each occurrence, plaintiff states that he purposely omitted such an allegation from his complaint.

Defendant's motion to dismiss the complaint on the ground that a school district is immune from liability for tort was sustained by the trial court, and a judgment was entered in favor of defendant. Plaintiff elected to stand on his complaint and sought a direct appeal to this court on the ground that the dismissal of his action would violate his constitutional rights. At that time we held that no fairly debatable constitutional question was presented so as to give this court jurisdiction on direct appeal, and accordingly the cause was transferred to the Appellate Court for the Second District. The Appellate Court affirmed the decision of the trial court and the case is now before us again on a certificate of importance.

In his brief, plaintiff recognizes the rule, established by this court in 1898, that a school district is immune from tort liability, and frankly asks this court . . . to abolish the rule *in toto*. . . .

.   .   .   .

Historically we find that the doctrine of the sovereign immunity of the state, the theory that "the King can do no wrong," was first extended to a subdivision of the state in 1788 in Russell v. Men of Devon, 2 Term Rep. 671, 100 Eng. Rep. 359. . . .

It should be noted that the Russell case was later overruled by the English courts, and that in 1890 it was definitely established that in England a school board or school district is subject to suit in tort for personal injuries on the same basis as a private individual or corporation. . . .

.   .   .   .

Coming down to the precise issue at hand, it is clear that if the above rules and precedents are strictly applied to the instant case, plaintiff's complaint, containing no allegation as to the existence of insurance, was properly dismissed. On the other hand, the complaint may be held to state a good cause of action on either one of two theories, (1) application of the doctrine of Moore v. Moyle, 405 Ill. 555, 92 N.E. 2d 81, or (2) abolition of the rule that a school district is immune from tort liability.

As to the doctrine of Moore v. Moyle, that case involved an action for personal injuries against Bradley University, a charitable education institution. Traditionally, charitable and educational institutions have enjoyed the same immunity from tort liability as have governmental agencies in Illinois. . . .

. . . .

The original basis of the immunity rule has been called a "survival of the medieval idea that the sovereign can do no wrong," or that "the King can do no wrong. . . ."

. . . .

The other chief reason advanced in support of the immunity rule in the more recent cases is the protection of public funds and public property. This corresponds to the "no fund" or "trust fund" theory upon which charitable immunity is based. . . .

We do not believe that in this present day and age, when public education constitutes one of the biggest businesses in the country, that school immunity can be justified on the protection-of-public-funds theory.

In the first place, analysis of the theory shows that it is based on the idea that payment of damage claims is a diversion of educational funds to an improper purpose. As many writers have pointed out, the fallacy in this argument is that it assumes the very point which is sought to be proved, *i.e.,* that payment of damage claims is not a proper purpose. "Logically, the 'No-fund' or 'trust fund' theory is without merit because it is of value only after a determination of what is a proper school expenditure. To predicate immunity upon the theory of a trust fund is merely to argue in a circle, since it assumes an answer to the very question at issue, to wit, what is an educational purpose? Many disagree with the 'no-fund' doctrine to the extent of ruling that the payment of funds for judgments resulting from accidents or injuries in schools is an educational purpose. Nor can it be properly argued that as a result of the abandonment of the common-law rule the district would be completely bankrupt. California, Tennessee, New York, Washington and other states have not been compelled to shut down their schools." . . .

. . . .

Neither are we impressed with defendant's plea that the abolition of immunity would create grave and unpredictable problems of school finance and administration. . . .

We are of the opinion that none of the reasons advanced in support of school district immunity have any true validity today. Further we believe that abolition of such immunity may tend to decrease the frequency of school bus accidents by coupling the power to transport pupils with the responsibility of exercising care in the selection and supervision of the drivers. . . . .

. . . .

We conclude that the rule of school district tort immunity is unjust, unsupported by any valid reason, and has no rightful place in modern day society.

Defendant strongly urges that if said immunity is to be abolished, it should be done by the legislature, not by this court. With this contention we must disagree. The doctrine of school district immunity was created by this court alone. Having found that doctrine to be unsound and unjust under present conditions, we consider that we have not only the power, but the duty, to abolish that immunity. "We closed our courtroom doors without legislative help, and we can likewise open them." Pierce v. Yakima Valley Memorial Hospital Ass'n, 43 Wash. 2d 162, 260 P. 2d 765, 774.

Guides for Class Discussion

1. See *Thomas* v. *Broadlands Community Consolidated School District, infra.*
2. Compare the reasoning of the court in its decision with that in *School District* v. *Rivera, supra;* with that in *Krutili* v. *Board of Education, supra.*
3. Are you in agreement with the court's holding? Give reasons.
4. Did the court, by rendering this decision, usurp from the legislature the legislative function?

11. "In 1962, the Supreme [Court] . . . in Minnesota abrogated the nonliability rule" (pp. 3-4).

SPANEL V. MOUNDS VIEW SCHOOL DISTRICT,
118 N.W. (2d) 795 (Minn.) (1962)
(Decided by the Minnesota Supreme Court)

[The facts of this case are easily gleaned from a reading of the opinion which follows.]

Otis, Justice.

Plaintiff sues on behalf of his 5-year-old son to recover damages from a school district and a teacher and principal employed by it for injuries resulting from the alleged negligence of defendants in permitting a defective slide to remain in the kindergarten classroom of an elementary school.

Plaintiff appeals from an order granting a motion to dismiss the action as to defendant school district on the ground the complaint fails to state a claim upon which relief can be granted against it.

The only issue before us is whether the doctrine of governmental tort immunity shall now be overruled by judicial decision.

. . . .

We hold that the order for dismissal is affirmed, with the caveat, however, that subject to the limitations we now discuss, the defense of sovereign immunity will no longer be available to school districts, municipal corporations, and other subdivisions of government on whom immunity has been conferred by judicial decision with respect to torts which are committed after the adjournment of the next regular session of the Minnesota Legislature.

All of the paths leading to the origin of governmental tort immunity converge on Russell v. The Men of Devon, 100 Eng. Rep. 359, 2 T. R. 667 (1788). This product of the English common law was left on our doorstep to become the putative ancestor of a long line of American cases beginning with Mower v. Leicester, 9 Mass. 247 (1812). Russell sued all of the male inhabitants of the County of Devon for damages occurring to his wagon by reason of a bridge being out of repair. It was apparently undisputed that the county had a duty to maintain such structures. The court held that the action would not lie because: (1) To permit it would lead to "an infinity of actions," [100 Eng. Rep. 362, 2 T. R. 671] (2) there was no precedent for attempting such a suit, (3) only the legislature should impose liability of this kind, (4) even if defendants are to be considered a corporation or quasi-corporation there is no fund out of which to satisfy the claim, (5) neither law nor reason supports the action, (6) there is a strong presumption that what has never been done cannot be done, and (7) although there is a legal principle which permits a remedy for every injury resulting from the neglect of another, a more applicable principle is "that it is better that an individual should sustain an injury than that the public should suffer an inconvenience." The court concluded that the suit should not be permitted *"because the action must be brought against the public."* (Italics supplied) There is no mention of the "King can do no wrong," but on the contrary it is suggested that plaintiff sue the county itself rather than its individual inhabitants. Every reason assigned by the court is born of expediency. The wrong to plaintiff is submerged in the convenience of the public. No moral, ethical, or rational reason for the decision is advanced by the court except the practical problem of assessing damages against individual defendants. The court's invitation to the legislature has a familiar ring. It was finally accepted as to claims against the Crown in 1947, although Russell had long since been overruled.

In 1812 when Mower's horse was killed by stepping in a hole on the Leicester bridge, counsel argued that "Men of Devon" did not apply since the town of Leicester was incorporated and had a treasury out of which to satisfy a judgment. The Massachusetts court nevertheless held that the town had no notice of the defect and that quasi-corporations are not liable for such neglect under the common law. On the authority of "Men of Devon" recovery was denied. It was on this shaky foundation that the law of governmental tort immunity was erected in Minnesota and elsewhere. In 1871 we held that one who was injured by a defective bridge *did* have a cause of action against a municipal corporation for its negligence, citing "Men of Devon." [Shartle v. City of Minneapolis, 17 Minn. 284.] A few years later we recognized the distinction between municipal corporations and quasi-corporations with respect to liability to individuals for the negligence of municipal officers or agents. Without citing any authority we held that a plaintiff injured on a defective courthouse sidewalk could not recover damages against the county basing our decision on what we said was a long-established doctrine which "the legislature alone should change." [Dosdall v. County of Olmsted, 30 Minn. 96, 14 N.W. 458.]

The following year we reverted to "Men of Devon" in finding a town not liable for its negligent failure to repair a bridge [Altnow v. Town of Sibley, 30 Minn. 186, 14 N.W. 877], defendant citing also Mower v. Leicester.

An 8-year-old boy was denied recovery for the loss of a leg injured on defendant's school grounds in Bank v. Brainerd School Dist., 49 Minn. 106, 109, 51 N.W. 814, 815. We held that the school district enjoyed the same tort immunity as towns and counties. . . .

. . . .

Some of the arguments advanced for retaining sovereign tort immunity are these: Stare decisis and stability in the law require it. There are no funds available to satisfy claims. The discretionary activities of administrative officials would be seriously circumscribed by the specter of tort liability for mistakes in judgment. The functions of government are mandatory under our system, involving many dangerous and hazardous undertakings, exposing vast numbers of persons to potential harm. It is a practical impossibility to police all of the activities of school children. Many units of government do not have sufficient resources to absorb a substantial loss without the threat of bankruptcy.

. . . .

Even in jurisdictions which adhere to the immunity doctrine, seldom is any justification advanced beyond the rule of stare decisis.

Our consideration of the origins of tort immunity persuade us that its genesis was accidental and was characterized by expediency, and that its continuation has stemmed from inertia. The development of governmental liability for proprietary functions was an acknowledgment that the original rule was unduly restrictive, and reflected an uneasiness in the corporate conscience. . . . It has been argued on behalf of defendants that if immunity is abolished public schools will be deluged with claims for injuries resulting from inadequate supervision, from frostbite while waiting for buses, from blows struck by other children, from forbidden and mischievous activities impulsively and foolishly inspired, and from a host of other causes. . . . The fact that subdivisions of government now enjoy no immunity in a number of areas of activity has not noticeably circumscribed their usefulness or rendered them insolvent.

. . . .

We recognize that by denying recovery in the case at bar the remainder of the decision becomes dictum. However, the court is unanimous in expressing its intention to overrule the doctrine of sovereign tort immunity as a defense with respect to tort claims against school districts, municipal corporations, and other subdivisions of government on whom immunity has been conferred by judicial decision arising after the next Minnesota legislature adjourns, subject to any statutes which now or hereafter limit or regulate the prosecution of such claims. However, we do not suggest that discretionary as distinguished from ministerial activities, or judicial, quasi-judicial, legislative, or quasi-legislative functions may not continue to have the benefit of the rule. Nor is it our purpose to abolish sovereign immunity as to the state itself.

Counsel has assured us that members of the bar, in and out of the legislature, intend to draft and secure the introduction of bills at the forthcoming session which will give affected entities of government an opportunity to meet their new obligations. . . .

. . . .

It may appear unfair to deprive the present claimant of his day in court. However, we are of the opinion it would work an even greater injustice to deny defendant and other units of government a defense on which they have had a right to rely. We believe that it is more equitable if they are permitted to plan in advance by securing liability insurance or by creating funds necessary for self-insurance. In addition provision must be made for routinely and promptly investigating personal injury and other tort claims at the time of their occurrence in order that defendants may marshall and preserve whatever evidence is available for the proper conduct of their defense.

Affirmed.

Guides for Class Discussion

1. Compare this case with *Molitor* v. *Kaneland Community Unit District, supra.*
2. Compare this case with *McGraw* v. *Rural High School District, infra.*
3. Do you approve the reasoning followed by the court in this case? Give reasons.
4. What is "the rule of stare decisis," to which the court referred?

12. "*Some courts take the position that if the principle is an historical anachronism and works injustice it should be abrogated but that the change should be made by the legislature and not by the courts*" (p. 4).

McGraw v. Rural High School District,
120 Kan. 413, 243 P. 1038 (1926)
(Decided by the Supreme Court of Kansas)

[Pertinent facts are to be founded in the material quoted.]

Burch, J.: The action was one for damages for personal injuries sustained by plaintiff while employed as a laborer to assist in the construction by the district of a high-school building. The petition alleged the injuries were occasioned by defendant's negligence. A demurrer to the petition was sustained, and plaintiff appeals.

The question presented is the old one of liability of a governmental agency for tort. It is contended the erection of the school building was not a governmental function, a distinction being made between providing school facilities and making use of provided facilities for educational purposes. It is further contended the petition presents a case of liability under a specific contract, not a case of violated public duty, citing *Williams* v. *Kearny County*, 61 Kan. 708, 60 P. 1046. Finally and chiefly, it is contended that, since the district had authority to erect the building and to employ plaintiff to do the work in which he was engaged when he was injured, the law of master and servant applies.

The school building was indispensable to keeping school, and providing the building for educational purposes was just as much a sovereign function as utilizing the building for educational purposes. The contract of employment contained no express convenant to return plaintiff to a status of good condition at expiration of his employment, and no implied convenant not to injure him, analogous to the convenants of the lease in the Williams case. While the contract of employment created the relation of master and servant, the relationship was not created for the private advantage of the incorporators of the school district, but to promote the general welfare through education of the young, a sovereign function to be exercised under immunity of the sovereign from tort liability.

If the doctrine of state immunity in tort survives by virtue of antiquity alone, is an historical anachronism, manifests an inefficient public policy, and works injustice to everybody concerned (Governmental Responsibility in Tort, by Edwin M. Borchard, 11 Am. Bar Assn. Jrl. 96, August 1925), the legislature should abrogate it. But the legislature must make the change in policy, not the courts.

The judgment of the district court is affirmed.

Guides for Class Discussion

1. Reconcile this decision with the one in *Molitor* v. *Kaneland Community Unit District, supra;* with *Spanel* v. *Mounds View School District, supra.*

2. Answer the contention that this case was one of liability under contract.

3. While the court recognized that the rule of immunity worked an injustice, it felt that the legislature was the one to abrogate the rule. Justify this position.

13. *"In some states . . . statutes have been enacted which abrogate the common-law rule and make school districts liable for injurie sustained as a result of the negligence of school officers, agents and employees" (p. 4).*

VENDRELL v. SCHOOL DISTRICT,
226 Ore. 263, 360 P. (2d) 282 (1961)
(Decided by the Supreme Court of Oregon)

[The facts of the case will be found in the first paragraph o the material which follows. In its decision, the court found i necessary to rule upon the question of whether a school distric was immune from liability. In so doing, it commented to the effec that the district would be held liable only in case of a statut to that effect. In discussing statutes relating to liability, the cour made it clear that, to hold the district liable, the statute would have to be clear and definite.]

O'CONNELL, Justice.

This is an action to recover damages for personal injuries suffered by plaintiff during the course of a football game between Nyssa hig school and the Vale high school, in which plaintiff was a participant a a member of the Nyssa high school team. The action is brought agains the school district as a corporate entity, the individual members of th board of directors of the district in their official capacity as board men bers, the superintendent of schools, and the principal of Nyssa hig school. The coach of the Nyssa football team was not made a part defendant.

Plaintiff was 15 years of age at the time of his injury. He bring this action in his own name after reaching the age of majority. Defend ants demurred to plaintiff's complaint. The demurrer was sustained an plaintiff, declining to plead further, appealed.

Plaintiff's injury occurred when he was tackled by two membe: of the Vale team. Among other injuries, he suffered a broken nec which resulted in paraplegia. . . .

. . . .

The only issue argued below and presented in the briefs and argu ment on appeal is whether ORS 332.180 is to be interpreted a impliedly providing for the waiver of the sovereign immunity o school district to the extent of the coverage of the insurance policy pu chased by the district. . . .

. . . .

Our Constitution is framed on the premise that the state is immune from suit and that if immunity is lifted it shall be done so by the action of the legislature. Article VI, § 24 provides as follows:

"Provision may be made by general law, for bringing suit against the State, as to all liabilities originating after, or existing at the time of the adoption of this Constitution; but no special act authorizing (sic) such suit to be brought, or making compensation to any person claiming damages against the State, shall ever be passed."

Since a school district is a political subdivision of the state, . . . the principle of immunity pronounced in the Constitution applies to it. . . .

Thus it is apparent that the doctrine of sovereign immunity exists in this state, not as the creation of the courts, but as a constitutional principle chosen by the people and which is subject to change only by general law. . . .

To determine, then, that a school district in this state may incur tort liability we must find that a provision waiving sovereign immunity has been "made by general law." The language of ORS 30.320 is broad enough to warrant an interpretation that the immunity of school districts has been waived, the statute, together with ORS 30.310, providing that an action may be maintained against a school district and other governmental units "for an injury to the rights of the plaintiff arising from some act or omission." However, our cases have interpreted the statute to permit recovery only when the governmental unit is acting in its proprietary as distinguished from its governmental capacity. . . . Since it is now established by Lovell v. School Dist. No. 13, 1943, 172 Or. 500, 507-508, 143 P. 2d 236 that a school district, when performing the duties imposed upon it by statute, always acts in a governmental capacity, ORS 30.320 does not operate to lift the school district's immunity from tort liability.

. . . .

. . . If the legislature had intended that the school district's immunity from tort liability was to be abrogated, it would seem that the statute would have been drafted to expressly so provide. We recognize that a different interpretation is possible. Thus in Molitor v. Kaneland Com. Unit Dist., 1959, 18 Ill. 2d 11, 163 N.E. 2d 89, 92 where the court likewise had before it a statute authorizing the school district to purchase insurance, the statute was interpreted "as expressing [the legislature's] dissatisfaction with the court-created doctrine of governmental immunity and an attempt to cut down that immunity where insurance is involved." We look at the matter differently. The legislature has undertaken to deal with the question of the school district's immunity; and we think that it is reasonable to assume that it considered the doctrine of immunity as a whole, at least as it related to school districts, and elected to lift immunity only to the extent of the insurance actually purchased.

Guides for Class Discussion

1. Compare the decision in this case with the one in *Molitor* v. *Kaneland Community Unit District, supra;* and *Hummer* v. *School City of Hartford City, infra.*
2. Are you in agreement with the court's reasoning?
3. Is the criterion that the statute must be definite too subjective to make for ease of application? Give reasons.

14. "*. . . where statutes have been enacted permitting school boards to carry . . . insurance, it has been held that . . . [these statutes] do not act to abrogate the common-law rule of immunity . . .*" (p. 4).

HUMMER V. SCHOOL CITY OF HARTFORD CITY,
124 Ind. App. 30, 112 N.E. (2d) 891 (1953)
(Decided by the Appellate Court of Indiana)

[This action for damages was brought against a school city by one who received personal injuries while attending a basketball game as a paid spectator. Among other things, he argued that the school city should be held liable because it carried liability insurance which it had purchased under statutory authority. The lower court ruled against plaintiff and the higher court affirmed the decision of the lower court.]

ACHOR, Judge.

. . . .

We now consider the . . . major question . . . , whether or not the Legislature by the enactment of § 39-1819, supra, made it possible for the appellee school corporation to waive its governmental immunity and, if so, whether or not appellant was entitled to allege and prove the fact of such insurance as constituting waiver. The rule is well established that governmental immunity may be abrogated or modified by legislative enactment unless prohibited by the Constitution, . . . and that the Legislature may establish circumstances under which schoc cities may waive the defense of immunity. . . . The rule is also well established that waiver must be affirmatively pleaded. . . .

The statute before us, § 39-1819, supra, is as follows:

"The state, or any municipal corporation thereof, is hereby empowered to purchase policies of insurance insuring the officers, appointees, agents and employees of the state or municipal corporation against loss or damage . . . , caused by accident and arising out of the ownership, maintenance, hire, or use of any motor vehicle owned by the state or such municipal corporation, and any real or other personal property whatsoever, owned, hired, or used by the state or such municipal corporation. . . . In no event shall the state or any municipal corporation thereof, be liable, in any case, in any amount in excess of the maximum amount of valid insurance in full force and effect and covering the particular motor vehicle or particular real or personal property involved in the accident causing such loss or damage. . . . No such policy of insurance shall be purchased by or issued or delivered to the state or to any municipal corporation . . . unless there shall be contained within such policy a provision that if there arises or may arise a claim, suit or cause of action in relation thereto, such insurance carrier will not set up, as a defense, the immunity of the state or of such municipal corporation. . . ."

This being a case of first impression in our state requiring construction of the above statute, we have searched the statutes and decisions of other states for guiding precedents upon this issue. . . .

. . . .

. . . our insurance statute . . . does not, in addition to providing for indemnity insurance, also affirmatively . . . create a primary liability on the part of the assured, or . . . provide for the filing of suit directly against the insurer, or . . . provide that the measure of liability can be determined by a limited judgment taken against the assured. The statute neither modifies nor expressly provides a remedy which waives or circumvents the immunity of the municipal corporation which insures itself against liability.

We conclude, therefore, that waiver of governmental immunity by a *school city* must be read into our statute, if at all, . . . by implication. . . .

. . . .

Appellant urges further in support of statutory waiver of governmental immunity by implication . . . that there would be no purpose in authorizing the purchase of insurance by school corporations if no liability for loss or damage were made to exist against such school cities and . . . that the following limitation in the statute would be a complete anomaly. The limitation referred to is as follows: . . . "In no event shall the . . . municipal corporation . . . be liable, in any case, . . . in excess of the maximum amount of valid insurance . . ." 39-1819, supra.

However, as heretofore stated, *personal* liability has been imposed upon the officials of school corporations. . . . These cases would seem to justify the procurement of insurance insuring its officials, etc. against the problematical "liability imposed by law" as provided in our statute, § 39-1919, supra. In this particular the statute has logical application to school cities as municipal corporations and must be so construed.

. . . .

In any event, as heretofore stated, it is an established rule of statutory construction that statutes which would modify so fundamental a rule of the common law must be clear and concise in their expression of such an intent, that intendment can not be supported by mere implication, and that if ambiguous, the statute must be construed against the modification of the rule. Consistent with this rule of statutory construction, numerous courts have held that statutes similar to our own and the procurement of insurance as therein authorized, have not had the effect of waiving the immunity of a governmental unit so as to permit judgment to be taken against it.

. . . .

The . . . cases [decided in other jurisdictions], although not controlling upon this court as to the construction to be placed upon our statute, are nevertheless persuasive that the common-law rule of governmental immunity from tort liability is not waived by a municipal corporation merely as the result of the procurement by it of liability insurance under a statute authoring the purchase of insurance insuring the officers, appointees, agents and employees of such municipal corporation. Such is the conclusion of this court.

Guides for Class Discussion

1. Compare this decision with the ones rendered in *Supler* v. *School District, infra; Taylor* v. *Knox County Board of Education, infra;* and *Thomas* v. *Broadlands Community Consolidated School District, infra.*
2. Are you in agreement with the court's reasoning? Give reason.

15. ". . . *where statutes have been enacted permitting school boards to carry . . . insurance, it has been held that . . . [although these statutes] do not act to abrogate the common-law rule of immunity, . . . school districts . . . [may be] held liable in an amount [not] in excess of the coverage of the insurance policy"* (p. 4).

TAYLOR V. KNOX COUNTY BOARD OF EDUCATION,
292 Ky. 767, 167 S.W. (2d) 700 (1942)
(Decided by the Court of Appeals of Kentucky)

[In Kentucky, the statute authorized the school board to "set aside funds" for liability and indemnity insurance against the negligence of the drivers and operators of school buses, for the purpose of paying any final judgment rendered against the insured for loss or damage to school property, or for injuries or death of any school child or other person, resulting from transportation accidents. In this case the court was called upon to interpret this statute—*i.e.*, to render a decision regarding whether the statute had the effect of waiving the school district's immunity under the common-law rule.]

REES, Justice

. . . .

. . . The Legislature may make school boards liable for their torts or the torts of their agents and employees, and we know of no reason why it may not taken [*sic*] a middle course and empower them to protect by liability insurance persons injured by the negligence of their bus drivers and to provide that the liability of the insurer shall be determined by the final judgment obtained by the injured person. The allegations of the petition as amended and the provisions of the insurance policy set out therein show that the insurance contract in the present case is not an indemnity policy, but is a liability policy issued for the benefit of injured third parties who may sue the insurer when the amount of liability has been determined by a final judgment against the insured. . . .

. . . .

The act does not make the board liable for the torts of its agents and employees, but it does permit the board to be sued and a judgment to be obtained which, when final, shall measure the liability of the insurance carrier to the injured party for whose benefit the insurance policy was issued. In no event, of course, can the judgment be collected out of school funds. . . .

Guides for Class Discussion

1. Compare this case with *Supler* v. *School District, infra;* and *Hummer* v. *School City of Hartford City, supra.* With which of these cases do you agree, and with which do you disagree?
2. Differentiate between the court's reasoning in this case and its reasoning in *Hummer* v. *School City of Hartford City, supra.*
3. How would the court have held had the legislature provided for an indemnity policy rather than a liability policy?

16. *"Where there is no statute authorizing the board to carry . . insurance . . . it has been held that a board may not spend it. funds to purchase liability insurance to protect itself against contingency that can never arise"* (p. 4).

BOARD OF EDUCATION v. COMMERCIAL CASUALTY INSURANCE CO.,
116 W. Va. 503, 182 S.E. 87 (1935)
(Decided by the Supreme Court of Appeals of West Virginia)

[A school board, questioning the authority of its predecessor to purchase liability insurance, brought this action against the company for the return of premiums paid. The lower court ruled in favor of the board, and the higher court affirmed its decision.]

MAXWELL, Judge.

. . . .

The basic inquiry is whether under West Virginia statutes which were in existence at the time of the purchase of this insurance a district board of education had authority to spend money for such purpose. The plaintiff denies that there was such authority; the defendant affirms.

Under the Code of 1931, a district board of education was vested with "general control and management of all the schools and the school interests of its district. . . ." Further, a board had authority "to provide at public expense for the transportation of pupils to and from such consolidated schools, or other schools where transportation of pupils may be necessary." . . . Can it be reasonably said that the said statute, by implication, created the right in a district board to purchase indemnity insurance by reason of its operation of school buses?

Because it is a public agency, an arm of the state, a school board is not liable for damages for personal injury, even though such injury may arise from neglect or nonfeasance. . . . It is therefore asserted on behalf of the plaintiff that inasmuch as the district board could not have been held liable for damages occasioned by the negligent operation of a school bus, there was nothing against which the policy of indemnification could operate; that it was without basis or justification. The defendant counters this position by urging that though there would be no primary liability of the board and therefore no basis for indemnification on that score, there are other elements of the policy which were of value to both the board and the public, namely, (1) to enable passengers and the public to enforce the personal liability of bus drivers for negligence; (2) to pay the expense of litigation and all costs taxed against the insured; (3) to investigate at the insurer's cost any accident to which the policy applies; (4) to defend any suit even if groundless; (5) to reimburse the assured for any surgical relief imperative at the time of an accident.

We are of opinion that under the law as it stood in 1932, when this insurance was purchased, there was no implied authority in a district board to procure insurance to facilitate the enforcement of bus drivers' liability. Since the date of the arising of this controversy, the statute has been enlarged. At present, a county board of education may "provide at public expense for insurance against the negligence of the drivers of school buses operated by the board." . . .

We are impressed that though the several services (items [2] to [5], supra) may have been undertaken by the insurer, they were of merely secondary importance. Even if they were matters as to which the district board might purchase insurance, they would not have justified the substantial premium paid for the policy. Primarily, the purpose of the policy was to indemnify the district board against legal liability which might be adjudged against it on account of the negligent operation of its school buses. The other items were incidental. . . .

We are dealing with a governmental agency of limited and circumscribed jurisdiction and authority. The scope of that authority is alone reflected in the statutes dealing with the subject. A function not expressly authorized can be justified only if it comes within clear and plain implications of the statute. . . .

.   .   .   .

There having been no warrant of authority on the part of the district board to purchase insurance to indemnify itself on account of the operation of school buses, nor to insure against the negligence of bus drivers, the benefits, if any, which remained were, in comparison with the major matter, mere shadows, wholly inadequate to support the defendant's claim for expenses of issuing and servicing the policy. . . .

Guides for Class Discussion

1. Compare the reasoning of the court in this case with that in *Thomas* v. *Broadlands Community Consolidated School District, infra.*
2. Evaluate the defendant's argument that, although the board had no liability, five elements of the policy were of value to both the board and the public.
3. The court stated that, since the cause of this action arose, the statute had been changed so as to authorize the board to carry insurance. Do you think such a statute is constitutional? Give reasons.

17. *"Where there is no statute authorizing the board to carry . . . insurance . . . it has been held that, because a school district is immune from tort liability, its purchase of liability insurance does not constitute a waiver of . . . immunity"* (p. 4).

SUPLER v. SCHOOL DISTRICT,
405 Pa. 657, 182 A. (2d) 535 (1962)
(Decided by the Supreme Court of Pennsylvania)

[This was an action against a school district for personal injuries suffered by a pupil as the result of the alleged negligence of an employee of the district. Plaintiff rested his case on the ground that, although the statute did not authorize or require it to do so, the district was covered by liability insurance. The lower court ruled in favor of the board and the higher court affirmed its decision.]

BELL, Chief Justice.

Plaintiffs seek damages for personal injuries suffered by minor plaintiff, Joseph W. Supler, as a result of alleged negligence on the part of defendant, W. A. Burson, an employee of defendant School District of North Franklin Township. Defendant School District filed an answer to plaintiff's complaint alleging under New Matter, that it is immune from suit for the negligence of its employees while engaged in the governmental functions of the School District and praying that the suit be dismissed. Plaintiffs then filed an Answer to New Matter averring that at the time of the occurrence of the injury the School District was fully *insured* against the risk involved in this case. Plaintiffs further averred that the insurance constituted a waiver of the defense of governmental immunity from suit and that in any event, by reason of such insurance, plaintiffs are entitled to maintain this action and recover a judgment against the School District to the extent of the insurance coverage. Defendant School District thereupon filed a motion for judgment on the pleadings. The Court en banc directed the entry of judgment in favor of defendant School District. From that judgment, plaintiffs took these appeals.

Since Ford v. Kendall Borough School District, 121 Pa. 543, 15 A. 812, 1 L.R.A. 607, was decided in 1888, this Court has always applied the rule that a School District is not liable in trespass for the negligence of its officers and employees while engaged in *governmental* functions. . . .

While plaintiffs recognize that these cases express the long and well settled law of Pennsylvania, they ask us to (1) to overrule them, which once again we refuse to do, or (2) if not, to modify the law and hold it inapplicable where the School District is covered by liability insurance. . . . In the Kesman case, this Court, in summarily dismissing appellants' contentions, said, (page 458, 29 A. 2d page 17):

"It has been repeatedly held that school districts are not liable for such negligence. . . . The same rule prevails in many other jurisdictions.

"In appellants' argument, it is suggested that as the defendant protected itself by liability insurance, it waived the immunity otherwise conceded to exist. No principle was suggested that would support a judgment against the defendant. . . ."

Plaintiffs further argue the rule should be modified because otherwise a School District which purchases liability insurance receives no value for the money it expends on premiums, if the district is protected by the doctrine of governmental immunity. The fallacy in this contention is demonstrated by Morris v. Mt. Lebanon Township School District, 393 Pa. 633, 144 A. 2d 737, supra, in which this Court held the School District liable for a tort committed in the performance of a proprietary function. It follows that a School District which purchases liability insurance does receive value since it protects itself against liability arising from its participation in proprietary functions. However, even if plaintiff's assumption were correct, it would not be a legally sufficient reason to justify a judicial change in the law.

If the Supreme Court were a super Legislature, which it is not, it would seem to many persons to be unjust to allow recovery to an injured person where the Governmental Authority carries insurance and to deny recovery to an injured person where the Governmental Authority is not insured. Under plaintiffs' theory the right to recovery at all, and the amount of the recovery, would depend not upon principles of Justice and the magnitude of the injury, but upon whether insurance was carried and, if so, the amount thereof.

If it is to be the policy of the law that the Commonwealth or any of its instrumentalities or any political subdivisions are to be subject to liability for the torts committed by their officers or employees while engaged in governmental functions, the change should be made by the Legislature and not by the Courts.

Judgment affirmed.

Guides for Class Discussion

1. Compare this decision with the one rendered by the court in *Morris* v. *School District of the Township of Mount Lebanon, infra;* with *Thomas* v. *Broadlands Community Consolidated School District, infra.*
2. Had the statute authorized or required the district to carry insurance, how do you think the court would have ruled? Give reasons.

18. *"Where there is no statute authorizing the board to carry . . . insurance . . . it has been held that where the district carries liability insurance . . . it can be held liable up to the amount of the insurance coverage"* (p. 4).

THOMAS v. BROADLANDS COMMUNITY CONSOLIDATED SCHOOL DISTRICT,

348 Ill. App. 567, 109 N.E. 2d 636 (1952)
(Decided by the Appellate Court of Illinois)

[The facts of this case will be found in the following quotation.]

O'Connor, Justice.

．　．　．　．　．　．　．　．　．　．　．　．　．　．　．

The plaintiff, a minor, sued, through his father as next friend for personal injuries received by him on October 4, 1950, while a student upon the playground, at the recess of the defendant, alleging negligence upon the part of defendant's agents, causing the loss of an eye to plaintiff. . . . The complaint alleged the carrying of liability insurance by defendant in an amount sufficient to pay any judgment recovered, and offered to limit collection of any judgment to the proceeds of such insurance policy. The defendant filed a motion to dismiss the complaint upon the ground that the defendant was created *nolen volens* by general law as a quasi-municipal corporation and as such is a part of the State of Illinois exercising governmental functions and not liable for the acts or negligence of its servants and agents. Upon June 15, 1951, the trial court sustained the motion to dismiss and, the plaintiff electing to abide by his complaint, final judgment was entered upon December 20, 1951, in favor of the defendant and for costs. The following questions were certified by the trial court and counsel for the respective parties to be the only questions of law to be determined upon this appeal:

1. Is the defendant immune from suit for negligence in this case?
2. If immunity exists, does the carrying of liability insurance remove this immunity either completely or to the extent of such insurance?

The decision upon the first question of law presented is free from complexity. Absent the question of insurance, the law in Illinois is clear that a School District, as a quasi-municipal corporation, is not liable for injuries resulting from tort. . . . We do not understand that plaintiff seriously contends the law is otherwise.

Does the liability insurance in force in behalf of the School District remove its immunity either totally or pro tanto? The answer to that question involves not only an analysis of decisions of this state, but also a research into the bases of the doctrine of governmental immunity.

It is the plaintiff's initial contention that Moore v. Moyle, 405 Ill. 555, 92 N.E. 2d 81, is, by analogy, decisive of this case. In the Moore case, supra, the Supreme Court of this State held that a complaint against a defendant charitable institution, alleged to be fully insured, so that a judgment, if obtained in a tort action, would not impair or diminish any funds held by the institution in trust for its charitable purposes, stated a cause of action. In that decision, the Court concluded that the sole object of the doctrine of immunity of charitable corporations from suit for tort was to protect trust funds of charities from depletion through the tortious conduct of their employees and agents. The Court indicated that the immunity granted to charitable corporations was not an absolute one and that such an immunity might be waived. The Court concluded that there was no intention shown in the previous decisions by it to extend the immunity granted to non-trust funds of the charity, and in holding that the plaintiff's complaint stated a cause of action against the charity, said in 405 Ill. on pages 565-566, 92 N.E. 2d on page 86:

> "We are of the opinion there is no justification for absolute immunity if the trust is protected, because that has been the reason for the rule of absolute immunity. Reason and justice require an extension of the rule in an attempt to inject some humanitarian principles into the abstract rule of absolute immunity. The law is not static and must follow and conform to changing conditions and new trends in human relations to justify its existence as a servant and protector

of the people and, when necessary, new remedies must be applied where none exist." (Italics supplied.)

We note that the doctrines of charitable immunity have had considerable effect on the doctrines pertaining to municipal immunity. . . .

. . . .

Text writers and at least one other case in Illinois have founded immunity upon the involuntary nature of the corporation, or upon the fact that in such a corporation its duties are wholly governmental in nature, that it is thus acting as an arm of the State which does not submit its action to the judgments of Courts and since the quasi-corporation is but a mere agent of the State it is likewise exempted. . . .

. . . .

The rule is, in regard to governmental functions of a municipal corporation, that no private action for tort will lie against the state since negligence cannot be imputed to the sovereign.

Defendant asserts in its brief that the basis for governmental immunity is that a State or subdivision thereof cannot be sued without its consent. In this defendant is only partially correct, for it has stated the rule and not the reason for the rule.

. . . .

Immunity of a municipal corporation cannot be justified upon the theory that the King can do no wrong, or any paraphrase thereof. Such a justification does not lend itself to the age in which we live, and its harsh consequences to society condemn it.

"The whole doctrine of governmental immunity from liability for tort rests upon a rotten foundation. It is almost incredible that in this modern age of comparative sociological enlightenment, and, in a republic, the medieval absolutism supposed to be implicit in the maxim, 'the King can do no wrong,' should exempt the various branches of the government from liability for their torts, and that the entire burden of damage resulting from the wrongful acts of the government should be imposed upon the single individual who suffers the injury, rather than distributed among the entire community constituting the government, where it could be borne without hardship upon any individual, and where it justly belongs." Barker v. City of Santa Fe, 47 N.M. 85, 136 P. (2d) 480. . . .

Guides for Class Discussion

1. Compare this case with *Supler* v. *School District, supra;* and *Board of Education* v. *Commercial Casualty Insurance Co., supra.*
2. Do you think this case represents "good" law? Give reasons.
3. On what ground did the court base its decision, primarily?

19. *"In a few instances the courts have held that recovery could be had [from a school district] in the case of injuries growing out of the performance of a proprietary function"* (p. 5).

MORRIS v. SCHOOL DISTRICT OF TOWNSHIP OF MT. LEBANON,
393 Pa. 633, 144 A. (2d) 737 (1958)
(Decided by the Supreme Court of Pennsylvania)

[The facts of this case will be found in the quotation which follows.]

COHEN, Justice.

For purposes of this appeal the following allegations are assumed to be true:

In the summer of 1953 the School District of the Township of Mount Lebanon conducted a recreation program open to the general public upon the payment of an admission fee. The program, which was not a part of the regular school curriculum, consisted of those activities normal to a summer day-camp, including arts and crafts, dancing and swimming. Plaintiff's minor decedent, Constance Morris, was duly enrolled in this recreation program upon payment by her parents of the weekly charges. On July 30, Constance drowned while playing in the water of the swimming pool. The failure of the defendant's employees in charge to give proper supervision and the rough and disorderly play in the water of those employees and others was alleged by Constance's father, the administrator of her estate, as the basis for the present action against the school district for wrongful death. Preliminary objections setting up the defense of the immunity of a governmental agency from tort liability were filed by the school district. The court below, *en banc*, sustained this objection and dismissed the complaint. Plaintiff has now appealed.

The doctrine of sovereign immunity and its application to local government law need not detain us here. The errors of history, logic and policy which were responsible for the development of this concept have been clearly exposed, and thoroughly criticized. Nevertheless, the solution of the problem of governmental responsibility in tort is too complex an undertaking to permit the partial and piecemeal judicial reform which the plaintiff seeks. Establishment of a comprehensive program by legislation applicable to the Commonwealth and to all of its sub-divisions is sorely needed to deal effectively with tort claims arising out of the conduct of governmental activities.

In conformity with the prevailing American view, we have long held that municipal corporations are not immune from liability in tort for the negligent acts of their servants committed in the course of the municipalities' proprietary functions. . . . Although early cases appear to have distinguished between municipal corporations proper, (cities and boroughs), and quasi-municipal corporations, (counties, townships and school districts), stating that the latter were subject to a *lesser liability,* these decisions meant no more than that as quasi-municipal corporations they exercised predominantly "governmental" functions, *the area of their potential liability was more limited.* It is clear that if these quasi-municipal corporations perform what can be said to be "proprietary" functions, the liability of a true municipal corporation attaches. . . .

Whatever may have been the governmental nature of the functions exercised by school districts in the past, their increased powers under the present School Code enable them to carry on many of the so-called proprietary endeavors characteristic of true municipal corporations. . . .

We must therefore consider whether the injury causing activity carried on by the school district in this case was an exercise of one such proprietary power.

Perhaps there is no issue known to the law which is surrounded by more confusion than the question whether a given municipal operation is governmental or proprietary in nature. Two reasons may be assigned therefor: First, the concept of proprietary functions has been viewed "liberally" and exceptions to the rule of non-liability for the conduct of governmental functions have been created because of judicial recognition that the losses caused by the torts of public employees should properly be treated, as in other cases of vicarious liability, as a cost of government administration. . . . Second, the tests yet devised for distinguishing between governmental and proprietary functions have proven unsatisfactory. . . .

In general, (and perhaps unhelpfully), it has been said that if a given activitity is one which a local government unit is not statutorily required to perform, or if it may also be carried on by private enterprise, or if it used as a means of raising revenue, the function is proprietary. . . .

In the instant case, although the nature of a summer recreation program has not before been judicially determined, the activity satisfies the requirements of a proprietary function. Thus, the school district in this case was not required by statute to undertake the recreation program, nor was the program even a part of the regular school curriculum. On the contrary, it was open to members of the general public residing both within and without the school district. Furthermore, the summer activity was of a type regularly conducted by private enterprises and a charge was made for participation therein.

We hold that these factors are sufficient to render the defendant subject to liability for the negligence of its employees as herein alleged. . . .

Guides for Class Discussion

1. Compare this case with *Richards* v. *School District of City of Birmingham, infra.*

2. What is your opinion of the criteria set up by the court for differentiating between governmental and proprietary functions? Are they defensible?

3. Do you think this concept of liability is likely to gain adherence among the courts of the various states?

20. *"The courts, however, have commonly held that a function carried on by a board of education does not lose its governmental nature and become a proprietary function merely because it yields some profit or produces some revenue"* (p. 5).

RICHARDS v. SCHOOL DISTRICT OF CITY OF BIRMINGHAM,
348 Mich. 490, 83 N.W. (2d) 643 (1957)
(Decided by the Supreme Court of Michigan)

[Plaintiff was injured while attending a football game between teams representing the high schools of Birmingham and Royal Oak, Michigan, when bleachers upon which he was seated collapsed. He then brought this action to recover damages. He alleged that the bleachers, which had been rented, were negligently constructed, and that the school district, who, by the leasing contract, had assumed responsibility for the erection of the bleachers, was negligent in so doing. Plaintiff contended that the district should be held liable on the ground that the injury grew out of the district's performance of a proprietary as opposed to a governmental function. The lower court ruled in favor of the school district and the Supreme Court, in a divided opinion, affirmed this decision.]

CARR, Justice.

· · · · · · · · · · · · · · ·

Plaintiff in the case at bar relies on the decision in Foss v. City of Lansing, 237 Mich. 633, 212 N.W. 952, 52 A.L.R. 185. There the defendant city, pursuant to resolution approved by vote of the electors, established a municipal garbage collection service, a fee of $1 per annum being specified by action of the city council as a charge for the use of cans or containers. To provide a means of disposing of the garbage the city purchased land outside the corporate limits, finally establishing on the property a piggery wherein the garbage was fed to hogs that were sold when ready for marketing. While returning to the city after conveying garbage to the piggery, a truck operated by a city employee collided with plaintiff's automobile. The suit was brought on the ground that the driver of the truck was negligent, and that the city was liable therefor. It appeared in the case that defendant realized a profit which was used to reduce the cost of garbage disposal. Under these circumstances this Court concluded that the city might be held liable, in the same manner as would a private corporation. Judgment in defendant's favor, entered on a directed verdict, was reversed and a new trial granted.

. . . .

The reasons supporting the decision in Daszkiewicz v. Detroit Board of Education, 301 Mich. 212, 3 N. W. 2d 71, 75, support the conclusion of the trial judge in the case at bar. There the administrator of the estate of a young man, who had been a student in the college of medicine operated by defendant in connection with Wayne University sued to recover damages because of the death of his intestate, due as it was alleged, to negligence on the part of defendant's employees At the conclusion of the testimony in the case motion for a directed verdict was made by defendant, the motion was taken under advisement, and the cause submitted to the jury. Verdict in favor of defendant was returned, and the court denied a subsequent motion for a new trial. It was the contention of the plaintiff, on appeal from the judgment entered, that the defendant in operating the public schools of the City of Detroit was performing an exclusively governmental function but that in operating the medical school it was engaged as a *quasi* municipality in a proprietary enterprise and, therefore, liable for the negligence of its employees because of the fact that the payment of tuition for attending said school was required. This Court, however rejected the claim, citing and quoting from Johnson v. Ontonagon County Road Commissioners, supra, and saying, further:

"The rule is generally recognized that a governmentally sponsored educational institution does not lose its immunity from tort liability by collecting tuition fees to assist in defraying the cost of such institution. Davie v. University of California Board of Regents 66 Cal. App. 693, 227 P. 243; Nabell v. City of Atlanta, 33 Ga App. 545, 126 S.E. 905; Todd v. Curators of University of Missouri 347 Mo. 460, 147 S.W. 2d 1063."

This decision must be construed as a clear recognition of the proposition that a school district created under the laws of the State of Michigan is not liable for the negligence of its employees even though income is received from tuition charged certain pupils. Obviously, the acceptance of a contrary theory would result in the diversion of monies raised by taxation for school purposes in any instance where such tuition is charged.

In the case at bar the defendant school district maintains a physical education department as a part of its facilities, and in connection therewith fosters and promotes athletics, including football, baseball, basketball, track and other activities. This is done in accordance with regulations of the State department of education, and as a part of the educational program of the defendant school district. It is not disputed that such activities have a proper place in education and in the physical and mental development of students. It is conceded that defendant has charged admission to football and baseball games, other athletic contests apparently being open to the public generally without charge.

An exhibit introduced by defendant district on the trial of the case, without objection, which exhibit was prepared by certified public accountants, discloses that the athletic activities program of the defendant school district for the year ending June 30, 1949, resulted in a net operating loss. The football game played on November 25, 1948, must be considered as a part of the athletic activities of the school rather than as an independent contest. It thus appears that such activities of the physical education department did not, for the year in question, result in a net profit. On the record in the case it may not be claimed that such activities are carried on for the purpose of making money for the benefit of defendant school district. Rather, the entire department is operated as a part of the school facilities and in furtherance of the objectives to be attained in educational lines. It may not be said that defendant district, in allowing athletic competition with other schools, is thereby engaging in a function proprietary in nature. On the contrary, it is performing a governmental function vested in it by law.

Under facts somewhat analogous to those in the case at bar, and involving the precise question of immunity from liability claimed here, it was held in Watson v. School District of the City of Bay City, 324 Mich. 1, 36 N.W. 2d 195, by an evenly divided Court, that the plaintiff was not entitled to recover. Judgment entered by the trial court notwithstanding the verdict of the jury was affirmed. The reasons advanced in the prevailing opinion are applicable here. Foss v. City of Lansing, supra, is for the reasons hereinbefore suggested not applicable. It may be noted in passing that Scott v. University of Michigan Athletic Ass'n, 152 Mich. 684, 116 N.W. 624, 17 L.R.A., N.S., 234, was not an action against the board of regents of the University of Michigan but was, rather, against an association composed of undergraduates, alumni and businessmen. In the decision of the case, reversing judgment entered on a verdict directed for defendant by the court, it was emphasized that the association, rather than the board of regents, was a proper party to the action because it was responsible for the erection of the bleacher that collapsed and stood in a position analogous to that of proprietor of a public resort. It may be noted also that in Robinson v. Washtenaw Circuit Judge, 228 Mich. 225, 199 N.W. 618, it was held that the board of regents was not liable for alleged malpractice on the part of a surgeon operating on plaintiff in the University hospital. It was held that said hospital was an adjunct to the medical department and was a State educational instrumentality maintained at public expense. We think the foregoing decisions clearly indicate the principles recognized in this State as controlling on the question under consideration.

Guides for Class Discussion

1. While recognizing that municipalities could be held liable in tort while engaged in the performance of a proprietary function, the court also held this was not the case with quasi-municipalities. Do you think the court was justified in differentiating between municipalities and quasi-municipalities, as it did?

2. Compare this case with *Morris* v. *School District of Township of Mount Lebanon, supra.*

3. What is the significance of the court's statement that athletics, including football, constitute a part of the physical education program and as such is a part of the educational program of the district?

21. "It has been held, too, that a school board does not lose its immunity from tort liability by engaging in a proprietary function where [for example] it leases an athletic field for playing baseball" (p. 5).

SMITH V. HEFNER,
235 N.C. 1, 16 S.E. (2d) 783 (1952)
(Decided by the Supreme Court of North Carolina)

[This was an action brought by the plaintiff to recover damages from the school district because of the alleged wrongful death of his intestate resulting from the fall of a stack of cement blocks that were piled near where he was sitting while engaged as a spectator at a league baseball game. The district had rented the field to the League Baseball Club. At the time of the accident the district was engaged in the construction of a grandstand. The cement blocks in question were to be used for this purpose

The lower court entered judgment in favor of the district, and the plaintiff appealed. The Supreme Court held that the district was without liability.]

JOHNSON, Justice.

. . . .

It is an established principle of jurisprudence, resting on grounds of sound public policy, that a state may not be sued in its own courts or elsewhere unless by statute it has consented to be sued or has otherwise waived its immunity from suit. . . .

By application of this principle, a subordinate division of the state, or agency exercising statutory governmental functions like a city administrative school unit, may be sued only when and as authorized by statute. . . .

It follows, therefore, that since there has been no statutory removal of the common law immunity from suit of the Trustees of the Hamlet City School Administrative Unit, the demurrer interposed by them as such trustees was properly sustained by Judge Clement.

Accordingly, we do not reach for decision the question, discussed in the briefs, as to whether, assuming the existence of general authority to sue a local agency of government like a city administrative school unit, such authority would extend only to such actions as are essentially incidental to the operation of the agency, and exclude causes of action sounding in tort. Suffice it to say, the decided weight of authority supports the view that an administrative school unit or school district may not be held liable for torts committed by its trustees or employees. . . .

Guides for Class Discussion

1. Compare this case with *Morris* v. *School District of Mount Lebanon, supra;* and *Richards* v. *School District of City of Birmingham, supra.* With which of these cases are you in agreement? Give reasons.
2. Outline the line of reasoning followed by the court.

22. "*Some courts, in the matter of tort liability of school districts, draw a distinction between ordinary negligence and wilful, positive misconduct . . . [and in] some instances . . . [they] have held school districts liable for trespass*" (p. 5).

FERRIS V. BOARD OF EDUCATION OF DETROIT,
122 Mich. 315, 81 N.W. 98 (1899)
(Decided by the Supreme Court of Michigan)

[The facts of this case are to be found in the first part of the following quotation.]

LONG, J.

Plaintiff for a number of years has owned and occupied, with his family, a house and lot on Lysander street, in Detroit. His house stands within three feet of the east line of his lot, and a sidewalk extends along that side, filling the space between his house and the lot line. In 1896 the defendant erected what is called the "Poe School Building" on its lot on the east of plaintiff's lot. This building stands within six feet six inches of the lot line next adjoining plaintiff's lot. . . . The school building is much higher than the plaintiff's house, and has a large amount of slate roof sloping towards plaintiff's lot. This roof, prior to the accident, had no projections or guards above the edge of the roof to interrupt the falling of snow and ice. During the winter months large quantities of snow and ice, when melting, slid down from this roof onto plaintiff's house and lot, and upon the sidewalk and steps which lead into the back part of plaintiff's house, and on one occasion his roof was injured by this falling ice and snow. Prior to the accident he notified different members of the school board of the injury to his premises by the snow and ice, and his wife also notified the secretary of the school board of the fact. Nothing was done about the matter, however. On February 22, 1898, snow fell during the day, but stopped in the afternoon, and plaintiff's wife cleaned it off this walk and back steps. Subsequently, and before the accident, large quantities of snow and ice slid from the roof of the school building down upon these steps. Plaintiff, who is a fireman in the employ of the city, came home to his supper in the evening, when his wife informed him of the falling of the snow and ice. He stepped out through the back door, and upon this snow and ice, and claims that by reason of that he fell heavily, breaking a rib and otherwise injuring himself. This action is brought against the board of education to recover damages for such injuries.

. . . .

The trial court was of the opinion that the defendant, being a municipal corporation, could not be held liable for negligent injuries under the common law, and, there being no liability created by statute, the plaintiff could not recover. It is conceded by counsel for plaintiff that municipal corporations are not generally held liable, under the common law, for negligent injuries to individuals arising from defective plans of construction of public works or failure to keep the same in repair; but it is contended that, where the injury is the result of the direct act or trespass of the municipality, it is liable, no matter whether acting in a public or private capacity. We are satisfied that counsel for plaintiff are right in this contention. The plaintiff had the right to the exclusive use and enjoyment of his property, and the defendant had no more right to erect a building in such a manner that the ice and snow would inevitably slide from the roof, and be precipitated upon the plaintiff's premises, than it would have to accumulate water upon its own premises, and then permit it to flow in a body upon his premises. It has been many times held in this court that a city has no more right to invade, or cause the invasion of, private property than an individual. . . .

If this action had been commenced for damages to the plaintiff's freehold, had any resulted, there could arise no doubt of his right to recover. The declaration alleges the damages to have accrued to the plaintiff by his slipping upon the ice which fell from the roof of the defendant's building upon plaintiff's premises, and that the defendant had had notice of the fact that snow and ice had from time to time been so precipitated upon the premises, and defendant had neglected, and continued to neglect, to take the steps necessary to prevent the same. The declaration, therefore, counts upon an actionable wrong. The cause of action is not a neglect in the performance of a corporate duty rendering a public work unfit for the purposes for which it was intended, but the doing of a wrongful act, causing a direct injury to the person of the plaintiff, while outside the limits of the defendant's premises. We think it must be said that the erection of the building without these barriers was the proximate cause of the injury. To entitle a party to exemption, he must show, not only that such injury might have happened, but that it must have happened if the act complained of had not been done. . . . In the present case it appeared that snow and ice must inevitably slide from this slate roof, as there were no barriers to prevent it. The school board had notice of it. It should have anticipated that the plaintiff or his family might receive an injury by the falling of the snow and ice, or that, by attempting to travel or go over it, they might be injured in that way. The defendant cannot now say that the injury must have happened [*sic*] the plaintiff if the snow and ice had not been thrown upon these premises.

Guides for Class Discussion

1. Compare the decision in this case with the decision in *Sestero* v. *Town of Glastonbury, infra;* and *Bingham* v. *Board of Education of Ogden City, infra.*

2. Differentiate between the reasoning of the court in this case and the reasoning of the courts in the two cases just mentioned. With which are you in agreement? Give reasons

23. "*In some instances . . . a school district has been liable for the maintenance of a nuisance*" (p. 5).

SESTERO v. TOWN OF GLASTONBURY,
19 Conn. Sup. 156, 110 A. (2d) 629 (1954)
(Decided by the Superior Court of Connecticut)

[This was an action for damages brought against the town of Glastonbury and the board of education of the town of Glastonbury, as well as a teacher, for injuries sustained by an elementary school pupil who, during a school recess, was pushed and fell. The board of education demurred to the complaint on the ground that in maintaining and managing public schools "it is a public quasi-corporation acting in the course of governmental or public duty and therefore immune or relieved thereby from liability for the harm alleged in the complaint." The lower court held that the action was really one in nuisance and, as a result, the common law rule of immunity of school districts did not avail the district.

HOUSE, Judge.

. . . .

The authorities cited by the defendant town of Glastonbury regarding the respective legal positions of towns and boards of education and the status of boards of education as agencies of the state and not of the towns in the maintenance and management of public schools would appear to support the legal position taken by the defendant town of Glastonbury. . . .

. . . .

The demurrer of the defendant board of education is based upon the defense of governmental immunity which attaches to the performance by a municipality or public body of a public duty for the public benefit and not for its own corporate profit. . . .

The defense of governmental immunity, however, does not avail against a cause of action founded on a nuisance created by a governmental body by positive act. . . .

The complaint to which the demurrer has been filed is in one count which sets out numerous ways in which it is alleged that the defendant was negligent. "A nuisance may have its origin in negligence. . . . It is not always easy to determine when the nuisance as distinguished from the negligence arises." Bush v. City of Norwalk, 122 Conn. 426, 428, 189 A. 608, 609. While the pleader has avoided the use of the word "nuisance" in the complaint, it does appear that the allegations of the complaint are sufficiently broad to set forth, in addition to allegations of ordinary negligence, the essentials of a claim of nuisance under the definition in Warren v. City of Bridgeport, 129 Conn. 355, 359, 28 A. 2d 1. . . . In addition to the allegations of failure to act, it is alleged that the condition or situation complained of was created by the positive act of the defendant and "increased greatly the probability of injury or harm," creating a hazardous and dangerous condition. While it is true that most of the allegations of the complaint allege a failure on the part of the defendant to take some action, positive acts of negligence on the part of the defendant in creating and maintaining the alleged hazardous and dangerous conditions are alleged and since the defense of governmental immunity does not avail as against a cause of action founded on a nuisance created by positive act, the demurrer is overruled.

Guides for Class Discussion

1. Compare this case with *Bingham* v. *Board of Education of Ogden City, infra;* and *Ferris* v. *Board of Education of Detroit, supra.*
2. Do you think the court was justified in ruling that the defense of governmental immunity does not avail in a case of nuisance?
3. Differentiate between "mere negligence" and "nuisance."

24. "Some courts hold that school districts are not liable in tort for trespass or the maintenance of a nuisance. These courts take the position that school districts are not liable for any kind of tort" (p. 5).

BINGHAM V. BOARD OF EDUCATION OF OGDEN CITY,
118 Utah 582, 223 P. (2d) 432 (1950)
(Decided by the Supreme Court of Utah)

[The main facts of this case will be found in the first paragraph of material quoted.]

LATIMER, Justice.

. . . .

The material facts pleaded in the complaint are as follows: That the defendant is a body corporate and owns the premises upon which the accident occurred; that on the day of the accident, and for some time prior thereto, the defendant maintained an incinerator for the purpose of burning old books, papers, debris, and other rubbish collected on the school premises; that these materials were deposited in the incinerator located in an unguarded place adjacent to a playground area and were burned at regular periods; that hot debris, embers and ashes were discharged or removed and allowed to accumulate over an area of several feet; that on the day in question the plaintiff, Marilyn Bingham, a child of the age of three years, was riding a tricycle and fell into the burning embers, receiving severe injuries; and that the operation of the incinerator in the dangerous and hazardous manner alleged constituted a nuisance.

. . . .

It frequently happens that the same act or omission may constitute negligence, and, at the same time, give rise to a nuisance. At times it is most difficult to determine whether an alleged state of facts establishes a nuisance or shows merely a lack of due care. Whether or not the allegations of this complaint picture a condition which, in law, is a nuisance or show merely negligent conduct, is a question not free from difficulty. Accordingly, we dispose of the liability of the school board regardless of the characterization of the negligence.

If the facts alleged in this action show ordinary negligence then, under previous statements made by this court, it would appear the demurrer was properly sustained. In the case of Woodcock v. Board of Education of Salt Lake City, 55 Utah 458, 187 P. 181, . . . the court said, . . . "The general law of this jurisdiction, as in most other jurisdictions, does not authorize actions for damages for personal injuries against school districts. School districts are corporations with limited powers, and act merely on behalf of the state in discharging the duty of educating the children of school age in the public schools created by general laws."

. . . .

While law writers, editors and judges have criticized and disapproved the . . . doctrine of governmental immunity as illogical and unjust, the weight of precedent of decided cases supports the general rule and we prefer not to disregard a principle so well established without statutory authority. We, therefore, adopt the rule of the majority and hold that school boards cannot be held liable for ordinary negligent acts.

Plaintiffs, however, contend that even if we follow the general rule they still have alleged a cause of action, as immunity from tort liability cannot be claimed when the act complained of reaches the level of a nuisance.

. . . .

The reasons given by most courts in holding boards of education immune from liability for negligence center around the proposition that school boards act in connection with public education as agents or instrumentalities of the state, in the performance of a governmental function, and consequently they partake of the state's sovereignty with respect to tort liability. If this reason be good to relieve boards of education from tort liability, then it should apply with equal force in cases involving personal injury caused by nuisances. The latter may involve more aggravated or continuous acts, but the right to recover should not be determined by the gradation of negligence or by the adjectives used in the complaint. If the strictness of the rule is to be relaxed in cases of nuisance, and if the schools are to be stripped of immunity, the stripping process should be by legislative enactment and not by court decree.

. . . .

The maintenance of a system of public schools within the state is a matter of statewide interest. Boards of education are created by the legislature to perform the function of educating the children residing in the state. As agencies of the state, their activities are restricted to the duties and powers specifically granted to them. They act without profit, are supported by taxes, and act solely in a governmental capacity. The legislature has not imposed responsibility upon them and this court cannot adopt a refined distinction between two torts, one sounding in mere negligence and one sounding in aggravated negligence and by such a judicial construction relieve the school board in one instance and impose liability in the other.

In the instant case, disposing of papers, rubbish and debris which collect daily on school grounds and in classrooms is reasonably within the scope of the duties imposed upon boards of education by the legislature. The burning of such rubbish and debris is an essential part of the sanitation of the school building and grounds. Since the acts complained of were committed in the performance of a governmental function, the rule of immunity applies, even though the firing of the incinerator was performed in such a negligent manner as may be characterized as maintaining a nuisance. We are aware that the allegations of the complaint portray a tragic and unfortunate case, and we are not without sympathy for the little girl and her father. However, under our constitution, the power to make departments of the state respond in damages for torts rests with the legislature, and without legislative enactment we are unable to impose any liability or obligation upon school districts.

Guides for Class Discussion

1. Compare this case with the decision in *Sestero* v. *Town of Glastonbury, supra,* and with the one in *Ferris* v. *Board of Education of Detroit, supra.*
2. Which one of the two cases just mentioned represents the soundest reasoning? Give reasons.
3. Differentiate between negligence and the maintenance of a nuisance.

25. "*Boards of education . . . have no inherent authority to contract*" (p. 6).

BARTH v. SCHOOL DISTRICT OF PHILADELPHIA,
393 Pa. 557, 143 A. (2d) 909 (1958)
(Decided by the Supreme Court of Pennsylvania)

[This was an action brought by a taxpayer to enjoin the defendant School District of Philadelphia from carrying out an agreement or contract between it and the City of Philadelphia. The school district and the city had entered into an agreement to establish and finance a Youth Conservation Commission for the purpose of curbing juvenile delinquency. The agreement provided for the organization of the Commission and also provided that the school district would pay up to a total of $125,000 for its support for the calendar year of 1958. Plaintiff—a citizen—contended that the agreement and the proposed appropriation were illegal for several reasons, but, primarily, because the district was without the authority to act as it did. He argued that a school district is possessed only of those powers specifically granted to it, and, because the power in question was not specifically granted to it, it was powerless to take the action it did. In other words, he contended that the school board, or the district, had no inherent authority to enter into this agreement or contract. The lower court agreed with plaintiff, and defendant appealed. The higher court agreed with the lower court and affirmed the decision rendered by it.]

BELL, Justice.

. . . .

A program to study and curb juvenile delinquency is not only worthy, but highly desirable. The crime wave which is sweeping our Country, and particularly the rise and extent of juvenile delinquency, and the vandalism and the atrocious crimes committed by juveniles has astonished, troubled and appalled our entire nation. Law and order, prevention, supression and punishment of crime, control of gangs, improvement of living conditions, rehabilitation of problem persons and persons with criminal tendencies—these are and since ancient times have been matters of the Sovereign (in our Country, local or State, and more recently, National Government), and have never heretofore been considered as a part of "Education." Futhermore a worthy objective does not justify the action of a School District or a public body, which has no fundamental or inherent powers of Government unless that action is authorized by the Constitution or by an Act of the Legislature.

A School District is not a Constitutional body. . . .

. . . .

A School District is a creature or agency of the Legislature and has only the powers that are granted by statute, specifically or by necessary implication. . . .

In Slippery Rock Area Joint School System v. Franklin Township School District, 389 Pa. 435, at page 442, 133 A. 2d 848, at page 852, supra, the Court said: "First it should be remembered that our entire school system is but an agency of the State Legislature—maintained by them to carry out a constitutional duty. . . . The school system, or the school district, then, are but agencies of the state legislature to administer this constitutional duty. Wilson v. Philadelphia School District, 328 Pa. 225, 230, [195 A. 90, 113 A.L.R. 1401]. Within that school system, a school district is an agency of the State, created by law *for the purpose of promoting education, deriving all of its powers from the statute, and discharging only such duties as are imposed upon it by statute.* . . ." [Italics supplied by the Court.]

. . . .

From the authorities cited and quoted . . . it is clear (1) that the School District of Philadelphia is an agent or creature of the Legislature; (2) that it has no inherent powers of government; and (3) that the only powers, functions and duties it possesses are those which are expressly or by necessary implication authorized by statute.

. . . .

Never heretofore have schools or school districts possessed or exercised, under the theory or name of Education, the wide basic powers, functions and duties of Municipal Government which are now claimed by the Board of Education, namely the prevention, suppression, correction, elimination and punishment of juvenile delinquency— euphemistic language to describe vandalism, misdemeanors and crimes committed by young persons—gang control and the improvement of living conditions. It is clear that the main purpose of this Agreement is, at best, very indirectly and very remotely connected with Education. . . .

. . . .

. . . a very worthy objective does not justify the action of a public body, such as a public school district, which has no inherent powers of government, unless that action is authorized by the Constitution or expressly or by necessary implication by an Act of the Legislature.

To particularize: A program to curb juvenile delinquency, and to control gangs, and to coordinate programs of various agencies of and throughout the City for the purpose of reducing juvenile delinquency, and to organize sensitive areas in the City on a block-to-block basis in an effort to improve living conditions—these are not and never have been a part of the function, power or duty of a school or a school district. They are a very important and essential part of municipal Government: They are not and never have been a part of or embraced within "Education" as that term has always been understood. . . .

. . . .

. . . The School District was properly enjoined, not because the Agreement represented an abuse of discretion, but because, being un-authorized by statute, it was beyond the legal power of the School Board.

Guides for Class Discussion

1. Are you in agreement with the court's reasoning? Give reasons.
2. Define "contract."
3. Do you think that contracts are implied within the meaning of the word "agreement" as used by the court?

26. "Where the statutes prescribe the mode of making a contract, as, for example, that it be reduced to written form or be made on the basis of competitive bidding, the mode of making the contract is the measure of power, and a contract made in any other mode cannot be enforced against the school district" (p. 6).

RICHARD D. KIMBALL CO. v. CITY OF MEDFORD,
240 Mass. 727, 166 N.E. (2d) 708 (1960)
(Decided by the Supreme Judicial Court of Massachusetts, Middlesex)

[In two actions an architect and an engineer attempted to recover fees of $1,000 and $1,500, respectively, for services rendered to the school committee of the city. The two were heard together. The lower court rendered judgment in favor of the architect and engineer, and the city appealed. The higher court overruled the lower court and rendered judgment for the defendant. Both the architect and engineer were notified of their appointment, following their selection by the committee, by a letter from the superintendent of schools. In neither case was employment evidenced by a written contract. One section of the General Laws—§ 33—which was a part of the city's charter, authorized the school committee to "make all repairs, the expenditures for which are made from the regular appropriations for the school department. . . ." Another section—§ 29—which was also a part of the city charter, provided that " 'All contracts made by any department, board or commission where the amount involved is one thousand dollars or more shall be in writing. . . .' " After first ruling that the powers conferred on the school committee by § 33, were subject to the limitations contained in § 29, the court held that the engineer and architect could not hold the city liable for their salaries because they were not employed by written contracts as required by statute.]

SPALDING, Judge.

. . . .

The judge ordered judgment for Tiffany in the sum of $1,500, and judgment for Kimball in the sum of $1,000. To these orders the city excepted. . . .

. . . .

It is familiar law that one dealing with a city or town cannot recover if statutory requirements such as are contained in the defendant's charter have not been observed, and the burden of proving compliance with such requirements rests upon the plaintiff. . . . Admittedly the requirements of § 29 were not satisfied. . . .

. . . .

The power of a school committee to make repairs is surely no broader than its power . . . to provide for transportation of pupils. . . . yet the statutes involved . . . were held to impose limitations on the powers of the school committee. What was said . . . in Eastern Mass. St. Ry. [v. Mayor of Fall River, 308 Mass. 232] . . . is pertinent here. "Contracting for the furnishing of transportation of school children bears only a secondary relation to education. . . . In general, these [contracts requiring the mayor's approval] are mere business transactions. They do not as a rule directly relate to methods of education or to the policy, conduct, regulation and discipline of the schools. Ordinary commercial contracts have never hitherto been held to belong in the field in which by long-established policy and tradition school committees have exercised exclusive and untrammeled control." We are of opinion that § 29 was intended to control contracts for repairs by placing the business affairs of the city in "centralized hands." School Comm. of Gloucester v. Gloucester, 324 Mass. 209, 218, 85 N.E. 2d 429.

. . . .

It follows that because the requirements of § 29 were not satisfied, the orders for judgment in favor of the plaintiffs were erroneous. This is a harsh result, as there is no suggestion that the plaintiffs did not fully and faithfully perform the services requested of them. But, as we said earlier, one who contracts with a municipality can recover only if the statutory safeguards governing its contracting powers are satisfied. Any other rule, however appealing it may be in an individual case, would in the long run render such safeguards worthless; it would be another instance of a hard case making bad law.

Guides for Class Discussion

1. Who was at fault in this case—the superintendent, the school committee, or the architect and engineer?
2. Do you think the court's decision denying recovery to the architect and engineer was equitable? Give reasons.

27. "*Where the statutes confer upon a board of education the performance of duties involving the exercise of judgment or*

discretion, the board is under obligation to perform the duties itself. . . . It follows that a board cannot delegate to its school superintendent, business manager, secretary, or to a committee of its own members, final authority to enter into a contract" (p. 6).

MURRY V. UNION PARISH SCHOOL BOARD,
185 So. 305 (La.) (1938)
(Decided by the Court of Appeal of Louisiana)

[This was an action against a school board for breach of contract, brought by one who alleged he had a contract with the board to transport pupils. According to custom, individual school board members selected those to transport children, and the parish superintendent executed contracts with them. In this case, plaintiff had been so selected and given a two-year contract which was never submitted to the school board for ratification. After he had served with apparent satisfaction for one year and had purchased a new bus, the board decided not to retain him, whereupon he brought this action. The board contended that its action was justified on the ground the contract, because not made or approved by the board, was illegal. The lower court ruled in favor of the plaintiff and the school board appealed. The court, here, held the board was not estopped to deny the contract's illegality and that the board could not ratify the contract, even if it wished to do so, since it was void.]

DREW, Judge.

. . . .

The custom of the School Board of Union Parish has been to allow the members from each Ward to select the school bus drivers and fix the price and, after such an agreement has been made, the superintendent executes a contract with the bus driver. It appears that such blanket authority has been given by the School Board to its superintendent and the members from each Ward. In this case the custom was followed and plaintiff at no time appeared before the School Board. . . . It was a contract between the School Board member from Ward 2 of Union Parish and the plaintiff, which contract was attempted to be ratified by the written contract executed and signed by the Superintendent of Education of Union Parish. The contract was never submitted to the school board as a body for its ratification.

. . . .

. . . the jurisprudence of this state is well settled and rightfully so that political bodies are not estopped by the unauthorized and illegal acts of their officers. School boards possess only delegated powers defined by statute and are not free to act as individuals, and it is not within the scope of their authority to ratify that which originally had no existence, such as a void contract.

Guides for Class Discussion

1. Do you agree with this decision? Give reasons.
2. What did the court mean when it said that "political bodies are not estopped by the unauthorized and illegal acts of their officers"?
3. Compare this case with *Seim* v. *Independent District of Monroe, infra.*

28. "*A board of education has no authority to enter into contracts which are clearly violative of public policy*" (p. 6).

Seim v. Independent District of Monroe,
70 S.D. 315, 17 N.W. (2d) 342 (1945)
(Decided by the Supreme Court of South Dakota)

[This was an action against a school district to collect for labor and materials used in the construction of a school building. The bidding specifications called for a base bid with three alternate proposals. Plaintiff secured the contract on the basis of his bid under one alternate proposal which excluded a stage. The contract provided that the board could authorize changes as the work progressed. Later, while the construction was in progress, the board decided to construct a stage opening. It did not advertise for bids. However, the contractor agreed to construct this opening for approximately $1,700. After the work was completed and the board failed to pay, the contractor brought this suit for the amount of the contract, covering the cost of the stage opening. The court ruled against him. It held that the change in the agreement was not incidental to the work agreed upon in the original contract but constituted a supplemental contract. It reasoned that, in the absence of competitive bidding which was the "fixed public policy," the original contract could not be amended to include the construction of the opening, under the clause authorizing changes as the work proceeded. As a result, it held that the contractor was not entitled to recover for labor and materials under *quantum meruit,* even though the parties appeared to have acted in good faith.]

ROBERTS, Judge.

. . . .

It is well settled that when by statutes the mode and manner in which contracts of a school district or other local subdivision may be entered into is limited and any other manner of entering into a contract or obligation is expressly or impliedly forbidden a contract not made in compliance therewith is invalid and cannot ordinarily be ratified. . . .

This court in Livingston v. School District No. 7, 11 S.D. 150, 76 N.W. 301, expressed the view that the obligation to do justice rests upon all persons, natural and artificial, and that the purchaser of an invalid bond the proceeds of which were used to construct a school house was entitled to recover on quantum meruit. Conceding the existence and justice of such a rule, it is without application where the contract is in violation of the express mandatory provisions of a statute. Where a contract is made contrary to a fixed public policy, there can be no implied promise to pay for labor and materials furnished. . . . The distinction appears from a discussion contained in Miller v. McKinnon, 20 Cal. 2d 83, 124 P. 2d 34. . . .

. . . .

The measure of the liability of defendant school district must therefore be sought in the terms of the original contract. Plaintiff seeks to sustain the validity of his claim upon the theory that he came within the terms of such contract. The right as we have stated was reserved in the board of education to "authorize changes in the work to be performed or the materials to be furnished pursuant to the provisions of the contract." Such provisions are not unusual in constructing contracts with school districts and other local subdivisions. . . . They may permit changes incidental to the complete execution of the work described in the contract, but cannot authorize supplemental contracts or district and independent work.

Guides for Class Discussion

1. Do you think that the court, in denying recovery even on the original contract, acted equitably? Give reasons.

2. How does the rule "The mode is the measure of the power" apply to this case?

29. "[If] *contracts of school boards . . . are prohibited or unauthorized by statute . . . [or if they] are made in violation of the exclusive statutory mode of making them, or . . . [if they] are violative of public policy . . . the school board will not, as a rule, be held liable . . . even though they have been fully performed and the school district retains the benefit of the performance'* (p. 6).

Goose River Bank v. Willow Creek School Township,
1 N.D. 26, 44 N.W. 1002 (1890)
(Decided by the Supreme Court of North Dakota)

[This was an action to test the validity of certain warrants issued to a teacher who was without a certificate, in payment for her services. The lower court held the warrants void and the higher court affirmed its decision.]

Corliss, C. J.
. . . The action was upon three school township warrants issued by the officers of the defendant. These warrants are void. They were issued to pay for the services of a teacher who held no lawful certificate of qualification. No such person can be employed to teach. The statute so declares, and any contract made in violation of this provision is void by the express terms of the same act. . . . There was therefore no consideration for these warrants. The teacher had no claim against the defendant, because the statute declares she should not be employed to teach, and every act in violation of this provision was a nullity, so far as the liability of the defendant is concerned. . . .

There is no force in the position that the defendant, having received the benefit of the teacher's service, is liable. Such a doctrine would defeat the policy of the law, which is to give the people of the state the benefit of trained and competent teachers. The law recognizes only one evidence that that policy has been regarded,—the certificate of qualification. If the defendant could be made liable by the mere receipt of the benefit of the services rendered, the law prohibiting the employment of teachers without certificates, and declaring void all contracts made in contravention of that provision, would be, in effect, repealed, and the protection of the people against incompetent and unfit teachers, which such statute was enacted to accomplish, would be destroyed. Where a contract is void because of the express declaration of a statute, or because prohibited in terms, the retention by a municipality of the fruits of such a contract will not subject it to liability, either under the contract or upon a *quantum meruit*. . . . This is particularly true in a case like the one at bar, where no person can teach without the certificate, without being actually or legally in collusion with local officers to defeat a wise and salutary statute enacted as a barrier against the employment of unqualified teachers. The person who teaches without the certificate has violated the letter and the spirit of the law. The wrong done is without remedy. The people who have thus had this barrier torn from about them have no redress. Shall the wrongdoer be compensated for aiding the school township officers in breaking down this barrier, thus depriving the people of the protection of this important law? . . . The judgment of the district court is affirmed.

Guides for Class Discussion

1. How do you think the court would have ruled had the teacher obtained a certificate before he completed his contract? Give reasons.

2. Should the court have permitted recovery under *quantum meruit?* Give reasons.

3. What did the court mean when it said there was "no consideration for these warrants"?

10. "*Where a school board has statutory authority to make a contract, but the contract is illegal because of some irregularity or invalidity in the making of it, courts of equity commonly permit recovery on quantum meruit or quantum valebant for the actual value of the services rendered or the goods delivered . . .*" (p.).

FARGO FOUNDRY CO. v. VILLAGE OF CALLOWAY,
148 Minn. 273, 181 N.W. 584 (1921)
(Decided by the Supreme Court of Minnesota)

[The facts of the case will be found in the material quoted.]

HALLAM, J. . . . Defendant is an ordinary village corporation. In November, 1917, it undertook to enter into a contract with plaintiff by which plaintiff was to furnish all labor and material for repairing a steel water tank belonging to the village for $580, and to furnish and install a new tubular boiler to carry steam to the tank for $420. The water tank was repaired and the boiler installed. The contract was void because not let upon competitive bids. . . . Plaintiff thereupon sued on quantum valebant alleging the value of the labor and material furnished to be of the sum of $1,267.34. No question was raised that labor and material of some value were furnished in the repair of the tank. The main defense was that the boiler as installed was wholly worthless, and, worse than that, that it became a burden to the extent that defendant was obliged to incur expense in removing it. The jury returned a verdict for $366.45.

The improvement served a municipal purpose and the contract was one that the city had power to make, and, had the essential requirements of the law been complied with, the contract would have been enforceable. In such a situation the village may be compelled to pay the value of what it has received. The express contract disappears from the case. The cause of action arises, not from any contract on the subject but from the general obligation to do justice which binds all persons natural and artificial. . . . The obligation to pay is measured by the benefit which the village has received.

Plaintiff urges that it is entitled to the full amount of its claim on the theory that the intrinsic value of the material furnished and the cost or value of the labor furnished were of that amount, that in law the benefit to defendant was this intrinsic value, irrespective of any use or failure of use as desired by the village, and that, whether the heating system performed the purpose desired by the village or not, its reasonable cost was the amount which the village must pay. We cannot sustain this contention. The heating plant was installed as a system. If as a system it was worthless and defendant was obliged to discard it at an expense, defendant has received no value for which it is required to pay. . . . Obligations such as this are sometimes called contracts implied in law, or quasi or constructive contracts. In fact they are not contracts at all, for there is no agreement. The obligation is imposed without regard to the assent of the party bound. The use of the term "contract" rests solely on a legal fiction. Such obligations were originally called contractual or quasi contractual in order to secure their enforcement by the common-law action of assumpsit at a time when it was considered that a right could not be enforced unless could be fitted into some existing form of remedy. To maintain assumpsit, it was necessary that there should be a promise and to meet this requirement the courts resorted to the fiction of a promise where none in fact existed. . . . Even now, long after the abolition of assumpsit as a form of action, these obligations are commonly expressed in terms of contract. . . . There is no necessity for doing so. Since technical forms of action have been abolished, the use of legal fiction is gone and the fiction ought to be abandoned. The village is obliged to pay on the same principle applied for money had and received, that is, that in equity and good conscience the defendant ought to pay. Heywood v. Northern Assurance Co., 133 Minn. 360, 158 N.W. 632, Ann. Cas. 1918D, 241.

Guides for Class Discussion

1. What did the court mean when it said "the express contract disappears from the case"?
2. What did the court mean by the fact that the contract rested solely on a legal fiction?
3. What was the basis on which the court arrived at its conclusions? Are you in agreement?
4. Do you think the court would have held as it did in case defendant had been a school district rather than a city?

31. *"As a general rule, courts of equity will . . . not permit recovery for the value of services rendered or goods delivered under a contract which violates the statutory mode of making it"* (p. 7).

REAMS v. COOLEY,
171 Cal. 150, 152 P. 293 (1915)
(Decided by the Supreme Court of California)

[A contract for plastering a school building had been let without competitive bidding as required by statute. Upon its completion, the board refused to pay the contractor who then brought this action. He recognized the fact he could not recover on the express contract, but argued that the district should be held liable on an implied contract in an action in *quantum meruit*.]

LORIGAN, J.

.   .   .   .

In presenting the merits of his appeal in this court appellant insists that even though the express contract entered into between himself and the school district was invalid for want of power in its board of trustees to enter into such a contract, except in the mode prescribed by . . . the Political Code, still the district, having received the benefit of the labor and materials of appellant in the construction of the school building, is liable therefor on an implied contract in an action on quantum meruit. But in view of the express limitation upon the power of the board to contract . . . the position of appellant is untenable. Undoubtedly, a school board, like a municipal corporation, may, under some circumstances, be held liable upon an implied contract for benefits received by it, but this rule of implied liability is applied only in those cases where the board or municipality is given the general power to contract with reference to a subject-matter, and the express contract which it has assumed to enter into in pursuance of this general power is rendered invalid for some mere irregularity or some invalidity in the execution thereof, and where the form or manner of entering into a contract is not violative of any statutory restriction upon the general power of the governing body to contract nor violative of public policy. In the absence of such restriction on the mode or manner of contracting, the same general rule applies to such inferior political bodies as to individuals, and the former will be held responsible on an implied contract for the payment of benefits it receives under an illegal express contract not prohibited by law. . . . But, while the doctrine of implied liability applies where general power to contract on a subject exists and the form or manner of doing so is not expressly provided by charter or statute, the decided weight of authority is to the effect that, when by statute the power of the board or municipality to make a contract is limited to a certain prescribed method of doing so, and any other method of doing it is expressly or impliedly prohibited, no implied liability can arise for benefits received under a contract made in violation of the particularly prescribed statutory mode. Under such circumstances the express contract attempted to be made is not invalid merely by reason of some irregularity or some invalidity in the exercise of a general power to contract, but the contract is void because the statute prescribes the only method in which a valid contract can be made, and the adoption of the prescribed mode is a jurisdictional prerequisite to the exercise of the power to contract at all and can be exercised in no other manner so as to incur any liability on the part of the municipality. Where the statute prescribes the only mode by which the power to contract shall be exercised the mode is the measure of the power. A contract made otherwise than as so prescribed is not binding or obligatory as a contract, and the doctrine of implied liability has no application in such cases. Zottman v. San Francisco, 20 Cal. 96, 81 Am. Dec. 96. . . .

. . . .

The rule announced in the Zottman Case and the other authorities in line with it must be applied here. While under sections 1617 and 1674 of the Political Code authority is given to school trustees to erect school buildings, there is at the same time by subdivision 22 of section 1617, applicable alike to boards of trustees of union high school districts as to boards of trustees of common school districts, a mode prescribed for exercising that power. By that subdivision where the work (as here) is to exceed the sum of $200, a valid contract can only be entered into with the lowest responsible bidder on competitive bidding after published notice therefor. Under the rule of the Zottman Case, this mode was the measure of the power. No contract, either expressly or impliedly, could be entered into by the school board except with the lowest bidder after advertisement, and, of course, no implied liability to pay upon a quantum meruit could exist where the prohibition of the statute against contracting in any other manner than as prescribed is disregarded.

It is urged in this case, as it invariably is in all such cases, that the application of this rule works a great hardship if the school district may retain the benefit of the work of the contractor and be relieved of liability to compensate him therefor. But the provision of the law limiting the power of school boards to validly contract, except in a prescribed mode, proceeds from a consideration of public policy not peculiar to such boards, but adopted as the policy of the state with reference to inferior boards and public bodies, and it would be difficult to perceive what practical public benefit or result could accrue by legislative limitation or prohibition on the power of such bodies to contract if courts were to allow a recovery where the limitation or prohibition is disregarded; in fact, the plea of hardship urged here was answered in the Zottman case by language as pertinent now as it was then, where the court said.

"It may sometimes seem a hardship upon a contractor that all compensation for work done, etc., should be denied him; but it should be remembered that he, no less than the officers of the corporation, when he deals in a matter expressly provided for in the charter, is bound to see to it that the charter is complied with. If he neglect this, or choose to take the hazard, he is a mere volunteer, and suffers only what he ought to have anticipated. If the statute forbids the contract which he has made, he knows it, or ought to know it, before he places his money or services at hazard."

Guides for Class Discussion

1. Compare the decision in this case with the one in *Farg[o]
   Foundry Co.* v. *Village of Calloway, supra.* Can they b[e]
   reconciled?
2. See *Seim* v. *Independent District of Monroe, supra.*
3. Is this decision ethically sound? Give reasons.

32. *"Where a board's authority to contract depends upon some
prior action by another board . . . most courts of equity hol[d]
that no recovery can be had for the actual value of goods or services which were delivered or rendered under a contract mad[e]
without the necessary prior action having been taken"* (p. 7).

EDWARDS v. SCHOOL DISTRICT,
117 Okla. 269, 235 P. 611 (1925)
(Decided by the Supreme Court of Oklahoma)

[This was an action brought by plaintiff to recover the sum o[f]
$1,200.00 for building a schoolhouse. In this case, it appears th[e]
board employed E. A. Lutes to build a schoolhouse for the distric[t]
and agreed to pay $1,200.00 for the same, but that it was withou[t]
funds. As a result, the board issued to Lutes, on September 1[0]
1907, a warrant in the sum of $1,200.00 which was later refuse[d]
for the lack of funds. Later he sold and delivered the warrant t[o]
plaintiff, Edwards. At the time the warrant was issued, no assessment had been made of the taxable property and no provision ha[d]
been made for funds with which to pay for the building of th[e]
schoolhouse or for the warrant. After it was constructed, th[e]
schoolhouse was turned over to the district and had been used fo[r]
school purposes previous to the time the action was brought. Th[e]
only disputed fact was whether or not the contract for buildin[g]
the schoolhouse was let with the knowledge and consent of th[e]
qualified electors of that district at a meeting held for that purpose
as required by statute.]

Threadgill, C. . . .

. . . .

Applying the provisions of this statute to the instant case, we see that, in order to authorize the contract for building the schoolhouse and make the warrant legal for the same, it was necessary to have a district meeting and the sort of house to be built agreed on by the qualified electors at such meeting before the district board could contract for it. The evidence shows that they had the meeting, and there were from six to ten electors present, but it is conflicting as to what action was taken, and the trial court evidently believed the testimony of Burr Hooker that the proposition to build a schoolhouse was rejected and voted down, or, if he believed the testimony of E. A. Lutes and W. E. Walters, he was warranted in believing that nothing definite was agreed upon except that the school board should go ahead and build a schoolhouse if funds could be provided for that purpose. There is nothing in their testimony to show a schoolhouse of any definite description for a definite price agreed upon. The court's general finding in favor of the defendant has the force and effect of a jury's verdict, and, where it is based upon conflicting testimony, and there is any evidence to support it, it will not be disturbed by this court on appeal. We must therefore conclude that the contract to build and the warrant issued to pay for building the schoolhouse were illegal, not being based upon an agreement of the district meeting as provided for in said section.

. . . .

It has been repeated many times by this court, but never to the contrary, that the officers of municipalities have their limitations fixed by law and all persons transacting business with them are charged with knowledge of such limitations, and when the officers and credit men exceed the legal limits in making contracts and debts against such municipalities such contracts and debts cannot be enforced by the courts; nor will the courts lend assistance to recover property furnished on such contracts. . . .

We are of the opinion that the judgment of the trial court should be sustained.

Guides for Class Discussion

1. Compare this case with *White River School Township* v. *Dorrell, infra*.
2. Do you think the rule followed by the court is a salutary one? Give reasons.

3. If no recovery can be had on a contract in a case of this sort, can the school district be required to return property furnished on such contracts?

33. *"In some states, courts of equity do not follow the general rule that no recovery can be had for the actual value of goods delivered or services rendered under an illegal or void contract . . . [on the ground] that a school district should not be permitted . . . to enjoy the benefits of the illegal contract without paying for the actual value of the goods or services"* (p. 7).

White River School Township v. Dorrell,
26 Ind. App. 538, 59 N.E. 867 (1901)
(Decided by the Appellate Court of Indiana)

[The facts of the case will be found in the material which follows.]

Robinson, J.

On August 4, 1896, appellant's [school district's] trustee was engaged in erecting a suitable and necessary school house in a certain school district having about 40 children of school age, and having no suitable school house. The contract price of the building was $1,300. The township had no funds belonging to the special school fund with which to pay for the completion of the building, and it required $500 to complete the building. The trustee represented to appellee that it was necessary for him to have such sum, and at the trustee's request and for the purpose of completing the building, appellee turned over to the trustee that sum, which was used in paying for the erection of the building under the contract, and was paid by the trustee to the contractor for the purpose of paying for the completion of the building and the township since that time and now retains the benefit derived from the use of such sum in the use of such school house for school purposes. Such sum was not in excess of the fund on hand to which the debt is chargeable and the fund derived from the tax assessed for the year 1896. The trial court held that appellee ought to be subrogated to the rights of the contractor to the extent of $500 with interest.

The right of subrogation is not founded upon contract, express or implied. It is based upon the principles of equity and justice, and includes every instance where one party, not a mere volunteer, pay for another a debt for which the latter was primarily liable, and which in good conscience and equity he should have paid. . . . The findings show that the money received by the trustee was paid out by him for property actually received by the school corporation and retained by it. The contract for building the house was such a contract as the trustee was authorized to make. The money was advanced to the trustee for the purpose of completing a necessary and suitable school house. The trustee had not the means in hand to complete the building, and the money advanced was, in fact, applied to that purpose. To permit a recovery in such a case is in no way recognizing a general power in the trustee to borrow money. There is no suggestion whatever of any fraud in the building of the house. Appellant has received and retains the benefit of the money so advanced, and the simplest principles of equity and justice require that it should repay it. . . .

Guides for Class Discussion

1. What is meant by "subrogation"?
2. On what grounds does the court justify its reasoning?
3. Are you in agreement with the court's thinking?
4. Do you think the court would have held as it did had there been fraud involved, or had the trustee not been possessed of the authority to build the building?

34. "*Where money has been paid to a school board in the performance of an illegal contract . . . and the money paid has not been spent or so mingled with other moneys of the board that it can no longer be identified, a court of equity will require its return to the original owner*" (p. 7).

BOARD OF TRUSTEES V. POSTEL,
121 Ky. 67, 88 S.W. 1065 (1905)
(Decided by the Court of Appeals of Kentucky)

[The facts of the case may be gleaned from the material quoted.]

HOBSON, C. J. In the year 1897 the trustees of the Fordsville graded common school district issued bonds to the amount of $4,000 on behalf of the district for the purpose of providing it with a lot, schoolhouse, and suitable furniture. The bonds were sold, and the trustees used the proceeds of the sale in buying a lot, building a schoolhouse, and furnishing it. But no vote of the legal voters of the district was taken before the issual of the bonds, and they were adjudged void under section 157 of the state Constitution: "No county, city, town, taxing district, or other municipality shall be authorized or permitted to become indebted in any manner or for any purpose, to an amount exceeding, in any year, the income and revenue provided for such year, without the assent of two-thirds of the voters thereof, voting at an election to be held for that purpose; and any indebtedness contracted in violation of this section shall be void. Nor shall such contract be enforceable by the person with whom made; nor shall such municipality ever be authorized to assume the same." The holders of the bonds, being in part the original purchasers and in part persons who had bought the bonds from them, instituted this action in equity asking that the lot, house and furniture which was purchased with the proceeds of the bonds be transferred to them; and, the court having adjudged them the relief sought, the school district appeals.

. . . .

No liability, direct or indirect, may be imposed upon the school district under the bonds in question. It is not liable on the bonds, nor can it be made liable by indirection in any way. But, if we ignore the bond transaction altogether, what have we? The district received $4,000 from the bondholders. The bonds being void, the district should have returned the money to the bondholders. If the bondholders had learned of the invalidity of the bonds while the district still had the $4,000 in its treasury which they had paid to it, manifestly a court of equity would have required the district to pay back their money to them. It was money obtained by a mutual mistake. While under the Constitution no liability would attach to the district for the money if it had lost it, or if it had spent it and the fund could not be identified and followed, where it may be followed and identified, there is no more reason why property which represents the fund should not be returned than there would be for not returning the money, if it had been placed in a bag and the district had the bag locked up in its safe. The purpose of the Constitution is not to enrich municipalities at the expense of innocent people who deal with them, and when they repudiate their bonds they must act honestly. A loss must not be placed upon the district; but, when justice may be done without inflicting any loss upon the district, equity will lay hold of the conscience of the parties and make them do what is just and right. . . .

Guides for Class Discussion

1. Was this decision equitable? Give reasons.
2. Compare the decision in this case with the one in *White River*

School Township v. *Dorrell, supra.*

3. Compare it with *Moe* v. *Millard County School District, infra.*

35. "*A court of equity will permit one who has delivered property to a school board under an illegal contract to recover it if the property can be restored without any substantial damage to the property of the district*" (p. 7).

MOE V. MILLARD COUNTY SCHOOL DISTRICT,
54 Utah 144, 179 P. 980 (1919)
(Decided by the Supreme Court of Utah)

[Plaintiff had furnished and installed certain heating, plumbing, and ventilating equipment for the defendant district under a contract which resulted in creating an indebtedness in excess of that permitted by the constitution. The district paid part of the bill but refused to complete payment on the ground that the contract was *ultra vires*. It also refused plaintiff's request to permit him to remove the equipment in question, on the ground that, because it was attached to the building, it became a fixture and was essential to the building's usefulness. Plaintiff then brought an action to enforce payment of the balance of the bill or to enforce his right to remove the equipment. The lower court upheld the position taken by the district, and plaintiff appealed. The higher court, here, reversed the decision of the lower court.]

BROWN, District Judge.

. . . .

It is conceded that under the provisions of our Constitution the plaintiff cannot recover upon the express contracts entered into for the installation of the property involved in this case, nor upon quantum meruit, for the reason that both express and implied contracts in violation of said provision are null and void. Respondent contends that . . Comp. Laws Utah 1907, §1875 (substantially a re-enactment of the constitutional provision), prohibit the recovery of the property for the reason that, if such recovery were allowed, persons selling property to a school district in violation of said provisions could indirectly compel the school district to pay for the same, and thus accomplish indirectly the very thing which both the Constitution and the statute prohibit. Appellant contends, on the other hand, that to deny such recovery would be most inequitable, and would permit a very salutary provision of law to be used by the school district as a means to acquire something for nothing.

. . . .

It might be conceded that most, if not all, of the property sought to be removed by this action would be classed as fixtures in a contest between parties where the application of the rules of law governing fixtures was admitted, such as between landlord and tenant, mortgagor and mortgagee, etc. A case of that kind is the case of *Filley* v. *Christopher*, 39 Wash. 22, 80 Pac. 834, 109 Am. St. Rep. 853, cited by respondent. But we cannot see how the doctrine of fixtures becomes applicable to this case so as to prevent a recovery of the property here sought. Why should not a school district be required to return real estate as readily as personal property which it had acquired under circumstances such as are shown by the facts in this case? If the contract were void because against public policy, such as a gambling contract, or was part of a fraudulent conspiracy between the parties to defraud others, the courts might refuse to aid either party, either by way of compelling performance, or the return of benefits; but even then we can see no difference as between personal property and real estate. Neither can we see that it makes any difference in this case whether the property has retained its character as personal property, or has, by being affixed to the freehold, become real estate. If it had become so affixed to the building, as it is admitted that some portions of it are, that its removal would cause material injury to the structure of the building itself, then it would seem to us that a recovery could not be had, not for the reason that the property had become a "fixture" in the ordinary meaning of that term, but for the reason that to permit its removal would work injustice upon the owner of the property to which it had been so affixed.

. . . .

However, to deny removal of this property, which is clearly subject to identification, easily removable without material injury to the structure of the building, not subject to any liens, when it is conceded that the plaintiff has no other remedy, would clearly be a subversion of the purpose for which the constitutional and statutory provisions in question were framed and would permit the taxpayers of the defendant school district improperly, because unnecessarily, to shift the burden of the education of the children of the district to the shoulders of those who in good faith have furnished the material for the completion of the school building, to the extent of the value of this property, which we think they would not desire, nor should they be permitted to do.

See *Bardwell* v. *Southern Engine & Boiler Works*, 130 Ky. 222, 113 S.W. 97, and annotation to same in 20 L. R. A. (N.S.) 110.

If the material furnished had been supplies which had been used or had been property which had become mingled with other property as to be not subject to identification, or have been so affixed as to be irremovable, that result might necessarily follow, because the plaintiff would be without remedy.

Guides for Class Discussion

1. What are "fixtures," of which the court made mention?
2. What line of reasoning did the court pursue in arriving at its conclusion?
3. See *White River School Township.* v. *Dorrell, supra.*
4. Under what conditions could the court permit the recovery of property that had been delivered to a school district under an illegal contract?

36. *"Where the statute prohibits a school board member from entering into a contract with the board of which he is a member, a contract entered into in violation of the statute is void and no recovery can be had . . . in a court of law, or on quantum meruit in a court of equity . . ." (p. 7).*

NOBLE v. DAVISON,
177 Ind. 19, 96 N.E. 325 (1911)
(Decided by the Supreme Court of Indiana)

[The facts of the case will be found in the material which follows.]

MORRIS, J. . . .

.   .   .   .

The complaint alleges that the plaintiff is a resident taxpayer of the city of Princeton; that defendants Noble, Yeager, and Fisher constitute the school board of the city of Princeton. . . .

The complaint further alleges that Noble is the president of defendant Noble Plumbing & Heating Company, which is a corporation organized and doing business under the laws of Indiana, and engaged in the business of plumbing and installing heating plants; that defendant Ernest E. Noble owns a large number of shares of the capital stock of the corporation, and is interested in all contracts made by the company with other persons and corporations. The complaint also alleges that on June 25, 1910, the school board, by its then acting trustees entered into a written contract with the defendant Noble Plumbing & Heating Company, by the terms of which the company agreed to install a steam-heating plant in a public school building in the city of Princeton for the price of $2,675; that by the terms of the contract the plant was to be installed by the 1st day of September, 1910; that the provisions of the contract cannot be more fully set out in the complaint, because the contract is in the possession of defendants.

* * * * * * * * *

Appellee claims the contract is void, because it violates section 2423, Burns' Stat. 1908; and also on grounds of public policy. The above section of the statute reads as follows: "Any . . . school trustee of any town or city . . . who shall, during the time he may occupy such office . . . be interested, directly or indirectly, in any contract for the construction of any . . . work of any kind, erected or built for the use of . . . any city . . . in the state, . . . shall be fined not less than three hundred dollars nor more than five thousand dollars, and be imprisoned in the state prison not less than two years," etc. Burns' Stat. 1908, §2423; Burns' Stat. 1901, §2136; R. S. 1881, §2049; 2 R. S. 1876, p. 454; Acts 1872, p. 26.

It has been repeatedly held that a contract executed in contravention of the provisions of this statute is absolutely void. . . .

* * * * * * * * *

Even in the absence of the statute, the contract would, as appellee maintains, be void, because contrary to public policy. Counsel for appellants say in their brief: "Public policy is a juridical ignis fatuus upon which a judicial decision is sometimes sought to be founded when no support can be found for it in the law; and it is resorted to frequently when the purpose is to take from one of the parties to the controversy that which is his by vested right, sometimes by constitutional guaranty. . . . It was an unhappy day for the law when the term was invented and given meaning as having the force of law." We cannot concur in any such suggestion. One has heedlessly considered the decisions of this court who would at this day assert such doctrine. This court has ever steadfastly adhered to the rule which invalidates all agreements injurious to the public, or against the public good, or which have a tendency to injure the public. Contracts belonging to this class are held void, even though no injury results. The test of the validity of such agreements is the tendency to public injury, regardless of the actual intent of the parties, and regardless of actual results.

Integrity in the discharge of official duty is zealously guarded by the law. It lends no aid to that which tends to corrupt or contaminate of-

ficial action, whether such action be judicial, legislative, or administrative. 9 Cyc. 485. And the tendency of contracts between municipal
corporations and officers thereof, for municipal improvements or supplies, is to mislead the judgments of the officers of the municipality, if
not to sully their purity.

. . . .

We see no reason for relaxing the rule adhered to so strictly by the
courts of this state. In fact, not only in Indiana, but elsewhere generally the principle is applied by the courts in a large and constantly in-
creasing number of cases. 9 Cyc. 482. As was said in State v. Windle,
supra: "The protection of the public interests requires that no exception
to this rule shall be allowed, nor any evasions tolerated."

It is maintained by counsel for appellants that one seeking equity
must do equity; that the school city holds the benefit of the labor
and materials furnished by the plumbing company, and it would be
inequitable to adjudge an avoidance of the contract without restoration
to the plumbing company of the reasonable value of all work done
and materials furnished. In answer to this contention, it is sufficient
to say that an equitable right cannot be founded on a violation of law.
Waymire v. Powell, supra. Equity follows the law, and assists no one
in obtaining or holding the fruits of an illegal agreement, but, on the
contrary, leaves such person where it finds him. . . .

Guides for Class Discussion

1. What did the court mean when it said "an equitable right cannot be founded on a violation of law"?
2. Compare this case with *Weitz* v. *Independent District of Des
   Moines, infra.*
3. By what line of reasoning did the court arrive at its decision?
4. How do you think the court would have held had there been
   no statute governing this situation?

37. "*In the absence of statute prohibiting it, a contract between a board and one of its members is commonly held to be contrary to public policy . . ., and no recovery can be had for benefits received under it*" (p. 7-8).

Weitz v. Independent District of Des Moines,
87 Iowa 81, 54 N.W. 70 (1893)
(Decided by the Supreme Court of Iowa)

[This was an action in equity brought by a resident and taxpayer to enjoin a school district from carrying out and performing an alleged contract with a member of the school board of the district. In this case the board had employed one of its members to superintend the erection of a schoolhouse in the district. No statute governed this situation. The court held, however, that the contract was void and that there could be no recovery under it.]

Rothrock, J. . . . It is argued and strenuously contended by counsel for the defendants that such a contract as this is voidable by the district, and not absolutely void; or that it is prima facie void, but may be made valid by showing that it was entered into by the parties thereto in good faith, was faithfully performed by the contractor, and that it should not in equity be repudiated by the district. It may be that if the taxpayers of this district had remained silent, and made no sign of disapproval until the contract was performed and the services fully rendered, it should not be held that the district should profit by the labor and skill of Whiting without compensation. But it is not necessary to determine that question in this case. We may refer, however, to the case of Moore v. Independent Dist., 55 Iowa, 654, 8 N.W. Rep. 631, where it was held that a member of the board of directors of a school district, who was employed to superintend the construction of a schoolhouse, had no right to recover from the district for services so rendered. That was an action upon a school order drawn by the district, and payable to said director for his services.

The case at bar presents no equitable considerations upon which the contract can be sustained, or upon which compensation can be made to Whiting for his services. There is nothing akin to estoppel in the whole record. Indeed, we regard the former opinion in the case as decisive of every question now presented. . . .

. . . It is apparent that there are no equitable considerations which require that this contract should be recognized or enforced. It is possible that the district would not be prejudiced by paying Whiting for his services. But that is not the question to be determined. If the way be opened by a decision of this court by which officers of counties cities, incorporated towns and school districts may let contracts to themselves, and recover thereon by showing that the contract was beneficial to the corporation, it would lead to the grossest abuses. . . . The defendants admitted in their answer that the board of directors had "paid to said Whiting at intervals the entire compensation agreed to be paid him for his services, except a small balance." This answer was filed on the 4th day of February, 1890. Whether the balance has since been paid does not appear. The contract price for the erection of the building was $52,425. Two per cent. of that amount would make the compensation of Whiting amount to $1,049. He claims in his testimony that the whole amount under his contract is "in the neighborhood of $1,300." The plaintiff excepted to the decree because the court did not order the money received by Whiting to be returned to the treasury of the district. Such an order should have been made. The defendant directors cannot be allowed to use the name of the district to defeat the action by paying the money to Whiting while the suit is pending, and then set up the claim that the action must fail because a taxpayer has no right to complain. We held in the former appeal that he had such right. In view of the fact that the evidence is not certain as to the exact amount paid to Whiting, we cannot render a judgment for any amount; but the decree in this court will direct, in general terms, that the full amount which has been paid to Whiting shall be refunded and paid back to the treasury of the school district within 60 days. The decree will be thus modified on plaintiff's appeal, and on defendants' appeal it is affirmed.

Guides for Class Discussion

1. Were the ends of justice served by the court?
2. How do you think the court would have held had no legal action been brought before the contract was completed?
3. Do you think the court should have required that Whiting repay the money already paid him by the district? Give reasons.

38. *"According to the weight of authority, however, a contract between a school board and one of its members is not void but merely voidable and, if the board permits performance of the contract, it will be held liable for benefits received"* (p. 8).

SMITH V. DANDRIDGE,
98 Ark. 38, 135 S.W. 800 (1911)
(Decided by the Supreme Court of Arkansas)

[The facts of the case will be found in the material quoted from the case.]

FRAUENTHAL, J. This was an action instituted by appellants, who were residents and taxpayers of the special school district of Paris, against the treasurer of the county in which the school district is situated and G. G. Dandridge, to enjoin the payment of a school warrant which had been issued by the president and secretary of said school district to said Dandridge for work and labor alleged to have been performed by him for the school district. The special school district of Paris had duly entered into a contract with certain contractors for the erection of a school building, and later it was deemed necessary to employ some one as superintendent to be present at the work and represent the school district to see that specifications as to the brick work were fully complied with. G. G. Dandridge was one of the directors of the school district, and, at the request of a number of the other directors he performed the duties of superintending this work, and later presented his claim for such services to the board of directors. His claim, amounting to $172.50 for 69 days' work, was allowed by the directors at one of the regular meetings of the school board. At that meeting four directors were present, one of whom was said Dandridge, and the other three members voted in favor of the allowance of the claim.

It is not claimed that there was any fraud practiced either in the selection of Dandridge or in the allowance of his claim, or that services of the kind performed by him were not required. . . . It is urged that Dandridge was one of the school directors, and, on that account, he could not enter into a contract for his own employment by the school district; and it is also urged that his claim was allowed at a meeting where either his vote or his presence was necessary to constitute a quorum, and on that account its allowance was not legally made, and for these reasons it is contended that the warrant issued for the payment of this claim is illegal and its payment should be enjoined. As a general rule it is unlawful for a director to enter into a contract with the school district in which he has a personal and individual interest. His relation to the school district as a director thereof is of a confidential and fiduciary nature. He represents the school district, and is its agent. On this account, he cannot place himself in a position where his own personal interests might conflict with those of the school district which he must represent. The law and public policy forbids him from making a contract with the school district in which he has an interest; and a contract so made by a director will not be enforceable. The principle upon which this public policy is founded is that, where one is acting in a fiduciary capacity for another, he will not be permitted to make a contract with himself in his individual capacity relative to the subject-matter of such employment. . . . But a director is disabled from making a binding contract with the school district, not because the thing contracted for is itself illegal or tainted with moral turpitude, but because his personal relation to the district as its agent requires that he should have no self-interest antagonistic to that of the district in making a contract for it. The contract, however, in such case is not absolutely void, but it is simply not a binding agreement and may be avoided. If under such voidable contract the school district has accepted and retained benefits, it would still be liable to make just compensation therefor, not because of the contract, but upon the principle that one ought to pay for valuable benefits received. . . .

In the case at bar, the appellee Dandridge is not endeavoring to recover under a contract made by him with the school district. . . . His right to receive compensation from the school district is not based on the contract, but it is grounded solely on the principle that he has rendered necessary services from which the school district has received real benefits and therefore should recover what those services are fairly and reasonably worth. This is not a suit brought by Dandridge to enforce any contract at law, but the appellants have by this action called upon a court of chancery for equitable relief. They cannot in a court of conscience ask for a relief the effect of which would work injustice. The services which Dandridge performed and for which he received the warrant as payment were entirely outside of the duties of his office as a director. There is no claim made that there was any fraudulent dealing either in selecting him to perform the services or in the amount of the claim therefor which he made. It is not claimed that the amount allowed him for the services is more than the services were fairly and reasonably worth. Under these circumstances, we think that he is justly and equitably entitled to payment for such services.

Guides for Class Discussion

1. Compare the decision in this case with *Fargo Foundry Co.* v. *Village of Calloway, supra.* Which of the two cases represents the best law? Why?

2. Was the court consistent in permitting recovery in this case

after saying "where one is acting in a fiduciary capacity for another, he will not be permitted to make a contract with himself in his individual capacity relative to the subject-matter of such employment"? Give reasons.

3. How did the court justify its decision in this case?

39. ". . . *a school board may ratify contracts which it had authority to make in the first instance*" (p. 8).

RYAN v. HUMPHRIES,
50 Okla. 343, 150 P. 1106 (1915)
(Decided by the Supreme Court of Oklahoma)

[This was an action brought by a teacher to compel the treasurer of the school district to register and pay a warrant in his favor. This warrant had been issued and signed by the director and clerk of said board. The treasurer refused to pay it on the ground the teacher did not have a legal contract. On the other hand, the teacher contended that the board had, by its actions, ratified the contract. The lower court held in favor of the teacher and the higher court upheld the decision of the lower court.]

ROBBERTS, C. . . .

. . . .

The contention of the respondent upon the first proposition, that the contract of employment was made without his knowledge or consent, by the other two members of the board, and at a time when a meeting of the board had not been legally called and was not in session, would ordinarily present a complicated and serious question. We are of opinion that the evidence clearly shows that the contract was made by Abbott and Gamble, as director and clerk of the district, in the absence and without the consent or knowledge of the respondent. Why this was done does not appear from the evidence. . . .

. . . .

This action of the board brings us to the question of its effect, in the way of ratification of the original contract entered into by Abbott and Gamble as director and clerk. In this connection it may not be out of place to say that the question of the power of municipal or quasi municipal corporations to ratify unauthorized contracts is one of the generally recognized controversies of the court and bar. The authorities are absolutely irreconcilable; and after careful study of the proposition the writer hereof acknowledges himself at sea, in the midst of the storm of high rolling waves of uncertainty; but we gather from the weight of the authorities that, where the corporation had the power to enter into the contract under consideration, and the manner of making it being the only question involved, such contract may, as a rule, be ratified by an acceptance of the benefits of the contract by corporations, and by a subsequent recognition and substantial performance of the acts and conditions required by law in the execution of the legal contract, or by acquiescence in the conditions and benefits obtained by virtue of the contract. . . .

. . . .

As stated before herein, this seems to be the rule followed and approved by the weight of authorities on the subject; and upon the facts in the instant case, as necessarily found by the trial court, sustained by these authorities, we hold that the contract of employment of the relator was fully ratified by the board, so far as it relates to the services involved herein, and such ratification is equivalent to authority originally existing, and renders the contract valid from its date.

Guides for Class Discussion

1. In general, what is the rule regarding the authority of a board of education to ratify an unenforceable contract?
2. Do you agree with the court's decision? Give reasons.
3. In its decision the court said that the "authorities are absolutely irreconcilable." What argument could you present on the other side of the question—*i.e.*, for a court taking the opposite point of view from that taken here?

40. "*A school board cannot, of course, ratify a contract that is ultra vires, violative of the statutory mode of making it, or violative of public policy*" (p. 8).

FIRST NATIONAL BANK v. WHISENHUNT,
94 Ark. 583, 127 S.W. 968 (1910)
(Decided by the Supreme Court of Arkansas)

[The facts of the case are included in that part of the decision quoted.]

FRAUENTHAL, J. This was an action instituted by appellant against school district No. 33 of Scott county and its three directors on two warrants or orders of said school district. On December 10, 1902, W. W. Tutwiler made a contract with two of the directors, by which he sold to the school district charts for $85. For the purchase money thereof three warrants of the school district were executed, one for $35 and the other two for $25 each. The warrant for $35 was paid immediately and the two other warrants are involved in this suit. These two warrants stated on their face the consideration thereof, and were made payable on August 1, 1903, and 1904, respectively. Some time after the execution of the warrants, the charts were received by, and were in the possession and use of, the school district at the time of the institution of this suit. The warrants were sold and transferred to appellant some time prior to August 1, 1903. It appears from the testimony that the electors of said school district did not authorize the expenditure for said charts at the annual election previous to the alleged purchase thereof, nor at any election thereafter; and it also appears from the testimony that no attempt was ever made to secure the approval of the state superintendent as to the price and merit of said charts. The cause was tried by the court sitting as a jury, who made a finding and rendered judgment in favor of appellees.

A school district is by the statutes of this state made a body corporate; but it is intended as an agency in the administration of public functions. It is a quasi public corporation, and can exercise no powers beyond those expressly conferred by statute or which arise therefrom by necessary implication. The powers and duties of the directors of a school district are derived only from legislative authority, and they can exercise no power that is not thus expressly or by necessary implication granted by statute. A contract entered into by the directors, therefore, which is beyond the powers conferred on them by statute to make, is null and void. . . . And all persons who deal with the school officers are presumed to have full knowledge of the extent of the powers of these officers to make the particular contract . . . By section 7620 of Kirby's Digest it is provided that the directors of a school district may expend annually out of the common school fund not more than $25 for maps, charts, etc., but it is there provided, further, that, before such expenditure can be made, the maps, charts, etc., must meet the approval of the state superintendent in price and merit, and the expenditure must also be authorized by a majority of the electors of the school district at the annual election previous thereto. . . .

It is urged by appellant that the contract has been ratified by the receipt and use of the charts by the school district. But, where a contract made by the directors of a school district is invalid because it was beyond the scope of their powers, it cannot be ratified by acceptance. The statute expressly provides that such contract can only be authorized by the electors at a meeting regularly called and by a vote cast at an election. This was a necessary condition to be observed before there could be any power to make such a contract, and it could not therefore be ratified except by the observance of those conditions that were essential to the making of a valid contract in the beginning, if it could be ratified in any event. . . .

In the case at bar the school directors were without power to enter into a contract for the purchase of the charts, and by statue were in effect, prohibited from doing so. Such a contract was not only unauthorized, but was contrary to law, and therefore void. Such a contract therefore could not be ratified or enforced because the charts were received by and are still in the possession of the school district.

Guides for Class Discussion

1. What is meant by a contract that is *"ultra vires"*?
2. Can an *ultra vires* contract be ratified?
3. Compare this case with *Edwards* v. *School District, supra,* and *Ryan* v. *Humphries, supra.* Can they be reconciled?

*41. "Where a school board has the authority to ratify a contract,
it may do so by formal resolution or by action that is incompatible
with any reasonable assumption other than that it intended to
ratify" (p. 8).*

Frank v. Board of Education of Jersey City,
90 N.J.L. 273, 100 A. 211 (1917)
(Decided by the Court of Error and Appeals of New Jersey)

[This was an action to collect from a school board for work done
and materials furnished it by unauthorized agents. The contracts
for such purchases were of a type that the district had the authority
to make. The agents in question were a supervising architect and a
vice principal of a high school. In making the purchases, the agents
were only doing what had been permitted " 'for a number of
years.' " Plaintiff had furnished other materials and done other
work for the board under similar circumstances, and the board had
always paid when billed. The board, in this case, did not deny the
authority of the agents in question until three years after the last
work had been performed. The lower court ruled in plaintiff's
favor, and the board appealed. The higher court affirmed the
decision of the lower court. In so doing it held there was an implied agency and that ratification could be implied from the board's
acts.]

BLACK, J.

. . . .

In the case under discussion, the School Law of the State . . .
provides that the board of education in a city school district such as
Jersey City is vested with the power of making contracts in and by
its corporate name and by section 50 every such board shall have
the supervision, control, and management of the public schools and
public school property in its district. It may appoint a superintendent
of schools, a business manager, and other officers, agents and employes,
as may be needed. Section 52 provides the board may at any time order
repairs to school buildings to an amount not exceeding $500, may
authorize the purchase of supplies to an amount not exceeding $250,
without advertisement. Section 72 provides for a business manager; who
shall supervise, if there be one, the construction and repair of all
school buildings, and shall report monthly to the board of education the
progress of the work; that repairs not exceeding the sum of $100 may
be ordered by the business manager, and repairs not exceeding the

sum of $500 may be ordered by the committee of the board having charge of the repair of school property, without the previous order of the board and without advertisement. In this statute, as will be seen, there is express authority for the appointment of an agent, a business manager. The term is immaterial. A supervising architect or vice principal might just as well be called an agent or business manager. . . . There is no evidence tending to show, and it is not even pretended, that all these various items, amounting in the aggregate to $684.30, can be treated as one contract, so as to bring the amount above the $500 limitation permitted by the statute for repairs of school property without the previous order of the board and without advertisement. It would be quite impracticable to require either a formal resolution for every possible small expenditure, or for the board to act by a majority in person. . . .

The literature of the law of agency is rich in adjudged cases. . . . The agency may be implied from the recognition or acquiescence of the alleged principal as to acts done in his behalf by the alleged agent, especially if the agent has repeatedly been permitted to perform acts like the one in question. . . . So ratification may be implied from any acts, words, or conduct on the part of the principal which reasonably tend to show an intention on the part of the principal to ratify the unauthorized acts or transactions of the alleged agent . . ., provided the principal in doing the acts relied on as a ratification acted with knowledge of the material facts. . . . The rule is particularly applicable, where it appears that the principal has repeatedly recognized and affirmed similar acts by the agent. . . . So a municipal corporation may ratify the unauthorized acts and contracts of its agents or officers which are within the scope of the corporate powers, but not otherwise. . . .

.   .   .   .

We think, as the board of education had the power, under the statute, to contract for the work done and material supplied in this case, there was created by conduct an implied agency, an agency in fact, on the part of Messrs. Rowland and Wilson, and further, that by implication the contracts of these unauthorized agents have been ratified by the acts and conduct of the school board; hence it was not error for the trial court to direct a judgment in favor of the respondent and against the appellant.

Guides for Class Discussion

1. What line of reasoning did the court follow in arriving at its decision? Are you in agreement with the court's thinking? Give reasons.

2. The court noted that the board knew that the materials were

furnished and the work done about the time when this happened. Do you think this affected the result? Why?

3. See *Ryan* v. *Humphries, supra.*

42. *"Where a board has authority to ratify a contract and does so, the contract is ratified in toto . . ."* (p. 8).

JONES v. SCHOOL DISTRICT,
7 Kan. App. 372, 51 P. 927 (1898)
(Decided by the Court of Appeals of Kansas)

[This was an action to recover wages earned as a teacher. The teacher in question—Jones—had entered into a written contract with the school board on July 22, 1891, to teach one of the defendant's schools for the ensuing term of nine months, beginning in September. On the 30th day of July, 1891, the annual school district meeting was held. At this time the electors voted that female teachers should be employed, but did not take action on any other proposition. Later the district board met and employed two female teachers who, with plaintiff and another lady that had been employed prior to the annual meeting, constituted the corps of teachers when school opened in September. With the full knowledge and consent of the board, plaintiff continued to teach for nine weeks when it was alleged she was dismissed without cause or excuse. She was paid for two months service. She then brought this action to recover the entire amount of her wages under contract. She contended the contract made was valid. The court found there was a division of opinion as to whether a contract made with a teacher before the annual district meeting was valid. It held, however, that it was not, but that the teacher could recover on the ground that the contract had been ratified.]

MILTON, J. . . .

. . . .

. . . Plaintiff alleges that she taught under this contract for nine weeks, and was twice paid as provided for therein; that the new board elected but two of the four teachers necessary, and that the plaintiff and another teacher were teaching under the contracts made with the board prior to the annual school meeting; that the electors at the annual meeting knew that plaintiff had been employed to teach for the ensuing term, and assented to such employment, and did not limit the power of the board except as to the sex of the teachers. It is evident that the contract set forth in plaintiff's petition is the basis upon which she taught, and was recognized and paid as a teacher by said board. Not being advised to the contrary, we presume that only one new member of the board was elected at the annual meeting. The contract bore the signature of two members of the new board. It was within the power of the two members at a regularly called meeting of the board to have adopted and ratified the said contract. If the board, with full knowledge that the contract was in existence, recognized and paid plaintiff as a teacher according to the terms thereof, did it not thus adopt that contract, and make it fully binding upon itself and the defendant district? . . . The case of Athearn v. Independent Dist., 33 Iowa, 105, is almost identical with the case at bar. Having taught for part of the term named in the contract, the teacher was discharged without just cause. There, as here, the plaintiff was paid for the time he actually taught under the contract. The board's answer denied that the contract was made under proper authority. The supreme court used this language: "But, if we concede that the contract was executed without authority upon the part of defendant's officers, it has nevertheless been ratified by defendant, and thereby became a binding instrument. Corporations may ratify contracts made without authority, and thus become bound thereby like natural persons; the same rule of law being applicable to each. . . . Performance of a contract, permission to the party with whom the corporation contracts to perform, the acceptance of the performance or the fruits of the performance by the corporation, acquiescence in the contract, payment to the other party, and the like, all operate as acts of ratification." . . . The contract in question, *if valid when made, was entire; if it became operative by adoption, it was likewise entire.* [Emphasis supplied.] The petition alleges that plaintiff was discharged without just cause or excuse. We think she is entitled to have the question raised decided on a trial of the case upon its merits. The judgment of the district court is reversed, and the case remanded with instructions to overrule the demurrer to plaintiff's petition. All the judges concurring.

Guides for Class Discussion

1. See *Ryan* v. *Humphries, supra;* and *Frank* v. *Board of Education of Jersey City, supra.*
2. Can the decision in this case be reconciled with the decisions in the cases just mentioned?

3. Can it be reconciled with *First National Bank* v. *Wheisehunt,
   supra?* Give reasons.

43. "*It has frequently been held that, where money has been paid
out in violation of an express constitutional or statutory prohibition
or for a purpose entirely outside the powers of the school district,
it may be recovered from the party or parties to whom it has been
paid in an action brought . . . on behalf of the district*" (p. 8).

Vick Consolidated School District v. New,
208 Ark. 874, 187 S.W. (2d) 948 (1945)
(Decided by the Supreme Court of Arkansas)

[This was an action brought to recover money allegedly due one
who served as a teacher but who was not properly licensed. Plaintiff, who was employed as superintendent, was given a supplemental
contract to teach three subjects that had been taught by a teacher
who had resigned. The board alleged that plaintiff had falsely
claimed he had the proper license and that, as a result, it had given
him the original contract and later the supplemental contract. It
prayed for a return of the money it had paid plaintiff under the
original contract. The statute provided: "'Any person who shall
teach in a public school in this state, without a legal certificate of
qualification to teach, shall not be entitled to receive for such services any compensation from revenues raised by tax. . . .'" The
court ruled that the board could recover the amount paid plaintiff
for teaching where he had no proper license.]

McFADDIN, Justice.

 . . . In those cases—where the contract was *not forbidden by
statute*—the court has allowed a recovery by the individual against the
governmental subdivision in a quantum meruit basis. Some such cases
are: Spearman v. Texarkana, 58 Ark. 348, 24 S.W. 883 . . .; Frick
v. Brinkley, 61 Ark. 397, 33 S.W. 527; Smith v. Dandridge, 98 Ark. 38,
135 S.W. 800. . . .
There are those cases in which an individual has dealt with the
district, council, board, or other governmental subdivision *in plain viola-*

tion of the letter of the statute and has received public money under a course of dealings *forbidden by statute*. In those cases the courts have not only refused the individual the quantum meruit for his services rendered, but have also allowed recovery by the governmental subdivision of any monies paid the individual, on a contract forbidden by statute. Some such cases are: Tallman v. Lewis, 124 Ark. 6, 186 S.W. 296. . . .

Tallman v. Lewis was a suit by a taxpayer to recover money previously paid by a district to one of the commissioners for services rendered. The law provided that no commissioner should be interested in any contract made by the district. Tallman, one of the commissioners, had served in lieu of an engineer, and had been compensated for such services. Lewis, a property owner, brought suit to recover the money so paid Tallman for his services. This court . . . said [124 Ark. 6, 186 S.W. 298]:

"The general rule is that, where a contract is expressly prohibited by law, and the statute in terms declares the contract to be null and void, no recovery can be had under it, and that a taxpayer has a right to maintain an action to recover back money illegally paid when its officers neglect or refuse to perform their duty in that respect. . . ."

Guides for Class Discussion

1. Are you in agreement with the rule laid down by the court in this case?
2. Is the rule equitable? Give reasons.
3. See *Culver* v. *Brown, infra.*

44. *"In some jurisdictions, however, it is held that money paid out on a contract made in violation of some statutory provision or of public policy cannot be recovered, where the facts show that the contract was made in good faith and the district retains and enjoys the benefits of its performance"* (p. 8).

CULVER v. BROWN,
259 Mich. 294, 243 N.W. 10 (1932)
(Decided by the Supreme Court of Michigan)

[The facts of this case are self-evident as one reads that part of the decision quoted.]

WIEST, J.

Defendant Vernon J. Brown, a director of school district No. 1, township of Vevay, city of Mason, furnished printing and supplies, through a copartnership of which he was a member, to the school district. This was illegal on his part. The statute, C. L. 1929, § 7692, provides: "It shall be illegal for any member of the board of education . . . to perform any labor except as provided in this act, or furnish any material or supplies for the school district in which he is an officer, or to be personally interested in any way whatever, directly or indirectly, in any contract with the district in which he holds office."

Plaintiff is a taxpayer in the district and filed the bill herein for an accounting and recovery of the money so expended. He invokes Act. no. 94, Pub. Acts 1929, which provides: "Any person or persons, firm or corporation, resident in any township or school district, paying taxes to such political unit, may institute suits or actions at law or in equity on behalf of or for the benefit of the treasurer of such political subdivision, for an accounting and/or the recovery of funds or moneys misappropriated or unlawfully expended by any public officer, board or commission of such political subdivision." This statute, instead of extending right to recover, restricts the right to mentioned instances.

The bill was dismissed and plaintiff appealed. The record presents no question of fraud or collusion or concert of purpose between the school board and defendants to evade the law. If it did, an entirely different question would be presented. The governing rule, here applicable and barring recovery, is founded upon the fact that the school district has received services and supplies wholly legitimate for school purposes and the money paid therefor has neither been misappropriated or expended for unlawful purposes. The vice here disclosed was not in the expenditure, but in the fact that defendant Vernon J. Brown, as an officer of the school district, was interested in furnishing needed and lawful printing and supplies.

This is not a case of enjoining payment because of the illegal act of defendant Vernon J. Brown. If it were, payment would be enjoined. . . .

Public funds, misappropriated or paid without value or for services not within the law, may be recovered; but there cannot be recovery for services or supplies required or authorized by law and furnished, paid for, and retained by the school district.

The decree dismissing the bill is affirmed, with costs to defendants.

Guides for Class Discussion

1. Compare this decision with *Jones* v. *School District, supra,* and *Vick Consolidated School District* v. *New, supra.*

2. Do you think the principle laid down by the court is equi-

table? Give reasons.
3. Had an attempt been made to enjoin payment under this contract, how do you think the court would have held?

45. *"A school board is a continuing corporate entity, and it may make contracts extending beyond the term of office of one or more of its members"* (p. 8).

Gardner v. North Little Rock Special School District,
161 Ark. 466, 257 S.W. 73 (1923)
(Decided by the Supreme Court of Arkansas)

[In May, 1919, the board of education of North Little Rock entered into a contract with one, Gardner, to serve as superintendent of schools for a two-year period beginning in July, 1919. Shortly after the contract was entered into, a school-board election was held. Gardner served until June, 1920, when he was discharged. He then brought this action to collect the remainder of the salary due him under his contract.]

McCulloch, C. J.

. . . .

The first question which presents itself is whether or not the directors of the district were empowered to enter into a contract with a school superintendent for a term of more than one year. This question was not expressly raised in the proceedings, but the denial of the execution of the contract itself is sufficient to raise the question of the legal power of the district to enter into the contract.

The statute governing single school districts and conferring authority upon the directors of such districts in the management and control of school affairs, authorizes the directors to "employ a superintendent of the schools, who may also be principal of any graded or high school that said board may establish." . . . It will be noted that there is nowhere found in the statute any express restriction upon the authority of the district in employing a superintendent so far as concerns the length of the term. If any such restriction exists, it must therefore be an implied one. In the case of *Gates* v. *School District*, 53 Ark. 468, 14 S.W. 656, 10 L.R.A. 186, this court held that the statute just referred to, conferring authority upon the board of directors to employ a superintendent of schools, does not limit the authority to an employment during the term of office of such directors, and that the statute does not forbid the board to make a contract with the superintendent for a term, beginning after some members of the board go out of office. The question of employment for a longer term than one year was not involved in that case, but the term fixed by the employment did, in fact, extend beyond the term of office of some of the directors then in office, and the reasoning of the court leads inevitably to the conclusion that the statute does not restrict the power of the board to the employment of a superintendent for a single year. . . .

. . . .

We are of the opinion that the authorities sustain the view that the statute, authorizing such an employment by a board of school directors or trustees, without any restrictions as to the length of term of the employment and duration of the contract, is not limited to the period of one year, nor to such a time as is within the term of office of all the members of the board at that time. . . .

. . . .

The proper rule seems to be that, unless the statute prescribes a time limit upon the duration of such a contract, the board may make a contract for a reasonable length of time, and the reasonableness of the contract is to be determined by all the circumstances. The mere fact that there are partial changes in the personnel of the board during the life of the contract does not of itself render it unreasonable in duration of time. Whether or not a contract extending beyond the incumbency of all of the members of the board then in office would be unreasonable we need not determine, for no such state of facts exists with respect to the contract now before us. In the present case the contract was made immediately before the school election in May 1919, and the term extended up to July 1, 1921. The terms of two of the directors then in office expired with the election in May, but if the contract with plaintiff had been for only one year, the board as constituted prior to the school election in 1920, which was a majority as it existed when this contract was made, could have made a new contract for another year, so the making of this contract did not extend the employment beyond the terms of even a majority of the members of the board, and . . . the contract was valid. The fact that it was within the power of a majority of the board who would remain in office past the time when the second year of the term might be contracted for affords a reason, if no other existed, for holding that the contract was not unreasonable. Our conclusion is that the contract was valid, and that there was no defense on that ground.

Guides for Class Discussion

1. How do you think the court would have ruled had the contract extended beyond the terms of all board members?
2. Do you think the court would have approved the contract had it begun after the expiration of the terms of some board members making it? Give reasons.

SELECTED BIBLIOGRAPHY

1. Edwards, Newton. *The Courts and the Public Schools,* rev. ed. Chicago: University of Chicago Press, 1955.
2. Garber, Lee O. *Handbook of School Law.* New London, Connecticut: Arthur C. Croft Publications, 1954.
3. Garber, Lee O. *Yearbook of School Law.* Danville, Illinois: The Interstate Printers and Publishers, Inc., annually since 1950.
4. Hamilton, Robert H. and Paul R. Mort. *The Law and Public Education,* rev. ed. Brooklyn: The Foundation Press, Inc., 1959.
5. Hamilton, Robert R. and E. Edmund Reutter, Jr. *Legal Aspects of School Board Operation.* New York: Bureau of Publications, Teachers College, Columbia University, 1958.
6. Lamb, Robert L. *Legal Liability of School Boards and Teachers for School Accidents.* Ottawa, Ontario: Research Division, Canadian Teachers Federation, Research Study No. 3, 1959.
7. Punke, Harold H. *Law and Liability In Pupil Transportation.* Chicago: University of Chicago Press, 1945.
8. Remmlein, Madaline Kinter. *School Law,* rev. ed. Danville, Illinois: The Interstate Printers and Publishers, Inc., 1962.
9. Reutter, E. Edmund, Jr. *Schools and the Law.* ("Legal Almanac Series," No. 17.) New York: Oceana Publications, Inc., 1960.
10. Rosenfield, Harry N. *Liability for School Accidents.* New York: Harper & Bros., 1940.
11. Weltzin, Joachim Frederick. *The Legal Authority of the American Public School.* Grand Forks, N. D.: Mid-West Book Concern, 1931.
12. *Who Is Liable for Pupil Injuries?* Washington, D. C.: Research Division, National Education Association, 1963.

SCHOOL LAW CASEBOOK SERIES—NO. 7

The Law Governing School Property and School-Building Construction

By

LEE O. GARBER

and

NEWTON EDWARDS

The Interstate
Printers and Publishers
Danville, Illinois

CONTENTS

INTRODUCTION

This casebook takes its place as the third in the second series of four books which, taken together, may be thought of as giving coverage to the field of "School Law." The earlier books in this series are "The Law Governing School Board Members and School Board Meetings" and "Tort and Contractual Liability of School Districts and School Boards." One more will follow. It will deal with School Finance.

Professors of School Law, who are seeking new and practical materials and who are desirous of using the case method of teaching, will welcome these casebooks as unique aids. Likewise, professors of Educational Administration who are interested in supplementing their instructional materials with additional materials of a legal nature should find these books exceedingly helpful.

The authors are well known for their work in this field—School Law. Newton Edwards is the author of the well-known textbook and reference work—*The Courts and the Public Schools.* Lee O. Garber is the author of *The Yearbook of School Law,* an annual publication since 1950. He has also been a regular contributor to *The Nation's Schools* since 1951.

Russell L. Guin,
Editor

Authors' Preface

This casebook follows the familiar pattern which characterizes the six that preceded it. It has two main sections—"Legal Principles" and "Court Decisions." From the legal principles mentioned in the first section, the most significant are selected and illustrated with appropriate court decisions in the second section.

The first four casebooks were designed to give coverage to the first half of a comprehensive course in School Law. This is the third in a projected series of four designed to give coverage to the last half of the School Law course.

The legal principles are selective and not exhaustive. Many of the cases selected illustrate more than one legal principle. Therefore, an instructor may become even more selective in his choice of cases for his class to consider if time is a matter of critical import.

It must be remembered that there is not, necessarily, uniformity of agreement among the courts on all questions. Courts deviate and, in the case of the most important deviations, court decisions are chosen to illustrate both points of view.

In addition to professors of School Law and School Administration, it is hoped that these casebooks will prove of both interest and value to practicing school administrators and school-board solicitors or attorneys.

Lee O. Garber
Newton Edwards

I.

LEGAL PRINCIPLES

The Law Governing School Property and School-Building Construction

Ownership and Control of School Property

Inasmuch as public education is a state function, public school property is state property held in trust for the state by local school authorities. It follows that the transfer of school property from one district to another by virtue of statutory authority does not deprive a school district or its inhabitants of property without due process of law. Whatever authority a school board may have over school property is authority which has been conferred upon it by statute.

Since education is a state and not a municipal function, cities and towns, even though they occupy the same territory as school districts, possess no inherent control over public schools; such authority as they may exercise over public schools and the buildings in which they are housed must be expressly and clearly conferred upon them by charter or statute. Cities and towns, unless authorized by statute, may not expend municipal funds for the construction of school buildings. Municipal officers have no inherent authority to control or manage school property. And this is true where a home-rule charter confers upon the city authority to regulate its local affairs. This follows from the fact that education is a state and not a local affair. A number of courts have held that school property is state property, subject to the exercise of the police power of the state residing in its local school boards; and the municipal authorities may not, therefore, require local school boards to obey their building ordinances or codes. But in some cases the courts have held that the police power of the municipality takes precedence over the police power of the school board where safety and sanitation are concerned.

State legislatures may authorize school boards to permit the use of school property for any purpose not prohibited by the constitution, and in a number of states the courts have sustained statutes authorizing a wide use of school buildings. In the absence of statutes authorizing the use of school buildings for other than school purposes, state courts have differed widely in their rulings. Some have

3

permitted the use of schoolhouses for religious meetings of one kind
or another provided there was no interference with the regular work
of the school, but others have held that no kind of religious exercise
could be held in a schoolhouse unless specifically authorized by
statute. The courts have been divided, too, on such matters as the
authority of school boards to permit the use of school buildings for
social and political meetings or to lease school property for a private
or commercial purpose. For example, they have approved the leasing
of school property for the drilling of oil and gas, although the
opposite has also been held.

Acquisition and Location of School Sites

As a rule, school boards are vested with specific statutory authority to acquire school sites, but even in the absence of such authority
the courts hold that authority to build school buildings carries with
it, by necessary implication, authority to purchase school sites.
Authority to purchase school sites carries with it by implication
authority to purchase the necessary playgrounds and athletic fields,
and these do not have to be adjacent to the lot on which the schoolhouse is situated. School boards are vested with authority to accept
donations of property to be used for school purposes, but when
school boards accept such a donation they will be required to
administer it perpetually according to the terms of the donor.

School boards, under statutory authority, may take private property by the exercise of the right of eminent domain; and, when they
do so, the courts will permit them a wide exercise of discretion both
with respect to the need of taking the property and the amount
to be taken. When property is taken by the right of eminent domain,
the courts will require the board to pay the owner a fair market
price for the property when put to its most profitable use; the owner
of land taken by eminent domain must be compensated for whatever
loss he suffers. When land is taken by eminent domain, the fee
remains with the original owner, unless the statutes provide otherwise, and when the property is no longer used for school purposes
it reverts to the original owner.

When property is conveyed to a school board and the deed clearly
provides for the reversion of the property to the original owner

when no longer used for school purposes, the board does not own the property in fee simple, and it reverts to the original owner or his heirs when no longer used for school purposes. But the courts do not look with favor on deeds that provide for reverter of school property, and such deeds will be construed strictly against the grantor. Where property was deeded to school districts "for school purposes only," "so long as the property shall be used for school purposes and no longer," or "to be used for school property in perpetuity," courts have held that the property did not revert to the grantor when no longer used for school purposes. Before a court will declare a forfeiture, it must be very clear that school authorities intended to abandon the use of property for school purposes. It has been held that property is no longer used for school purposes when it has been sold or leased and the proceeds are being used to maintain a school.

In the exercise of its discretion to select school sites, a school board will not have its discretion controlled by the courts so long as it is exercised in good faith and not abused. A school board must be free to exercise its discretion and best judgment at the time it makes the determination of a school site; it cannot limit its discretion in this respect by prior commitments or understandings with the public.

Employment of Architects

Authority of a school board to build school buildings carries with it, by implication, authority to employ architects. In employing an architect, a school board need not resort to competitive bidding in the absence of statute to the contrary. Contracts with architects, like all other contracts, must be made by the board in its corporate capacity and not by an individual member or committee of the board. It is well settled that, where an architect agrees to furnish plans and specifications for a building that can be built at a cost closely approximating a given amount, or not to exceed a certain sum, he cannot recover under the contract unless the building he designs can be erected for the sum stipulated, or unless the increased cost is due to some special circumstance. Some courts hold—and their decisions appear to be the most reasonable—that a contract

between a school board and an architect to prepare general draw
ings and specifications for a school building is valid even though th
board may not, at the time, have the necessary funds to build th
building and the building may never be built. These courts reaso
that the plans and specifications of the architect are necessary t
enable the school board to determine what the kind of buildin
desired would cost; even if the projected building is never erecte(
the architect's fee would be chargeable to the general fund. Som
courts take the position, however, that a contract between a scho(
board and an architect is invalid where the plans and specification
call for a building which would cost more than the board coul
legally spend for that purpose.

Where a school board breaks a contract with an architect, th
rule is that he is entitled to recover the contract price, less whateve
payments have been made and less what it would cost him to pe
form the contract.

Bids on Building Contracts

Where the statutes do not require school boards to let buildin
contracts on the basis of competitive bidding, a school board ma
or may not, at its discretion, advertise for bids. And in such case:
the board may reject all bids unless its advertisement is so worde
as to constitute an offer to accept the lowest bid. In case the statute
require school boards to advertise for bids on school-building cor
tracts and to award such contracts to the lowest responsible bidde
the mode of making the contract is the measure of the board
power to make it, and if the statute is disregarded, the contracte
cannot recover on the contract. As a rule, under such circumstance
the contractor cannot recover on *quantum meruit*, in a court (
equity, the actual value of the building. In order to have competitiv
bidding, plans and specifications must be sufficiently definite t
enable those who bid to bid on a common basis; otherwise there
no competition. A school board may ask for bids on alternate pla
and proposals, and there is competitive bidding even though onl
one bid is received. Where the statutes require that bids be let t
the lowest responsible bidder, in deciding who is the lowest respon
sible bidder, the board should take into consideration cost, financia

standing, experience, resources, and all other factors necessary for it to form a judgment on the bidder's responsibility. Where a school board acts in good faith and its judgment is based upon substantial fact, the courts will not overrule its discretion in determining the lowest responsible bidder. The mere passage of a resolution by a board to accept a bid does not constitute a contract—there is no contract until the bidder has been officially notified that his bid has been accepted—and a board may rescind its resolution awarding the contract at any time before such notification. If a contractor makes an honest mistake in calculating the cost of a school building and the mistake goes to the essence of the contract, a court of equity will annul the bid and put the parties *in statu quo.* After bids have been accepted, courts will permit minor, but not major, changes in the specifications; to permit major changes would be equivalent to letting a new contract without competitive bidding.

Illegal and Void Building Contracts

School boards have only such powers as are conferred upon them by statute; when a school board enters into a contract for the purchase of school property in excess of its statutory authority, the contract is *ultra vires.* In some states a school district will not be bound under an *ultra vires* contract even though it retains and enjoys the use of property obtained under such a contract. The courts in some states, however, hold that a district must pay for property retained and used under an *ultra vires* contract.

Ratification of School-Building Contracts

If a school board makes a contract for the erection of a school building or for the purchase of other school property which it had no authority to make, it cannot later ratify the contract by any act of its own so as to make it binding on the board. But if a school board enters into a contract for the purchase of school property which it had authority to make and the contract is unenforceable because of some irregularity in the making of it, the board may later ratify it. Formal action to ratify is not necessary; ratification takes place when a board so acts that its action is incompatible with any other assumption than its intent to ratify.

Defective Performance of Building Contracts

A school board may not refuse to accept a schoolhouse if the contractor has acted in good faith and substantially performed his contract. It is difficult to determine what constitutes substantial performance of a building contract but the courts are agreed that there is no substantial performance unless the building is such as to accomplish the purpose for which it was built. Where there is substantial performance, a board will be required to pay the contractor the contract price, less deductions to cover omissions in performance. Even though a school building has been accepted and paid for, it has been held that a school board may sue the contractor for defective performance.

Contractors' Bonds

Authority to build schoolhouses carries with it by implication authority to require a contractor to whom a building contract is let to give a bond guaranteeing the faithful performance of the contract and the payment for all labor and materials used in the construction of the building. As a rule, the obligation of a surety on a bond to insure the performance of a building contract is measured by the terms of the contract; but where the liability in the contract is broader than in the bond, many courts have held that the bond is the measure of the surety's liability. An accommodation surety—one who receives no pay—is a favorite of the law, and if there is any doubt with respect to the obligations under the bond it will be resolved in his favor; but contracts for suretyship will be construed more strictly against a surety for pay. When the bond is given by a surety company for pay, the bond is interpreted as are other contracts with a view of giving effect to the true meaning of the parties. Under the common law it was originally held that any change in a contract without the consent of the surety released the surety from all liability. With the rise of bonding companies for pay, however, the rule has been changed, and now it is generally held that the surety will be relieved entirely only if the change in the contract increases his liability materially; and, if the change is not great enough to relieve the surety entirely, he will be relieved *pro tanto—i.e.,* to the amount of his extra obligation.

A surety who gives a bond guaranteeing the performance of a building contract and the payment for labor and materials will not be relieved of his obligation to laborers and materialmen by any alteration in the original contract to which they did not give their consent. In a number of states the statutes require a contractor to give a bond to pay for labor and materials. Where there is evidence from surrounding circumstances or some provision in the bond that the contractor intended to give a statutory bond, the terms of the statute will generally be read into the bond and the surety will be held liable to pay for labor and materials. But other courts interpret the bond strictly and will not read the terms of the statute into it. Where a contractor agrees to provide the labor and materials used in the construction of a school building and gives a bond to guarantee that his contract will be performed, he does not definitely agree to pay for the labor and materials, and there is no right of action against his surety. Where a contract to construct a school building provides that the board retain each month a certain percentage of what is due the contractor in order to insure the completion of the building, and the contractor defaults, the contractor's surety has a claim on the retained percentage superior to that of laborers and materialmen or of a bank to which the contractor has assigned his rights to the retained percentage.

It is commonly held that a school district will not be held liable for failure to take a bond conditioned to pay for labor and materials even though a statute requires that such a bond be taken. Where the statutes require a school board to take a bond conditioned to pay for labor and materials going into the construction of a school building, members of the board will not, as a rule, be held personally liable for failure to take such a bond, although the opposite has been held.

II.

COURT DECISIONS

COURT DECISIONS

1. "Inasmuch as public education is a state function, public property is state property held in trust for the state by local school authorities" (p. 3).

PRITCHETT V. COUNTY BOARD OF SCHOOL TRUSTEES,
5 Ill. (2d) 356, 125 N.E. (2d) 476 (1955)
(Decided by the Supreme Court of Illinois)

[This was an action involving the constitutionality of certain statutes relating to the reorganization of school districts. In arriving at its decision, the court found it necessary to comment on the legal status of school property.]

DAILEY, JUSTICE.

. . . .

A frequently cited proposition is that the State may, with or without the consent of the inhabitants of a school district, or against their protest, and with or without notice or hearing, take the school facilities in the district without compensation and vest them in other districts or agencies. The State may hold or manage the facilities directly or indirectly. The area of the district may be contracted or expanded, it may be divided, united in whole or in part with another district, and the district may be abolished. All this at the will of the legislature. The "property of the school district" is a phrase which is misleading. The district owns no property, all school facilities, such as grounds, buildings, equipment, etc., being in fact and law the property of the State and subject to the legislative will.

Guides for Class Discussion

1. Compare this decision with the one in *Ross* v. *Adams Mills Rural School District, infra.*
2. Do you agree with the court? Give reasons.

2. "... *the transfer of school property from one district to another by virtue of statutory authority does not deprive a school district or its inhabitants of property without due process of law*" (p. 3).

Ross v. Adams Mills Rural School District,
113 Ohio St. 466, 149 N.E. 634 (1925)
(Decided by the Supreme Court of Ohio)

[When part of one rural district that had a bonded indebtedness was transferred to a second rural district, the second district was ordered to pay $25,000 toward the reduction of the indebtedness of the first district. The second district refused to do so, but the county auditor levied the tax on all the property of the district. To enjoin the levy and collection of the tax, this action was brought. The court refused to enjoin the levy and collection. In arriving at its decision the court saw fit to comment on the effect of a statute that provided for the transfer of school property from one district to another.]

Matthias, J. . . .

. . . .

It seems to be the clear purpose and intent of the provisions of section 4692, General Code, to require that any of the indebtedness of the district from which territory is transferred shall be apportioned between the districts from which and to which such territory is transferred. Indeed, it is impossible to make that provision of the statute effective if not so interpreted and applied.

When such division was made the indebtedness became the indebtedness of the Adams Mills district and of the Jefferson district, as apportioned. Under the provisions of section 4692, General Code, the "legal title of the property of the board of education shall become vested in the board of education of the school district to which such property is transferred," and, when an equitable division of the indebtedness was made, all the property in each district became liable for its respective proportion thereof. There is no statutory provision which would authorize a tax levied upon only a portion of a district or subdivision and no method has been prescribed, and none has been suggested, whereby that could be done. It would be contrary to the provisions of all tax levying and tax limitation statutes. In accordance with the familiar principles of statutory construction, section 4692, General Code, will be so construed as to make it a valid enactment for all purposes, and proceedings thereunder will, if possible, be so construed as to accomplish a valid result. Just as legislation enacted subsequent to the issuance of bonds that would remove a portion of the security thereof, and thereby impair the obligation of contract, would be invalid as against the holders of said bonds so also would a proceeding under this statute which undertook to transfer a portion of the district be a nullity against holders of the bonds, if it did not provide for the apportionment of the indebtedness and payment of the bonds as contemplated in the original proceeding for the issuance thereof, as required by the constitutional and statutory provisions heretofore referred to.

The contention that such statutory provision is violative of the due process clause of the federal Constitution has been considered in numerous cases and decided adversely thereto. In Hunter v. City of Pittsburgh, 207 U. S. 161, 28 S. Ct. 40, 52 L. Ed. 151, it was held:

"There is no contract, within the meaning of the contract clause of the Federal Constitution, between a municipality and its citizens and taxpayers that the latter shall be taxed only for the uses of that corporation and not for the uses of any like corporation with which it may be consolidated."

The language of Justice Moody, who rendered the opinion of the court, is pertinent here. After referring to the powers conferred upon municipal corporations and their status as political subdivisions of the state, he said, at page (28 S. Ct. 46):

"The State, therefore, at its pleasure may modify or withdraw all such powers, may take without compensation such property, hold it itself, or vest it in other agencies, expand or contract the territorial area, unite the whole or a part of it with another municipality, repeal the charter and destroy the corporation. . . . Although the inhabitants and property owners may by such changes suffer inconvenience, and their property may be lessened in value by the burden of increased taxation, or for any other reason, they have no right by contract or otherwise in the unaltered or continued existence of the corporation or its powers, and there is nothing in the federal Constitution which protects them from these injurious consequences."

Guides for Class Discussion

1. Do you think the court's decision was equitable? Give reasons.
2. What is meant by the due-process-of-law clause?
3. Had there been no statute governing the matter, what rule would the court have undoubtedly followed?
4. Compare the decision in this case with that rendered in *Pritchett* v. *County Board of School Trustees, supra.*

3. "*Since . . . cities and towns . . . possess no inherent control over public schools, such authority as they may exercise over public schools and the buildings in which they are housed must be expressly and clearly conferred upon them by charter or statute*" (p. 3).

Salt Lake City v. Board of Education of Salt Lake City,
52 Utah 540, 175 P. 654 (1918)
(Decided by the Supreme Court of Utah)

[This action was brought by a city to enjoin a board of education from proceeding further in the construction of a school building. It was contended that, because the building did not meet the requirements of certain building ordinances, the district could not erect it. The lower court ruled for the city and enjoined the district. On appeal the higher court reversed the lower court. It held that, in the absence of authority granted it by statute, the municipality had no control over the public schools.]

Frick, C. J. . . .

. . . .

The contention of appellants' counsel can perhaps be best stated in their own language as contained in their printed brief. They say:

"The question for decision is as to whether the plaintiff city, acting in pursuance of the police powers conferred upon it by general law, may impose building restrictions or regulations upon the defendant board of education in the erection of school buildings. . . .

. . . .

Respondent's counsel . . . contend that the power of police regulation is exclusively vested in the cities and that the boards of education possess no such power. . . .

. . . .

. . . the mere fact that no police powers are vested in the boards of education [is not] decisive of the question of whether the state has in fact surrendered to the cities plenary police power over our public school buildings.

. . . Counsel for respondent insist that such power is clearly conferred in the several subdivisions of [the statute]. . . . A careful reading and consideration, however, of the provisions contained in [these] subdivisions . . . in our judgment clearly shows that it was not the intention of the Legislature to make those provisions applicable to public school buildings. . . .

. . . .

In connection with the principles just quoted, another one must not be overlooked which is admirably expressed by the Court of Appeals of Kentucky in the case of Kentucky Institution for Education of Blind v. City of Louisville, 123 Ky. 767, 97 S.W. 402, 8 L. R. A. (N. S.) 533, in the following words:

"The principle is that the state, when creating municipal governments, does not cede to them any control of the state's property situated within them, nor over any property which the state has authorized another body or power to control."

. . . .

. . . In this connection it is perhaps but just and fair to counsel for respondent to state that they concede that the ordinances of respondent would have no application to what they call state buildings, although such buildings are located within the limits of the city. This concession is made in deference to the principle quoted from the Kentucky case to which we have referred. Under our Constitution and statutes, however, we can conceive of no distinction between what are denominated by counsel state buildings, such as the buildings of the State University, or the Capitol, and our school buildings. True, the control of the university is placed in the hands of a board of regents whose duties and powers are perhaps defined with more particularity and detail than are the powers of the boards of education. That may perhaps also be true respecting the State Capitol. Be that as it may, however, the public school buildings and their control are of as much concern to the state as are the other buildings. . . . If it be conceded, therefore, as it is and must be, that the state has not surrendered the control over its buildings to the cities, then it necessarily follows that the terms "public buildings" and "all buildings" used in the statute] . . . do not embrace all buildings within the cities. Moreover, if state buildings must be excluded, then public school buildings must likewise be excluded from those terms.

Guides for Class Discussion

1. What basic line of reasoning did the court follow in arriving at its decision?
2. Compare this case with *Community Fire District of St. Louis County* v. *Board of Education, infra.*

3. In your opinion is the law, as propounded by the court in this
   case, equitable and fair? Give reasons.

4. *"Cities and towns, unless authorized by statute, may not expend
   municipal funds for the construction of school buildings"* (p. 3).

NELSON v. MAYOR ETC. OF TOWN OF HOMER,
48 La. Ann. 258, 19 So. 271 (1896)
(Decided by the Supreme Court of Louisiana)

[When the Town of Homer attempted to appropriate funds for
the support and maintenance of a school, its actions were questioned
in court. In arriving at its decision, the court ruled that the municipality, without express permission so to do, may not spend its
funds for educational purposes.]

McENERY, J.

The plaintiffs, who are taxpayers in the town of Homer, bring this suit
to annul certain ordinances of the corporation establishing a high school,
and the ordinances assessing and appropriating five mills of the taxes of
1895 for the support and maintenance of the school. The reason for the
nullity of the ordinance is that the corporation of the town of Homer was
without power and authority to enact said ordinances, to levy said amount,
and appropriate the same for educational purposes. The defense is that
under article 209 of the constitution municipal corporations have the power
and authority to levy and collect taxes to the amount of 10 mills for
municipal purposes, and that an assessment for educational purposes is a
municipal regulation. It is further alleged that the corporation, in accordance with Act. No. 110 of 1880, amended its charter, and incorporated
this power in it. Under the general welfare clause of the charter, as originally granted, the district judge rendered a judgment in favor of defendants, maintaining the legality of the ordinances and the assessment and
appropriation of the tax. The plaintiffs appealed.

. . . Corporations are the creatures of legislative will, and can do no
act not authorized by their charters, unless it is by implication necessary
to carry out conferred powers. In the original charter there was no grant
of any right to the corporation of Homer to erect a school building and

maintain a high school. It cannot, by its own act, usurp powers not granted. There was no authority under the act for the corporation to so amend its charter as to authorize the levying of a tax for the maintaining of a high school, or for any other educational purpose. . . . A high school is not essential to municipal government. A system of education is not a part of municipal regulation, and the power of the corporation to establish a public school cannot be inferred from any power necessary for municipal existence. The judgment appealed from is annulled, avoided, and reversed, and it is now ordered that there be judgment for plaintiffs decreeing the nullity of the ordinances mentioned in the petition, and on which the taxing power and assessment is exercised for the levying of the five-mill tax complained of.

Guides for Class Discussion

1. On what basis did the court arrive at its decision?
2. Was the court's reasoning sound?
3. What are the educational implications of this case?

5. *"Municipal officers have no inherent authority to control or manage school property"* (p. 3).

State v. Zeidler,
268 Wis. 34, 66 N.W. (2d) 652 (1954)
(Decided by the Supreme Court of Wisconsin)

[In Milwaukee, Wisconsin, the Board of School Directors, an independent public body, was, by statute, charged with the function of purchasing sites and erecting school buildings. "The schoolhouses and the sites on which they are situated . . . [were] the property of the city," and deeds were made to the city. In 1946 the school district purchased a piece of property to be used as a site for a new building. In 1954, the board not having erected the building, the Common Council of the City of Milwaukee declared the property was no longer needed for public purposes and ordered the proper city officers to sell and convey the property. When the

Mayor and City Clerk refused to execute and sign the deed, on the ground the school directors and not the city council had control of the property and must consent to its conveyance, an action in mandamus was brought to compel them to do so. The trial court issued the writ of mandamus, and the defendants appealed.]

STEINLE, JUSTICE.

. . . .

Under the statutes the Board alone is vested with authority to acquire real estate for school purposes. The Common Council has been granted no power in such respect. However, when property is acquired for such purpose, the title is not taken in the name of the Board, but in that of the city. When acquired, the Board utilizes, manages, and controls the property. Jurisdiction to function in such regard has not been granted to the Common Council. . . .

. . . .

The respondents contend that the signing and delivery of the deed by the Mayor and City Clerk constitute ministerial action, the performance of which they may not refuse. It is further contended that it was not within the province of these city officers to "pass upon" the validity of the Common Council resolution. . . .

. . . .

It is especially noted that in his official capacity the Mayor is charged with the responsibility of "taking care that the laws of the state are duly observed and enforced." Were he to knowingly fail in such regard, his conduct might well be construed as nonfeasance in office.

As hereinbefore declared, the Common Council of the city of Milwaukee is not empowered by law to validly direct the conveyance of real estate in control of the Board of School Directors without that body's consent. Were the Mayor to sign the deed, he too would participate in the illegal action of the Common Council and violate the law, the observance of which he is specifically charged to "take care of." . . . It is clear that when the Common Council of the city of Milwaukee by resolution acts legally and within the four corners of its authority in directing a conveyance of property by the Mayor—whether the Mayor signs the resolution, or fails to return it in five days thereby effectuating its passage, or whether it is passed over his veto—then the Mayor thereafter is not in a position to exercise further discretion and decline to sign or deliver the deed. We note that in all of the cases which have come to our attention wherein a Mayor has been compelled by *mandamus* to perform a duty in nature of a ministerial act, the compulsion is based upon mandate of *valid* authority to direct such act. . . .

It seems to us that when it appears that an ordinance or resolution is *invalid*, a Mayor charged with the responsibility of "taking care" that the laws of the state are duly observed and enforced, and that the officers of the city properly discharge their duties, is not to be compelled by *mandamus* to execute a contract provided by an *invalid* ordinance or resolution. Consequently, we conclude that the remedy of *mandamus* does not lie to compel the Mayor of the city of Milwaukee to sign and deliver the deed in question. . . .

Guides for Class Discussion

1. Do you agree with the court in this case? Give reasons.
2. Would a statute authorizing the city council to take the action it did be held constitutional? Why or why not?

6. ". . . *education is a state and not a local affair*" (p. 3).

STATE EX REL. CLARK v. HAWORTH,
122 Ind. 462, 23 N.E. 946 (1890)
(Decided by the Supreme Court of Indiana)

[This was an action against a school trustee to compel him to obey a uniform text book law. He based his refusal to comply with the statute on the ground that it was unconstitutional because it was in violation of the right of local self-government. The lower court held in his favor, but, on appeal, the lower court was reversed, and the act was declared constitutional.]

ELLIOTT, J. . . .

The act assailed does not impinge in the slightest degree upon the right of local self-government. The right of local self-government is an inherent, and not a derivative, one. Individualized, it is the right which a man possesses in virtue of his character as a free man. It is not bestowed by legislatures, nor derived from statutes. But the courts which have carried to its utmost extent the doctrine of local self-government have never so much as intimated that it exists as to a matter over which the constitution has given the law-making power supreme control; nor have they gone beyond the line which separates matters of purely local concern from those of state control. Essentially and intrinsically, *the schools* in which are educated and trained the children who are to become the rulers of the commonwealth *are matters of state, and not of local jurisdiction.* In such matters the state is a unit, and the legislature the source of power. The authority over schools and school affairs is not necessarily a distributive one, to be exercised by local instrumentalities; but, on the contrary, it is a central power, residing in the legislature of the state. It is for the law-making power to determine whether the authority shall be exercised by a state board of education, or distributed to county, township, or city organizations throughout the state. With that determination the judiciary can no more rightfully interfere than can the legislature with a decree or judgment pronounced by a judicial tribunal. The decision is as conclusive and inviolable in the one case as in the other; and an interference with the legislative judgment would be a breach of the constitution which no principle would justify, nor any precedent excuse. [Emphasis supplied.]

Guides for Class Discussion

1. Do you think the courts, today, would accept this decision? Give reasons.
2. What is meant by the "right of local self-government"?
3. Which branch of state government has the authority to determine how the public school system will be organized?
4. What is the real significance of this case?

7. "*A number of courts have held that school property is state property, subject to the exercise of the police power of the state residing in its local school boards; and the municipal authorities may not, therefore, require local school boards to obey their building ordinances or codes*" (p. 3).

City of Bloomfield v. Davis County Community School District,
119 N.W. (2d) 909 (Iowa) (1963)
(Decided by the Supreme Court of Iowa)

[The facts of the case will be found in the material quoted.]

Garfield, Chief Justice.

This is an action in equity by the City of Bloomfield to enjoin defendants, Davis County Community School District, and its contractor, Boatman, from installing in a restricted residence district in plaintiff city a bulk storage tank for gasoline and a pump to supply its school buses therewith. ... By cross-petition defendants sought to enjoin the city from interfering with their construction of the "facility" and, if a permit therefor is necessary, to compel its issuance by mandamus. Following trial to the court there was a decree for plaintiff from which defendants appeal.

On September 19, 1933, the council of plaintiff city passed ordinance 84 designating and establishing a restricted residence district in the city. Section 2 of the ordinance provides: "That no buildings or other structures, except residences, school houses, churches, and other similar structures shall hereafter be erected, reconstructed, altered, repaired or occupied within said district without first securing from the city council permit therefor . . . ."

. . . .

The only contention of defendants we find it necessary to consider is that ordinance 84 should not be held applicable to them to prevent installation on this school-owned site of this gasoline facility for servicing its school buses because the school district is an arm of the state and proposes to use its property for a governmental purpose.

The ordinance was obviously enacted under the authority of what are now sections 415.1-3, Codes 1958, 1962, I. C. A. and is an exercise of the police power delegated to the city. . . .

The law seems quite well settled that a municipal zoning ordinance is not applicable to the state or any of its agencies in the use of its property for a governmental purpose unless the legislature has clearly manifested a contrary intent. . . .

. . . .

The underlying logic of some . . . authorities is, in substance, that the legislature could not have intended, in the absence of clear expression to the contrary, to give municipalities authority to thwart the state, or any of its agencies in performing a duty imposed upon it by statute.

There can be no doubt the school district is an arm or agency of the state and that the maintenance of public schools, including providing transportation to the pupils entitled to it as required by statute is a governmental function. . . .

. . . .

We think furnishing economical transportation to pupils entitled to it is as much a school matter, over which the district has exclusive jurisdiction, as maintenance of the school buildings or location of the high school football field. (Plaintiff concedes a football stadium is generally held to come within the meaning of a schoolhouse. See also Livingston v. Davis, 243 Iowa 21, 27, 50 N.W. 2d 592, 27 A. L. R. 2d 1237.)

The evidence is undisputed it is economical for the school district to own its buses. It can save eight to ten cents a gallon from buying gasoline for them in bulk and putting it in the buses itself. Bloomfield is maintenance headquarters for the buses the district owns. Many of them have been parked over night for a year or more on the tract where it is proposed to locate this tank and pump. As stated, the district owns the ground. It is most convenient to the school and can be supervised with the same personnel. The school board carefully considered the matter of installing the facility on this site. The state department of public instruction recommended the action the board took. The state fire marshall approved the plans prepared by the architect. No abuse of discretion on the part of anyone is claimed or shown.

Guides for Class Discussion

1. Compare the decision in this case with the one in *State* v. *Zeidler, supra.*
2. Compare the decision in this case with the one in *Community Fire Protection District St. Louis County* v. *Board of Education, infra.*
3. Do you think that this represents "good law"? Give reasons.
4. Under what conditions might a city require a school district to obey a municipal building ordinance?

8. ". . . in some cases the courts have held that the police power of the municipality takes precedence over the police power of the school board where safety and sanitation are concerned" (p. 3).

COMMUNITY FIRE PROTECTION DISTRICT OF ST. LOUIS COUNTY v. BOARD OF EDUCATION,
315 S.W. (2d) 873 (Mo.) (1958)
(Decided by the St. Louis Court of Appeals)

[The Missouri courts have consistently refused to follow the general rule that, in the absence of statute to the contrary, other municipalities may not exercise police power over school buildings

In this case it was held that the police power of a fire district—a municipal corporation—takes precedence over that of the school board.]

James D. Clemens, Special Judge.

· · · · · · · · · · · · · · · · · ·

The issue prescribed for us . . . is whether it is the Fire District or the School District to whom the Legislature has granted authority to determine minimum standards for fire protection in the construction of . . . [a] school building.

· · · · · · · · · · · · · · · · ·

This precise conflict of authority between a statutory fire district and a reorganized school district, has not yet been resolved by our courts. However, our courts have previously dealt with the principle of conflicting authority of public corporations. . . .

Thus, the case of Kansas City v. School District of Kansas City, 356 Mo. 364, 201 S.W. 2d 930, 932, involved the right of the city to exact fees from the school district for inspecting furnace boilers located in the schools. That right depended upon whether the State has reposed in the City or in the school district, "the power and the responsibility of taking measures to protect the people and the property of the people of Kansas City from conflagrations, explosions, smoke nuisances, noxious gases, and casualties which might be caused or occasioned by the facilities of the public school buildings." The Supreme Court analyzed the status of each party and ruled that the school district was not a municipal corporation with diversified powers, but a quasi-public corporation, "the arm and instrumentality of the state for one single and noble purpose, viz., to educate the children of the district." By contrast, the city was held to be possessed of police power, charged with maintaining the safety, health and general welfare of its populace—to be "a miniature state" within its authorized sphere of action. The court then ruled in favor of the city, saying:

"Since the State itself has taken no precautionary measures, and City has been vested with the regulatory and supervisory responsibilities of the exercise of the police power, and School District (having no police power) has not been expressly and specifically given full duty to attend to these responsibilities, we think the Legislature is content in the thought the measures to be taken are within the police power vested in City. . . ."

In the case of Smith v. Board of Education of City of St. Louis, 359 Mo. 264, 221 S.W. 2d 203, 205, the issue was the conflict of powers between the city and the board to regulate school restaurants. By ordinance the city provided for inspection and regulation of all restaurants as to food, utensils, waste disposal and the health and cleanliness of food handlers. By statute, all schools were empowered to operate restaurants, and the commissioner of school buildings in St. Louis was charged with the care of school buildings and was responsible for the sanitary condition thereof. The Supreme Court did not make a specific distinction between the city's possession of police power and the school board's lack thereof, but ruled the conflict in favor of the city as to regulation of the school restaurants because the Legislature had not "expressly and specifically" given the school board "full duty to attend to these responsibilities."

.   .   .   .

. . . Applying here the principles settled in those . . . cases, it is clear to us that the Legislature has subjugated the School District's general power to construct buildings to the Fire District's specific power to regulate the construction of buildings in the furtherance of fire prevention. This is so because of the comparative status of the parties, the Fire District being a municipal corporation endowed with police powers in the field of fire prevention, and the School District being a quasi-public corporation without police power with only the limited power of public education. Inasmuch as the Fire District is exercising police power delegated to it by the State, the School District is just as subservient thereto as if the provisions of the Fire District's ordinances had been prescribed by the State itself. Also, we note that the language granting powers to the School District as to school buildings is directive and elastic, and it is certainly no mandate to erect school buildings in disregard of reasonable building regulations, which the Fire District has been empowered to ordain. So, this result must also prevail because the Legislature, by granting specific power to the Fire District to ordain fire prevention measures is deemed to have denied contrary power to the School District.

.   .   .   .

The respondent School District . . . relies heavily on the case of Salt Lake City v. Board of Education, 52 Utah 540, 175 P. 654. The issue there was quite similar to the case at bar and the city was denied the right to enforce its building restrictions upon the school board. Suffice to say that our Supreme Court has denounced the principle set forth in this Utah case, and said in Kansas City v. School District of Kansas City, supra [356 Mo. 364, 201 S.W. 2d 935]: "We are not disposed to here further analyze these opinions so ably reasoned and written; however, the tendency of decision in harmony with ours herein seems to us more likely to promote the public safety, health and welfare."

.   .   .   .

We conclude that as between these parties, the Legislature has granted to the Fire District the authority to determine the minimum standards for fire prevention and fire protection in the construction of the school building.

Guides for Class Discussion

1. What was the reasoning of the court?
2. Compare this decision with the one in *Salt Lake City* v. *Board of Education of Salt Lake City, supra.* Which represents the "better" law? Give reasons.

9. "*State legislatures may authorize school boards to permit the use of school property for any purpose not prohibited by the constitution, and in a number of states the courts have sustained statutes authorizing a wide use of school buildings*" (p. 3).

Nichols v. School Directors,
93 Ill. 61 (1879)
(Decided by the Supreme Court of Illinois)

[The facts at issue will be found in the quoted material which follows.]

Mr. Justice Sheldon delivered the opinion of the Court:

This was a bill for an injunction by complainant as a citizen, taxpayer and freeholder of the school district of which defendants were directors, to restrain them from allowing the school house of that district to be used by any society or organization for the purpose of a religious meeting house.

The grievance as set forth in the bill is, that the defendants have, as such directors, given permission to different church organizations to hold religious services in the school house, against the protest of complainant and other tax-payers of the district; that under this permission some of the church organizations purpose holding stated meetings in the school house; that by this means complainant is compelled to aid in furnishing a house of worship, and for religious meetings, contrary to the law of the land; that he is opposed to such use of the house by the societies, and that such meetings are about to be held in the same contrary to his wishes, wherefore he prays the injunction.

A demurrer was filed to the bill, which the circuit court sustained, and dissolved the temporary injunction which had been granted, and dismissed the bill. The complainant appealed to this court.

By statute, the supervision and control of school houses is vested in the school directors of the district, and "who may grant the temporary use of school houses, when not occupied by schools, for religious meetings and Sunday schools, for evening schools and for literary societies, and for such other meetings as the directors may deem proper." Rev. Stat. 1874, p. 958, § 39.

There is clearly sufficient warrant in the statute, if that be valid, for the action of the school directors.

But the statute is assailed as being unconstitutional.

The clauses of the constitution which are pointed out as being supposed to be violated by this statute are the following only:

"No person shall be required to attend or support any ministry or place of worship against his consent, nor shall any preference be given by law to any religious denomination or mode of worship." Art. 2, #3.

Art. 8, #3, forbidding, among other public bodies, the General Assembly or any school district from ever making any appropriation or paying from any public fund whatever anything in aid of any church or sectarian purpose, etc.; and forbidding the State or any public corporation from making any grant or donation of land, money or other personal property to any church or for any sectarian purpose.

. . . .

Religion and religious worship are not so placed under the ban of the constitution that they may not be allowed to become the recipient of any incidental benefit whatsoever from the public bodies or authorities of the State. That instrument itself contains a provision authorizing the legislature to exempt property used for religious purposes from taxation and thereby, the same as is complained of here, there might be indirectly imposed upon the tax-payer the burden of increased taxation, and in that manner the indirect supporting of places of worship. In the respect of the possibility of enhanced taxation therefrom, this provision of the constitution itself is even more obnoxious to objection than this permission given by the school directors to hold religious meetings in the school house. There is no pretence that it is in any way in interference with the occupation of the building for school purposes.

We think the court rightly sustained the demurrer and dismissed the bill, as making no case for an injunction.

The decree will be affirmed.

Decree affirmed

Guides for Class Discussion

1. Do you think the court today would hold as did the court in this case? Give reasons.

2. Are you in agreement with this decision? Give reasons.

10. *"Some [courts] have permitted the use of schoolhouses for religious meetings of one kind or another provided there was no interference with the regular work of the school"* (pp. 3-4).

Southside Estates Baptist Church v. Board of Trustees,
115 So. (2d) 697 (Fla.) (1959)
(Decided by the Supreme Court of Florida)

[The facts of this case will be found in the material quoted.]

Thornal, Justice.

Appellants, who were plaintiffs below, seek reversal of a final decree dismissing their bill of complaint by which they sought an injunction against the temporary use of a public school building for religious meetings.

We must determine whether a Florida public school can be used temporarily as a place of worship during non-school hours.

The appellee, Board of Trustees, permitted several churches to use various school buildings during Sunday non-school hours. The authorization was for the temporary use of the buildings pending completion of construction of church buildings. The record does not show whether the religious groups paid rent nor does it reflect any direct expense to the school trustees. It is clear that the use of the buildings did not interfere with the operation of the school system. The public school system was not in any fashion employed as a medium for the promotion of any religion. The appellants as plaintiffs, sought to enjoin the use of the school buildings for religious purposes. The Chancellor granted a motion to dismiss the amended complaint with prejudice. Reversal of this decree is now sought.

. . . .

While admittedly, there are some differences of view regarding the matter of religious meetings in school houses during non-school periods, we think that logic, as well as our traditional attitudes toward the importance of religious worship, justifies our alignment with those courts which permit such use. . . .

We ourselves have heretofore taken the position that an incidental benefit to a religious group resulting from an appropriate use of public property is not violative of Section 6, of the Declaration of Rights of the Florida Constitution. . . .

In the instant case the Legislature has endowed the trustees of the school district with a reasonable discretion to permit the use of school property during non-school hours "for any legal assembly." We think that the religious observances described in the complaint are well within the category of "legal assembly." . . .

We, therefore, hold that a Board of Trustees of a Florida School District has the power to exercise a reasonable discretion to permit the use of school buildings during non-school hours for any legal assembly which includes religious meetings, subject, of course, to judicial review should such discretion be abused to the point that it could be construed as a contribution of public funds in aid of a particular religious group or as the promotion or establishment of a particular religion.

We think that what we have said disposes also of the contention that the conduct of the appellee trustees is violative of the First Amendment to the Constitution of the United States, which provides in part that, "Congress shall make no law respecting an establishment of religion, or prohibiting the free exercise thereof; . . ." as the same has been made applicable to the states under the due process provision of the Fourteenth Amendment. We find nothing in the conduct of the appellee trustees to suggest the involvement of public funds or property in the establishment of a religion or in preferring one religious faith over another. We agree with those courts which have observed that in the ultimate the American people are basically religious. Their spiritual or theological views might differ, but by and large, they are committed to the ideal that there should be a place for any and all religions in the scheme of our community and social life.

The Chancellor ruled correctly in dismissing the amended complaint with prejudice. His decree is, therefore, affirmed.

Guides for Class Discussion

1. Compare this case with *Spencer v. Joint School District, infra.*

2. Are you in agreement with the court's thinking in this case? Give reasons.

3. What are some of the implications which this case has for school administration?

11. *"Some [courts] . . . have held that no kind of religious exercises could be held in a schoolhouse unless specifically authorized by statute" (pp. 3-4).*

SPENCER V. JOINT SCHOOL DISTRICT,
15 Kan. 259 (1875)
(Decided by the Supreme Court of Kansas)

[This was an action brought to restrain the defendant district from leasing its school building for other than school purposes. Primarily, the objection related to the use of the building for religious purposes. The district demurred, and the trial court sustained the demurrer. On appeal, this decision of the trial court was overthrown.]

BREWER, J.: . . . .

. . . .

. . . . the question as it comes before us, may fairly be thus stated: May the majority of the taxpayers and electors in a school-district, for other than school purposes use or permit the use of the school-house built with funds raised by taxation? The question is one which in view of the times, and the attacks made in so many places, and from so many directions, upon our public-school system, justifies, as it has received at our hands, most serious consideration. We are fully aware of the fact, that all over the state the school-house is, by general consent, or at least without active opposition, used for a variety of purposes other than the holding of public schools. Sabbath schools of separate religious denominations, church assemblies, sometimes political meetings, social gatherings, etc., are held there. Now none of these can be strictly considered among the purposes for which a public building can be erected, or taxation employed. But it often happens, particularly in our newer settlements, that there is no other public building than the school-house—no place so convenient as that. The use for these purposes works little damage. It is used by the inhabitants of the district whose money has built it, and used for their profit or pleasure. Shall it be said that this is illegal? . . . The public school-house cannot be used for any private purposes. The argument is a short one. Taxation is invoked to raise funds to erect the building; but taxation is illegitimate to provide for any private purpose. Taxation will not lie to raise funds to build a place for a religious society, a political society, or a social club. What cannot be done directly, cannot be done indirectly. As you may not levy taxes to build a church, no more may you levy taxes to build a school-house and then lease it for a church.

Nor is it an answer to say that its use for school purposes is not interfered with, and that the use for the other purposes works little, perhaps no immediately-perceptible injury to the building, and results in the receipt of immediate pecuniary benefit. . . . The use of a public school-house for a single religious or political gathering, is, legally, as unauthorized as its constant use therefor. True, a court of equity would not interfere by injunction after a single use, and where there was no likelihood of a repetition of the wrong, for it is only apprehended wrongs that equity will enjoin. Here the unauthorized use is charged as a frequent fact, and one likely to occur hereafter. It is unnecessary to pursue this discussion further, for it would be simply traveling over a road already well worn and dusty. . . .

The judgment of the district court will be reversed, and the case remanded for further proceedings in accordance with the views herein expressed.

Guides for Class Discussion

1. Trace the line of reasoning followed by the court.
2. Compare this decision with the one rendered by the court in *Southside Estates Baptist Church* v. *Board of Trustees, supra.*

12. *"The courts . . . have approved the leasing of school property for the drilling of oil and gas, although the opposite has also been held"* (p. 4).

WILLIAMS v. McKENZIE,
203 Ky. 376, 262 S.W. 598 (1924)
(Decided by the Court of Appeals of Kentucky)

[In Kentucky, where the statute gave a county board of education the authority to hold and dispose of school property for the use and benefit of the district, its authority to execute a lease for the drilling of oil on school lands was questioned. The lower court held that the board did not have the authority in question and, on appeal, the higher court reversed its decision.]

TURNER, C. . . .

. . . .

But it is earnestly argued that, the county board of education being the creature of the statute for a specific purpose, its only duty and authority lies in the administration of educational affairs; that it is not authorized to go into the field of speculation and engage in hazardous industrial affairs, even though such activities might result profitably, and for that reason alone the oil lease given by the school board was invalid and properly cancelled. . . .

In support of this argument reliance is had upon the case of Herald v. Board of Education, 65 W. Va. 765, 65 S.E. 102, 31 L. R. A. (N. S.) 588. In that case it was held by a majority of the Supreme Court of West Virginia that a school board under the statutes of that state had no power to lease a schoolhouse lot for oil and gas purposes, even though the school authorities had the absolute fee-simple title thereto.

. . . .

Oil and gas are fugitive minerals; they are connected by underground streams or crevices by which they may be drained from one property onto another, and there brought to the surface. There can be no sound or practical reason given that will deprive school authorities who own property under which there are valuable minerals from entering into contracts for its development, and particularly would this seem to be true when the character of the mineral is such that adjoining landowners may profit at the expense of the school property by the failure of the school authorities to enter such contracts. . . . There was, however, in the West Virginia case referred to, a strong dissenting opinion, in which we fully concur. That opinion, after discussing the West Virginia statute, said:

"I think the statute not only expressly but impliedly gives this board ample power to lease this property. This ought especially to be so where the product, as in this case, is oil and gas, fugitive in nature and which will be drained and carried away by operations on adjoining lands."

We are of the opinion, therefore, that under the statute in existence at the time the title was conveyed to the school authorities the board of education had the right to execute the lease in question, and, having the right to do so, it was its duty to do so to prevent the valuable mineral product on the school property from being appropriated by others.

Guides for Class Discussion

1. Do you agree with the court, or do you prefer the decision of the West Virginia court in the case cited? Give reasons.

2. Do you agree with the court when it says the board not only
   had the authority or right to take the action it did, but it had
   the duty of so doing? Give reasons.

13. "*As a rule, school boards are vested with specific statutory
authority to acquire school sites, but even in the absence of such
authority the courts hold that authority to build school buildings
carries with it, by necessary implication, authority to purchase
school sites*" (p. 4).

STATE v. BOARD OF EDUCATION,
71 W. Va. 52, 76 S.E. 127 (1912)
(Decided by the Supreme Court of Appeals of West Virginia)

[Pertinent facts will be found in the following quotation.]

BRANNON, P.

The school district of Clarksburg by vote authorized the incurrence
of a debt and the issue of bonds for its payment for the purpose of building
one high school and two graded schools. The bonds were sold, and their
proceeds are in the treasury. The board of education refused to build
the high school and one graded school out of such money, on the ground
that to do so would call for the purchase of ground for their erection,
and the board doubted its power to use any of the money coming from
said bonds in acquiring such ground. Howard Post asks of this court a
mandamus to compel the board to build said high school and graded
school, and to acquire sites for them, and use such bond money in
doing so.

Act 1908, c. 27, § 13 (Code Supp. 1909, c. 45, § 1571), says that the
board of education of every district shall provide by purchase or condemnation "suitable schoolhouses and grounds." Act 1911, c. 70, allows the board
to "borrow money and issue bonds for the purpose of building, completing
enlarging, repairing or furnishing schoolhouses." . . . When the statute says
that the money may be used to build houses, it means that it may be used
to acquire land for schoolhouses. Necessarily so. It is a necessary implication, if the words do not per se mean land, as here used. Commanded to
build schoolhouses, it is an incidental power because indispensable to

attain the end. You cannot build a schoolhouse without land on which to build it.

In view of the law above stated, and in view of the purpose which must have been in the minds of the legislators who enacted the bond section, we hold that the word "schoolhouses" includes land for schoolhouses. We hold that the section in giving the board of education power to apply the money arising from the bonds "for the purpose of building, completing, enlarging, repairing or furnishing schoolhouses" meant to give the board power to acquire land on which to build schoolhouses. We can see that the Legislature never designed to limit the use of the money to work and material of construction, and deny its use in acquiring the ground indispensable and preliminary to work of construction. This ground is the first thing requisite in carrying out the purpose of the statute —a sine qua non. Otherwise the statute might be abortive. . . . Think of the intent and purpose, as we must do when construing a statute. Think of the evil to be remedied, the object to be accomplished, and give such a statute such a construction as will effectuate its purpose. We think the other construction would be cramped and technical, forgetful of the spirit, sticking to the mere letter.

Guides for Class Discussion

1. Compare this case with *Reiger* v. *Board of Education, infra.*
2. Do you agree with the court's decision? Give reasons.

4. "*Authority to purchase school sites carries with it by implication authority to purchase the necessary playgrounds and athletic fields, and these do not have to be adjacent to the lot on which the schoolhouse is situated*" (p. 4).

REIGER V. BOARD OF EDUCATION,
287 Ill. 590, 122 N.E. 838 (1919)
(Decided by the Supreme Court of Illinois)

[The board of education of Springfield, Illinois, purchased certain real estate, which was a block and a half from the nearest schoolhouse and was not acquired as a schoolhouse site. When it began to erect improvements necessary to the conversion of the property into recreational grounds and athletic fields, this action was brought to restrain the board from completing the payment for the property. Plaintiffs did not deny that playgrounds and athletic fields were "necessary grounds" within the meaning of a statute authorizing the board " 'to buy or lease sites for schoolhouses with the necessary grounds' etc.," but they contended that such power could only be exercised "in connection with the buying or leasing of 'sites for schoolhouses' and that the 'necessary grounds' must be connected with and a part of the school site and actually contiguous to the same." The lower court ruled in favor of the board, and the court, here, upheld its decision.]

DUNCAN, C. J. . . .

. . . .

. . . We cannot agree that a reasonable construction of clause 5 of section 127 requires that necessary school grounds shall be purchased in connection with the purchase of a school site or that such necessary grounds must be contiguous to a schoolhouse site already purchased. It is very easy to conceive of a situation where it would not be possible to acquire additional necessary school grounds contiguous to a site already purchased by reason of the surrounding property being held by other property owners and not obtainable at a reasonable figure. Said clause 5 empowers the board to buy or lease sites for schoolhouses, with the necessary school grounds, and it contains no requirement that the necessary school grounds must all be contiguous to the schoolhouse site. We are therefore not authorized to give it such an interpretation, particularly in cases where it might be shown that it is not possible to purchase other suitable grounds contiguous to one or more sites already purchased. The statute necessarily gives a board of education large discretion in the selection of school grounds, and where there are a number of schools in a school district it is clearly evident that grounds not connected with any of the school sites might be used as playgrounds for the pupils of a number of schools, and would serve the necessity of such schools equally as well, or better, than if contiguous to any one site and at very much less cost.

Guides for Class Discussion

1. Do you think the court would have held as it did had the facts indicated that the property in question was to be used for the benefit of the pupils enrolled in a single school?

2. Would the court have held as it did if there had been no statute authorizing a school board to obtain sites and construct buildings? Give reasons for your answer.

15. *"School boards are vested with authority to accept donations of property to be used for school purposes, but when school boards accept such a donation they will be required to administer it perpetually according to the terms of the donor"* (p. 4).

MAXCY v. CITY OF OSHKOSH,
144 Wis. 238, 128 N.W. 899 (1910)
(Decided by the Supreme Court of Wisconsin)

[A grant was made to the City of Oshkosh, Wisconsin, for the purpose of constructing a manual training school, contingent upon the city raising and providing an additional $50,000. When the common council passed a resolution accepting the gift and providing for the issuance and sale of bonds in the amount of $50,000 to meet its obligation, an action was brought to restrain the city from using the proceeds of the bond sale for this purpose. The court, here, commented at some length on the responsibility of the municipality in case it accepted the donation.]

BARNES, J. . . .

. . . .

It is further urged that, a trust in perpetuity being created by the will, the property devoted to the charitable use must always be applied to such use, and that it is beyond the power of the city of Oshkosh to raise money to build a manual training school which must be forever maintained as such. This contention raises one of the most difficult questions in the case. The general rule of law is that money or property devoted to a charitable use where a trust is created must, if the gift is accepted, be irrevocably devoted to such use, and that in case of attempted diversion a court of equity will intervene, and if necessary name a new trustee to carry out the objects and purposes of the trust. In other words, the term "perpetuity" as applied to charitable trusts has retained its original significance, in that it means an inalienable and indestructible interest. Generally speaking, any limitation that suspends the power of alienation beyond the period allowed by law creates a perpetuity; but we are not dealing with a perpetuity of this kind.

However, this general language in reference to the meaning of a perpetuity as applied to a charitable trust cannot be taken too literally. . . . No one is wise enough to say what social changes the mutations of time may bring about or what political or other cataclysms the future may witness. . . . We must presume that the city of Oshkosh will live and thrive, and that the system of free district schools guaranteed by the Constitution will be maintained therein. We must also presume that instruction in the languages, in mathematics, and in other subjects now taught therein will be continued. The tendency of the times is to enlarge the school curriculum instead of reducing it. It is fair to assume that any branch of knowledge that has been firmly ingrafted in our system of education has come to stay, and there is nothing in the record to indicate that manual training in our public schools has not come to stay. Of course laws may be passed in the future that will prohibit the teaching of manual training; but the testatrix knew of this possibility when she made her gift and was willing to take the chances. . . . Mrs. Beach knew when she made her will that the school building she was providing for might not, and in fact could not, endure for all time. Fire might destroy it, and, if it did not, time would disintegrate it and render it unfit for use. Conditions might demand that a newer, more commodious and more modern building should be constructed at some time in the future, even before the building provided for had ceased to be serviceable. All the city will have to do to comply with the terms of the will will be to place such a memorial tablet in the new building as was placed in the old, and carry on a system of instruction therein in harmony with the expressed wish of the testatrix. . . . The undertaking of the city of Oshkosh to perpetually maintain this school is not contrary to the letter of the law. . . . When the city of Oshkosh accepted its charter, it subjected itself to the burdens imposed by the Constitution. One of those burdens was the maintenance of a system of district schools in which education should be free to all pupils of school age, so long as the city existed and so long as the provision of the Constitution survived; or, in other words, in perpetuity. . . .

Guides for Class Discussion

1. Do you think the fact that the municipality had been authorized to maintain schools by virtue of its charter affected the thinking of the court? If so, how?

2. Had the grant been made to a school district instead of a city, do you think the court would have ruled as it did? Give reasons.

16. "*School boards, under statutory authority, may take private property by the exercise of the right of eminent domain; and, when they do so, the courts will permit them a wide exercise of discretion both with respect to the need of taking the property and the amount to be taken*" (p. 4).

STATE V. STOJACK,
53 Wash. (2d) 55, 330 P. (2d) 567 (1958)
(Decided by the Supreme Court of Washington)

[A school district, to condemn land contiguous to a 73-acre site which it already owned, brought a condemnation action. The trial court refused to enter a decree of public use and necessity which would have permitted the district to condemn the property. In an original proceeding for a writ of certiorari for a review of the trial court's order, the higher court approved the district's efforts at condemnation.]

WEAVER, Justice.

.   .   .   .

A municipal corporation does not have an inherent power of eminent domain. It may exercise such power only when it is expressly authorized to do so by the state legislature. . . .

Of course, by statute, the state may delegate the power of eminent domain to one of its political subdivisions, but such statutes are strictly construed. . . .

.   .   .   .

The trial court erred when it concluded that the school district was not entitled to condemn defendant's property because the district already owned 73 acres of land.

.   .   .   .

Public education is a public use for which private property may b appropriated under the power of eminent domain. If an attempt is made t take more property than is reasonably necessary to accomplish the purpos then the taking of excess property is no longer a public use, and a certifi cate of public use and necessity must be denied.

In the selection of a site, the board of directors had the authority t determine the area of land reasonably necessary to accommodate suitabl buildings, play grounds . . ., student activity areas, and related facilities t establish an adequate senior high school in accordance with present da educational requirements. . . .

Generally, the action of a public agency or a municipal corporatio having the right of eminent domain in selecting land for a public use wi not be controlled by the courts, except for a manifest abuse of discretio violation of law, fraud, improper motives, or collusion. This court ha frequently held that, in eminent domain proceedings, selection of land t be condemned by the proper public agency is conclusive in the absence bad faith, or arbitrary, capricious, or fraudulent action.

Guides for Class Discussion

1. What, in your mind, is the real significance of this decision?
2. As a result of this decision, what limitations, if any, are place on the board's authority to take property by eminent domain

17. *"When property is taken by the right of eminent domain, t courts will require the board to pay the owner a fair market pri for the property when put to its most profitable use; the owner land taken by eminent domain must be compensated for whatev loss he suffers"* (p. 4).

SARGENT v. TOWN OF MERRIMAC,
196 Mass. 171, 81 N.E. 970 (1907)
(Decided by the Supreme Judicial Court of Massachusetts, Essex

[This was an action against the Town of Merrimac for co pensation for land taken by defendant for a water supply. T main question before the court was the value of the land in questi for the special purpose to which it could be put. In its decision, the court commented on the need for properly compensating the owner for the property taken.]

LORING, J. This is a petition to obtain compensation for the taking of a lot of land by the defendant town for a water supply. The lot in question contained good water adapted in quantity and quality for the supply of the town. There was evidence that the water in question was the only ground water in the neighborhood fit for the needs of the defendant town, but that there was a lake or pond of water which would be fit in respect of quantity and quality if treated by filtration. The case is here on exceptions taken by the petitioner.

. . . .

What the petitioner was entitled to receive was the fair market value of the land of her testator as it was at the time of the taking. Market value in this connection does not mean the same thing that market value means when the market value of flour or other things dealt in daily in the market is spoken of. A lot of land cannot have a market value in that sense of the word. What is meant by the market value of land is the value of the land in the market; that is to say, for the purposes of sale.

The market value to which the petitioner was entitled was made up of the value of the land apart from its special adaptability for water supply purposes, plus such sum as a purchaser would have added to that value because of the chance that the land in question might be some day used as a water supply. Moulton v. Newburyport Water Co., 137 Mass. 163.

Guides for Class Discussion

1. What did the court hold with respect to the determination of the value of property taken? Do you agree?

2. Do you think the rule laid down by the court is applicable to a case where the property is taken by a quasi-municipal corporation such as a school district, rather than by a municipal corporation? Justify your answer.

18. *"When land is taken by eminent domain, the fee remains with the original owner, unless the statutes provide otherwise, and when the property is no longer used for school purposes it reverts to the original owner"* (p. 4).

MULLIGAN V. SCHOOL DISTRICT,
241 Pa. St. 204, 88 A. 362 (1913)
(Decided by the Supreme Court of Pennsylvania)

[This was an action to recover the money paid to a school district for property which the district had previously taken as the result of the exercise of the right of eminent domain. Some years after taking the property the district abandoned it for school purposes and sold it to one Morris for $1,000. The officials of the district executed a deed to Morris purportedly conferring a fee and "containing a convenant of general warranty." Later, the heirs of one Lazarus who had earlier purchased from the owners of the property their right, title, and interest in it, brought an action of ejectment against Morris, to recover the land. This resulted in a judgment in favor of Lazarus' heirs. Morris subsequently died and his heirs brought this action against the district to recover the $1,000 which Morris had paid for the property. The trial court ruled for plaintiff but its decision was overruled on appeal. At issue was the nature of the title which the district took following the exercise of the right of eminent domain.]

MOSCHZISKER, J. . . .

. . . .

The statement of claim shows that the plaintiff's action was expressly founded upon a breach of the covenant of general warranty contained in the deed to their decedent. School districts are creatures of the statute and only have such powers as are thereby given to them. They are "corporations of lower grade and less power than a city, have less the characteristics of private corporations and more of a mere agent of the state. They are territorial divisions for the purposes of the common school laws; and their officers have no power except by express statutory grant and necessary implication." Erie School District v. Fuess, 98 Pa. 600, 606. No act of assembly has been cited to us, and we know of none, which either expressly or impliedly grants or attempts to grant the right or confer the power upon a school district to convey in fee property acquired by it in

he exercise of the power of eminent domain, or in such a case to enter
nto a covenant of general warranty of title; and in law the plaintiff's
lecedent must have been aware of this when he accepted the deed and
paid the purchase money. Moreover, even though from all the facts in the
case the inference might be deduced that a conveyance to the purchaser
aad been authorized by action of the school board, the plaintiffs were
unable to produce the minutes and there were no proofs from which it
could justifiably be found that the officials who signed the deed had been
ormally authorized to bind the district by a covenant of general warranty.
The conclusion we are forced to is hard upon the estate of the plaintiff's
lecedent, but it is clear beyond doubt that the referee and the learned
court below erred when they permitted a recovery in this case.

Guides for Class Discussion

1. While the court ruled that the board did not have the right
   to "convey in fee property acquired by it in the exercise of the
   power of eminent domain," it ruled against plaintiffs. Why?
2. How do you think the court would have held if, by statute,
   the board had been authorized to take title in fee simple?
   Give reasons.

9. "*When property is conveyed to a school board and the deed
learly provides for the reversion of the property to the original
wner when no longer used for school purposes, the board does not
wn the property in fee simple, and it reverts to the original owner
r his heirs when no longer used for school purposes*" (pp. 4-5).

CONSOLIDATED SCHOOL DISTRICT v. WALTER,
243 Minn. 159, 66 N.W. (2d) 881 (1954)
(Decided by the Supreme Court of Minnesota)

[This was an action to enjoin defendants from entering upon cer-
ain real estate which, in 1863, had been conveyed to a school
istrict for use as a site for a schoolhouse. The original conveyance
rovided that whenever the tract of land ceased to be used as the
te for a schoolhouse it should revert to the owner, " 'his wife,

their heirs and assigns.' " Subsequently the executor of the estat of the original owner conveyed the entire tract of land to on Hartley Mars. By other conveyances, the land eventually came int the hands of defendant. None of the deeds to the tract of land mad reference to the part conveyed to the district in 1863. Defendan acting upon the assumption that the district ceased to make use the property as a public school took possession of the propert Plaintiff district then brought this action to have the ownership the school site determined. The district court ruled in favor defendant and the plaintiff appealed. The higher court reversed th lower court, holding that a possibility of reverter was not alienabl and defendants, as a result, acquired no interest in the site. It rule that only the grantor and his heirs could recover the property whe it ceased to be used as a school site.]

DELL, Chief Justice.

. . . .

We choose to determine first what interests passed under the Ayres dee made in 1863. Clearly the intent was to create a charitable trust—the Ayr being the settlors; the school district, the trustee; and the inhabitants the district, the beneficiaries. . . .

. . . .

It appears to us that the intent of the grantor, as expressed in the dee and in light of the surrounding circumstances, was to convey the land the school district in fee for so long as it was needed for the purpose give It does not appear tenable to us that he merely intended to give the scho district a right of user in the land, retaining ownership in himself. The va majority of cases involving similar grants of land to school districts hav reached the same conclusion.

Whether the qualified fee involved here is a fee determinable by special limitation, or a fee subject to a condition subsequent, does n materially affect the result in this case. However, the failure to proper distinguish these two types of qualified fees has caused unnecessary co fusion and is worthy of brief comment. Theoretically, if the grantor inten to insure compliance with a condition by providing for forfeiture up breach, a fee upon condition subsequent arises; but if the intent is to gi the property as long as it is needed for a specified use and no longer, th a determinable fee is created. The practical distinction between the tv rests largely in their manner of termination. Under a condition subseque the grantor or his heirs must exercise his right of reentry upon breach the condition or the estate continues in the grantee. There is no su election by the grantor in a determinable fee. In the latter case, t property reverts back to the grantor or his heirs automatically without any action on his part upon the happening of the special limitation. It is often difficult to ascertain the intent of the grantor, and exhaustive study could, no doubt, uncover factually identical cases with opposite results. The deed in this case does not contain the common indicia for creating a fee subject to a condition subsequent nor does it provide for the right of reentry, although this provision has been held not to be essential. On the other hand the deed does provide that "whenever said School House ceases to be used . . ." the estate will "determine" and "revert." This language, although not technically precise, more closely resembles that used in a conveyance of a determinable fee. Cases with similar facts support this construction. . . .

. . . .

Despite vigorous criticism of the rule, the authorities generally concede that possibilities of reverter were not alienable at common law, and this was apparently assumed to be the law in Minnesota prior to 1937. The reason commonly given for the common-law rule was that possibilities of reverter were too nebulous to be conveyed unless coupled with a reversionary interest. . . .

Guides for Class Discussion

1. Compare this decision with the one in *Washington City Board of Education* v. *Edgerton, infra.*
2. Distinguish between this decision and the one in *Scott County Board of Education* v. *Pepper, infra.*
3. Differentiate between a fee determinable by a special limitation and a fee subject to a condition subsequent.
4. Do you think that the court, in distinguishing between these two types of qualified fees, was guilty of recognizing a "distinction" without a "difference"? Give reasons.

20. ". . . *the courts do not look with favor on deeds that provide for reverter of school property, and such deeds will be construed strictly against the grantor*" (p. 5).

WASHINGTON CITY BOARD OF EDUCATION v. EDGERTON,
244 N.C. 576, 94 S.E. (2d) 661 (1956)
(Decided by the Supreme Court of North Carolina)

[This was an action by a board of education to determine title to a city lot which defendant agreed to purchase from the board. The lower court held the board had the right to convey the property free of any reversionary interest. The higher court upheld this decision. The facts of the case will be found in the material quoted.]

DEVIN, Justice.

In 1808 by an act of the General Assembly of North Carolina, Chapter LXXV, the trustees of the Washington Academy were created a corporate body, and as such acquired fee simple title to the land described in the pleadings, and erected thereon a building which was used thereafter by the trustees for conducting a school. In 1904 successor trustees of the Washington Academy conveyed this property by deed to the Board of School Trustees of the Town of Washington and their successors for a nominal consideration "upon condition that the same shall be held and possessed by the party of the second part only so long as the said property shall be used for school purposes."

Thereafter a 3-story brick school building was erected on the property and continuously used for school purposes until March, 1956, when the building was sold and removed, a new school building having been erected on another site, and the land was offered for sale at public auction in accord with the statute. The defendant Edgerton became the last and highest bidder in the amount of $77,800. It was stipulated that the plaintiff, the Washington City Board of Education, a body corporate, is one and the same as the Board of Trustees of the Washington City Administrative Unit and the Board of School Trustees of the Town of Washington, by virtue of pertinent statutes.

. . . .

After a careful study of all the facts and circumstances in this case in the light of previous decisions of this Court, we reach the conclusion that the language used in the habendum clause in the deed of 1904 was not intended to impose rigid restrictions upon the title or to create a condition subsequent, but that it was intended by the parties thereby to indicate the motive and purpose of the transfer of title. It expresses no power of termination or right of re-entry for condition broken.

"A clause in a deed will not be construed as a condition subsequent, unless it expresses in apt and appropriate language the intention of the parties to this effect . . . and a mere statement of the purpose for which the property is to be used is not sufficient to create such condition." Hall v. Quinn, 190 N.C. 326, 130 S.E. 18, 20; Oxford Orphanage v. Kittrell, 223 N.C. 427, 27 S.E. 2d 133.

. . . .

The law does not favor a construction of the language in a deed which will constitute a condition subsequent unless the intention of the parties to create such a restriction upon the title is clearly manifested. . . . And where the language in the deed merely expresses the motive and purpose which prompted the conveyance, without reservation of power of termination or right of re-entry for condition broken, an unqualified fee will pass.

Guides for Class Discussion

1. Compare this decision with the one rendered in *Scott County Board of Education* v. *Pepper, infra.*
2. On what basis did the court arrive at its decision?

21. "*Where property was deeded to school districts 'for school purposes only,' 'so long as the property shall be used for school purposes and no longer,' or 'to be used for school property in perpetuity,' courts have held that the property did not revert to the grantor when no longer used for school purposes*" (p. 5).

Scott County Board of Education v. Pepper,
311 S.W. (2d) 189 (Ky.) (1958)
(Decided by the Court of Appeals of Kentucky)

[This was an action brought by a board of education to quiet title to a tract of land that had been conveyed to it in 1915 " 'for the purpose of a common school house, and for no other purpose.' " The conveyance was made following the receipt of $225 paid by the board, and the deed was signed by the grantor whose heirs now claimed title to it as reversioners. There appeared to be no reason why the board should deny that it had ceased to use the land for the purpose of a common school, and it had attempted to sell the site for $3,000. The only question was whether the board's interest continued in the property after it ceased to use it or whether it reverted to the grantor's heirs.]

MILLIKEN, Judge.

．　．　．　．　．　．　．　．　．　．　．　．　．　．　．

The question is whether the Board obtained a fee simple title by the conveyance or some type of defeasible fee. The criteria applicable here are summarized in the Restatement of the Law of Property, Section 44, note m., pages 129-130:

"When a limitation merely states the purpose for which the land is conveyed, such limitation usually does not indicate an intent to create an estate in fee simple which is to expire automatically upon the cessation of use for the purpose named. Additional facts, however, can cause such an intent to be found. Among the facts sufficient to have this result are clauses in other parts of the same instrument, the relation between the consideration paid for the conveyance and the market value of the land in question, and the situation under which the conveyance was obtained.

"Illustrations:

"18. A, owning Blackacre in fee simple absolute, transfers Blackacre 'to B and his heirs to and for the use of the C Church and for no other purpose.' B has an estate in fee simple absolute and not an estate in fee simple determinable."

The quoted words from the deed to the Board are not the usual words of limitation such as "during," "as long as," "until," and the like which result in creating an estate upon limitation, automatically terminating at the time specified. . . . Nor are they the usual words of condition such as "on condition that," "provided that" or "on these express conditions," which technically require an ejectment or re-entry to cause the title to revert. . . . In fact, it is the general rule that conveyances of land for stated purposes, and for no other, do not create fees upon limitations or express provisions for reverter when such uses cease. . . .

This court has consistently held to the general rule in deeds of this nature and refused to create a right of reversion where none was expressly stated or inescapably implied.

Guides for Class Discussion

1. Do you agree with the reasoning of the court in this case? Give reasons.

2. What does this case add to your knowledge of the subject of "reversion"?

22. *"Before a court will declare a forfeiture, it must be very clear that school authorities intended to abandon the use of property for school purposes"* (p. 5).

HARRIS v. CONSOLIDATED SCHOOL DISTRICT,
328 S.W. (2d) 646 (Mo.) (1959)
(Decided by the Supreme Court of Missouri)

[This was an action to quiet title to property conveyed to a school district by a deed which contained a reverter clause. The main issue was whether a school district had abandoned the use of school property so as to make it possible for the title to revert to the heirs of the original grantor, or rather, to one holding a quit-claim deed from the heirs. The trial court ruled that, even though classes ceased to be taught in the school building located on the site in question, and some rooms in the building were used for the storage of miscellaneous materials, and one room was rented for use as a grocery store, the district had not abandoned the property. The higher court upheld the decision of the lower court, in an appeal by plaintiffs.]

EAGER, Judge.

. . . .

We have determined that the trial court was correct in holding that no reverter had been shown as of the date of filing suit. The reverter clause, as a whole, must be construed to mean that the property shall revert when, and only when, it is no longer used "for a school site"; the last part of the clause merely says "when they fail and cease *using* it . . ." (without specification of purpose), but we must fairly infer the purpose previously stated. A cessation of use, as so referred to, is not a momentary or casual one; we think that such a clause necessarily implies a thought and intent of permanency in the change. No one could well claim that a cessation of classes for a day, a week, a month, or even for a term, would effect a reverter, if they were to be resumed thereafter. . . . The dominant issue is whether the building has, with a reasonable prospect of permanency, ceased to be a school, in view of its continued use for school storage, and the considered possibility of its future use for classes. . . . We shall not presume to fix any date when abandonment would take place. A school district may not arbitrarily retain title to property under such a conveyance unless it is done in good faith and with some reasonable purpose and intent. We do hold that neither at the filing of the suit nor at the time of the trial had there been a reverter. This, however, is no adjudication for all future times. The use of one room as a grocery concerned the trial court considerably; it held that the evidence was not competent because the pleadings had not been amended to show a reliance thereon as an abandonment. . . . On the merits we do not consider the temporary use of one room of the building as a grocery store as in any way controlling. It is apparent that the district was thereby able to effect some repairs to the building, without expending public money; the occupancy could be terminated promptly on notice. We all know that ordinarily a building is better preserved when occupied than when vacant. Actually, the parties simply agreed to mitigate the loss and damage from deterioration. We hold that such temporary occupancy did not affect the status. If more were needed, we might look to the admitted oral agreement that this occupancy should not affect the present litigation; presumably, that bound the parties plaintiff and defendant. We may note here that plaintiff, in adopting this theory of the materiality and competency of subsequent events (and plaintiff still urges the point here), is also precluded from objecting to our consideration of such expressed discussions and intentions of the board as may have occurred after suit was file [*sic*]. We, therefore, hold that as of the date of the judgment there had been no abandonment or reverter.

Guides for Class Discussion

1. Distinguish between this case and the three that precede it.
2. Do you agree with the court's thinking? Give reasons.

23. *"In the exercise of its discretion to select school sites, a school board will not have its discretion controlled by the courts so long as it is exercised in good faith and not abused"* (p. 5).

PIKE COUNTY BOARD OF EDUCATION v. FORD,
279 S.W. (2d) 245 (Ky.) (1955)
(Decided by the Court of Appeals of Kentucky)

[When the plaintiff school board attempted to obtain certain land for a site for a schoolhouse it could not agree with the owner concerning the price, and it brought a condemnation proceedings. The trial court set the price at $12,000 and awarded damages in the amount of $1,000, and an appeal was taken to the circuit court, which found the value of the land to be $15,350 and made no award for damages. This appeal was from that judgment. In arriving at its decision, here, the court found it necessary to comment on the authority of a board to condemn property.]

CAMMACK, Judge.

. . . .

A school board is vested with the authority to select public school sites, subject only to the limitation that it cannot act arbitrarily or beyond the pale of sound discretion. . . . In the case of Perry County Board of Education v. Deaton, 311 Ky. 227, 223 S.W. 2d 882, 883, we said:

"County Boards of Education are given broad discretion under KRS 160.160 and 160.290 in the selection of school sites and in the establishment of schools as they deem necessary for the promotion of education and the general welfare of the pupils. As stated in Phelps v. Witt, 304 Ky. 473, 201 S.W. 2d 4, and Justice v. Clemons, 308 Ky. 820, 215 S.W. 2d 992, when the Board has obtained the approval of the Superintendent of Public Instruction of its plans for a new building (KRS 162.060) courts will not interfere with the proposed plans unless there is positive proof of fraud, collusion or a clear abuse of discretion. The obligation of locating school sites rests with the County Board of Education. It is not for the courts to say whether the Board has acted wisely or unwisely in determining where the school should be located. The only question for the courts' determination is whether the Board is exceeding its authority or is acting arbitrarily."

The testimony of Paul W. Thurman, Director of School Building Grounds for the State Department of Education, shows that the superintendent of Public Instruction was consulted about the proposed site and that the location was approved by the Department. There is no evidence showing fraud, collusion or abuse of discretion on the part of the School Board. Consequently, the court exceeded its authority when, on its own motion, it undertook to question the wisdom of choosing this particular site for the school. . . .

We think also that the court erred in holding that the Board was without authority to condemn the land under lease to the Columbian Fuel Corporation. An authority with the power to condemn is not limited to its immediate needs only, but it may, and indeed should, give consideration to future needs. . . .

   .   .   .   .

The fact that a portion of the land taken will continue to be put to private use by a public utility, holding a lease thereon until the needs of the Board require its use, does not destroy the right of eminent domain. The Board had authority to take whatever interest the appellees had in the property and to leave for future negotiation the question of the corporation's interest. . . .

Guides for Class Discussion

1. Do you think it proper that the court should not interfere with a school board in the selection of a school site in the absence of evidence that the board abused its discretion or acted arbitrarily? Justify your answer.
2. Compare this case with *Sarratt* v. *Cash, infra.*

24. *"A school board must be free to exercise its discretion . . . at the time it makes the determination of a school site; it cannot limit its discretion in this respect by prior commitments or understandings with the public"* (p. 5).

SARRATT v. CASH,
103 S.C. 531, 88 S.E. 256 (1916)
(Decided by the Supreme Court of South Carolina)

[This was an action to enjoin a board of education from locating a school building on a certain site near the center of the district. Plaintiffs alleged that those who circulated the petition upon which an election for approving a bond issue was ordered, "represented to the electors that the new building would be located in the west end" of the district, and that but for this representation the bond issue would not have been approved. For violating this alleged understanding, they attempted to enjoin the board.]

HYDRICK, J. . . .

.   .   .   .

Assuming . . . as we must for the purpose of this inquiry, that the representations were made with the effect alleged, the question is: Should that preclude the trustees from now exercising the judgment and discretion vested in them by law to locate the building where they believed it ought to be located to best subserve the educational interests of the district as a whole? Or, stating the proposition differently, must they now, because of those representations, abuse their discretion by locating the building where, in their judgment, it will not be for the best interests of the district? They are bound, under the statute and their oath of office, to exercise their discretion and judgment, in the language of the statute (Civ. Code, § 1761) "so as best to promote the educational interests of their district." This power and duty is continuing and inalienable. They could not, therefore, bind themselves by promises or representation, so as to divest themselves of the right to a free and untrammeled exercise of their judgment and discretion for the best interests of their district at the time they were required to act as a body. . . . It would be contrary to public policy to allow public officers who are charged with the duty of exercising their judgment and discretion for the benefit of the whole district to bind or fetter themselves by promise or representation to individuals or to electors of a section of the district so that they could not, at all times, act freely and impartially for the benefit of the whole district. The power was conferred upon them for public purposes, and it could not be lawfully bartered away to influence signatures to the petition or votes in the election. The electors are presumed to have known this. Therefore they had no legal right to rely upon the alleged representations, or to be influenced by them in signing the petition or in voting in the election.

Guides for Class Discussion

1. Do you think the ends of equity and justice were served in this case? Give reasons.
2. On what ground did the court arrive at its decision?

25. *"Authority of a school board to build school buildings carries with it, by implication, authority to employ architects"* (p. 5).

PEOPLE EX REL. KIEHM V. BOARD OF EDUCATION,
190 N.Y.S. 798, 198 App. Div. 476 (1921)
(Decided by the Supreme Court, Appellate Division,
Fourth Department, New York)

[This was an action brought to collect a bill for architectural services from a school board. The board had employed the architect but, when he presented his bill, the board disapproved it on the basis of an opinion of the corporation counsel that it was not legal. This opinion was based, in part, on the fact there was no statutory authority granting to boards the authority to employ architects, although they did have the authority to construct new buildings.]

HUBBS, J. . . .

. . . .

It is quite apparent from the petition and return . . . that the board did not disallow the claim upon its merits, but based its refusal to allow it upon the ground that it was not a legal claim. . . .

. . . .

Undoubtedly the board, having the power and authority to build a new building, had power and authority to employ architects to draw the necessary plans and to make the necessary estimates and specifications. Without such services the board could not make out its estimates of the cost of the proposed building. The board, acting within its authority, did, by resolution, employ the relators who furnished plans, estimates, and specifications which were used by the board in preparing the proposition to submit to prospective bidders. The board then refused to audit the relators' claim upon the ground that it did not have the legal right so to do. It says that the contract with the relators was void, prohibited by subdivision 8 of section 875, aforesaid, and unenforceable, as the amount involved was over $1,000 and the board did not advertise for estimates. It is clear that the section referred to does not apply to a situation like this involving professional services.

Guides for Class Discussion

1. Are you in agreement with the court's reasoning? Give reasons.

2. Compare this decision with the one in *Cobb* v. *Pasadena City Board of Education, infra.*

26. *"In employing an architect, a school board need not resort to competitive bidding in the absence of statute to the contrary"* (p. 5).

COBB V. PASADENA CITY BOARD OF EDUCATION,
134 Cal. App. 93, 285 P. (2d) 41 (1955)
(Decided by the District Court of Appeal,
Second District, Division 2, California)

[The facts of the case will be found in the material quoted.]

MOORE, Presiding Judge.

The question here presented is whether a board of education is required to advertise for competitive bids before it may contract with an architect for his professional services to prepare plans for the city's school extension program.

By his complaint, appellant sought an injunction to prevent respondent from disbursing public funds as architect's fees for services rendered and to be performed in connection with the proposed Pasadena school extension program. . . .

.   .   .   .

The contention here made has long since been denied judicially and legislatively. It has been held that because an architect is an artist, that his work requires taste, skill and technical learning and ability of a rare kind, it would be bad judgment to advertise and get many bids when the lowest bidder might be also the least capable and most inexperienced and his bid absolutely unacceptable and therefore "the employment of a person who is highly and technically skilled in his science or profession is one which may properly be made without competitive bidding." . . . Because all contracts for the construction of improvements must be subject to competitive bidding, and because such contracts must conform with the procedure prescribed in sections 18051 and 18052, supra, it does not follow that in the employment of an architect to prepare plans for a public building a board must comply with those sections. . . . Where competitive proposals do not produce an advantage, a statute requiring competitive bidding does not apply. . . .

.   .   .   .

The contention that respondent improperly employed architects who neither reside in Pasadena nor do business there is based on no authority. . . . Such employment, therefore, lies within the discretion of the board, with which courts will not interfere in the absence of fraud or abuse of discretion in the exercise of its legislative powers. . . .

Guides for Class Discussion

1. What line of reasoning motivated the court?
2. Do you think its reasoning is sound? Give reasons.

27. *"Contracts with architects, like all other contracts, must be made by the board in its corporate capacity and not by an individual member or committee of the board"* (p. 5).

DIERKS SPECIAL SCHOOL DISTRICT v. VAN DYKE,
152 Ark. 26, 237 S.W. 428 (1922)
(Decided by the Supreme Court of Arkansas)

[This was an action by an architect to recover fees allegedly due him from a board of education for services in preparing plans for and supervising the construction of a school building. At issue was the legality of the contract, which it was not shown was either voted by the board or ratified by it while acting in its corporate capacity. The court held the contract was illegal.]

HART, J. . . . It is settled in this state that no contract can be made by a school board except at a board meeting, and that no meeting can be held unless all the directors are present, or the absent member, or members, have been duly notified. It has been further held that notice of a regular meeting is, however, unnecessary where regular meetings are held at stated times fixed by the board. . . . This is in application of the general rule that where persons are authorized by statute to perform a public service, as board or as an organized body, which requires deliberation, they must be convened in a body that they may have the advice of every member although they may not all be of the same opinion as to the matter in hand.

While there is in the record in the present case a contract signed by Van Dyke and the president and secretary of the Dierks special school district, employing him as architect in the construction of a new school building, it is not shown that this contract was authorized at a regular meeting of the school board, or at a special meeting where all the directors were present, or where each of them had been duly notified of the meeting. In the application of the rule above stated it is conceded by counsel for the plaintiff, Van Dyke, that he is not entitled to recover on the contract just referred to, but it is claimed by him that the contract in question was ratified by the members of the school board, and that therefore he is entitled to recover upon it just as if it had been legally executed in the first instance.

. . . .

. . . The record shows that on the 4th day of September, 1918, at a meeting of the school board in which four members were present, the board voted to receive the contract presented by the architect, V. B. Van Dyke, and instructed the president and secretary of the school board to sign the same, and that the president and secretary did so. There is nothing to show, however, that this was at a regular meeting of the school board, or that all the members of the board were duly notified to be present at it. It will be noted that two of the members were absent, and it is not shown that they received any notification whatever to be present. This is the only evidence in the record from which to find that the board of directors of said special school district ratified the contract which its president and secretary made with Van Dyke, and this testimony is not sufficient to show a ratification of the contract. As we have already seen, such a contract could only be made or ratified by the board at a regular meeting, or at a call meeting of which all the members of the board were present or had been given due notice.

Guides for Class Discussion

1. On what basis did the court arrive at its decision?
2. Do you think the reasoning of the court was sound? Give reasons.
3. What are the implications of this case for school administration?

28. "*It is well settled that, where an architect agrees to furnish plans and specifications for a building that can be built at a cost closely approximating a given amount, or not to exceed a certain sum, he cannot recover under the contract unless the building he designs can be erected for the sum stipulated, or unless the increased cost is due to some special circumstance*" (p. 5).

PIERCE v. BOARD OF EDUCATION,
211 N.Y.S. 788, 125 Misc. Rep. 589 (1925)
(Decided by the Supreme Court, Orleans County, New York)

[Plaintiffs—architects—brought this action to recover for services rendered defendant "pursuant to an agreement for furnishing preliminary studies, general plans, and specifications for the construction" of two schoolhouses. After completing plans, plaintiffs informed defendant that the elementary-school building could, they thought, be built within the amount of $20,000 and that the combination junior high and elementary building could be constructed for about $75,000. After bids were opened, it was found that the lowest bid for the grade-school building was $38,413, and for the combination building, $101,651.09. Therefore the defendant abandoned the project, and plaintiffs brought this action. They contended that they were entitled to three and one-half per cent of the lowest bids. Defendant contended that it was the duty of plaintiffs to furnish plans so that the building project could be carried out within the appropriation previously voted by the district, the amount of which the plaintiffs knew or should have known.]

EDWARD R. O'MALLEY, J. . . .

. . . .

It seems to be well settled that, where plans are required for a building not to cost more than a certain sum, or are accepted on condition that it can be erected for a given amount, there can be no recovery by the architect, unless the building can be erected for the sum named, or unless the increased cost is due to special circumstances, or to a change of plan by direction of the owner. . . .

In the instant case there was no express stipulation made by the defendant limiting the cost of the buildings to be constructed, but it is claimed that, where the employer is a municipal corporation, as in the case at bar, such a provision is implied in the contract of employment, and this claim is based on the general rule of law that one dealing with the agent of a municipal corporation has no right to presume that the agent is acting within the line of his or its authority, and that it is the duty of one so dealing to ascertain the nature and extent of the agent's authority to contract, and that there were certain specific limitations in the Education Law on the defendant's authority and power to contract for the construction of school buildings, among which was that the expense of the buildings must be within the appropriation voted by the district, and that plaintiffs were bound to know these limitations as a matter of law, and that in fact they did know of these express limitations. . . .

. . . .

The resolution voted upon by the district expressly provided that the total cost of the sites and the buildings was not to exceed $125,000, and the plaintiffs were bound under the law to know that the erection of the buildings and their right to recover under their contract were conditioned on the expense coming within the appropriation. The bids submitted show that the costs would have exceeded the appropriation. The sum of the lowest bids received was 47 per cent. higher than plaintiffs' estimate of the cost of the buildings. The result was that the defendant could not erect the buildings within the appropriation or the estimate given by the plaintiffs, or for a sum that would reasonably approximate the appropriation or the estimate. This being so, the defendant had no power to proceed with the building portion of the project. . . .

. . . .

The limitation contained in the resolution as to costs was binding on both the plaintiffs and the defendant, and I am of the opinion that all of the limitations upon the authority of the defendant to deal with the plaintiffs must be read into and made a part of the contract. If these conclusions are correct, the plaintiffs cannot recover for their services . . . because of a failure on their part to perform the contract.

Guides for Class Discussion

1. Compare the decision in this case with the ones in *Fiske* v. *School District, infra*; and *Ritter* v. *School District, infra*.
2. Are you in agreement with the court? Give reasons.

29. "*Some courts hold—and their decisions appear to be the mos*
reasonable—that a contract between a school board and an architec
to prepare general drawings and specifications for a school buildin
is valid even though the board may not, at the time, have th
necessary funds to build the building and the building may neve
be built" (pp. 5-6).

FISKE v. SCHOOL DISTRICT,
59 Neb. 51, 80 N.W. 265 (1899)
(Decided by the Supreme Court of Nebraska)

[The facts of this case will be found in that portion of th
decision which is included herein.]

HARRISON, C. J. . . .
In this action the plaintiff sought a recovery for services alleged to hav
been rendered to the defendant in preparing plans, drawings, and specifi
cations for school buildings, pursuant to the terms of a contract betwee
the parties. . . .
For a statement of the case, we refer to the former opinion. It need no
be repeated here. It will be noticed that the controverted questions relat
mainly, if not entirely, to the right of the plaintiff to recover for prelimi
nary plans, drawings, and specifications, which were not used or followe
in the construction of any buildings. . . . It is asserted . . . that the authorit
of school-district boards or officers to contract in regard to erection o
buildings or any subject which will or does involve the expenditure o
money is limited by statute, and must be within the statutory terms; that i
must be within the funds provided or on hand to meet the propose
expenditures; and that the party who contracts with the board or office
does so at his peril, and must take notice of its or their requisite authorit
or the lack thereof. . . . The projected buildings were never erected; th
preliminary plans and drawings could not be said to be a part of an
construction of buildings; and, if not, the expense of them was not any pa
of a building, or necessarily to be paid from a building fund. They wer
ordered for the use of the district, and were necessary as much so as man
other articles or services which come within the general expenses of
school district, and must be paid for from the general fund. There is
fund from which all such expenses are paid, and we may call it a "genera
fund." It is so recognized and designated in the general school law, an
payments directed to be made from it. Comp. St. c. 79, subd. 4, § 13. Ther
was a legitimate expense and charge against the district, and funds fro
which it could be properly paid. The facts of this case, as stated in th
petition, place it clearly without the direct terms or the principle of th
cases cited, to which we have hereinbefore referred.

Guides for Class Discussion

1. Compare this case with *Ritter* v. *School District, infra.* With which do you agree? Give reasons.
2. What line of reasoning did the court follow in arriving at its decision?

30. "*Some courts take the position . . . that a contract between a school board and an architect is invalid where the plans and specifications call for a building which would cost more than the board could legally spend for that purpose*" (p. 6).

RITTER v. SCHOOL DISTRICT,
291 Pa. 439, 140 A. 126 (1928)
(Decided by the Supreme Court of Pennsylvania)

[This was an action by an architect to recover his commission on a school building which was never built, and for which he did not even prepare definite and finished plans."]

SCHAFFER, J. . . .

. . . .

The insurmountable block in plaintiff's way to recovery is that what he contemplated would result in an unlawful increase in the indebtedness of the school district. It had but $417,000 available for the building. His plan contemplated an expenditure of $800,000. Such an outlay the school board could not have made. The case at bar differs from Sauer v. McKees Rocks School Dist., 243 Pa. 295, 90 A. 150, in which an architect sued for commissions for services in connection with a school building and where the cost of the structure exceeded the 2 per cent. borrowing capacity of the district. There the architect originally claimed commissions on the completed cost of the building. By leave of court he amended his claim so as to recover only for the services actually performed, and he was permitted to recover that amount. Had the plaintiff here made a like claim, which on the trial he expressly declined to do, he might have succeeded.

Appellant's counsel argue that his contract was separate from that for the erection of the building and in itself did not exhaust the borrowing capacity of the school district. With this we do not agree. Plaintiff's contract was inseparably bound up with the whole building program, and by express reference made a part of it. When he planned a building as part of the program for which it was beyond the power of the defendant to contract, he could not recover his commissions on the cost of it.

Guides for Class Discussion

1. Are you in agreement with the decision in this case? Give reasons.
2. Compare the decision in this case with the ones in *Fiske* v. *School District, supra,* and *Pierce* v. *Board of Education, supra.*

31. *"Where a school board breaks a contract with an architect, the rule is that he is entitled to recover the contract price, less whatever payments have been made and less what it would cost him to perform the contract"* (p. 6).

PAGE v. HARLINGEN INDEPENDENT SCHOOL DISTRICT,
23 S.W. (2d) 829 (Tex.) (1929)
(Decided by the Court of Civil Appeals of Texas)

[In this case a school board entered into a contract with an architect to draw plans for and supervise the construction of three school buildings. After two had been completed, the board repudiated its contract covering the third. To recover for the alleged wrongful and illegal repudiation of the contract, the architect brought this action. The first question before the court was the legality of the contract. Having decided it was legal, the next question the court was called upon to answer was the amount plaintiff was entitled to recover.]

COBBS, J. . . .

. . . .

. . . we think the facts establish a valid contract for all the work done by appellants, and that the act of the school board in setting aside appel lants' contract and giving it to another violated the contractual relation existing between the appellants and appellee.

. . . .

On account of the breach of the contract by appellee under the circumstances, appellants are entitled to recover damages; the contract price less what appellee district has paid them, and less the amount it would cost appellants to carry out their contract. Gould v. McCormick, 75 Wash. 61, 134 P. 676, 47 L. R. A. (N. S.) 765, Ann. Cas. 1915 A, 710; Jacobberger v. School District, 122 Or. 124, 256 P. 652; Phelps v. Connellee (Tex. Com. App.) 285 S.W. 1047; Id. (Civ. App.) 278 S.W. 939.

In the Jacobberger and Gould Cases, supra, the rule stated is: "The damages for wrongfully discharging an architect who had undertaken to draw plans for and superintend the construction of a building for a percentage of its cost are the difference between the contract price and what it would have cost them to complete their undertaking at the time of their discharge." On motion for a rehearing in the Phelps v. Connellee Case, supra, the appeals court modified this holding to the extent that a further deduction of whatever amount the architect may have saved himself by finding other employment should be made from the recovery. But the Supreme Court reversed the Court of Civil Appeals' opinion as rendered on rehearing, and held that an architect wrongfully discharged is entitled to recover his contract price, less whatever payments have been made, and what it would cost him to perform his contract; and that such further mitigation of damages was a matter of defense to be pleaded by the defendant.

. . . .

Appellants have shown a legal right to recover the sum of $8,033.52, therefore the judgment of the trial court is reversed, and judgment here rendered for appellants for the said sum of $8,033.52.

Reversed and rendered.

Guides for Class Discussion

1. Do you think the rule laid down by the court for determining the amount of damages to which the architect was entitled was equitable? Give reasons.
2. Do you think a court today would follow this same rule?
3. Had the contract been illegal, how much damages could the architect have recovered?

32. *"Where the statutes do not require school boards to let build-ing contracts on the basis of competitive bidding, a school board may or may not, at its discretion, advertise for bids"* (p. 6).

SMITH v. BOARD OF EDUCATION,
405 Ill. 143, 89 N.E. (2d) 893 (1950)
(Decided by the Supreme Court of Illinois)

[This was an action to restrain a board of education from proceed-ing with a contract for the construction of a new high school build-ing. Among other things, plaintiff contended the contract was illegal because it was not based upon competitive bidding. The lower court ruled in favor of the defendant, and the higher court affirmed it decision.]

SIMPSON, Justice.

· ·

The legislature has provided for the creation of boards of education and has delegated to such boards the power to build schoolhouses, upon receiv-ing authority to do so from a majority of the electorate of the school dis-trict, subject to the approval of the county superintendent of schools respecting certain health and safety measures. . . . The method to be employed in letting contracts for the construction of school buildings has been left to the discretion of the school boards of the respective school districts. Appellant attacks the wisdom of permitting the board of education of a high school district to negotiate contracts for building schoolhouses without limitation as to size, cost, or methods to be employed in the letting of such contracts. It is insisted that the unrestrained acts of the board of education, in such cases, is contrary to public policy. Where no limitation has been placed upon a school board by the vote of the people of the district, it has the right to use its discretion as to the character and cost of a school building which shall be adequate and proper for the use of the district. . . .

The remaining question to be determined is whether the allegations of the complaint are sufficient to charge the Board of Education with fraud in awarding the construction contract to Arnold Lies Company, Inc. While the words, "fraud," "fraudulently," and "conspiracy," are used repeatedly a careful reading of the complaint compels the conclusion that these charges are based on two main allegations, first, that the Board of Educa-tion eliminated competitive bidding, and second, that the contract was awarded for a substantially larger sum than might have been bid by other contractors. In the absence of allegations of facts showing fraudulent acts or conduct in connection with the awarding of the contract, this was not sufficient to charge fraud. We have already pointed out that the legislature delegated the authority to build schoolhouses, under proper circumstances, to boards of education without requiring that contracts for their construction be awarded as a result of competitive bidding. Where the language used in a statute is plain and certain it must be given effect by the courts and we cannot legislate but must interpret the law as announced by the legislature.

Guides for Class Discussion

1. Are you in agreement with this decision? Give reasons.
2. Compare this case with *Coward* v. *Mayor, etc., of City of Bayonne, infra.*

33. ". . . *the board may reject all bids unless its advertisement is so worded as to constitute an offer to accept the lowest bid*" (p. 6).

COWARD V. MAYOR, ETC., OF CITY OF BAYONNE,
67 N.J.L. 470, 51 A. 490 (1902)
(Decided by the Supreme Court of New Jersey)

[In this case an attempt was made to invalidate a contract for the construction of a school building made by the board of education. The board employed an architect and, after he had finished drawing up the specifications, advertised for bids. In the advertisement the board reserved the right to reject all bids. Following the rejection of the bids, new specifications were drawn up and the contract again was submitted for bidding. In awarding the contract, certain changes were made in the specifications from those included in the architect's drawings. On the ground that the contract was illegal, this action was brought to restrain the board from proceeding as it planned to do. The court held the contract was legal.]

GARRETSON, J. . . .

* * * * * * * * * * * * * * * * * * *

The board of education of Bayonne are not required by the charter of that city, or by any general law of the state, to advertise for proposals for doing any of the work which they are authorized to do. The only provision is in section 91 of the charter, supra, and, although the board did actually advertise for proposals, they were not required to award the contract to the lowest bidder; and the award of the contract to a higher or the highest bidder, or to some one who did not bid at all, would not, in the absence of bad faith and corruption, be regarded as such an abuse of that discretion conferred upon them by law as to justify interference by this court. The employment of an architect to prepare plans and specifications, and the soliciting of bids, may have been a proper method of ascertaining the most favorable contract that could be obtained for the city. It is the method which a private person would pursue as to his own affairs. And after the bids had been received there was nothing to prevent the board from so modifying the specifications that a better contract might be made for the city. The board had the right to purchase for use in the building any article or apparatus of a specific make, even though it was patented or the product of an exclusive manufacture. City of Newark v. Bonnell, 57 N. J. Law, 424, 31 Atl. 408. Nor do we think that a statement in the advertisement that only union labor should be employed (such a condition not being contained in the contract) would vitiate the contract. The evidence fails to disclose that the board of education had any motive in awarding the contract, other than that of making the best bargain possible for the city. We think that they exercised the discretion conferred upon them by law with good faith and honesty.

Guides for Class Discussion

1. On what basis did the court arrive at its decision? Was this sound?

2. Compare this decision with the one rendered in *Smith* v. *Board of Education, supra.*

3. Had the advertisement for bids not included the statement that the board reserved the right to reject all bids, would the court have held as it did?

34. *"In case the statutes require school boards to advertise for bids on school-building contracts and to award such contracts to the lowest responsible bidder, the mode of making the contract is the measure of the board's power to make it, and if the statute is disregarded, the contractor cannot recover on the contract"* (p. 6).

YODER v. SCHOOL DISTRICT OF LUZERNE TOWNSHIP,
399 Pa. 425, 160 A. (2d) 419 (1960)
(Decided by the Supreme Court of Pennsylvania)

[In this case a contractor brought an action against a school district to recover for work done and supplies and materials furnished in connection with the paving of certain school playgrounds. Plaintiff was low bidder on a contract for the paving job and was awarded the contract. Specifications called for 4,379 square yards of six-inch base, at a total cost of $29,882.45. The contract stated no extra work would be done unless so ordered in writing. Without complying with the statute respecting advertising and bidding, the area surfaced by plaintiff was increased to 10,240 yards and the base was changed from six inches to four. These changes were made pursuant to oral orders of the board members "who singly or in groups, visited the job sites from time to time." The final bill was for $44,174.60 instead of the $29,882.45 originally agreed upon. Plaintiff received $29,174.60 and brought this action to recover the $15,000 which he contended was still due him. The district's refusal to pay was based upon its contention that the extra work had not been performed in conformity with the statute requiring public advertisement for bids and formal corporate action in the letting of the bids. The trial court sustained the defendant district's position and the contractor appealed. The higher court upheld the lower court's decision.]

BENJAMIN R. JONES, Justice.

. . . .

These sections [of the statute relating to bidding and the method of contracting] are mandatory, not directory. Similar provisions in other statutes have been uniformly construed as mandatory. . . . This Court said in Commonwealth v. Zang, 142 P. Super 566, 571, 16 A. 2d 741; 744: ". . . the purpose and public policy behind these provisions of the School Code are to protect the school district from any possible collusion and dishonesty, and to insure that where material or supplies . . . are purchased they will be obtained at the best possible price. . . . To permit contracts to be entered into and expenditures made without compliance with the provisions of the act would defeat the very object the legislature had in mind in inserting them. In re Summit Hill School Directors, [258 Pa. 575, 102 A. 278]. . . ." "The infirmities of human nature, the natural disposition to favor friends, personal and political, and the various motives which influence public officers to depart from a strict and rigid adherence to the obligations that rest upon them . . . should be held strictly within the limits of the powers conferred upon them.": Smith v. City of Philadelphia, 227 Pa. 423, 76 A. 221, 223.

In Luzerne Township v. County of Fayette, 330 Pa. 247, 251, 199 A. 327, 329, we said "All contracts by county commissioners involving an expenditure exceeding $100 must be in writing. Act of June 27, 1895, P. L. 403, § 10 as amended . . . and embodied in the General County Law of May 2, 1929, P. L. 1278, § 348 . . . . This provision of the law is not merely directory, but mandatory, and a contract which does not comply with it imposes no liability upon the county. Where a statute prescribes the formal mode of making public contracts it must be observed; otherwise they cannot be enforced against the governmental agency involved. . . ."

Guides for Class Discussion

1. Are you in agreement with the court's thinking? Give reasons.
2. See *Reams* v. *Cooley, infra.*

35. *"In case the statutes require [competitive bidding] . . . the mode of making the contract is the measure of the board's power . . . , and if the statute is disregarded . . . the contractor cannot recover on quantum meruit, in a court of equity, the actual value of the building"* (p. 6).

REAMS v. COOLEY,
171 Cal. 150, 152 P. 293 (1915)
(Decided by the Supreme Court of California)

[In this case a contract for plastering had been let without bidding, as required by statute. Upon its completion, the board refused to pay the contractor, on the ground the contract had been made improperly, and he brought this action. The court held in favor of the district, and the contractor appealed.]

LORIGAN, J. . . .

. . . .

. . . While under sections 1617 and 1674 of the Political Code authority is given to school trustees to erect school buildings, there is at the same time by subdivision 22 of section 1617, applicable alike to boards of trustees of union high school districts as to boards of trustees of common school districts, a mode prescribed for exercising that power. By that subdivision where the work (as here) is to exceed the sum of $200, a valid contract can only be entered into with the lowest bidder on competitive bidding after published notice therefor. . . . No contract, either expressly or impliedly, could be entered into by the school board except with the lowest bidder after advertisement, and, of course, *no implied liability to pay upon a quantum meruit could exist where the prohibition of the statute against contracting in any other manner than as prescribed is disregarded.* [Emphasis supplied.]

It is urged in this case, as it invariably is in all such cases, that the application of this rule works a great hardship if the school district may retain the benefit of the work of the contractor and be relieved of liability to compensate him therefor. But the provision of the law limiting the power of school boards to validly contract, except in a prescribed mode, proceeds from a consideration of public policy not peculiar to such boards, but adopted as the policy of the state with reference to inferior boards and public bodies, and it would be difficult to perceive what practical public benefit or result could accrue by legislative limitation or prohibition on the power of such bodies to contract if courts were to allow a recovery where the limitation or prohibition is disregarded; in fact, the plea of hardship urged here was answered in the Zottman case [20 Cal. 96] by language as pertinent now as it was then, where the court said:

"It may sometimes seem a hardship upon a contractor that all compensation for work done, etc., should be denied him; but it should be remembered that he, no less than the officers of the corporation, when he deals in a matter expressly provided for in the charter, is bound to see to it that the charter is complied with. If he neglect this, or choose to take the hazard, he is a mere volunteer, and suffers only what he ought to have anticipated. If the statute forbids the contract which he has made, he knows it, or ought to know it, before he places his money or services at hazard."

Guides for Class Discussion

1. Are you in agreement with the court's reasoning? Give reasons.
2. Compare this decision with the one in *White River School Township* v. *Dorrell, infra.*
3. Compare this decision with the one rendered in *Yoder* v. *School District of Luzerne Township, supra.*

36. *"In order to have competitive bidding, plans and specifications must be sufficiently definite to enable those who bid to bid on a common basis; otherwise there is no competition"* (p. 6).

HOMAN v. BOARD OF EDUCATION,
3 N.J.M. 301, 127 A. 824 (1925)
(Decided by the Supreme Court of New Jersey)

[This was an action to set aside the award of a contract by a school board.]

PER CURIAM. The writ of certiorari was issued to review the action of the defendant in awarding the contract for the erection of a schoolhouse known as the Rosedale School on the 24th day of September, 1924. The prosecutors' bid, after public advertisement, was $197,330. The defendant' bid was $198,689.

The ground upon which the prosecutors seek to set aside the award of the contract is that it is in violation of the statute which provides:

"All contracts shall be awarded to the lowest responsible bidder." . . .
This provision limits the power of the board. . . .

What constitutes responsibility within the meaning of the statute is
fully discussed and illustrated in the cases of Paterson Contracting Co.
v. City of Hackensack, 122 A. 741; Peluso v. Hoboken, 98 N.J. Law, 706,
126 A 623; Harrington's Sons Co. v. Jersey City, 78 N.J. Law, 610, 75 A.
943.

Under these cases it is not shown in the record that the prosecutors
were not "responsible bidders" within the meaning of the statute, and in
the defendant's brief, it is stated, at the very outset let it be made clear
that the financial responsibility of the H. John Homan Company is not
questioned.

. . . .

The advertising for bids, however, requested that the time be stated
in the contract within which the building would be finished.

As was said by this court in the case of Armitage v. Mayor, etc., of
Newark, 86 N.J. Law, 6, 90 A. 1035, the general vice of this course is
that no common standard for the competition is set up. . . . Testimony
was taken which is urged as a justification of the board's action, viz. that
the prosecutors delayed the completion of prior contracts with the board,
but this is no legal excuse for not complying with the plain mandate of
the statute.

For these reasons the award of the contract in this case is set aside,
with costs.

Guides for Class Discussion

1. Do you think the court acted equitably in ruling that common
   standards for competition must be set up in order to constitute
   responsibility in bidding? Give reasons.
2. See *Yoder* v. *School District of Luzerne Township, supra.*

37. "*Where the statutes require that bids be let to the lowest responsible bidder, in deciding who is the lowest responsible bidder, the board should take into consideration cost, financial standing, experience, resources, and all other factors necessary for it to form a judgment of the bidder's responsibility*" (pp. 6-7).

MEYER v. BOARD OF EDUCATION,
221 N.Y.S. (2d) 500 (1961)
(Decided by the Supreme Court, Special Term,
Nassau County, Part I)

[This was an application for an order to cancel an award of a contract made by the defendant board to Werther Electrical Contracting Co., Inc., and to direct the award of this contract to the plaintiff. Plaintiff was the lowest bidder when bids were solicited and he contended he should receive the contract. The court held that the record failed to show that defendant was arbitrary in its awarding of the contract.]

MARIO PITTONI, Justice.

. . . .

The basic facts are not in dispute. On Wednesday, August 2, 1961, the bids were received by the Board of Education, and the Board, not being familiar with either of the two bidders involved, and anxious to have the work completed before the fall session began, instructed its architect to immediately investigate and report on each of these bidding contractors. On August 7, 1961 the architect submitted his report to the Board that he had requested the petitioner to supply the names of architectural firms to which inquiries could be directed concerning recent projects which the petitioner had completed; that the petitioner supplied the names of two architectural firms; that when the school architect communicated with both of these references one responded that the petitioner had done a project for that firm over 10 years prior to the inquiry, and the other said that he would not recommend the petitioner. The second said that although the petitioner had once been a good contractor he had experienced difficulties in the last few years, was having difficulty in getting approval of his work from underwriting laboratories, and that after being awarded an electrical contract as a low bidder he submitted estimates for extra work, which were not included in the plans and specifications and which were too high in price. The investigating architect also reported that his investigation showed that Werther had a good reputation in the industry for its work and had received the highest recommendation from well-known engineers and architects. Upon the report and recommendation of its architect the Board then proceeded, at its August 7, 1961 public meeting, to award the contract to Werther as the lowest responsible bidder. Another public hearing at the petitioner's request was held on August 28, 1961. The petitioner and his attorney were heard and the Board adhered to its original decision.

The key word in Section 103 of the General Municipal Law and in the decision of the Board is "responsible." Without question it means "accountable" or "reliable." The Board came to its decision that Werther was the lowest responsible bidder after considering the report of its architect who was designated or appointed to seek facts as to the responsibility of the bidders involved. The Board concluded that upon the facts in hand Werther was a responsible bidder and the petitioner was not.

The Board used a common sense approach and method in making its determination and this court cannot say that it was wrong in the method chosen; nor will it define or limit the standards the Board should have used as guides so long as the method chosen was reasonable.

The burden of proof was on the petitioner to show that he was a responsible bidder. There was no burden on the Board to go out and investigate blindly as to the bidder's responsibility. He submitted two persons as references, and upon interview these persons supplied information which failed to show that the petitioner was a responsible person.

. . . .

Accordingly, it cannot be said that the Board was arbitrary, capricious or unreasonable in making its decision. . . .

Guides for Class Discussion

1. Do you think the court would have ruled as it did had the board made the investigation itself, rather than requested the architect to make it? Give reasons.

2. Compare this decision with *Joseph Rugo, Inc.* v. *Henson, infra.*

38. *"Where a school board acts in good faith and its judgment is based upon substantial fact, the courts will not overrule its discretion in determining the lowest responsible bidder"* (p. 7).

JOSEPH RUGO, INC. v. HENSON,
148 Conn. 430, 171 A. (2d) 409 (1961)
(Decided by the Supreme Court of Errors of Connecticut)

[This was an action by a contractor to compel defendant to award to him a contract for the construction of a new high school. Defendant demurred, and the lower court sustained the demurrer. The plaintiff appealed, and the higher court here held that the board, which had reserved the right to reject any and all offers, was justified in rejecting all bids where it felt they were excessive, even if the action was arbitrary and capricious, so long as it was not fraudulent.]

BORDON, Associate Justice.

. . . .

Although there are three assignments of error, the only question to be determined is whether there was error in sustaining the demurrer. On the face of the record, it appears that the court sustained the demurrer on grounds other than those claimed by the defendants. If, however, a proper conclusion was reached, the ruling may be upheld. . . . In passing on a demurrer, the court should consider only the grounds specified. . . . Upon appeal, we consider the whole record and give judgment for the party who, on the whole, appears to be entitled to it. . . .

There is no allegation in the complaint which overcomes the recognized principle of law that where municipalities reserve the right to reject any or all bids they are empowered to do so. . . . It is true that certain paragraphs of the complaint allege arbitrariness, capriciousness, and similar conduct, but such conduct, if there was any, by the empowered officers is immaterial, since the right to reject all bids was asserted in the invitation to bid. . . . Courts have relaxed the application of the established principle of law only where fraud or corruption has influenced the conduct of the officials. No allegation of fraud or corruption appears in this complaint.

All that is required of officials is that they observe good faith and accord all bidders just consideration, thus avoiding favoritism and corruption. An honest exercise of discretion will generally not be disturbed. Courts will only intervene to prevent the rejection of a bid when the

bvious purpose of the rejection is to defeat the object and integrity
of competitive bidding. . . .

Guides for Class Discussion

1. Do you think the court was right in holding that, as long as
the board did not act fraudulently or corruptly, its actions
would be upheld in this case? Justify your answer.
2. What did the court have to say, indirectly, concerning the
purpose of a competitive-bidding statute?

39. *"The mere passage of a resolution by a board to accept a bid
does not constitute a contract—there is no contract until the bidder
has been officially notified that his bid has been accepted—and
a board may rescind its resolution awarding the contract at any
time before such notification"* (p. 7).

WAYNE CROUSE, INC. V. SCHOOL DISTRICT
OF BOROUGH OF BRADDOCK,
341 Pa. 497, 19 A. (2d) 843 (1941)
(Decided by the Supreme Court of Pennsylvania)

[In Pennsylvania, where the statute required that building contracts be reduced to writing, a school board, after advertising for
bids for plumbing and heating, voted to award the contract to
plaintiff, who was the lowest bidder. Later, before the contract
was reduced to writing and signed, the board rescinded its action
on the ground plaintiff was not the lowest responsible bidder, and
his action was brought to compel the board to enter into the
contract with plaintiff. The court ruled against plaintiff.]

MAXEY, Justice.

. . . .

The school district through its secretary verbally notified the plaintiff
to proceed to execute the written contracts prepared and secure materialmen and performance bonds. The officers of Plaintiff Corporation proceeded to do this the morning after the meeting at which the award
was made to it. The Plumbers' Union protested to the school board that
the school district persisted in the award, labor difficulties would be

experienced. The secretary and architect consulted with the plaintiff corporation's representatives but the latter's efforts with the union were unsuccessful and the school district was so notified.

The following appears on the minutes of the meeting of the Board of Directors of the school district held on March 10, 1938: "It was regularly moved and seconded by Wrobleski and Andolina that the actions of the board in awarding the plumbing contract . . . to Wayne & Crouse Inc. . . . be rescinded because of the finding after investigation that they are not the lowest responsible bidder, in that they cannot perform the said contract. All ayes. . ." . . . .

. . . .

When a municipal body advertises for bids for public work and receives what appears to be a satisfactory bid, it is within the contemplation of both bidder and acceptor that no contractual relation shall arise therefrom until a written contract embodying all material terms of the offer and acceptance has been formally entered into. The motion whose adoption is evidenced by the minutes of the school district in the instant case meant merely that the proposal was accepted subject to the preparation and execution of a formal contract or subject to the motion being rescinded before the contract was executed. A preliminary declaration of intention to enter into a formal contract, which was all the motion amounted to, did not in any way limit the school directors' freedom of future action.

Guides for Class Discussion

1. Are you in agreement with this decision? Give reasons.
2. What line of reasoning motivated the court?

40. *"If a contractor makes an honest mistake in calculating the cost of a school building and the mistake goes to the essence of the contract, a court of equity will annul the bid and put the parties in statu quo"* (p. 7).

BOARD OF EDUCATION v. HOOPER,
350 S.W. (2d) 629 (Ky.) (1961)
(Decided by the Court of Appeals of Kentucky)

[The facts of this case will be found in the material quoted.]

CULLEN, Commissioner.

Appellees Hooper and Burchett, partners, submitted a bid to the Board of Education of Floyd County for the construction of a school building

As required by the specifications, the bid was accompanied by a bid bond, with appellee Travelers Indemnity Company as surety, conditioned that f the bid be accepted the bidders would execute a contract for the work n accordance with their bid and the specifications. Upon the opening of he bids the Hooper-Burchett bid, in the amount of $73,978.90, was found to be the lowest and was accepted by the board of education. The following day Hooper and Burchett notified the board that by inadvertence the price of the steel required in the construction, amounting to $12,000, had been omitted from their bid, and by reason thereof they could not execute a contract for their bid price. Three days later, without readvertising for bids, the board let a contract to the next lower bidder, whose bid was $78,000. Thereafter the board brought this action against Hooper and Burchett and the surety on their bid bond, seeking to recover the amount of the bond (which was five percent of the bid price). The court entered judgment for the defendants and the board has appealed.

Hooper and Burchett testified that the mistake in their bid arose from the fact that they had divided between them the work of preparing the bid estimates and each had assumed that the other had included the price of the steel in his estimates.

The facts in this case cannot be distinguished from those in Board of Regents of Murray State Normal School v. Cole, 209 Ky. 761, 273 S.W. 508, where in submitting a bid of $207,787 the bidder by inadvertence omitted the cost of cut stone in the amount of $21,066. It was held that the bidder was entitled to be relieved from his bid . . . .

. . . The rationale of the case is that even though the mistake is unilateral, the bidder may be relieved from his contract if the mistake is one of material substance and of such consequence that enforcement of the contract would be unconscionable; if the mistake involved mere ordinary negligence and not gross carelessness; if the other party will suffer no damage other than the loss of the bargain; and if the bidder gives prompt notice of the mistake.

. . . The fact that notice of the mistake is not given until after acceptance of the bid will not preclude relief. . . . .

It is our opinion that the trial court properly denied recovery on the bid bond.

.   .   .   .

The judgment is affirmed.

Guides for Class Discussion

1. On what ground did the court arrive at its decision?
2. As a result of this decision, could one who had been the low bidder change his mind and thereby avoid his obligation?

41. *"After bids have been accepted, courts will permit minor, but not major, changes in the specifications. . ." (p. 7).*

HIBBS V. ARENSBERG,
276 Pa. 24, 119 A. 727 (1923)
(Decided by the Supreme Court of Pennsylvania)

[This was an action to restrain a board of education from carrying out a contract for the construction of a school building that was let to one who was not the lowest bidder. Among other things, it was charged that the architect's specifications regarding materials were not sufficiently definite so as to insure that all bidders were bidding on the same basis, and that changes in the specifications were made after the contract was let. In arriving at its decision, the court commented on the effect of modifying or changing the specifications after a bid has been accepted.]

KEPHART, J. . . .

. . . .

It is averred, in the bill to restrain the school directors from awarding the contract to construct a badly needed school building in a school district in Fayette county, that the architect's plans and specifications do not fully state the kind, quality, and quantity of materials required. One special item reads:

"The face brick . . . to be a thoroughly vitrified, wire-cut, face brick of such color as will be selected by the architect and school board; . . . to cost not more than $34.00 per thousand."

We see no reason why an intelligent bid could not be made on this item. Vitrified, wire-cut, face brick has a definite meaning; the contract preserved the right of inspection and rejection of materials; and there was little opportunity to slight the quality. If a certain make of brick had been selected, or several makes, we can readily see a charge of a different character might be presented.

That the directors later decided to use a little more expensive brick would not condemn the letting, or cause the directors to be liable for the increased price, or avoid the purchase. There was no such departure from the general purpose as would require reletting. Unforeseen contingencies or new ideas sometimes make it necessary to change the character or quality of material or a part of a structure from the original plans. A certain flexibility in the power of officials to take care of these matters is intended to be granted, that the law relating to public letting may not become an instrument of oppression through a too rigid construction. These officers must act honestly, reasonably, and intelligently, and a new departure must not so vary from the original plan or be of such importance as to constitute a new undertaking, which the act controls, and where fairness could only be reached through competitive bidding. Courts, however, will be slow to interfere unless it appears the officers are not acting in good faith.

Guides for Class Discussion

1. What conditions must prevail for the courts to approve the making of minor changes in specifications after a contract has been let?
2. Do you think this decision represents "good" law? Give reasons.

42. *"In some states a school district will not be bound under an ultra vires contract even though it retains and enjoys the use of property obtained under such a contract"* (p. 7).

HONEY CREEK SCHOOL TOWNSHIP v. BARNES,
119 Ind. 213, 21 N.E. 747 (1889)
(Decided by the Supreme Court of Indiana)

[The facts of this case will be found in that part of the decision reproduced.]

OLDS, J. This action is brought by the appellees against the appellant. The complaint is in one paragraph, and alleges that on the 1st day of February, 1884, one Benjamin King, at that time the legal and acting school trustee of said school township, bought of the plaintiffs books for the use of the schools of said township; that said books were received and used by the schools of said township, and that the same were necessary for such township in its schools, at and for the price of $56.25; that upon said date said trustee, as such, executed to the plaintiffs, in the firm name and style of A. S. Barnes & Co., his written obligation to pay the same out of the special school fund of said township on or before the 20th day of January . . . . It further averred that George W. Kemp was elected trustee as the successor of King, and a refusal to pay the amount. . . . Appellant filed a demurrer to the complaint, which was overruled and the ruling assigned as error. The question presented is as to whether a township school trustee has authority to purchase school books and bind the school township for the payment of the same.

It is contended by counsel for appellee that section 4444, Rev. St. 1881, authorizes the township trustee to purchase necessary school books for the schools of his township. So much of said section as is material in the consideration of this case is as follows: "The trustees shall take charge of the educational affairs of their respective townships, towns, and cities. They shall employ teachers, establish and locate conveniently a sufficient number of schools for the education of the white children therein, and build or otherwise provide suitable houses, furniture, apparatus, and other articles and educational appliances necessary for the thorough organization and efficient management of said schools." . . .

The uncontroverted evidence in the case shows the books purchased to be 75 copies of Monteith's Popular Science Readers; that they were used by the pupils in their reading exercises, as contended by counsel, "to give the pupils a change in reading exercises, to draw out new thoughts, and an additional incentive to new exertion." The same could be said of any new readers or text-books purchased by the trustee and put in use in the schools. They would produce a change and stimulate the mind and divert the line of thought from the subjects in the old books, but it must be admitted, and it is too plain to require argument to demonstrate the proposition, that if the trustee has the authority to purchase this class of books he may purchase any other readers, spelling-books, or any other class of text-books; that he may supply all the text-books used in the schools of his township at the expense of his school township. This may be the proper system for our state to adopt. That is not for us here to determine, but the trustees cannot pursue such a course and bind the school township without some further legislation on the subject. . . . School townships are corporations with limited statutory powers, and all who deal with a trustee of a school township are charged with notice of the scope of his authority, and that he can bind his township only by such contracts as are authorized by law. . . .

The fact that the books were received by the trustee, and used under his direction, creates no liability. . . .

Guides for Class Discussion

1. Compare this decision with the one rendered in *White River School Township* v. *Dorrell, infra.* Which do you think represents the "better" law? Give reasons.
2. Considering the date of this decision—1889—do you think it would still be followed in some jurisdictions?
3. What is the rationale of this decision?

43. "The courts in some states . . . hold that a district must pay or property retained and used under an ultra vires contract" p. 7).

WHITE RIVER SCHOOL TOWNSHIP v. DORRELL,
26 Ind. App. 538, 59 N.E. 867 (1901)
(Decided by the Appellate Court of Indiana)

[The facts of the case will be found in the material which follows].

ROBINSON, J. . . .

On August 4, 1896, appellant's [school district's] trustee was engaged in erecting a suitable and necessary school house in a certain school district having about 40 children of school age, and having no suitable school house. The contract price of the building was $1,300. The township had no funds belonging to the special school fund with which to pay for the completion of the building, and it required $500 to complete the building. The trustee represented to appellee that it was necessary for him to have such sum, and at the trustee's request, and for the purpose of completing the building, appellee turned over to the trustee that sum, which was used in paying for the erection of the building under the contract, and was paid by the trustee to the contractor for the purpose of paying for the completion of the building, and the township since that time and now retains the benefit derived from the use of such sum in the use of such school house for school purposes. Such sum was not in excess of the fund on hand to which the debt is chargeable and the fund derived from the tax assessed for the year 1896. The trial court held that appellee ought to be subrogated to the rights of the contractor to the extent of $500 with interest.

The right of subrogation is not founded upon contract, express or implied. It is based upon the principles of equity and justice, and includes every instance where one party, not a mere volunteer, pays for another debt for which the latter was primarily liable, and which in good conscience and equity he should have paid. . . . The findings show that the money received by the trustee was paid out by him for property actually received by the school corporation and retained by it. The contract for building the house was such a contract as the trustee was authorized to make. The money was advanced to the trustee for the purpose of completing a necessary and suitable school house. The trustee had not the means in hand to complete the building, and the money advanced was, in fact, applied to that purpose. To permit a recovery in such a case is in no way recognizing a general power in the trustee to borrow money.

There is no suggestion whatever of any fraud in the building of the house. Appellant has received and retains the benefit of the money so advanced, and the simplest principles of equity and justice require that it should repay it. . . .

Guides for Class Discussion

1. What is meant by "subrogation"?
2. On what grounds does the court justify its reasoning?
3. Are you in agreement with the court's thinking?
4. Do you think the court would have held as it did had there been fraud involved, or had the trustee not been possessed of the authority to build the building?

44. "*If a school board makes a contract for the erection of a school building or for the purchase of other school property which it had no authority to make, it cannot later ratify the contract by any act of its own so as to make it binding on the board*" (p. 7).

SCHOOL DIRECTORS v. FOGELMAN,
76 Ill. 189 (1875)
(Decided by the Supreme Court of Illinois)

[This was an action by the successors of certain school directors against the directors of a school district questioning the validity of three orders which they had drawn in favor of defendant. Each order was purported to be in part payment for the construction of a school house. It was contended that the directors had acted illegally, since no vote of the electors had been taken on the matter as required by statute.]

Mr. JUSTICE BREESE delivered the opinion of the Court:

.   .   .   .

It is conceded no vote of the people of the district was had authorizing the building of this school house. The orders purport, on their face, to be for such purpose, and it was no difficult matter for any person about negotiating them to ascertain if a vote had been taken. The returns of such an election are, by law, made to the town treasurer, the officer on whom they are drawn, and if inquiry had been made of him as to this fact, he would have informed the inquirer, as he testified, that no vote had been taken.

Section 48 of the act of 1865, which was in force when this contract was made, is most explicit. It declares it shall not be lawful for a board of directors to purchase or locate a school house site, or to purchase, build or remove a school house, etc., without a vote of the people, at an election to be called, etc. If this is the lawful course to be pursued, any other course to accomplish the object was necessarily unlawful, and the act null and void. These bodies can exercise no other powers than expressly granted, or such as may be necessary to carry into effect a granted power. Glidden et al. v. Hopkins, 47 Ill. 529. And it is fortunate for the people this power is so restricted. If, in the face of this law, a board of directors can lawfully contract for building a school house, to cost six hundred dollars, the contract price of the one in question, what is to prevent them to contract for a structure to cost sixty thousand dollars, or any other sum, and draw their orders on the treasurer at ten per cent in payment? We know of no limit to their power.

. . . .

It is also urged by appellee that the school house was accepted by the directors who incurred the debt, and that school was kept in it. That does not legalize the act, or bind the tax-payers. The question here presented is a question of power, and no act of the kind set up can make it valid for any purpose. Nor can the beneficiary in this case resort to such acts in support of his claim. In the absence of power to do the act, there can be no innocent holder of this paper. He should have looked to the authority to make the contract in satisfaction of which the orders are drawn.

There is no ground on which a recovery can be had against this board of directors, the appellants.

Guides for Class Discussion

1. On what basis did the court arrive at its decision?
2. Was the rule laid down by the court equitable from the point of view of the contractor?
3. See *Sullivan* v. *School District, infra.*

45. ". . . *if a school board enters into a contract for the purchase of school property which it had authority to make and the contract is unenforceable because of some irregularity in the making of it, the board may later ratify it*" (p. 7).

SULLIVAN v. SCHOOL DISTRICT,
39 Kan. 347, 18 P. 287 (1888)
(Decided by the Supreme Court of Kansas)

[This was an action to recover from a school district money owed a materialman by a contractor who had absconded from the state before the building for which he had contracted with the board had been completed. The district completed the building and had since occupied it. When the district refused to pay the materialman, he brought this action. The board contended there could be no recovery because the original contract with Eley, the contractor who absconded, was not made in the manner prescribed by statute. It had been made between Eley and a single member of the board, although there was evidence tending to show that the board had later ratified it. The real issue before the court was whether the board could legally ratify such a contract which had been irregularly made.]

VALENTINE, J. . . .

It must be remembered that the case was disposed of in the court below merely upon a demurrer to the plaintiffs' evidence. Hence the only real question for us now to consider is merely whether that portion of the evidence most favorable to the plaintiffs tended to prove the aforesaid ratification and confirmation or not, and not whether the whole of the evidence in the case in fact proved the plaintiffs' case or not. . . . It is admitted that the original contract with Eley was, at the time it was made, void, for the reason that it was not made by the entire school board, but only by a portion thereof. . . . But it is claimed by the plaintiffs that the evidence introduced in the court below tended to show a ratification of the contract by the entire school board, and also by the entire school-district. We think such a contract might be ratified, and might be made binding upon the school-district. . . . We think the evidence tended to prove that the contract was ratified by the school board, and also by the school-district. . . . We might say, however, that almost everything seems to have been done irregularly in that school-district. In some cases the director ignored both the other members of the school board, and generally the director and the treasurer ignored the clerk, and the clerk often failed to make entries. It seems that the school-district and its officers permitted, and perhaps even authorized these irregularities; and hence the courts should not construe these irregularities, or these separate acts of the separate members of the school board, too critically.

Guides for Class Discussion

1. Are you in agreement with the court? Give reasons.
2. See *School Directors* v. *Fogelman, supra.*
3. Do you think that the history of irregularities mentioned influenced the court's decision?

46. *"Formal action to ratify is not necessary; ratification takes place when a board so acts that its action is incompatible with any other assumption than its intent to ratify"* (p. 7).

FRANK V. BOARD OF EDUCATION OF JERSEY CITY,
90 N.J.L. 273, 100 A. 211 (1917)
(Decided by the Court of Error and Appeals of New Jersey)

[This was an action to collect from a school board for work done and materials furnished it by unauthorized agents. The contracts for such purchases were of a type that the district had the authority to make. The agents in question were a supervising architect and a vice principal of a high school. In making the purchases, the agents were only doing what had been permitted " 'for a number of years.' " Plaintiff had furnished other materials and done other work for the board under similar circumstances, and the board had always paid when billed. The board, in this case, did not deny the authority of the agents in question until three years after the last work had been performed. The lower court ruled in plaintiff's favor, and the board appealed. The higher court affirmed the decision of the lower court. In so doing it held there was an implied agency and that ratification could be implied from the board's acts.]

BLACK, J. . . .

.   .   .   .

In the case under discussion, the School Law of the State . . . provides
that the board of education in a city school district such as Jersey City
is vested with the power of making contracts in and by its corporate
name and by section 50 every such board shall have the supervision,
control, and management of the public schools and public school property
in its district. It may appoint a superintendent of schools, a business
manager, and other officers, agents and employes, as may be needed.
Section 52 provides the board may at any time order repairs to school
buildings to an amount not exceeding $500, may authorize the purchase
of supplies to an amount not exceeding $250, without advertisement.
Section 72 provides for a business manager, who shall supervise, if there
be one, the construction and repair of all school buildings, and shall report
monthly to the board of education the progress of the work; that repairs
not exceeding the sum of $100 may be ordered by the business manager,
and repairs not exceeding the sum of $500 may be ordered by the com-
mittee of the board having charge of the repair of school property, without
the previous order of the board and without advertisement. In this statute,
as will be seen, there is express authority for the appointment of an agent,
a business manager. The term is immaterial. A supervising architect or
vice principal might just as well be called an agent or business manager.
. . .

The literature of the law of agency is rich in adjudged cases. . . . The
agency may be implied from the recognition or acquiescence of the alleged
principal as to acts done in his behalf by the alleged agent, especially
if the agent has repeatedly been permitted to perform acts like the one
in question. . . . So ratification may be implied from any acts, words, or
conduct on the part of the principal which reasonably tend to show an
intention on the part of the principal to ratify the unauthorized acts or
transactions of the alleged agent . . . , provided the principal in doing
the acts relied on as a ratification acted with knowledge of the material
facts. . . . The rule is particularly applicable, where it appears that the
principal has repeatedly recognized and affirmed similar acts by the agent
. . . So a municipal corporation may ratify the unauthorized acts and
contracts of its agents or officers which are within the scope of the
corporate powers, but not otherwise. . . .

Guides for Class Discussion

1. What line of reasoning did the court follow in arriving at its
   decision? Are you in agreement with the court's thinking? Give
   reasons.
2. The court noted that the board knew that the materials were

furnished and the work done about the time when this happened. Do you think this affected the result? Why?
3. What limitation to the general rule, that ratification may be implied from the board's actions, did the court recognize?

7. *"It is difficult to determine what constitutes substantial performance of a building contract but the courts are agreed that there . . . substantial performance . . . [if] the building is such as to accomplish the purpose for which it was built"* (p. 8).

STATE v. GOODMAN,
351 S.W. (2d) 763 (Mo.) (1961)
(Decided by the Supreme Court of Missouri)

[In Missouri a school board and a contractor, who had been awarded the contract for the construction of a combination gymnasium and music building, found it impossible to agree and litigation was resorted to. The contractor had substantially completed the building when the district took it over. It had been using the building for approximately three years when this action was brought. The real question before the court was the amount due the contractor by the board. In its decision the court commented on the meaning of "substantial completion" or "substantial performance" it outlined the method for determining the amount due the contractor at the time of final settlement.]

STORCKMAN, Judge.

. . . .

. . . the evidence showed that on September 6, 1957, plaintiff's architect, defendant, and the attorneys for the parties went through the building together and that the architect "made up a list of what remained to be done." This was referred to as the "punch list" and was introduced in evidence as plaintiff's Exhibit Y. No evidence was offered, however, as to cost of completing the items on the punch list. As to these items the opinion states, 336 S.W. 2d loc. cit. 101: "As of September 21, 1957, the architect compiled a list of items (a punch list) necessary to finally complete

the building in accordance with the plans and specifications. Aside fro
the defective roof (eliminated by the stipulation of the parties) the larg
of this long list of items was '5 doors missing,' replacing certain oth
doors with doors of another type wood, painting in places, grouti
certain windows and numerous other small items. The district was entitl
to a completed building, including these items, and the list establish
that the building was not complete. Nevertheless the architect had certifie
as the contract contemplated, that there was 'substantial completion'
the building. . . ."

Paragraph III of plaintiff's pleading having been voluntarily dismisse
the items on the "punch list" so far as the record shows, were the only or
needed to make the building conform to the plans and specifications. T
architect had certified to the board that the building was substantia
complete as of May 21, 1957. *The building was substantially comple
when it had reached the stage in its construction when it could have be
put to the use for which it was intended* even though comparatively min
items remained to be furnished or performed in order to make it confor
to the plans and specifications of the completed building. . . . [Empha
supplied.]

Guides for Class Discussion

1. What constitutes "substantial performance"?
2. Compare this decision with the one rendered in *Dodge
   Kimball, infra.*
3. What was meant by the statement "The district was entitl
   to a completed building . . ."?

18. "A school board may not refuse to accept a schoolhouse if the contractor has acted in good faith and substantially performed his contract . . . [but, in such a case] the board will be required to pay the contractor [only] the contract price, less deductions to cover omissions in performance" (p. 8).

DODGE v. KIMBALL,
203 Mass. 364, 89 N.E. 542 (1909)
(Decided by the Supreme Judicial Court of
Massachusetts, Berkshire)

[This was an action to recover payment on the balance of the contract for the construction of a building. Plaintiff became a bankrupt and never completed the building. There were at least 0 different particulars in which the contract was not performed. By agreement of all parties concerned, the matter was referred to a referee whose determination of matters of fact was final, but his decisions of law were subject to review by the courts. He ruled that plaintiff was not entitled to recover, and plaintiff appealed his decision to the courts. In making its ruling, the court was forced to consider whether there had been substantial compliance and whether defendant could be required to pay for that part of the contract which was performed.]

KNOWLTON, C. J. . . .

. . . .

It is to be noticed, first, that the question whether there was a substantial performance of the contract is to be determined in reference to the entire contract. . . . The referee might well find that the plaintiff failed to perform the contract substantially, in view of all his departures from it. . . . The validity of the finding must be determined in reference to all the facts of the case. But as the referee indicates that this breach is the principal reason for his decision we will consider this branch of the case by itself.

Formerly it was generally held in this country, as it is held in England, that a contractor could not recover under a building contract, unless there was a full and complete performance of it, or a waiver as to the parts not performed, and that he could not recover on a quantum meruit after a partial performance from which the owner had received benefit, unless there had been such subsequent dealings between the parties as would create an implied contract to pay for what had been done. . . . But i most of the American states a more liberal doctrine has been establishe in favor of contractors for the construction of buildings, and it is generall held that if a contractor has attempted in good faith to perform his contrac and has substantially performed it—although by inadvertence he has faile to perform it literally according to its terms—he may recover under th contract, with a proper deduction to the owner for the imperfections o omissions in the performance. . . . It would seem that in cases of thi kind, while the plaintiff recovers under the contract, not the contract price but the contract price less the deduction, he ought to aver, not absolut performance, but only substantial performance of his contract and a righ to recover only the balance after allowing the owner a proper sum fo the failure to do the work exactly in the way required. . . . The rule ver generally adopted is that, to entitle the plaintiff to recover, he needs t show only that he proceeded in good faith in an effort to perform th contract, and that the result was a substantial performance of it, althoug there may be various imperfections or omissions that call for a consider able diminution of the contract price. The reason for this construction o such contracts is in part the difficulty of attaining perfection in the qualit of the materials and workmanship, and of entirely correcting the effec of a slight inadvertence, and the injustice of allowing the owner to retai without compensation the benefit of a costly building upon his real estate that is substantially, but not exactly, such as he agreed to pay for. I none of the courts of this country, so far as we know, is the contractor lef remediless under conditions like those above stated. The recovery per mitted is generally upon the basis of the contract, with a deduction fo the difference between the value of the substantial performance show and the complete performance which would be paid for at the contrac price.

Guides for Class Discussion

1. While this case did not involve a school building, did thi have any effect on the decision?
2. How did the court arrive at its decision?
3. Are you in agreement with this decision? Give reasons.

49. *"Even though a school building has been accepted and paid for, it has been held that a school board may sue the contractor for defective performance"* (p. 8).

RUBINO v. BOARD OF TRUSTEES,
12 Cal. Rptr. 690 (1961)
(Decided by the District Court of Appeal,
Third District, California)

[This was an action brought by a contractor, who constructed a school plant and playground, to recover for additional work performed by him in order to remedy a defect. The defect was discovered after the contract had been completed and the work accepted by the board. The cost of repairing the damage was $973.40. It was to collect this amount that this action was brought. The plaintiff contended that, when the board accepted the building it discharged him from all obligations, even though the contract had been defectively performed; and that the board was liable for the cost of repairs. The board contended otherwise. The trial court ruled in favor of the board and against the contractor. On appeal, its decision was upheld by the higher court.]

SCHOTTKY, Justice.

. . . .

The trial court found that "the proximate cause of the damage to the southwest corner of the playground area was the overflowing of the water from the ditch due to the inadequacy of the eight-inch well casing to carry the flow of the ditch." The court found further that the school district ordered Plaintiffs to repair the damage aforesaid in January, 1969 [sic], maintaining that this damage was caused through the fault of the Plaintiffs; that Plaintiffs disclaimed any responsibility for the damage but, without admitting liability or responsibility and because it was raining and in order to avoid additional damages, the Plaintiffs caused repairs to be made." The repairs cost $973.40 and this action was brought to recover this amount. As stated recovery was denied.

Appellants contend that acceptance of the work precludes recovery on behalf of the school district for any later discovered defects. Appellants rely on cases such as City Street Improvement Company v. City of Marysville, 155 Cal. 419, 101 P. 308, 23 L. R. A., N. S., 317, and Hagginwood Sanitary District v. Downer Corporation, 179 Cal. App. 2d 756, 3 Cal. Rptr. 873. Both involved contracts with provisions to the effect that the work was to be done under the direction and to the satisfaction of an engineer. Both held that acceptance by the engineer precluded recovery for any defective work except if fraud were proved. In Hagginwood Sanitary District v. Downer Corporation, supra, the court stated at page 760 of 179 Cal. App. 2d, at page 876 of 3 Cal. Rptr: "It is the rule in this state that the decision of an engineer or superintendent approving or disapproving the work as performed under a contract is in the absence of fraud, bad faith or mistake conclusive and binding on the parties where the contract either expressly provides that it shall be final and conclusive or in plain language shows that it was the intention of the parties that the person to whom the question is submitted shall be the final arbiter of it. Brown v. Aguilar, 202 Cal. 143, 259 P. 735. . . ."

We do not believe that the decisions relied upon by appellants are determinative of the instant appeal. The appeal is on the judgment roll and the contract is not a part of the record. The question of whether the acceptance operated as a discharge of the defectively performed contract was a question of fact for the trial court to resolve . . . , and we must assume that the evidence supports the findings and judgment of the court denying recovery.

The judgment is affirmed.

Guides for Class Discussion

1. Do you think this decision is equitable? Give reasons.
2. Had the defect been discovered as much as five or ten years after the building had been accepted, do you think the court would have held as it did? Why?

50. *"Authority to build schoolhouses carries with it by implication authority to require a contractor to whom a building contract is let to give a bond guaranteeing the faithful performance of the contract and the payment for all labor and materials used in the construction of the building" (p. 8).*

BOARD OF PRESIDENT AND DIRECTORS OF THE ST. LOUIS PUBLIC SCHOOLS v. WOODS,
77 Mo. 197 (1883)
(Decided by the Supreme Court of Missouri)

[When a contractor, who had agreed to construct a schoolhouse, failed to perform the duties required of him under the contract, the school board brought this action to collect from his sureties. Specifically, it was charged that the contractor failed to pay all just claims of sub-contractors and materialmen, items covered by the bond. Defendants argued that the bond, in so far as it authorized plaintiffs to bring this suit, was void because plaintiffs were only authorized, by statute, to contract for the construction of the building and payment therefor. The main question before the court was the authority of the board or district to require a bond in the absence of statute so authorizing it to do.]

MARTIN, C. . . .

. . . .

I am unable to adopt the conclusion reached by the learned counsel for the appellant, to the effect that the bond now sued on was beyond the powers of the board to accept, or that it "is repugnant or inconsistent with the objects of its creation." By the act of incorporation, the board is vested with "the charge and control of the public schools and all the property appropriated to the use of public schools within said city." It is also empowered "to do all lawful acts which may be proper or convenient to carry into effect the object of the corporation." . . .

The board of public schools certainly has the power to build school houses. It has the right to make contracts with contractors for the erection of school buildings. And as germane to these powers, I think it has the right like any other proprietor, to exact conditions from its contractors, which shall tend to secure and pay off the material men and laborers, who unquestionably contribute most to the erection of such buildings. Viewed from the narrow standpoint of private economy, this must be the cheapest way to erect such costly and commodious structures. Otherwise as the statutes furnish no security to material men or laborers in the mechanics' lien law, as against the board, on account of its being a municipal corporation, they will be compelled to add something to the materials and labor going into the school buildings, on the well known principle which prevails throughout the business world, that high prices and high interest always attend bad security. In a wider sense, I think, the bond is germane to the corporate objects of the school board. . . . I must decline to hold that the school board in the conduct of its business transactions ought to be controlled by such a phlegmatic sense of justice toward its builders, as the learned counsel for the appellants think so appropriate to it as a public corporation. The object and purpose of the bond being entirely within the powers of the board, and the board being constituted the trustee of an express trust in the bond, the right to sue on it ought not to be questioned.

Guides for Class Discussion

1. Is this decision equitable? Give reasons.
2. By what line of reasoning did the court arrive at its decision?

51. "... the obligation of a surety on a bond to insure the performance of a building contract is measured by the terms of the contract; but where the liability in the contract is broader than in the bond, many courts have held that the bond is the measure of the surety's liability" (p. 8).

DUNLAP v. EDEN,
15 Ind. App. 575, 44 N.E. 560 (1896)
(Decided by the Appellate Court of Indiana)

[This was an action by a contractor against a sub-contractor and his surety upon a performance bond. In this case, the contract provided that the sub-contractor would be responsible for paying for any and all materials, but the bond contained no such provision. The question before the court was whether surety's liability was governed by the terms of the contract or the bond.]

Davis, C. J. . . .

. . . .

The rule is that where a written instrument is the foundation of a
pleading, and is made an exhibit, its statements will control the allegations
of the pleading. . . . Therefore, in determining the liability of the sureties
in this action, we are governed by the terms and conditions of the bond,
and not by the allegations in relation thereto in the complaint. The contention of counsel for appellant is that the contract and bond, having been
executed contemporaneously, are treated as one instrument, and that the
sureties on the bond are bound for the performance of all the terms and
conditions of the contract. Assuming that the bond and contract should be
read and construed together, it does not follow that the obligors on the
bond are liable for all the debts contracted by Eden in the execution of
the contract. They are only bound to the extent that they guarantied the
payment of such debts. . . . In this case, under the terms and conditions
of the contract, Eden was to complete the work, pay for the work and
material, and indemnify Waggener against loss, etc.; but, under the
terms of the bond, the obligors were bound only that Eden should complete the work, and indemnify Waggener. In other words, as before
observed, there is no provision in the bond that Eden shall pay for the
work and material. There is no general condition in the bond that Eden
shall in all things fully keep and perform the contract between himself
and Waggener. There is no provision therein of similar import. The
language of the bond is clear, plain, and explicit, and there is no aver-
ment that there was any mistake in drawing the bond, by reason of which
the condition that Eden should pay for labor and material was omitted.
It is a familiar rule that where a bond appears to be complete and perfect
on its face, with conditions fully expressed, a new condition, in the absence
of mistake, cannot be added.

Guides for Class Discussion

1. While this decision was rendered in a case brought by a contractor against a sub-contractor, do you think the court would
   have followed the same rule had the case involved a school
   district and a contractor instead? Give reasons.
2. What implications does this case have for school administration?

52. ". . . *contracts for suretyship will be construed . . . strictly against a surety for pay*" (p. 8).

Phoenix Indemnity Co. v. Board of Public Instruction,
114 So. (2d) 478 (Fla.) (1959)
(Decided by the District Court of Appeal of Florida, First District)

[This was an action against a contractor and his surety on a performance bond for the purpose of recovering unpaid insurance premiums for workmen's compensation, public liability, and property damage insurance taken out by the contractor. The contractor was required by statute to carry the insurance and to furnish the bond. In fact, the contract was made a part of the bond. In addition to the conditions prescribed by the statutes, the bond was also conditioned to guarantee the payment of "all bills for '*services* furnished to the principal in connection with the contract.'" The question before the court was whether the surety under the bond, could be held liable for the cost of the insurance mentioned. The court held it could.]

STURGIS, Judge.

. . . .

While this is a case of first impression in Florida, it is the general rule that whether a surety for compensation will be held liable for unpaid insurance premiums depends strictly upon the terms of the bond as construed in the light of applicable statutes.

. . . .

In the last case [McCrary v. Dade County, 8 Fla. 652, 86 So. 612, 614] it was held that the phrase "supplying labor and materials in prosecution of the work" is not limited in meaning to the structure, building or thing produced in which the labor or material must actually enter and become an integral part. Adhering thereto, we hold that the liability of the surety for the insurance premiums involved in this suit must be construed in accordance with the terms and qualifications of the formal public work contract for the performance of which the bond was given, or in the light of the special circumstances under which the insurance was furnished. And as the bond in suit is conditioned to pay bills for "services" and to complete all "work comprehended by the contract free and clear of all liens for labor or materials, or otherwise," we are persuaded that it contemplates performances and a guaranty beyond those specifically required by F.S. Section 255.05, F. S. A.

Contracts of suretyship for compensation are to be construed most strongly against the surety and in favor of the indemnity which the obligee has reasonable grounds to expect. They are regarded in the nature of an insurance contract and are governed by rules applicable to such contracts. The maxim that "sureties are favored in the law" has no application to contracts of suretyship by one engaged in the business for hire. The provisions of the bond should be considered as a whole and given that effect which was logically intended by the parties as shown by the entire instrument. . . .

Guides for Class Discussion

1. Compare this decision with the one rendered in *Dunlap, Eden, supra*.

2. On what basis did the court arrive at its decision?

53. *"When the bond is given by a surety company for pay, the bond is interpreted as are other contracts with a view of giving effect to the true meaning of the parties"* (p. 8).

BLYTH-FARGO CO. v. FREE,
46 Utah 233, 148 P. 427 (1915)
(Decided by the Supreme Court of Utah)

[In an action to recover on a bond given pursuant to a contract to construct a tunnel, the primary question before the court related to the interpretation of the bond. In arriving at its decision, the court gave considerable attention to how a bond should be interpreted.]

FRICK, J. . . .

. . . .

Counsel for appellant insist that the bond in question is an indemnity bond pure and simple, and was intended to indemnify and save harmless the company for any damages it might suffer in case the contractor did not, in the particulars specified in the bond, comply with its conditions.

. . . Respondent contends that, inasmuch as appellant copied a certain provision contained in the contract into the bond, it was bound to copy it correctly, or suffer the consequences. . . .

. . . Taking the bond as it is written, and under the pleadings and evidence, we must arrive at the intention of the parties from the bond as written, can the respondent sustain this action? Counsel contend that in view that the appellant is engaged in the business of furnishing such bonds for profit, and for the reason that it determines upon the language and phraseology that is used therein, therefore such bonds are to be liberally construed in favor of the beneficiary. A number of cases are cited in support of the contention. While some courts use the expression that bonds given under such circumstances are to be liberally construed in favor of the beneficiary, yet that is not precisely what the courts mean. The rules or canons of interpretation which are resorted to by the courts to aid them in arriving at the meaning or intention of any written document, instrument, contract, or statute, are precisely the same in every case. Where, however, the intention or meaning is once ascertained, then the application of the contract to the subject-matter is in certain cases and under certain circumstances perhaps more liberal than under others. It has many times been decided that sureties are favorites of the law, and that "the contract of a surety is strictissimi juris, and it is not to be extended beyond the express terms in which it is expressed." . . . This is all that the courts mean when they use the somewhat loose expression, which they sometimes do, that the contract of a surety is to be "strictly construed." Moreover, what is meant by the expression that the surety or indemnitor who executes such bond for profit does not come within the rule of strict construction is that, as against such surety or indemnitor, when the meaning or intention of the parties to such an instrument is once ascertained the bond will be applied neither strictly nor liberally, but with the view of effectuating the object or purpose for which it was given. Although a surety under such a bond is entitled to have the meaning and intention of the parties determined by the same rules that the meaning and intention of parties to other instruments are determined, yet in case of an ambiguity in the language used, or, if a doubt arises by reason of the use of a particular term or phrase, the doubt may be, and usually is, resolved against the surety for profit, whereas it may be, and usually is, otherwise as against a voluntary surety.

Guides for Class Discussion

1. While this case did not involve a school district, do you think the court would have followed a different line of reasoning if it had?

2. Compare this decision with the one rendered in *Dunlap v. Eden, supra;* with *Phoenix Indemnity Co.* v. *Board of Public Instruction, supra.*

54. *"Under the common law it was originally held that any change in a contract without the consent of the surety released the surety from all liability"* (p. 8).

INDEPENDENT DISTRICT OF MASON CITY v. REICHARD,
50 Iowa 98 (1878)
(Decided by the Supreme Court of Iowa)

[This was an action to recover on a bond to secure the performance of a school-building contract entered into by a contractor with a school board. Some time after the signing of the contract the board and the contractor entered into a new agreement altering the terms of the original contract. When the contractor failed to complete the project, this action was brought to collect from him and his surety. The surety contended that, because the contract for which the bond had been given was altered, it was relieved of all liability, and the court agreed.]

DAY, J. . . .

. . . .

This contract was signed by Jacob Reichard [contractor] and by the board of directors of plaintiff, and attested by their secretary. There is no proof that the sureties upon the bond assented to this contract, and it is not claimed that they ever did assent thereto. The changes made by this agreement are material. By the original contract defendant Jacob Reichard was to have twenty thousand dollars in bonds as soon as he gave bond, with sureties, for the proper performance of his contract. Under this supplemental agreement no payment was to be made until twenty days after the agreement was signed, and then only twelve thousand dollars was to be paid. Of the balance, the payment of six thousand dollars was to be postponed until the walls of the building were completed and ready for the joists; one thousand dollars was not to be paid until the building was accepted; and the remaining one thousand dollars was to be allowed to the school board for negotiating the bonds. We think it is very clear that these changes operated to discharge the sureties upon the bond.

"Any alteration, however *bona fide*, by the creditor and the principal, without the assent of the surety, of the terms of the original agreement, so far as they relate to the subject-matter in respect of which the surety became responsible for the principal, will exonerate the surety." Chitty on Contracts (11th Ed.), 776. "And this doctrine seems to hold, although the new terms thus substituted vary only in a slight degree from those of the original agreement." Id., 777. In regard to this principle, in *Miller v. Stewart*, 9 Wheat., 680, it is said: "It is not sufficient that he" (a surety) "may sustain no injury by a change in the contract, or that it may even be for his benefit. He has a right to stand upon the very terms of his contract and if he does not assent to any variation of it, and a variation is made, it is fatal."

Guides for Class Discussion

1. Do you think this decision was equitable? Give reasons.
2. Had surety approved the changes in the contract, do you think the court would have held it liable on the bond, or would it have required a new bond?
3. The court noted that the changes made in the contract were "material." Do you think it would have held as it did had they been "immaterial"? Give reasons.

55. ". . . *it is generally held that [if any change in a contract is made without the consent of the surety for pay] the surety will be relieved entirely only if the change in the contract increases his liability materially; and, if the change is not great enough to relieve the surety entirely, he will be relieved pro tanto—i.e., to the amount of his extra obligation*" (p. 8).

MARYLAND CASUALTY CO. v. EAGLE RIVER UNION FREE HIGH SCHOOL DISTRICT,
188 Wis. 520, 205 N.W. 926 (1925)
(Decided by the Supreme Court of Wisconsin)

[The nature of the action and issue before the court is clearly stated in the quotation which follows.]

OWEN, J. . . .

. . . .

The appellant claims, generally, that it was discharged from its obligation by reason of breaches of the contract on the part of the school district in paying out money contrary to the provisions of the contract. It claims that money was paid to the contractor in violation of the contract provision that payment should be made only once a month, and then only upon architects' certificates, and only to the extent of 90 per cent. of the material and labor entering into the construction of the building. It also claims that a complete new contract was made between the school district and the contractor in March, 1923, when the school district agreed to advance money in the manner set forth in the statement of facts, to enable the contractor to prosecute the work of construction. . . .

At the outset of our consideration of this case it is well to have in mind the general principles of law touching the liability of paid sureties upon bonds of this nature, at least so far as they can be invoked to work a discharge of the surety. It is thoroughly established by the decisions of this court that contracts of this kind, entered into for a consideration by surety companies engaged in such business, are in effect contracts of insurance, and the contracts are not to be construed according to the rules of law applicable to the ordinary accommodation surety. . . . Sureties were favorites of the common law, because their liabilities were gratuitously assumed. The rules and principles of the common law declaring the rights and liabilities of sureties were developed in an atmosphere surcharged with sympathy for the surety. Accordingly it was held that any conduct prejudicial to the surety resulted in the total discharge of the surety from any liability. . . .

The number of cases coming to the courts, in which paid sureties are urging their complete discharge by reason of some infraction of the contract on the part of the indemnified, suggests that a more specific rule concerning their rights and liabilities be stated. . . . While the contract between the parties should govern their rights and liabilities, such contract should no longer be construed strictly in favor of the surety. This has often been declared. It would seem too, that not every circumstance prejudicial to the interests of the surety should work a total discharge of the surety, without any reference or consideration to the extent to which the interests of the surety were in fact prejudiced by such circumstance. In other words, a paid surety should not suffer damage by breach of any duty or obligation resting upon the indemnified; but neither should the surety be permitted to profit thereby. If the breach on the part of the indemnified results in damage to the surety, the surety should be compensated for such damage, but no further.

. . . We must not be understood as saying that there can be no conduct on the part of the indemnified which will result in the absolute discharge of the paid surety; but we say that, as a general proposition, considerations of justice are fully met when the surety is recouped to the extent of the losses actually sustained by reason of misconduct on the part of the indemnified.

Guides for Class Discussion

1. Do you think the rule laid down by the court is equitable? Give reasons.
2. On what basis did the court arrive at its decision?
3. See *Dunlap* v. *Eden, supra;* and *Phoenix Indemnity Co.* v. *Board of Public Instruction, supra.*

56. "*A surety who gives a bond guaranteeing the performance of a building contract and the payment for labor and materials will not be relieved of his obligation to laborers and materialmen by any alteration in the original contract to which they did not give their consent*" (p. 9).

United States Fidelity & Guaranty Co. v. Cicero Smith Lumber Co.,
290 S.W. 307 (Tex.) (1927)
(Decided by the Court of Civil Appeals of Texas, Amarillo)

[This was an action by a lumber company against a contractor and his surety for an unpaid bill for lumber used in the construction of a schoolhouse. The bond in question was made for the use of those furnishing material under the contract. The bonding company denied liability on several grounds, one of which was based on the contention that, inasmuch as the board had not retained 20 per cent of the contract price until the building was completed, as it had agreed to do, surety was relieved of its liability. The question before the court was the effect of the alteration of the original agreement, to which the materialman did not consent, on the liability of surety.]

Hall, C. J. . . .

. . . .

The first proposition urged in the brief is that sureties upon a contractor's bond for the construction of a public school building are discharged where the trustees of the district fail to retain 20 per cent. of the contract price until after the building was completed, as required by the contract. We overrule this contention, for the reason that the bond recites that it was made for the use of all persons who might furnish material under the contract, and further provides that any one furnishing material could sue upon the bond, though not specifically named as an obligee therein. In answer to special issue No. 2, the jury found that the payment of more than 80 per cent. of the contract price had been made by the school trustees without the knowledge and consent of the lumber company. While such excess payment by the trustees would have released the sureties from all liability to the owners of the building, the rule is otherwise as to parties furnishing material to be used in the building. The rule is that, where the obligation names materialmen and laborers as obligees, the sureties are not discharged from liability to them by reason of the owner having made payments in violation of the bond, unless such obligees knew of such violation at the time they furnished the material.

Guides for Class Discussion

1. How do you think the court would have ruled had the school district, instead of a materialman, been the complainant?
2. Do you think this decision is equitable? Give your reasons.

57. *"Where there is evidence . . . that the contractor intended to give a statutory bond, the terms of the statute will generally be read into the bond and the surety will be held liable to pay for labor and materials"* (p. 9).

COLLINS v. NATIONAL FIRE INSURANCE COMPANY OF HARTFORD,
105 So. (2d) 190 (Fla.) (1958)
(Decided by the District Court of Appeal of Florida, Second District)

[At issue in this case was the question of whether a performance bond that did not specifically contain the statutory provision that it guaranteed payment to all persons supplying labor, material, and supplies to the contractor or subcontractors, protected laborers and materialmen. The court held that it did, on the ground that the bond should be construed in light of the law or statute requiring it and the purpose it is supposed or expected to accomplish.]

KANNER, Chief Judge.

. . . .

The purpose of the provision contained in section 255.05, that a contractor shall promptly make payments for labor, material, and supplies, is to protect laborers and materialmen whose labor and material are put into public buildings or projects on which they can acquire no lien. A contractor's bond should be construed in the light of this section and must be supposed to accomplish its purpose. . . .

. . . .

In the case of the City of Ocala for Use of Standard Oil Co. v. Continental Casualty Co., 1930, 99 Fla. 736, 127 So. 326, 77 A. L. R. 8, the action was against the contractor's surety and the contractor to recover for material and services rendered to the contractor in connection with street improvements, which action involved the question of the sufficiency of the bond. In that case, it is stated, quoting from 127 So. at page 328:

"There was no duty or obligation of the surety company to enter into the bond that the statute requires the contractor to execute 'before commencing' the 'public work.' If a surety company executes a penal bond purporting in terms or in substance or by sufficient reference to be in accordance with or for the purpose of complying with the requirements of the statute in cases of such contracts, as to 'additional obligation that such contractor shall promptly make payments to all persons supplying him labor, material and supplies used directly or indirectly in the prosecution of the work provided for in the contract,' the surety company will be liable as provided by the statute. . . ."

. . . .

In the Ocala case the bond contained no language to meet the requirement to protect the laborers or materialmen, nor was there language in the contract to fulfill this deficiency. However, it is clearly indicated that where a surety company executes a penal bond which appears by sufficient reference to be in compliance with or for the purpose of fulfilling the statutory bond conditions designed to protect laborers and materialmen in cases of public improvement, the surety company will be liable as provided by the bond.

Where a written contract refers to and sufficiently describes another document, that other document or so much of it as is referred to, may be regarded as a part of the contract and therefore is properly considered in its interpretation. Also where a contract expressly provides that it is subject to the terms and conditions of other contracts which are definitely specified, such other contracts must be considered in determining the intent of the parties to the transaction. . . . The bond here specifically referred to and described the contract and expressly stated that the contract was annexed to it. The contract was so annexed. Under the stated principles, we hold that the language contained in the surety bond here sufficiently by reference incorporates into the bond the language of the contract hereinabove quoted from article 7.

Guides for Class Discussion

1. Compare this decision with the one rendered in *Tennessee Supply Company* v. *Bina Young & Son, infra.*
2. Are you in agreement with the line of reasoning adopted by the court? Give reasons.

58. *"Where there is evidence . . . that the contractor intended to give a statutory bond, . . . [some] courts interpret the bond strictly and will not read the terms of the statute into it"* (p. 9).

TENNESSEE SUPPLY COMPANY v. BINA YOUNG & SON,
142 Tenn. 142, 218 S.W. 225 (1919)
(Decided by the Supreme Court of Tennessee)

[This was an action against a contractor and the security on his bond by a materialman to collect for materials furnished the contractor and used in the construction of a school building. The bond had apparently been taken to meet the statutory requirement, although the bond itself was not as broad as the statute. The question before the court was whether the bond should be interpreted strictly, or whether the terms of the statute should be read into it. The court held that the bond should be interpreted strictly.]

MCKINNEY, J. . . . .

. . . .

Later . . . [the school commissioners] charged that the contractors had not erected said building according to contract, and asked that they be decreed damages on account of such breach.

They also charged in said cross-bill that it was the intention of the parties to have said bond drawn so as to comply with chapter 182 of the Acts of 1899, and prayed that said bond be reformed accordingly.

.   .   .   .

We will first dispose of the assignments of error made by the school commissioners, the first of which is as follows:

"The court erred in refusing to decree a reformation of said bond so as to expressly show that said contractors were to pay the materialmen and furnishers for the material used in construction of said building, and to have said bond so expressly provide."

.   .   .   .

A bond was executed by the contractors and delivered to Mr. Graf, the architect. This bond is not embodied in the transcript in this cause, and the record does not show the provisions and conditions thereof. However, Mr. Graf, acting for the school board, declined to accept said bond, but submitted a bond which had been prepared by his attorney, and which was executed by said contractors and their surety without any change or alteration. Mr. Graf testified that he had never heard of the act of 1899, and hence he could not have had same in mind.

The surety company executed the bond prepared by the obligees, and without any agreement as to the terms and conditions to be contained therein further than appears by the bond itself, which was prepared by the agent of the obligees, and it would be unfair and unjust to the surety company to reform the bond so as to make it different from the one which the parties agreed upon.

The second assignment of error is as follows:

"The court erred in holding and decreeing that said bond is not in compliance with chapter 182 of the Acts of 1899, and that therefore said surety company is not liable on said bond for the material and labor that went into the Jellico school building, and in failing to grant appellants a decree against said surety company for the aggregate amount of the decree in this cause for materials furnished Bina Young & Son by materialmen, to wit the sum of $3,980.77 and interest thereon and costs of the cause."

It has been held by this court that a bond of this character does not comply with chapter 182 of the Acts of 1899. . . .

.   .   .   .

It is apparent in this case that the bond was executed for the benefit of the owner, and not for the benefit of the laborers and materialmen, and since complainants are not parties to the bond, nor beneficiaries thereunder, they have no cause of action against the surety on said bond, and the chancellor was correct in dismissing that part of their bill.

Guides for Class Discussion

1. Compare this decision with the one rendered in *Collins* v. *National Fire Insurance Company of Hartford, supra.*
2. See *Green Bay Lumber Co.* v. *Independent School District, Infra.*
3. What line of reasoning motivated the court?

59. *"Where a contractor agrees to provide the labor and materials used in the construction of a school building and gives a bond to guarantee that his contract will be performed, he does not definitely agree to pay for the labor and materials, and there is no right of action against his surety"* (p. 9).

GREEN BAY LUMBER CO. v. INDEPENDENT SCHOOL DISTRICT,
121 Iowa 663, 97 N.W. 72 (1903)
(Decided by the Supreme Court of Iowa)

[This was an action by one who furnished materials to a contractor engaged in constructing a school building against a contractor and the sureties on his bond. The contract provided that the contractor would furnish labor and materials. "The sureties demurred on the ground that the bond was executed solely for the benefit of the district." The trial court sustained the demurrer, and its action was upheld on appeal.]

LADD, J. . . .

The sole question on this appeal is whether the bond executed by the contractor to the school district was also intended for the benefit of subcontractors furnishing labor and materials. If not so intended, the sureties are not liable, and the demurrer was properly sustained. It will be observed that the contract merely required Weaver to provide materials and perform the labor, but contains no stipulation in relation to the payment therefor by him. A condition for compliance therewith imposed on the bondsman no liability to the subcontractors. . . . The bond exacted first the erection of the building in compliance with the contract, and its "delivery free from any liens or claims of any kind." As no liens or claims might be asserted against the building, the sureties were safe in pledging that it should be without them. . . . Certainly an agreement to discharge them cannot be implied from a contract that a building shall be delivered clear of liens and claims, and it is inferred therefrom that payment shall be made of claims which could in no event be asserted against the building. . . . Neither the bond nor the contract in suit exacts of the contractor payment of labor or materials used in the building. . . . by no fair construction can the language be said to bind the contractor to pay any liens or claims whatever. It binds him to do no more than repay the district what it has been compelled to pay for the purposes mentioned. A careful reading of the bond leads to the inevitable conclusion that the sole object had in its execution was the indemnity of the school district. Not having been executed for the benefit of the labor and material men, they cannot recover thereon. . . .

Guides for Class Discussion

1. Do you think the rule laid down by the court in this case is equitable?
2. See *Tennessee Supply Company* v. *Bina Young & Son, supra.*
3. How could sureties have been made liable for labor and material?

60. "Where a contract . . . provides that the board retain each month a certain percentage of what is due the contractor in order to insure the completion of the building, and the contractor defaults, the contractor's surety has a claim on the retained percentage superior to that of laborers and materialmen or of a bank to which the contractor has assigned his rights to the retained percentage" (p. 9).

LEVINSON v. LINDERMAN,
51 Wash. 855, 322 P. (2d) 863 (1958)
(Decided by the Supreme Court of Washington,
Department 2)

[In this case a contractor defaulted and his surety completed the contract at a cost of $89,159.70. The district still owed—*i.e.*, it had retained—$62,200.29. This it deposited in the court's registry. Plaintiff and others had obtained a judgment against the contractor for $3,413.54. In addition, a bank had loaned the contractor $15,000 upon his promissory note, secured by the assignment of a progress payment. The question before the court was the distribution of the amount retained by the district. The trial court subordinated the claims of the surety to the judgment creditor and contract creditor just mentioned, whereupon surety appealed. The court, here, reversed the lower court and held that where the surety completed the contract, the funds retained by the board belonged to the surety by right of subrogation.]

Foster, Justice.

. . . .

The bank could not fail to know that the contract was for the construction of school buildings and that a performance bond was required by RCW 39.08.010 at the time of the execution of the contract. Inquiry would have shown that the contract prohibited the assignment in question, and that the school district had the right under the contract, in the event of the contractor's default, to complete the buildings and to use all sums unpaid for that purpose.

. . . .

The funds distributed by the judgment belong to the surety and not to the contractor, and, therefore, the bank acquired nothing by the assignment because the contractor had nothing to assign. . . .

*   *   *   *   *   *   *   *   *   *   *   *

There is another compelling reason for reversal. This is not a case of priorities between assignees under separate assignments of moneys belonging to the contractor, for the surety completed the buildings at a cost of $89,159.70, with only $62,200.29 remaining unpaid on the contract, and the deposited funds belong to the surety by right of subrogation.

The school district had the right to complete the work in any way it chose and to use the unpaid balance therefor. When the surety completed the construction, it was subrogated to the rights of the school district to the unpaid balance, and all of the funds in the court's registry belong to it.

*   *   *   *   *   *   *   *   *   *   *   *   *   *

The judgment must be reversed because the assignment was prohibited by contract and is, therefore, void, and the funds involved are those of the surety by right of subrogation. Upon the contractor's default, the school district had the right to apply the entire unpaid balance to the completion of the construction, and the surety on the performance bond completing the contract is subrogated to all its rights.

The judgment of respondent Osina under the writ of garnishment falls for the same reason, for at the time of the service of the writ, October 24, 1955, more than a year after the contractor's default and the completion of the work by the surety, the school district was not indebted to the contractor; hence, the respondent Osina obtained nothing by the garnishment.

Guides for Class Discussion

1. What is meant by the "right of subrogation"?
2. Are you in agreement with the court's reasoning? Give reasons.

61. *"It is commonly held that a school district will not be held liable for failure to take a bond conditioned to pay for labor and materials even though a statute requires that such a bond be taken"* (p. 9).

FREEMAN v. CITY OF CHANUTE,
63 Kan. 573, 66 P. 647 (1901)
(Decided by the Supreme Court of Kansas, Division No. 1)

[In this action an attempt was made to hold a municipality liable for loss sustained by one as the result of furnishing material to a contractor engaged in the construction of a public building. The municipal officers, in spite of a statute that required all persons who contracted to construct public improvements to give a bond, failed to require the contractor in question to provide the bond. On the ground that, because the district failed to obey the law, it should be held liable for loss sustained by a materialman, this action was brought. The court held the district not liable and ruled against the plaintiff.]

GREENE, J. . . .

. . . There are two kinds of duties which are imposed upon a municipal corporation. One is of that kind which arises from the grant of a special power, in the exercise of which the municipality is a legal individual. The other is of that kind which arises or is implied from the use of political rights under the general law in the exercise of which it is a sovereign. The former power is quasi private, and is used for private purposes; the latter is public, and used for public purposes. . . . In the exercise of its quasi private or corporate power a municipality is like a private corporation, and is liable for a failure to use its power well, or for an injury caused by using it negligently. In building its waterworks, gas, electric light plants, sewers, and other internal improvements which are for the exclusive benefit of the corporation, it is in the exercise of its quasi private power, and is liable to the same extent as are private corporations. . . . But in the exercise of the political or public power conferred upon it as an arm of the state for the benefit of all the people its officers, although appointed or elected by the city, paid and subject to be discharged by it, are not the agents of the municipality, but of the state, and the corporation is not liable either for their misfeasance or nonfeasance. . . .

The duty of taking the bond provided for in the statute . . . is not imposed upon the corporation. It is not taken for the benefit of the corporation or its inhabitants, but is for the benefit of any person who shall perform labor or furnish material to the person or persons who contracts with a public officer to construct any public improvements, whether such person be a resident of the city or elsewhere. The duty is a public one in the interest of the public, imposed by statute upon public officers, and with which the corporation in its private capacity has no concern.

Guides for Class Discussion

1. Compare this decision with the one in *Plumbing Supply Co.* v. *Board of Education, infra.*
2. The defendant in this case, it will be noted, was the city of Chanute. Do you think the court would have held the same had it been a school district? Give reasons.
3. Are you in agreement with this decision? Give reasons.

62. "*Where the statutes require a school board to take a bond conditioned to pay for labor and materials . . . members of the board will not, as a rule, be held personally liable for failure to take such a bond . . . .*" (p. 9).

PLUMBING SUPPLY CO. v. BOARD OF EDUCATION,
32 S.D. 270, 142 N.W. 1131 (1913)
(Decided by the Supreme Court of South Dakota)

[This was an action questioning the personal liability of school board members for failure to take a bond when the statute made it the duty of all public corporations to require that a contractor, when awarded a contract for the construction of a school building, put up a bond conditioned for the payment of labor and materials. The court here held that the school board members could not be held liable individually for their failure to obey the statute.]

McCoy, J. . . .

We are of the opinion that there is not now and never was any common-law liability against officers of this class, individually, for neglect to perform official duties. At common law the king could not be sued without his consent. Neither could any officer who represented the king. The same principle has been applied to the sovereign power of the state in this country. Members of a board of education fall within this class of officers who represent the king or who represent the sovereign power of the state in a public official capacity. Liability for negligence and suit therefor against the individual officer can only exist by virtue of an express statute creating the individual duty of such officer, and also authorizing the maintenance of a suit for failure to perform such duty. No such individual duty, as charged in the complaint, has ever been imposed upon such officers as members of a board of education as individuals, in this state. From a close reading of chapter 245, Laws 1909, it will be observed that the duty to take a contractor's bond, as alleged in the complaint, is imposed on the corporation only, and not on the officers thereof as individuals. . . .

. . . .

School districts are state agencies exercising and wielding a distributive portion of the sovereign power of the state, and the officers of school districts are the living agencies through whom the sovereign state act is carried into effect. A school district officer in the performance of his duties acts in a political capacity, as much so as the Governor of a state, and is not liable for negligent acts of omission occurring in the performance of such political or public duties, unless the sovereign power of the state has authorized and consented to a suit for such negligence. Now, in the matter of letting building contracts for the repair or construction of a public school building, and the taking of a contractor's bond, we are of the opinion that the members of a board of education act in a public and political capacity, as an agent of the state, in the carrying out of a portion of the distributed functions of state government, and are not liable to suit for negligent acts of omission, unless the state has by express statute consented to such suit. It therefore necessarily follows that there is no common-law liability for such negligent acts as are complained of in this case against the members of the board of education, as personal individuals, or as officers composing the board, and that if any such liability exists at all it must be based upon statute.

Guides for Class Discussion

1. Compare the decision in this case with the one in *Warren* v. *Glens Falls Indemnity Co., infra.*

2. Compare this decision with the one in *Freeman* v. *City of Chanute, supra.*
3. Which of these cases represents the "best" law? Give reasons.

63. *"Where the statutes require a school board to take a bond conditioned to pay for labor and materials . . . members of the board will [in some jurisdictions] . . . be held personally liable for failure to take such a bond"* (p. 9).

WARREN v. GLENS FALLS INDEMNITY CO.,
66 So. (2d) 54 (Fla.) (1953)
(Decided by the Supreme Court of Florida,
Special Division B)

[This was a suit against sureties on the official bonds of members of a County Board of Public Instruction, to recover loss incurred by plaintiff who furnished materials to a contractor on a school construction project and was unable to collect therefor. He based his claim on the ground the board failed to perform a ministerial duty, required by statute, of taking a bond from the contractor to guarantee payment of labor and materials. The lower court held against plaintiff, who appealed. The higher court reversed the lower court. It held the duty of taking the bond was mandatory and failure to follow the statute made the board members individually liable in tort.]

DREW, Justice.

. . . .

Section 255.05, Florida Statutes, 1951, F. S. A., has been on the statute books for many years. It was placed there to protect laborers and material-men who incorporate their labor and materials in public buildings on which they can have no lien. This section is extremely broad in its scope. It concerns itself with all public buildings and we find nothing in the School Code to even infer that it was not intended to apply to school buildings. On the contrary, section 237.31(4) can, and should, be construed to make this section, 255.05, a part thereof because, in section 237.31(4) it is ex pressly provided that the contractor *shall* provide bond "in such amount and for such purposes as [*shall be*] *prescribed by law* . . . ." (Emphasis supplied.) . . .

It is urged upon us by defendants below that the statute, 255.05, supra, does not place a ministerial duty on the board to require the bond; they say:

". . . ; it does not say that the board of public instruction shall require a person entering into a contract to execute a particular type bond. It was incumbent upon the contractor to furnish the proper bond and of course the school board would have approved of his bond if the bond furnished had complied with the regulations as set out in the School Code. . . ."

We wholly disagree with this argument. The provision in the statutes that the bond shall be required before commencing work is patently and clearly the same as saying that the school board shall see to it that the contractor does not begin work until the bond is executed, posted and duly approved. Only it would have such authority. The purpose is quite obviously to protect those who incorporate their labor or material in the structure. If there is any doubt as to the duty of the board in this respect, such doubt is completely dissipated by the concluding two sentences of the section making it the duty of the public body to furnish a copy of such bond to interested persons.

It is therefore our conclusion that it was the mandatory duty of the school board members to see to it that the bond required by said section 255.05 was posted before work was commenced; that the duty to do so was ministerial; that the failure to do so was a breach of the duty to faithfully perform the duties of the office and that persons suffering loss because thereof had a remedy against such board members individually in tort.

Guides for Class Discussion

1. Compare the holding in this case with that in *Plumbing Supply Co.* v. *Board of Education, supra.*
2. Which case represents the better law? Give reasons.
3. Compare this case with *Freeman* v. *City of Chanute, supra.*

SELECTED BIBLIOGRAPHY

1. Edwards, Newton. *The Courts and the Public Schools,* rev. ed. Chicago: University of Chicago Press, 1955.
2. Garber, Lee O. (Ed.) *Law and the School Business Manager.* Danville, Ill.: The Interstate Printers & Publishers, Inc., 1957.
3. Garber, Lee O. *Yearbook of School Law.* "School Property." Danville, Illinois: The Interstate Printers & Publishers, Inc., annually since 1950.
4. Hamilton, Robert H. and Paul R. Mort. *The Law and Public Education,* rev. ed. Brooklyn: The Foundation Press, Inc., 1959.
5. Hamilton, Robert R. and E. Edmund Reutter, Jr. *Legal Aspects of School Board Operation.* New York: Bureau of Publications, Teachers College, Columbia University, 1958.
6. Punke, Harold H. *The Courts and Public-School Property.* Chicago: University of Chicago Press, 1936.
7. Reutter, E. Edmund, Jr. *Schools and the Law.* ("Legal Almanac Series," No. 17.) New York: Oceana Publications, Inc., 1960.

SCHOOL LAW CASEBOOK SERIES—NO. 8

The Law Governing the Financing of Public Education

By

LEE O. GARBER

and

NEWTON EDWARDS

The Interstate
Printers and Publishers
Danville, Illinois

CONTENTS

INTRODUCTION

The publication of this book marks the completion of a series of eight casebooks, which, taken together, give a complete coverage to the field of "School Law." The first four books—constituting the first series—deal with school law for teachers, and are entitled: "The Public School in Our Governmental Structure"; "The Law Relating to the Creation, Alteration, and Dissolution of School Districts"; "The Law Governing Teaching Personnel"; and "The Law Governing Pupils." Earlier books in this second series deal with law for the school administrator primarily, and are entitled: "The Law Governing School Board Members and School Board Meetings"; "Tort and Contractual Liability of School Districts and School Boards"; and "The Law Governing School Property and School Buildings."

The authors, who have prepared all eight casebooks, need no introduction. Newton Edwards, the pioneer and foremost authority in the field of School Law, is the author of the leading textbook in the field—*The Courts and the Public Schools*. Lee O. Garber is the author of the *Yearbooks of School Law*, which have appeared annually since 1950. He is also the author of other books in this field and has served as a regular contributor to *The Nation's Schools* for over a decade.

Russell L. Guin
Publisher

Authors' Preface

With the publication of this casebook a long-standing ambition of the authors has been fulfilled. For a number of years they have felt the need for case material that could be used in conducting courses in School Law for teachers and administrators. In the eight casebooks which comprise the entire series, the essential material is now available in useful form for one desiring to make use of the case method in teaching School Law.

The books may be thought of as comprising two series. The first, including the first four books, gives coverage to a course in "School Law for Teachers." The last, consisting of the last four books, gives coverage to a course in "School Law for School Administrators."

Not only should these casebooks find a place for themselves in courses using the case method, but it is hoped that they will be found useful in supplementing the reading of students regardless of the method of teaching employed. In addition, these books are already being employed in some school-administration courses where law, instead of being taught separately, is integrated with the content of other courses.

Like the seven preceding books, this book is organized into two main parts. Part I is devoted to a statement of significant legal principles. Part II consists of portions of court decisions which have been selected to illustrate the various principles. Introducing each case is a quotation taken from Part I—Legal Principles—that gives the key to the reason for selecting the case. Following each case is a series of questions or comments designed to focus attention on the case itself. These are only suggestive—they are not intended to be comprehensive.

The hope of the authors is that, as the result of making this case material available, they may have succeeded in making some little contribution toward encouraging the establishment of courses in School Law as a part of the professional training of teachers and administrators. If so, they will feel amply rewarded for all of their efforts.

Lee O. Garber
Newton Edwards

I.

LEGAL PRINCIPLES

The Law Governing the Financing
of Public Education

Taxes and Taxation

Authority to Tax for School Purposes.—A state legislature, in the absence of some constitutional restriction, has plenary power with respect to the financing of the state's educational system. The state may act through direct legislative enactments or it may delegate its authority with respect to school finance to such local units of government as school districts, counties, or municipalities. It follows that the power to levy taxes for school purposes is never inherent in a school district; the power to tax must be expressly granted or necessarily implied from a specific grant. As a general rule, the fiscal powers delegated to a school district will be strictly construed by the courts. Thus, it has been held that a school board cannot use its taxing power to build up, year by year, a surplus fund to be used later for building purposes. And where taxes are authorized for a specific purpose, such as the construction of a school building or for general educational purposes, they must be used for that purpose and no other.

School taxes are state taxes even though they have been levied and collected by a school district or a municipality. And since education is a state and not a local or municipal function, school districts, counties, or municipalities may be required without their consent to levy taxes for school purposes. A local taxpayer has no interest in school district funds beyond seeing that they are used for the purpose for which they are levied and raised.

So long as school boards act within the scope of their statutory authority, the courts will not control their discretion with respect to the amount of taxes to be levied and collected or with respect to the purpose for which the taxes may be applied.

The Municipality and School Finance.—As a general rule, cities and school districts are distinct legal entities even though they may embrace the same territory; each has its own peculiar function. A city is a municipal corporation proper created primarily for purposes of local government; a school district is a quasi-corporation,

3

created to accomplish a state purpose locally. Since education is not a municipal function, a city may exercise only those powers with respect to school finance which have been conferred upon it by charter or statute. A statute requiring a board of education to submit its budget to a city council for approval will be strictly construed; unless the statute clearly indicates the intent of the legislature to authorize the council to reduce the budget, the courts will hold that the statute merely confers a ministerial duty upon the council and will not permit it to reduce the budget. But where a statute requires a school board to submit its budget to a city council for approval and the statute is so worded as to indicate clearly the intent of the legislature to confer upon the council a broad discretion with respect to the amount to be raised for school purposes, the council may reduce the budget to any extent that it deems wise. Authority of a city council to fix the amount of a school budget does not mean that the council may direct an itemized expenditure of the gross amount authorized; the board of education may spend the funds at its disposal in any manner and for any purpose permitted by law.

The Levying, Collection, and Disposition of Tax Money.—The statutory requirements governing the levying of taxes should be followed with particular care; otherwise the tax may be illegal. Where the statutes require the giving of notice of a special election to determine whether taxes shall be levied, the giving of the required notice is mandatory and failure to give it will, in most jurisdictions, render the tax void. Irregularities in conducting an election to determine whether taxes shall be levied or for any other purpose will not render the election void unless it can be shown that the irregularities could have affected the results. In some jurisdictions where the statutes require that taxes be levied on or before a certain date the courts hold that failure to levy the tax by the prescribed date renders the tax illegal; in other jurisdictions the courts hold that failure to levy the tax within the prescribed time does not render the tax void.

Authorities whose duty it is to levy taxes should keep a written record of their proceedings, for, as a rule, parol evidence is inadmissible to prove that a tax has been properly levied.

The location of property for purposes of taxation is so much determined by the domicile of the owner that one needs a clear conception of what constitutes domicile. One's domicile is the place where one actually resides with the intent of living there for an indefinite time. The general rule is that tangible personal property is taxable at the domicile of the owner even though it may be temporarily located in another state. It is well settled that tangible personal property which is definitely and more or less permanently located in a state other than that in which the owner is domiciled may be taxed by the law of the place where it is found. Then, too, a state legislature may make tangible personal property taxable elsewhere than in the domicile of the owner; and, where it is made taxable in a state other than the one of the owner's domicile, it cannot be taxed in both states.

Intangible personal property, such as stocks, bonds, and mortgages are taxable at the domicile of the owner. The state legislature may provide that intangible personal property shall be taxed where located, and intangible personal property may attain a business situs in a state other than the owner's domicile and if so it is taxable there. A state may tax the income earned within its borders by a resident of another state.

Where illegal taxes are paid voluntarily or merely under protest they cannot be recovered; if illegal taxes are paid under duress they may be recovered. It has been held that funds derived from athletics or other extra-curricular activities must go into official accounts of the school treasurer and be subject to audit the same as other funds. A taxpayer will not be permitted to enjoin the collection of a tax on the ground that the proceeds will be used for an illegal purpose, but a taxpayer may enjoin the collection of an illegal tax. A statute which provides for the collection of a state-wide tax and for its distribution to the various districts on such bases as seem wise in order to equalize educational opportunities is not unconstitutional on the ground that it violates the principle of uniformity, provided the mode of distribution is made to apply to all districts in the same class or category.

School Bonds and the School Debt

Authority to Issue Bonds.—Authority to finance the costs of education by the issuance of school bonds is an authority that is not usually implied; and authority to borrow money does not, as a rule, authorize a school board to issue bonds. As a general rule, the authority to issue bonds must be clearly and expressly conferred by statute upon a school board. The legislature may prescribe the conditions under which school bonds may be issued, and failure to conform to the prescribed conditions will render the bonds illegal. Where bonds are authorized for a particular purpose, the funds derived from their sale must be used for that purpose and no other. In case the voters of a school district authorize the sale of bonds in an amount greater than the law permits, the authorization is not therefore illegal, and the school board may issue bonds in the amount authorized by statute. It has been held that where a school board has statutory authority to call an election to determine whether bonds shall be issued, if the proposition is defeated at the election the board may call as many additional elections as it sees fit. Failure to issue bonds for several years after they have been authorized will not render them void. A taxpayer may bring action to enjoin the issuance of illegal bonds.

Validity of School Bonds.—While earlier decisions generally held that where statutes authorizing the issuance of school bonds prescribed the procedures to be followed, these statutes were mandatory, and failure to follow the procedures rendered the bonds illegal, more recent decisions hold that a substantial compliance with such statutes is all that is required and minor irregularities, questioned after the election has been held, will not void the election. Elections to authorize the issuance of school bonds must be called by the proper authorities or the bonds will be void. Statutory provisions governing the giving of notice of elections for the issuance of bonds should be strictly followed, but courts are reluctant to hold bond elections void for mere irregularities and will not do so unless it can be shown that the irregularities complained of could have affected the results of the election. In case the voters of a school district are called upon to authorize the issuance of bonds, the proceeds of which are to be used for separate and distinct purposes, they must be given the opportunity to vote on each proposition separately; otherwise the election will be held void because it violates the general principle that double propositions cannot be submitted as one. Frequently the courts are asked to rule on whether a stated purpose of two or more parts constitutes a single proposition.

The Binding Force of Recitals in School Bonds.—School bonds commonly have in them statements to the effect that they have been issued in conformity to statutory requirements—that all the conditions required to make them legal have been complied with. Where recitals in school bonds relating to matters of fact, and made by those having authority to make them, contain statements that all conditions for their legal issuance have been complied with, the recitals estop the district from denying the validity of the bonds even though the recitals may in fact be false. But in case a school bond contains a recital with respect to a matter of law it will not bind a school district if it is false; in such a case there can be no such thing as an innocent purchaser because everyone is bound to determine the law for himself.

Rights of a Holder of an Illegal Bond.—The holder of an illegal bond, one that has been issued without authority or in violation of some constitutional or statutory provision, cannot recover on the bond against the district even though he may be an innocent purchaser. In some states, however, it has been held that where illegal bonds have been sold and the proceeds applied to the purposes of the district, the holder of a bond may recover on *quantum meruit.* Generally, the courts permit the purchaser of an illegal bond to recover the money paid for it if it has not been so commingled with the other money of the district that it cannot be identified; and they will also permit the purchaser of an illegal bond to recover property bought with the proceeds from the sale of such a bond provided no other money of the district was used to purchase the property.

In determining whether the indebtedness limit of a school district has been exceeded, the courts commonly hold that the limitation is upon the net and not the gross debt—the gross debt includes all legal obligations of the district including bonds, contracts, and interest accrued; the net debt is determined by subtracting from this gross debt, cash on hand in a sinking fund, taxes levied but not yet collected, property of the district which is not being used for school purposes, and any other assets which may be applied to the payment of debts. Some courts hold that delinquent taxes may be regarded as deductible assets, but others hold that they cannot be so regarded. Most courts hold that refunding bonds do not increase a school district's indebtedness; they merely change its form. Some courts, however, hold that refunding bonds do increase the indebtedness of a school district. In determining whether the amount of bonded indebtedness is within the debt limit, it is generally held that it is the amount of such indebtedness that exists at the time the bonds are issued and not at the time they are voted that governs.

II.

COURT DECISIONS

Court Decisions

1. "*A state legislature, in the absence of some constitutional restriction, has plenary power with respect to the financing of the state's educational system*" (p. 3).

MILLER v. CHILDERS,
107 Okla. 57, 238 P. 204 (1924)
(Decided by the Supreme Court of Oklahoma)

[The facts of this case are readily gleaned from the first two paragraphs of the material that follows.]

LYDICK, J. This action was begun in the district court of Oklahoma county by Fred L. Miller to enjoin the state treasurer and others from permitting moneys to be paid out of the state treasury under the provisions of House Bill No. 19, chapter 103, Session Laws of Oklahoma of 1924, entitled "An act providing aid for weak school districts, making appropriation for the year ending June 30, 1924."

The plaintiff asserts that the act is violative of the provisions of our state Constitution, and therefore void. The lower court sustained defendant's demurrer to plaintiff's petition, and dismissed his action, and he brings the case here on appeal.

.   .   .   .

The state had the right, in the first instance, to contract this indebtedness. In a sense it is a misnomer to label this appropriation as an aid to weak school districts. Less appropriately it is true, but not without some reason, might we designate as an aid to the state the school funds raised by a school district's own tax levy for the promotion of public school work. This we say for the very good reason that, under section 1 of article 3 of the Constitution, the duty rests primarily upon the state Legislature to "establish and maintain a system of free public schools wherein all the children of the state may be educated." This implies an efficient and sufficient system, with competent teachers, necessary general facilities, and school terms of such duration as may be necessary to properly implant in the minds of our youth such degree of learning that when the work is done they may be educated young men and women.

.   .   .   .

The state Legislature may, where not otherwise limited by organic law, choose its own agencies and methods for this work. It has chosen the school district officers and teachers who did the work of the school district

11

to do the added work which it ordered to be done. The Constitution has specifically authorize [*sic*] each school district to levy and collect a 15-mill tax levy, to be by it expended in carrying on this work. There the Constitution terminates the expenditure by a school district, and from there, where the school district's work must end, the Legislature must "carry on" to the point where we can say that there is satisfied the constitutional mandate for the maintenance of a free public school system. . . .

.   .   .   .

While the Congress of the United States may do only that which the federal Constitution has granted unto it the power to do, the Legislature may, in a general sense and as to rightful subjects of legislation, do all except that which by the Constitution it is prohibited from doing. See Cooley's Constitutional Limitations, 241, 242.

It is true that the teachers to be paid by this act rendered their services before the date when the act became effective, to wit, 90 days from its passage and approval by the Governor. The services, however, for aught that appears in the pleadings, were rendered after the act had been properly enacted. For years the Legislature had been providing for such services in similar manner, and these teachers rendered these services in good faith, depending upon the Legislature to do its constitutional duty in the premises, and through which the state would acknowledge its laborers to be worthy of their hire. And so, for the good reasons stated, we hold that the act of the Legislature in assuming to pay these obligations was one calling for the exercise of its own wisdom and discretion, and which it is not within our province to disturb. The act is not violative of article 10, § 14, of the state Constitution.

Guides for Class Discussion

1. See *Marion & M. Rg. Co.* v. *Alexander, infra.*
2. Are you in agreement with the court's reasoning? Give reasons.

2. " . . . *the power to levy taxes for school purposes is never in-herent in a school district; the power to tax must be expressly granted or necessarily implied from a specific grant*" (p. 3).

MARION & M. RY. CO. v. ALEXANDER,
63 Kan. 72, 64 P. 978 (1901)
(Decided by the Supreme Court of Kansas)

[The facts of this case will be found in the quoted sections which follow.]

CUNNINGHAM, J. The plaintiff in error in this action seeks to enjoin the collection of all taxes levied for school purposes in school district No. 79, Marion County, Kan., in excess of 2 per cent. on the taxable property owned by it in said district. A graded school district, No. 79, had been organized, identical in boundaries and inhabitants with school district No. 79; such organization being authorized by article 7, c. 92, of the General Statutes of 1889. That article generally provided for the organi-zation of union or graded schools. . . .

. . . it is contended by plaintiff in error that while the inhabitants of one or more school districts may form a union or graded district, and create machinery to run the same and to maintain any and all schools therein, the total levy "for the various school purposes" cannot exceed 2 per cent. on the taxable property in any one district annually. It is contended by the defendants in error that the various sections quoted, conferring as they do upon the various members of the graded school district board all the powers of like officers of ordinary district boards, and erecting a separate entity for the purpose of managing a separate school, and conferring upon that entity the power to levy taxes as found in section 110, give the power to such graded school district to make within its bounds an additional levy not to exceed 2 per cent.; that is, that it may levy as much as the original school district may, and this in addition to what the original district levies, and not that the total of both levies must be the limit fixed in section 28. The court below took this view of the question. In this we do not agree. . . . We may say that the question is not one entirely free from doubt, but can hardly believe that the legisla-ture would have left in it that condition, had its purpose been to confer the right to so largely increase the burden of taxation. The authority to levy taxes is an extraordinary one. It is never left to implication, unless it is a necessary implication. Its warrant must be clearly found in the act of the legislature. Any other rule might lead to great wrong and oppres-sion, and when there is a reasonable doubt as to its existence the right must be denied. Therefore to say that the right is in doubt is to deny its existence. . . .

The levies sought to be enjoined are those for the years 1894 and 1895, and our conclusion is that the judgment of the district court must be reversed, and it be directed to make the injunction perpetual, enjoining all of the defendants from collecting all of said school taxes in excess of 2 per cent. All the justices concurring.

Guides for Class Discussion

1. What did the court mean when it said: "The authority to levy taxes is . . . never left to implication, unless it is a necessary implication"?
2. Do you agree with the court that if the right to levy taxes is in doubt it does not exist? Give reasons.

3. *"As a general rule, the fiscal powers delegated to a school district will be strictly construed by the courts. Thus, it has been held that a school board cannot use its taxing power to build up, year by year, a surplus fund to be used later for building purposes"* (p. 3).

Cleveland, C., C. & St. L. Ry. Co. v. People,
208 Ill. 9, 69 N.E. 832 (1904)
(Decided by the Supreme Court of Illinois)

[This was an action to collect certain delinquent taxes against a railway company—the appellant. Among other things defendant contended that the tax ostensibly levied for building purposes was not in reality levied for such purposes, because "at the time of the levy it was not the intention or purpose of the board of directors to use the said sum, or any part thereof, for building purposes, for the reason no schoolhouse had been built or was being built."]

Hand, C. J. . . . .

. . . .

It is . . . contended that the $1,000 tax levied for "building purposes" is invalid, on the ground that the tax thus sought to be raised is to be used, when collected, to pay the bonded indebtedness, and interest thereon, of the district, or in the erection of a schoolhouse which had not been agreed upon by the board of directors at the time the tax levy was made. The evidence shows that said district, at the time of the tax levy, had three bonds, of $500 each, outstanding, which bore interest at 5 per cent, per annum, maturing, respectively, in 1904, 1905, and 1906, and that the proceeds of said school bonds had been used by the district for the purpose of erecting a school house, which was then in use by the district. . . . Here . . . it was shown the board of directors did not intend to use the $1,000 levy for "building purposes" with which to pay said bonds and interest, but that it was their intention to use the fund thus raised to erect a schoolhouse, the erection of which they had in contemplation, but the erection of which they had not fully agreed upon. We think it clear the board of directors of a school district cannot levy a tax for "building purposes" with a view to accumulate a fund to be used at some time in the future with which to build a schoolhouse, the erection of which they have in contemplation, but which they have not decided to build at the time the tax levy is made, and which has an existence only in the minds of the several members of the board of directors at the time of the tax levy. The section of the statute under which the levy for building purposes was made designates the levy as an "annual tax levy," and the section, as a whole, clearly indicates that the levy made by virtue thereof is intended to provide for the wants of the school district for the ensuing school year only, and not for its further future needs. The taxpayer has the right to be informed, when he is called upon to pay a tax, what the tax is levied for and how the money paid by him is to be expended by the board of directors. The record in this case shows no bonds of the district would mature in the year 1903; that it was not the intention of the board of directors to use the money raised for "building purposes" by said tax levy in payment of outstanding bonds of the district; and that the erection of a schoolhouse had not been determined upon by the board of directors at the time the tax levy for "building purposes" was made. There was therefore no basis for a valid tax levy for "building purposes" existing in said school district at the time the levy for that purpose was made; hence the tax of $1,000 for "building purposes" was void.

Guides for Class Discussion

1. Compare this decision with the one rendered in *Marion & M. Ry. Co.* v. *Alexander, supra.*
2. This decision could have the effect of prohibiting a school board from adopting a "pay-as-you-go" plan for financing school buildings. Do you think this is desirable? Give reasons.

4. ". . . *where taxes are authorized for a specific purpose, such as the construction of a school building or for general educational purposes, they must be used for that purpose and no other*" (p. 3).

SAN BENITO INDEPENDENT SCHOOL DISTRICT v. FARMERS' STATE BANK
78 S.W. (2d) 741 (Tex.) (1935)
(Decided by the Court of Civil Appeals of Texas, San Antonio)

[This was an action brought by a school district against a bank and the banking commissioner to recover some $13,000—the amount of the balance of funds on deposit in the bank in three different accounts. Plaintiffs asked that the amount of the unpaid warrants held by the bank against a fourth fund, which had been exhausted, be offset against the claims of the district against the bank, thereby leaving a balance of $9,975.91, for which net amount the district asked a judgment. The bank had been closed, and its affairs had been taken over by the state banking commissioner, for administration. At the time it was closed, the school district had four separate checking accounts in the bank. The first was an "interest and sinking fund account," the second a "local maintenance fund account," the third an "interest and penalty refunding account," and the fourth a "state available warrant fund account." In the first account there was a balance of $12,942.68; in the second there was a balance of $318.25; in the third there was a balance of $124.16. In the case of the fourth fund, the bank held unpaid district warrants drawn against it in the amount of $3,409.18. In defendants' defense, the bank and banking commissioner set up a claim for the $3,409.18 represented by the unpaid district warrants, and contended that "that claim against that fund could not legally be applied as an offset against the district's claim upon deposits in the other three specific fund accounts." Therefore, they prayed for a direct judgment upon said warrants. The trial court rendered judgment in favor of the district for the amount of its deposits in the bank and in favor of the banking commissioner for the amount of the unpaid warrants, denying the district's contention that the latter be applied as an offset against the former. The district appealed. The higher court upheld the decision of the lower court.]

Sмiтн, Justice.

. . . .

It is too well settled to require citation, or any extended discussion, that a public fund collected and allocated for a particular public purpose cannot be lawfully diverted to the use of another particular public purpose. Under that wise rule, when applied here, when the taxpayer pays a certain tax for the specific purpose of liquidating a particular public bonded indebtedness of his school district, the funds derived therefrom cannot lawfully be used for the purpose of paying teachers' salaries, chargeable under the law to a different public fund; when lawful interest and penalties have been collected from the taxpayers and segregated into a particular fund, and is required by law to be refunded to the taxpayer, as is the case here, that fund may not lawfully be diverted to the payment of teachers' salaries chargeable to another specific fund, as is sought to be done by appellant; when a specific tax has been levied and assessed by a school district and paid by the taxpayers, for the particular purpose of "local maintenance" (exclusive of teachers' salaries), and the fund so collected has been segregated and allocated to that purpose, as was done here, the district may not divert that fund to another for the purpose of paying teachers' salaries, as is sought to be done by the district in this case.

So when the bank acquired the warrants against the district's "state available fund" account, which was exhausted, at least for the time being, it could not lawfully collect them by charging the amounts thereof to the accounts of the interest and sinking fund, or the local maintenance fund, or the interest and penalty refunding fund; it could only hold the warrants until the account against which they were drawn was replenished, and it was so holding them, as among its assets, when it ceased to do business.

The corporate school district, as are all municipal corporations, is but a trustee or guardian of the public funds coming into its possession under the law, and may disburse those funds only in the manner and for the purposes prescribed by law. As the funds in question were gathered in, the district, in obedience to law, allocated them to the several purposes for which they were paid in, and deposited them with the bank in appropriate separate accounts kept for each specific fund. When so segregated into separate accounts, the district had no power or authority to transfer any part of the funds from either account and apply it to the purposes of any other account, any more than a trustee of several persons or estates could divert the funds of one cestui que trust to the use of another. Nor could the bank, in this case, lawfully pay the warrants drawn on one particular account out of the funds of another particular account, any more than it could charge the draft of one individual depositor to the account of another. The rights, capacities and interests of the respective parties are thus fixed by settled principles of law, and there being no mutuality of rights, interests and capacities between the district as trustee of the "available state" fund and account, and the same entity as trustee of the other three specific funds and accounts, it could not appropriate the one to the uses of the others.

Guides for Class Discussion

1. What line of reasoning motivated the court?
2. Are you in agreement with the court's conclusions? Give reasons.

5. *"School taxes are state taxes even though they have been levied and collected by a school district or a municipality" (p. 3).*

CITY BOARD OF EDUCATION OF ATHENS V. WILLIAMS,
231 Ala. 137, 163 So. 802 (1935)
(Decided by the Supreme Court of Alabama)

[This case had its origin when a city board of education claimed its right to control school funds administered by it which were on deposit in a bank at the time the bank was liquidated. The real question before the court was the nature of such funds. The case came to the higher court on appeal from the lower court. The lower court's ruling and additional facts in the case are to be found in the material which follows.]

FOSTER, Justice.

.   .   .   .

We think that the error which affected the decree of the court in finding that the funds were not state school funds was the emphasis placed upon the contention that the city board of education was an agency of the city and not the state, and should be placed in the same classification as a city in respect to this question. But whatever may be its classification, as a city or state agency, and whether its creation is a feature of the charter powers granted to the cities by law or the Constitution, and whether it is a voluntary organization as an integral part of a city which is voluntary, questions which we do not consider controlling, the inquiry is dependent, we think, upon the qualities of the fund it is administering. Any person or authority, however set up, may be designated for the purpose of administering state funds, and the nature of the fund may not be affected by the constituent qualities of the agency.

.   .   .   .

If the Constitution raises the fund and directs its use in furthering a state function, it continues to be such a state fund regardless of the sort of agency designated to administer it. Likewise if the Legislature makes an appropriation of the state's funds to be so used.

. . . .

The agreed statement of facts here is to the effect that the amount of $668.75 . . . represents money received from the tax collector of Limestone county, collected under assessments in district No. 34 of that county, being the city of Athens. . . . That is the three-mill tax authorized by constitutional amendment. . . . Such funds shall be used for the exclusive benefit of the public schools of such district; in rural districts by the county board; in cities by the city board. . . . Their nature and qualities are not affected by the circumstance that the county board or city board shall administer them, nor by characteristics of the administering board.

The facts further show that the item of $210.10 represents money appropriated to the city board of Athens by the county board . . . and by the city council of Athens. . . . The fund thus apportioned by the county board remains a portion of the state school fund.

When the city makes an appropriation to school purposes . . . and causes it to be set apart and held by its treasurer as treasurer of the school fund . . . it is no longer a part of the city funds, but at once becomes as other funds so in possession of the treasurer of the city board. . . . All such money is then held by it for the state system of schools, regardless of its source, to be expended directly for the benefit of those situated in that city.

Guides for Class Discussion

1. What are the implications of the legal principle enunciated by the court in this case for school administration in general?
2. Do you think the principle is sound? Give reasons.

6. ". . . *since education is a state and not a local or municipal function, school districts, counties, or municipalities may be required without their consent to levy taxes for school purposes*" (p. 3).

REVELL v. MAYOR, ETC., OF CITY OF ANNAPOLIS,
81 Md. 1, 31 A. 695 (1895)
(Decided by the Court of Appeals of Maryland)

[This case was an action against the mayor, counselor, and aldermen of the city of Annapolis to compel them to issue city bonds to raise money for the purpose of erecting a public school building in the city. The defendants demurred, and plaintiffs appealed. The question was whether the legislature had the power to direct that the city authorities should issue bonds to raise money to be applied to the erection of a public school building in the city. Defendants denied the right of the legislators so to do, on the ground that it was not competent for the legislature to require a municipal corporation to levy a tax or to create a debt "for a local purpose, in which the state has no concern, or to assume a debt not within the corporate powers of a municipal government." The court stated that the erection of buildings necessary for public schools was not necessarily a matter of purely local concern in which the state had no interest. On this basis, largely, it held in favor of plaintiffs. In arriving at its decision the court found it necessary to consider the nature and authority of municipal corporations in some detail.]

ROBINSON, C. J. . . . What is a municipal corporation? It is but a subordinate part of the state government, incorporated for public purposes, and clothed with special and limited powers of legislation in regard to its own local affairs. It has no inherent legislative power, and can exercise such powers only as have been expressly or by fair implication delegated to it by the legislature. The control of highways and bridges within the corporate limits; the power to provide for an efficient police force; to pass all necessary laws and ordinances for the preservation of the health, safety, and welfare of its people; and the power to provide for the support of its public schools by local taxation,—are all among the ordinary powers delegated to municipal corporations. And the public schools in Baltimore city are not only under the control and supervision of the city authorities, but are mainly supported by municipal taxation. It is no answer to say that the public schools in Annapolis are under the control of the school commissioners of Anne Arundel county, and that under its charter it has no power to create a debt or levy taxes for their support. The legislature may, at its pleasure, alter, amend, and enlarge its powers. It may authorize the city authorities to establish public schools within the corporate limits, and direct that bonds shall be issued to raise money for their support, payable at intervals during a series of years. There is no difference in principle between issuing bonds and the levying of a tax in one year sufficient to meet the necessary expenditure. It would be less burdensome to the taxpayers to issue bonds payable at intervals than to levy a tax to raise $10,000 in any one year. This, however, is a matter of detail, within the discretion of the legislature, and over which the courts have no control.

If the legislature has the power to direct the city authorities to create a debt for a public school building, the exercise of this power in no manner depends upon their consent or upon the consent of the qualified voters of the city. We recognize the force of the argument that the question whether a municipal debt is to be created ought to be left to the discretion and judgment of the people who are to bear the burden. We recognize the fact that the exercise of this power by the legislature may be liable to abuse. But this abuse of a power is no argument against its exercise. The remedy, however, in such cases, is with the people to whom the members of the legislature are responsible for the discharge of the trust committed to them. It is a matter over which the courts have no control. If the debt to be created was for a private purpose, that would present quite a different question, for it is a fundamental principle, inherent in the nature of taxation itself, that all burdens and taxes shall be levied for public, and not for private, purposes. Be that as it may, it is well settled in this state that the legislature has the power to compel a municipal corporation to levy a tax or incur a debt for a public purpose, and one within the ordinary functions of a municipal government.

Guides for Class Discussion

1. Compare the decision in this case with the one rendered in *City Board of Education of Athens* v. *Williams, supra.*
2. Are you in agreement with the court's thinking that education is a state, and not a local, function?

7. "*A local taxpayer has no interest in school district funds beyond seeing that they are used for the purpose for which they are levied and raised*" (p. 3).

LINDGREN V. SCHOOL DISTRICT OF BRIDGEPORT,
170 Neb. 279, 102 N.W. (2d) 599 (1960)
(Decided by the Supreme Court of Nebraska)

[This was an action to enjoin a school district from carrying out an order of the county school superintendent detaching certain lands belonging to plaintiffs from one district and attaching them to another district. The court, in upholding the legality of the county superintendent's action, found it necessary to rule on plaintiffs' interest in the tax funds levied and collected by the district in which their land was previously situated.]

CARTER, Justice.

This is a suit by a landowner and his wife to enjoin the defendants from giving effect to an order of the county superintendent of schools detaching certain lands of plaintiffs from School District No. 50 and annexing such lands to the School District of the city of Bridgeport. The trial court held the proceedings void and granted injunctive relief. The School District of the city of Bridgeport and the members of its board of education have appealed.

. . . .

The fixing of boundaries of school districts is a legislative function. The Legislature may, in the exercise of its control over school district boundaries, provide a method for changing such boundaries, and the method provided may properly authorize such change to be initiated by petition of the required percentage of the voters of the district. Such a method must, however, provide a means for determining whether the proposed change in boundaries is for a public purpose, and a means by which an aggrieved property owner, whose property is injuriously affected, may have his rights judicially determined. . . . In the instant case the Legislature has provided a method for transferring lands from one school district to another. It has provided for notice and hearing before the county superintendent, which hearing is judicial in character, and which may be reviewed by error proceedings to the district court. This constitutes due process of law. The fact that lands being transferred from one school district to another may thereby be subjected to a higher rate of taxation poses no question of unconstitutionality since the transfer has been made by a means consistent with due process. Nor does the fact that the school district from which the lands were attached retains tax funds, previously levied and collected, affect the validity of the transfer. *A voter or tax-payer of a school district has no interest in the tax funds of a district other than to see that they are used for the public purpose for which they were levied.* The provision that tax funds previously levied and collected shall remain the property of the district remaining after the proper transfer of a part of its lands to another school district is clearly within the province of the Legislature. [Emphasis supplied.]

Guides for Class Discussion

1. Do you think the rule laid down by the court here is a wise one? Give reasons.
2. Compare the decision in this case with the one rendered by the court in *Revell* v. *Mayor, etc., of City of Annapolis, supra.*

8. "*So long as school boards act within the scope of their statutory authority, the courts will not control their discretion with respect to the amount of taxes to be levied and collected or with respect to the purpose for which the taxes may be applied*" (p. 3).

WHARTON V. SCHOOL DIRECTORS OF CASS TOWNSHIP,
42 Pa. St. 358 (1862)
(Decided by the Supreme Court of Pennsylvania)

[This was an action to recover property seized by a tax collector for non-payment of taxes, which plaintiffs contended were "not necessary to keep the schools of the district in operation for ten months in the year, and is a much larger sum than is required for any lawful purpose." The lower court dismissed plaintiffs' action, and an appeal was taken to the higher court, on the ground that the lower court had erred in dissolving the injunction for want of jurisdiction. The court, in rendering its decision, saw fit to consider at some length the nature of school districts and the authority of school boards to levy and collect taxes.]

WOODWARD, J. . . .

School districts are not, strictly speaking, municipal corporations, for they have neither a common seal nor legislative powers, both of which are characteristics of such corporations. They are territorial divisions for the purposes of the common school laws, consisting generally of boroughs and townships, though frequently subdivided into smaller districts, and are governed by a board of directors chosen by the people. They belong to that class of *quasi* corporations to which counties and townships belong—exercising within a prescribed sphere many of the faculties of a corporation . . . and the directors are invested with various discretionary powers in execution of the school laws, for which they are responsible only to the people whose representatives they are. Clearly the courts have no control over these discretionary powers, but the judicial authority to restrain *illegal* acts by the school directors, is as unquestionable as it is to restrain wrongdoing by any other class of men. . . .

But does the record present a case of illegal conduct on the part of the directors? The complaint is that they have laid a school-tax of eleven mills on the valuation of the plaintiff's property in Cass township, and are proceeding to collect it. The directors answer, that they assessed eight mills for school purposes for the year 1861, and three mills for building purposes, and that this rate was necessary for the purpose of carrying on the schools of the district, repairing and building school-houses, and paying debts of former years.

. . . .

. . . The power of taxation, altogether legislative and in no degree judicial, is committed by the legislature in the matter of schools, to the directors of school districts. If the directors refuse to perform their duties the court can compel them. If they transcend their powers the court can restrain them. If they misjudge their power the court can correct them. But if they exercise their unquestionable powers unwisely, there is no judicial remedy.

Guides for Class Discussion

1. Compare the decision in this case with the one rendered by the court in *Board of Education of Alton Community School District* v. *Alton Water Company, supra.*
2. In light of the position taken by the court, do you think there is any danger that the board of directors might abuse its authority with respect to taxation? Give reasons.

, *"As a general rule, cities and school districts are distinct legal
ntities even though they may embrace the same territory; each has
s own peculiar function" (p. 3).*

State ex rel. Harbach v. Mayor of
City of Milwaukee,
189 Wis. 84, 206 N.W. 210 (1925)
(Decided by the Supreme Court of Wisconsin)

[Where a school district has boundaries coterminous with those of
municipal corporation such as a city, problems frequently arise
oncerning the authority of the city in matters of an educational
ature. In general, courts agree, in such cases, that the school dis-
·ict and the city are separate agencies and that each has its own
eculiar function. The district, acting as an arm of the state, carries
ut a state or governmental function, while the city carries out a
ocal or municipal function.

[In this case an action was instituted by one Harbach, secretary
f the Milwaukee board of education, against the mayor and city
ouncil of the city of Milwaukee. A writ of mandamus was asked
or in order to compel the mayor and city council to levy a tax of
75,000 for the purpose of making repairs on school buildings in
he city. In 1921 a law was passed providing that in cities of the
rst class a maximum of .8 of one mill on each dollar of assessed
aluation could be levied for such purpose. In 1925 this law was
hanged and the maximum was changed from .8 of one mill to one
nill. The council refused to levy more than .8 of one mill. The
mount asked by the board exceeded .8 of one mill but was less
han one mill. The mayor and council contended that the act of 1925
vas unconstitutional on the ground that it violated the following
ection of the constitution: "Cities and villages organized pursuant
o state law . . . are hereby empowered to determine their local
ffairs and government, subject only to this Constitution and to such
nactments of the Legislature of state-wide concern as shall with
niformity affect every city or every village."

[It was claimed that because the act of 1925 applied only to
ities of the first class, rather than to all cities and villages, it violated
his section of the constitution. It was also claimed by the defendants

that the repair of school buildings was a local purpose and that the legislature was prohibited from legislating upon that subject except by general laws. The court reasoned differently and granted the writ.]

Owen, J. . . .

. . . .

It is contended that the repair of school buildings constituted a local affair of the city of Milwaukee, and that by the constitutional provision just quoted the Legislature is prohibited from legislating upon that subject except by general law, which "shall with uniformity affect every city or every village"; that as chapter 285, Laws 1925, affected only cities of the first class, it was not a law which "uniformly affected every city or every village."

It is obvious that the limitation placed upon the power of the Legislature, with reference to laws which "shall with uniformity affect every city or every village," is confined to the "local affairs and government" of cities and villages. With reference to all subjects that do not constitute "local affairs," or relate to the government of cities and villages, the Legislature has the same power of classification that it had before the adoption of the Home Rule Amendment. Respondents' contention, therefore, must rest upon the proposition that the repair of school buildings within the city of Milwaukee is a local affair of said city. If not, respondents' contention must fall. In undertaking a consideration of this question we shall not attempt any general definition of the term "local affairs," or to set the boundaries thereof. We shall address ourselves solely to the proposition of whether the repair of school buildings in the city of Milwaukee constitutes the "local affairs" of said city within the meaning of the constitutional provision here under consideration.

Turning to the provisions of the Constitution as they existed at the time of the adoption of the so-called Home Rule Amendment, we find that by section 3, art. 11, it was made the duty of the Legislature "to provide for the organization of cities and incorporated villages," and that by section 3, or article 10, it was provided that:

"The 'Legislature shall provide by law for the establishment of district schools, which shall be as nearly uniform as practicable; and such schools shall be free and without charge for tuition to all children between the ages of four and twenty years; and no sectarian instruction shall be allowed therein.' "

. . . .

. . . With reference to the interest of the state in the two fields there is a wide difference. Local municipalities are organized for the purpose of dealing with matters of local concern. In such matters the state has little or no interest. The state, however, does have an interest in the education of its entire citizenship—an interest so deep and substantial that the framers of the Constitution not only made provision for the establishment of district schools, but made provision for the creation of a school fund, the income of which should be devoted to the maintenance of district schools throughout the state.

The city attorney frankly admitted that the city of Milwaukee could not close up the schools of the city, nor could it abolish the board of education. . . . The city attorney, while conceding that the city may not abolish the board of education, contended that the maintenance of the school buildings of the city is more distinctly local, and that there must be some point where the state's interest ceased and the authority of the city attached. This contention involves the degree of interference rather than the power to interfere at all. If the field of legislation upon the subject of education belongs to the state, it belongs to it in its entirety. If the cause of education is not a subject of municipal regulation, the municipality cannot touch it or interfere with it in the slightest degree. School buildings are an essential agency in the state's educational scheme, and to allow municipalities a voice in the construction, repair, control, or management of the school buildings within their borders is to yield to them the power to frustrate the state's plan in promoting education throughout the state. If power be granted to interfere in this respect, there would be no logical limitation to municipal interference with the district schools. This court has held that the ward schools of the cities of the state are district schools, within the meaning of article 10, § 3, of the Constitution. . . . It has also held that a free high school district is a quasi corporation, a somewhat independent unit of school government, whose corporate identity is not merged in that of any town, city, or village. . . .

These considerations lead irresistibly to the conclusion that, although the boundaries of a school district may be coterminous with the boundaries of a city, there is no merger of the school district affairs with the city affairs. They remain separate and distinct units of government for the purpose of exercising separate and distinct powers and for the accomplishment of separate and distinct purposes. It follows that the so-called Home Rule Amendment imposes no limitation upon the power of the Legislature to deal with the subject of education, and this applies to every agency created or provided, and to every policy adopted by the Legislature, having for its object the promotion of the cause of education throughout the state.

Guides for Class Discussion

1. What did the court say with respect to the merger of the affairs of the city and the school district?
2. How can one justify the court's comments regarding the authority of the municipality and the school district, respectively, over education?

3. How does this case reinforce the concept of education as a state and not a local function?

4. What are some implications of this case for educational administration?

10. *"A city is a municipal corporation proper created primarily for purposes of local government; a school district is a quasi-corporation, created to accomplish a state purpose locally"* (pp. 3-4).

BOARD OF EDUCATION OF ALTON COMMUNITY SCHOOL DISTRICT v. ALTON WATER CO.,
314 Ill. 466, 145 N.E. 683 (1924)
(Decided by the Supreme Court of Illinois)

[This was a case brought to collect water rental from the Alton (Ill.) Community Consolidated School District. In 1906 the Alton Water Company accepted a franchise from the city of Alton. Among other things, this franchise provided the water company would furnish free a reasonable quantity of water to all public and parochial schools located in the City of Alton. In 1922 the water company put into effect a new schedule of rates. When the State Commerce Commission entered an order requiring the water company to continue furnishing water free to the schools, it brought an action appealing the order. The Circuit Court of Madison County, Illinois, held the order unlawful and set it aside, and the school district appealed.]

HEARD, J. . . . .

. . . .

It is contended by appellants that the ordinance of March 31, 1906, and its acceptance by appellee, constituted a valid and binding contract for the benefit of appellants, by which appellee was obligated to furnish water free to appellants during the life of the franchise, and that such contract could not be abrogated by the city council by resolution. The city council of a city is a body of limited powers, and can only exercise such powers as are conferred upon it by the Legislature, either expressly or impliedly. . . .

. . . .

. . . By the ordinance of March 31, 1906, it was not provided that the water to the schools should be furnished as a donation by appellee, but it was provided that "such water is furnished free as a part of the consideration for the said hydrant rental, which is deemed to cover water to be taken from hydrants, and in such public or parochial buildings and watering troughs." In other words, the water was not to be furnished free by appellee, but was to be paid for by the city of Alton under the terms of the ordinance as to hydrant rental. Even if the ordinance and its acceptance by appellee be construed as a contract between the city of Alton and appellee, to the effect that during the life of the franchise hydrant rental should be paid by the city at the rate fixed by the ordinance, and that such rate should cover the cost of water furnished to the public and parochial schools, the city council was powerless to enter into such contract.

By the ordinance of March 31, 1906, the hydrant rental, covering water furnished to the public and parochial schools, was to be paid by taxation. A municipality has no inherent power to raise public funds by means of taxation, but such power is derived only by grant from the state. . . . A municipal corporation holds its property in trust for public uses, and its funds can be used only for corporate purposes. They cannot be diverted to private use. Nor can the municipal authorities or the electors give away the money or property of the municipality. . . .

. . . The city of Alton and the appellant board of education are separate corporate entities, each clothed with the power of taxation for its corporate purposes and for none other. They are organized under different laws, each for a specific purpose. The parochial schools are purely private institutions, and neither municipal corporation has any authority to contract or levy a tax for their benefit. The board of education would have no power to levy a tax for the purpose of maintaining a city waterworks system or any purpose for the sole benefit of the city in its corporate capacity, nor would the city have any authority to levy a tax for the maintenance of a community high school.

The ordinance of March 31, 1906, in so far as it provided for the furnishing of water to appellants, was not a valid, binding contract upon the city and appellee, which would prevent the city, at any time during the continuance of the franchise, from changing its rates for hydrant rental according to law.

Guides for Class Discussion

1. Compare this case with *State ex rel. Harbach* v. *Mayor of City of Milwaukee, supra.*

2. Do you agree with the court's reasoning? Give your reasons.
3. What did the court say about the function or purpose of a municipal corporation?
4. What limitations does this case place upon the activities of a municipal corporation?

11. *"Since education is not a municipal function, a city may exercise only those powers with respect to school finance which have been conferred upon it by charter or statute" (p. 4).*

BOARD OF EDUCATION OF NASHUA v. VAGGE,
102 N.H. 457, 159 A. (2d) 158 (1960)
(Decided by the Supreme Court of New Hampshire)

[See the quoted material for a statement of facts which gave rise to this litigation.]

KENISON, Chief Justice.

The plaintiff states the issue in this case in the following language: "The question before this Court is whether the Board of Education of the City of Nashua has the sole and exclusive power to select a site for the erection of a junior high school, and also whether, having selected unused land owned by the City of Nashua for the erection of a junior high school, the Board of Education can compel the Board of Aldermen to convey and transfer the selected site to the Board of Education."

It is the defendant's position that the question requires a negative answer, while the plaintiff maintains that the question should be answered in the affirmative. . . .

. . . .

We are aware of the policy favoring financial independence for school districts recommended in Report of the [legislative] Commission to Study the State Educational System (1946). "School districts that are fiscally dependent on finance committees, city councils and other agencies of the local government lose at once their major administrative responsibility." . . .

However the extent to which school administration is subject to control by the mayor and board of aldermen is determined by the general statutes and the charter provisions in each city. Toussaint v. Fogarty, 80 N.H. 286, 116 A. 636. That it varies from city to city and is dependent on the subject matter involved is illustrated by City of Franklin v. Hinds, 101 N.H. 344, 143 A. 2d 111, where the city council of Franklin was sustained in its refusal to appropriate funds for additional teachers. See Garber, Yearbook of School Law, 1960, p. 90.

"In any particular instance the degree of control to be exercised by either school board members or municipal officers must be ascertained by reference to statutory and charter provisions. Under no circumstances, however, will municipal officers be permitted to exercise any greater degree of control over school finance than that clearly intended by the legislature." Edwards, The Courts and Public Schools (Rev. ed. 1955), p. 106 quoted with approval in City of Franklin v. Hinds, 101 N.H. 344, 345, 143 A. 2d 111. Applying this principle of statutory construction to this case we nevertheless find no provisions in the city charter as amended or in RSA 199:2 which compel the city to transfer the land selected by the board of education regardless of the action taken by the mayor and the board of aldermen.

Guides for Class Discussion

1. From this decision may it be concluded that the city council or board of aldermen, regardless of the title of a city's administrative body, has the authority to deny a school board the right to use unused city property for school purposes? Give reasons.

2. See *Board of Education of City of Saginaw, East Side* v. *Board of Estimates of City of Saginaw, infra;* and *Board of Education of Town of Stamford* v. *Board of Finance of Town of Stamford, infra.*

12. "A statute requiring a board of education to submit its budget to a city council for approval will be strictly construed; unless the statute clearly indicates the intent of the legislature to authorize the council to reduce the budget, the courts will hold that the statute merely confers a ministerial duty upon the council and will not permit it to reduce the budget" (p. 4).

BOARD OF EDUCATION OF CITY OF SAGINAW, EAST SIDE v. BOARD OF ESTIMATES OF CITY OF SAGINAW,
230 Mich. 495, 203 N.W. 68 (1925)
(Decided by the Supreme Court of Michigan)

[The facts underlying this case will be found in that part of the decision which is quoted.]

CLARK, J. Within the city of Saginaw are two school districts. The city has a board of estimates. . . . The statute gives the board of education of the district very broad powers relating to acquiring and disposing of real estate, borrowing money, making contracts, and to general management and control of the affairs of the district. . . .

. . . .

Plaintiff, board of education of the city of Saginaw, East Side, made its estimate for 1924 and submitted it to the board of estimates, which board cut out items, chiefly of teachers' wages and of proposed building, aggregating about $50,000, and approved the remainder of the estimate. Plaintiff brought mandamus to compel approval of the entire estimate. The case involves a construction of the last provision of the part of section 23, quoted, relating to approval by the board of estimates.

Plaintiff contends that the board of estimates has no discretion, beyond determining if the estimate is within the tax limit and if it is otherwise within the law. Defendant contends, in effect, that it is for the school board to propose, and for defendant to dispose, and that it has general discretion in passing upon any and all items of the estimate. A judgment for defendant is reviewed on certiorari.

If defendant is right, then the Legislature must have intended, in effect, to take from the school board and to give to the board of estimates the power to determine, from which no right of review or appeal is given, the length of the school year under the statute, the number and compensation of teachers, the fiscal plans and policies, and the character and quantity of materials, supplies, and equipment for the district; for, if the board of estimates has power to say upon the estimate how much and for what purpose money may be raised, it is, by its absolute power of veto, virtually the master of the affairs of the plaintiff district.

This was not intended. If it were, we might expect to find a clear legislative expression to that effect. . . .

The plaintiff is right. The board of estimates, finding the estimate to be within the tax limit and otherwise legal, must approve it.

Guides for Class Discussion

1. Are you in agreement with the court's thinking with respect to the question involved?
2. Under this line of reasoning, will the court approve legislation authorizing a city administrative authority to reduce the school budget?
3. See *Board of Education of Town of Stamford* v. *Board of Finance of Town of Stamford, infra.*

13. "*. . . where a statute requires a school board to submit its budget to a city council for approval and the statute is so worded as to indicate clearly the intent of the legislature to confer upon the council a broad discretion with respect to the amount to be raised for school purposes, the council may reduce the budget to any extent that it deems wise*" (p. 4).

BOARD OF EDUCATION OF TOWN OF STAMFORD v. BOARD OF FINANCE OF TOWN OF STAMFORD,
127 Conn. 345, 16 A. (2d) 601 (1940)
(Decided by the Supreme Court of Errors of Connecticut)

[This was an action brought by a board of education against a town for the purpose of determining the respective powers of the two boards with respect to expenditures for school purposes. Specifically, the board of education, among other things, questioned the legality of the action of the board of finance in reducing the estimates submitted by the board of education in its budget which, by statute, the board of finance was required to approve.]

MALTBIE, Chief Justice.

. . . .

A town board of education is an agency of the state in charge of education in the town; to that end it is granted broad powers by the legislature; and it is beyond control by the town or any of its officers in the exercise of those powers or in the incurring of expense, to be paid by the town, necessitated thereby, except as limitations are found in statutory provisions. . . . The issue presented is, then, whether the General Assembly has narrowed the powers of boards of education by its statutes . . . establishing and defining the powers of town boards of finance and . . . providing for the submission of estimates to that board by boards of education. In Groton & Stonington Traction Co. v. Groton, [115 Conn. 151] . . . the question of the respective powers of a town board of education and a town board of finance was directly presented. Speaking by Hinman, J., we reviewed the applicable statutes; and without quoting the opinion, it may be briefly summed up, as applicable to such a case as the one now before us, as follows: Where a town board of education includes in the estimates it submits to a board of finance expenditures for a purpose which is not within statutory provisions imposing a duty upon it nor within one which vests it with a discretion to be independently exercised, the board of finance may, if in its judgment, considering not only the educational purpose to be served but also the financial condition of the town, it finds that the expenditure is not justified, decline to recommend an appropriation for it; where, however, the estimate is for an expenditure for a purpose which the statutes make it the duty of the board of education to effectuate or they vest in the board of education a discretion to be independently exercised as to the carrying out of some purpose, the town board of finance has not the power to refuse to include any appropriation for it in the budget it submits and can reduce the estimate submitted by the board of education only when that estimate exceeds the amount reasonably necessary for the accomplishment of the purpose, taking into consideration along with the educational needs of the town, its financial condition and the other expenditures it must make. The board of finance in such a case must exercise its sound judgment in determining whether or to what extent the estimates of the board of education are larger than the sums reasonably necessary and if it properly exercises its discretion and the budget is approved by the town the board of education has no power to exceed the appropriations made.

Guides for Class Discussion

1. Compare the decision in this case with the one rendered by the court in *Board of Education of City of Saginaw, East Side*

v. *Board of Estimates of City of Saginaw, supra.* Are they in conflict?

2. In cases such as the one here, what is the main point at issue?

14. "*Authority of a city council to fix the amount of a school budget does not mean that the council may direct an itemized expenditure of the gross amount authorized; the board of education may spend the funds at its disposal in any manner and for any purpose permitted by law*" (p. 4).

LYNCH V. CITY OF FALL RIVER,
336 Mass. 558, 147 N.E. (2d) 152 (1958)
(Decided by the Supreme Judicial Court of Massachusetts, Bristol)

[When a school committee decided to increase teachers' salaries and pay the increase out of unexpended funds in the salary item of the budget, the mayor refused to approve the payrolls. The court, ruling in favor of the committee, commented on the authority of municipal officers to control the expenditure of the budget it had approved.]

WILKINS, C. J.

.   .   .   .

No question is made as to the traditional supremacy of the school committee in the field of education, nor is it controverted that the school committee have the absolute right to fix the salaries of public school teachers. . . . The city's contention is that such right must be exercised prior to the adoption of the annual budget. Reliance is placed upon § 33A of the municipal finance act, G.L. (Ter.Ed.) c. 44, as appearing in St. 1955, c. 358, which reads in part, "The [annual] budget shall include sums sufficient to pay the salaries of officers and employees fixed by law or by ordinance." The school teachers' salaries, however, were fixed not "by law or by ordinance," but by contract. . . .

.   .   .   .

The city also urges that a supplemental appropriation was necessary, because until the end of the year there coulud [*sic*] be no true "balance" or "surplus" from which the increased amounts voted could be paid. The

plaintiff counters that the original appropriation was sufficient, and th
the school committee have the power to expend it for teachers' salaries
any way they see fit. It should be noted, if material, that the wor
"balance" and "surplus" appear only in the argument of the city, and we
not used by the school committee in the votes.

The case at bar is controlled by *Leonard v. School Committee*
Springfield, 241 Mass. 325, 135 N.E. 459. There the school committe
submitted to the mayor estimates for expenses of the public schools whic
among other things, included an increase in compensation for many teac
ers, as well as salaries of additional teachers. The mayor reduced th
amount in transmitting his budget to the city council. After the budg
became effective, the school committee, in order to provide money for th
increased salaries, voted to eliminate summer schools and kindergarte
and to curtail expenses under other separate headings in the budget. A
page 327 of 241 Mass., at page 460 of 135 N.E. it was said, "The preci
question to be decided is whether the school committee has power th
to carry out its policy as to the management of the school system
whether it is bound by the action of the mayor and city council to th
items set forth in the budget without power to modify or change them
any substantial particular." In deciding the question in favor of the scho
committee, the court said, 241 Mass. at page 332, 135 N.E. at page 46
the opinion being by Chief Justice Rugg: "It is to be noted that x
question here is raised as to an attempt by a school committee to spe
more than a total appropriation made for the support of the public schoo
The school committee only assert a right to fix the salaries of teachers
conformity to their own sound discretion without being restricted in th
regard to particular items specified in the budget. That contention
sound. . . ."

The case at bar is a stronger one for the school committee, becau
here no money was taken from other headings in the budget to pay th
increased salaries.

Guides for Class Discussion

1. See *Board of Education of Town of Stamford* v. *Board of F
nance of Town of Stamford*, *supra*.
2. Do you think the court's reasoning is sound? Give reasons.

5. "Where the statutes require the giving of notice of a special *ection* to determine whether taxes shall be levied, the giving of *e* required notice is mandatory and failure to give it will, in most *risdictions*, render the tax void" (p. 4).

BRAMWELL V. GUHEEN,
3 Idaho 347, 29 P. 110 (1892)
(Decided by the Supreme Court of Idaho)

[The facts of this case will be found in the material which *llows*.]

HUSTON, J. This action was brought by the plaintiff to enjoin the de- *ndant*, who is the assessor and tax collector of Bingham county, from *llecting* a school tax assessed on certain real estate of plaintiff by the *oard* of trustees of school-district No. 15 of said county.

The ownership and description of the real estate is set forth in the *omplaint*, as are, also, the facts constituting the claimed illegality of the *vy* and assessment; and the complaint further alleges that such tax con- *itutes* a cloud upon the title to said real estate of plaintiff, etc. A general *emurrer* was filed to the complaint, which, after argument, was over- *led* by the court; the court holding that the complaint stated facts suffi- *ient* to warrant the relief prayed for. This ruling was correct, we think.

. . . .

Subdivision 7 of section 667 of the Revised Statutes of Idaho provide *s* follows: "They [the trustees] may, by giving ten days' notice in writing, *osted* in three conspicuous places in their district, call, at any time prior *o* the second Monday of September, an election of the legal votes of their *istrict*, for the purpose of deciding whether or not a special tax, specify- *ng* the rate proposed to be collected, which must not exceed ten mills on *ne* dollar of the taxable property, be levied on said district for the build- *ng* or repairing of school-houses or for the support of public schools in *ne* district; and they may appoint two judges and a clerk of said election. *he* voting at each election must be by ballot, on which ballot must be *vritten* or printed "Tax, yes," or "Tax, no"; and none but actual free- *olders* or heads of families of said district are entitled to vote at such *lection*," etc. The notice of the meeting, as the same appears in the *ecord*, is as follows: "Notice. There will be a school-meeting held in the *istrict* school-house in the 15th district on May 17th, 1890, at 12 o'clock *harp*, to take into consideration the voting of a tax of ten mills. W. H. *)YE*, Clerk of the Board of Trustees. N. W. McMILLAN." . . .

Where the statute provides for the levying of a special tax, all the *equirements* of the statute in regard to the making of such levy must be strictly followed. Burroughs, Tax'n, p. 396, and cases cited; Cooley, Tax'n, p. 334 et seq. The notice was not for an election, but for a meeting "to take into consideration the voting of a tax of ten mills." Nothing is said in the notice as to the purpose for which the tax is to be raised, nor is there anything said in the notice about an election. Twenty-five persons met at the place and at the time indicated, and informally talked and discussed the subject; and this seems to have been all that was contemplated by the notice "to take into consideration the voting of a tax of ten mills." Having, as they doubtless thought, sufficiently considered the matter, they dispersed. Thereafter eight other persons convened at the same place, organized a meeting, appointed officers of election, and proceeded to hold what is claimed to have been an election. The court finds that a vote was taken by ballot, but this finding is not sustained by the record of the meeting. The certificate of the trustees states "that it was moved and carried that the vote of tax be ten mills on the dollar"; and, further on, "the vote then being taken, the judges reported as follows, to-wit: Tax, yes—eight; tax, no—none." It does not appear that any vote by ballot was taken. While, in considering the acts of boards and meetings of this character, considerable latitude should be given, in this case there was such a complete abnegation of the plain provisions of the statute as to make it imperative upon the court to hold the proceedings to levy the tax in question invalid, and the tax levied thereunder void.

Guides for Class Discussion

1. See *Moser* v. *White, infra.*
2. Are you in agreement with the thinking of the court in this case? Give reasons.

16. *"Irregularities in conducting an election to determine whether taxes shall be levied or for any other purpose will not render the election void unless it can be shown that the irregularities could have affected the results"* (p. 4).

SHELTON V. SCHOOL BOARD,
43 Okla. 239, 142 P. 1034 (1914)
(Decided by the Supreme Court of Oklahoma)

[In this case the legality of an election for the issuance of school bonds was questioned. The main ground on which the election was questioned was that 41 women were permitted to vote. It was contended that this was illegal. The court ruled that while it was illegal it did not invalidate the election as the result would not have been changed had the irregularity not occurred.]

BLEAKMORE, J. . . .

.   .   .   .

Qualified electors, as defined by the Constitution of Oklahoma, are male and not female citizens. It is apparent that while under section 3, art. 3, of the Constitution, supra, it was intended to permit women who possessed all the qualifications of electors, except sex, to vote at school district elections and meetings, yet the power to restrict or entirely deprive them of such right was remitted to the Legislature; and it is clear from the language used in section 21, art. 6, c. 219, Sess. Laws 1913, that in providing that only qualified electors should vote upon the question of the issuance of bonds, as in the instant case, the Legislature intended to take away from the female citizens of this state the privilege of participating in such elections. This intent is clearly manifested by the language used in section 27 of said article and chapter, wherein it is specifically provided that all persons, male and female, possessing the other qualifications provided in the Constitution and laws of the state, may vote for elective school officers only.

The evidence discloses that 41 women, who were not entitled to vote, actually voted at said election. It is urged by the plaintiffs in error that because of the fact that this number of disqualified voters were allowed to participate in the election that the entire poll should be rejected and the election held invalid. This is not the law. As was held by this court, in Martin v. McGarr, 27 Okla. 653, 117 Pac. 323, 38 L.R.A. (N.S.) 1007:

"The general rule obtaining throughout all the states of the Union is that an election is not to be held invalid except as a last resort; the correct doctrine being announced by Judge Brewster, in the case of Batturs v. McGary, 1 Brewster, 162, as follows: 'The courts have the power to reject an entire poll, but only in the extremest case—as where it is impossible to ascertain the true vote. Impossibility is the test.' "

And again in the same opinion:

"When fraud on the part of the officers of the election is established, the poll will not be rejected, unless it prove impossible to purge it of the fraud."

.   .   .   .

In the case at bar, if the votes cast by those persons disqualified be eliminated, still the bond issue carried by a large majority of votes over the requisite number provided by law, and therefore it is not only not "impossible to ascertain the true vote" in this election but it is clearly impossible not to do so.

Guides for Class Discussion

1. Are you in agreement with the court's reasoning in this case? Give reasons.
2. If the result of the election might have been changed had the irregularity not occurred, how do you think the court would have held? Justify your position.

17. "*In some jurisdictions where the statutes require that taxes be levied on or before a certain date the courts hold that failure to levy the tax by the prescribed date renders the tax illegal . . . (p. 4).*

SMITH v. CANYON COUNTY,
39 Idaho 222, 226 P. 1070 (1924)
(Decided by the Supreme Court of Idaho)

[This was an action seeking to have a special tax that had been levied declared invalid. One ground for so doing was that the tax had not been levied at the proper time.]

McCARTHY, C. J. . . . .

. . . .

The remaining question, and the vital one, is: Was a tax levied by school district No. 34 for 1920? C. S. § 878, provides that the electors in annual meeting shall determine whether a special tax shall be levied; and section 875 provides this annual meeting shall be held on the third Monday in April. Section 880 provides the board of trustees shall have power to levy a special tax when the annual meeting shall neglect or refuse to do so. This clearly contemplates that before the trustees have power to levy the tax, the annual meeting shall have been held and shall have neglected or refused to act, or at least that the electors shall have neglected or refused to hold an annual meeting. The electors attempted to hold an annual meeting on September 20, 1920, for the purpose of levying the tax.

It is contended by respondent that the provisions of the statute in regard to the time of the annual meeting are merely directory and a meeting held at any other time is valid. In Shoup v. Willis, 2 Idaho (Hasb.) 120, 6 Pac. 124, this court said:

"It is a well-settled principle of law that taxes cannot be levied or collected at any other time, or in any manner, nor for any other purpose, than that designed by law."

. . . .

The authorities generally hold that where the statutes authorize the electors of a district to hold an annual meeting at a certain time of the year for the election of officers or levying of taxes, a meeting held and action taken at a different time are invalid. . . . The principle underlying these decisions is the elementary one that the powers of such subdivisions as school districts proceed entirely from statutes and cannot be exercised unless the statutory requirements are substantially complied with. We are constrained to hold that the electors of the district had no power to hold an annual meeting and levy a tax in September, 1920.

Guides for Class Discussion

1. *See Bramwell v. Guheen, supra.*
2. Compare this decision with the one rendered in *Rural High School District v. Raub, infra.* Which represents the better law? Give reasons.

18. *"In some jurisdictions . . . the courts hold that failure to levy the tax within the prescribed time does not render the tax void"* (p. 4).

RURAL HIGH SCHOOL DISTRICT V. RAUB,
103 Kan. 757, 176 P. 110 (1918)
(Decided by the Supreme Court of Kansas)

[The facts in this case will be found in the material quoted.]

PORTER, J. The question for determination is whether it is the duty of the county clerk to extend upon the tax rolls a levy which is not made by a rural high school district until after the third Monday in April, and not certified to the county clerk until long after the 25th day of July.

Rural high school district No. 93 of Jefferson county was organized at an election held on August 5, 1918. . . . The board of directors of the district at a called meeting held on the 14th day of September, 1918, made a levy of taxes for the expenses of the current year, and the clerk of the board duly certified the levy to the county clerks of the three counties.

The defendant as clerk of Shawnee county, being doubtful as to his authority, declines to extend the levy upon the tax rolls.

The statute provides that the board of each rural high school district shall meet annually on the third Monday in April and make the necessary levy for taxes. . . .

It is the school district's contention that the provisions of these statutes with respect to the time when the levy shall be made and certified are directory only, and not mandatory, and that the validity of the levy is not affected by the failure to have the levy certified and extended within the designated time. The rule relied upon is stated in Endlich on the Interpretation of Statutes, § 433, as follows:

"But when a public duty is imposed, and the statute requires that it shall be performed in a certain manner, or within a certain time, or under other specified conditions, such prescriptions may well be regarded as intended to be directory only, when injustice or inconvenience to others who have no control over those exercising the duty, would result, if such requirements were essential and imperative."

. . . Provisions of this nature specifying the time in which public officers shall perform their duties are generally regarded as directory "unless the nature of the act to be performed, or the phraseology of the statute, is such that the designation of time must be considered as a limitation of the power of the officer." Sutherland on Statutory Construction, § 448. The provisions with respect to time are, under such circumstances, considered merely as a direction with a view simply to orderly and prompt conduct of official business. . . .

. . . We think . . . that in view of the general principles upon which the reason for the rule of interpretation referred to rests, and the interests of the public in a case like the present, we are fully warranted in holding that the provisions in respect of time in which the officers shall act are directory only, and not mandatory.

Guides for Class Discussion

1. Compare the decision in this case with the one rendered in *Smith* v. *Canyon County, supra.* Which represents the better law? Why?

2. What line of reasoning motivated the court?

3. Do you think a court today would accept this decision as precedent?

19. *"Authorities whose duty it is to levy taxes should keep a written record of their proceedings, for, as a rule, parol evidence is inadmissible to prove that a tax has been properly levied"* (p. 4).

MOSER V. WHITE,
29 Mich. 59 (1874)
(Decided by the Supreme Court of Michigan)

[The facts of this case may be gleaned from the material which follows.]

CAMPBELL, J.

Plaintiff recovered a judgment before a justice of the peace in Macomb county, against the village authorities of Mt. Clemens for trespass in seizing and selling his property to pay an illegal village tax. This judgment was reversed on certiorari in the circuit court, and is now brought before us by writ of error.

The questions of informality in the tax-roll on which reliance was chiefly made for reversing the justice's judgment, become unimportant in view of the conceded fact that the council of the village of Mt. Clemens never passed any resolution and took no action of record to determine what taxes should be raised for the year in question.

The village charter authorizes the village council to lay taxes for village purposes. But such a body can only act by resolution or by-law, adopted at a meeting, and the proceedings of such meetings cannot be left in parol. *Every essential proceeding in the course of a levy of taxes must appear in some written and permanent form* in the records of the bodies authorized to act upon them. Such a thing as a parol levy of taxes is not legally possible under our laws. [Emphasis supplied.]

Guides for Class Discussion

1. Do you think the court was correct in holding as it did? Give reasons.
2. It will be noted that this case was decided in 1874—almost 100 years ago. Do you think courts today would accept it as precedent? Give reasons.
3. See *Bramwell v. Guheen, supra.*

20. *"One's domicile is the place where one actually resides with the intent of living there for an indefinite time"* (p. 5).

HOLT v. HENDEE,
248 Ill. 288, 93 N.E. 749 (1911)
(Decided by the Supreme Court of Illinois)

[This was an action by plaintiff seeking to restrain the county clerk of Lake County, Illinois, from extending any taxes against him for personal property for the year 1909. He did not, during 1909 or during previous years, list any personal property for taxation in Lake County. The board of review, however, caused him to appear before it and, when he refused to list his property, it levied an assessment against him. He contended he was not subject to the tax for the year in question because at that time he was a resident of the state of California. As a result, the court was required to rule on the question of his domicile for tax purposes.]

COOKE, J. . . .

. . . .

. . . The testimony of other witnesses tends to show that appellant has been in Lake Forest a large portion of the time since 1885; that from 1901 to 1907 he spent at least 75 per cent. of each year in Lake Forest, and was seen upon the streets of Lake Forest the same as other business men having their place of business in Chicago and their residence in Lake Forest; that he has been active in municipal affairs affecting the water-works company of which he is president; that he conducted his business in Chicago and resided in Lake Forest, traveling back and forth on the train, and, according to his own testimony, frequently purchasing and using monthly tickets between Lake Forest and Chicago; that during that period he attended church at Lake Forest 75 per cent. of the Sundays, taking an active interest in the selection of the pastor, and was a regular attendant at the weekly prayer meeting on Wednesday night.

It seems to us apparent from a consideration of all the evidence that the house at Lake Forest, in which appellant owns an undivided interest, is, and has been for several years at least, his real home, and that he maintains no establishment at any other place, especially in California, which could be considered as such. In Hayes v. Hayes, 74 Ill. 312, it is said that, according to authoritative text-writers, the term "domicile," in its ordinary acceptation, means the place where a person lives or has his home, and that in a strict legal sense that is properly the domicile of a person where he has his true, fixed, permanent home and principal establishment, and to which, whenever he is absent, he has the intention of returning. It is further said in the same case that, in order to effect a change of domicile, there must be an actual abandonment of the first domicile coupled with an intention not to return to it, and there must be a new domicile acquired by actual residence within another jurisdiction coupled with the intention of making the last acquired residence a permanent home. In order to bring about a change of residence, it is necessary that there be not only an intention to change the residence, but the change must actually be made by abandoning the old and permanently locating in the new place of residence. . . . The intention is not necessarily determined from the statements or declarations of the party but may be inferred from the surrounding circumstances, which may entirely disprove such statements or declarations. On the question of domicile less weight will be given to the party's declaration than to his acts. . . . Applying these rules to the case at bar, we are of the opinion that the acts of appellant and the circumstances shown by the evidence wholly disprove his statements that he changed his place of residence to San Diego county, Cal., in 1904, and has ever since been a resident of that county. . . .

Guides for Class Discussion

1. Differentiate between "domicile" and "residence."
2. Are you in agreement with the court's holding? Give reasons.
3. See *Commonwealth* v. *American Dredging Co., infra.*

21. *"The general rule is that tangible personal property is taxable at the domicile of the owner even though it may be temporarily located in another state"* (p. 5).

COMMONWEALTH V. AMERICAN DREDGING CO.,
122 Pa. St. 386, 15 A. 443 (1888)
(Decided by the Supreme Court of Pennsylvania)

[This was an action to determine whether certain personal property consisting of a tugboat, dredges, and scows, owned by a Pennsylvania corporation, not located within the state were taxable in the state of Pennsylvania.]

PAXSON, J. The court below correctly held that the defendant company was not liable to taxation upon so much of its capital stock as was represented by lands and buildings situate in the state of New Jersey; but we are of opinion that the learned judge erred in his ruling that the $92,000 of said stock, represented in the form of dredges, tug-boat, and the 11 scows, conceding that they, or at least a part of them, were built outside the state, and have never been within it, were not liable to taxation. This is not because of the technical principle that the *situs* of personal property is where the domicile of the owner is found. This rule is doubtless true as to intangible property, such as bonds, mortgages, and other evidences of debt. But the better opinion seems to be that it does not hold in the case of visible, tangible, personal property, permanently located in another state. In such cases it is taxable within the jurisdiction where found, and is exempt at the domicile of the owner. Goods and chattels, horses and cattle, and other movable property of a tangible or visible character, are liable to taxation in the jurisdiction of the state wherein the same are and are ordinarily kept, irrespective of the residence or domicile of the owner. Legal protection and taxation are reciprocal; so that such personal property and effects of a corporeal nature, or that may be handled and removed, as receive the protection of the law, are liable to be taxed by the law where they are thus protected. Ror. Int. St. Law, 204, and cases there cited; Potter, Corp. §§ 189, 190; Pierce, R. R. 472. No fault is found with this principle; but does it apply to the facts of this case? It must be conceded that the property in question must be liable to taxation in some jurisdiction. If it were permanently located in another state, it would be liable to taxation there. But the facts show that it is not permanently located out of the state. From the nature of the business, it is in one place to-day and another to-morrow, and hence not taxable in the jurisdiction where temporarily employed. It follows that, if not taxable here, it escapes altogether.

Guides for Class Discussion

1. Compare this decision with the one in *Fennell* v. *Pauley, infra.* Distinguish between them.
2. See also *Colbert* v. *Board of Supervisors, infra;* and *Scripps* v. *Board of Review, infra.*

22. *"It is well settled that tangible personal property which is definitely and more or less permanently located in a state other than that in which the owner is domiciled may be taxed by the law of the place where it is found"* (p. 5).

FENNELL V. PAULEY,
112 Iowa 94, 83 N.W. 799 (1900)
(Decided by the Supreme Court of Iowa)

[This was an action to have an assessment, made against property belonging to the plaintiff, canceled. Plaintiff, a resident of Missouri, had brought cattle into Iowa for feeding purposes and objected when they were assessed for purposes of taxation in the state of Iowa. He contended that, because he was a resident of Missouri, the *situs* of the cattle for purposes of taxation was Missouri and not Iowa.]

WATERMAN, J. In the years 1895-96 plaintiff was a resident of the state of Missouri. In December, 1895, he brought into Fremont county, in this state, 202 head of cattle for feeding purposes, and kept them upon land owned by him. In April, 1896, the cattle were taken back to the state of Missouri. Plaintiff claims that these cattle were assessed to him in the state of Missouri, and the tax there paid by him. But we think the court may well have found from the evidence that this was not the fact; that these particular cattle were never assessed anywhere save in this state. The contention is that this property, belonging to a nonresident and being only temporarily in this state, was not taxable here. Section 812, Code 1873, provides that all personal property shall be taxed in the name of the owner on the 1st day of January. That property of this nature is taxable is fixed by sections 797-801, and section 817 requires personal property in the hands of an agent to be listed by the assessor. Section 823 requires the assessor to return all personal property found in his township. We understand that property in transit through the state cannot be taxed here, nor can such as belongs to a nonresident, which is here only as an incident of its transfer elsewhere. To give the right to assess the personal property of a nonresident found within this state, it must be located here with something like permanency, or for some purpose other than merely aiding its transit. The general rule is that personalty is taxed where the owner resides. Ament v. Humphrey, 3 G. Greene, 255; Rhyno v. Madison Co., 43 Iowa, 632. But to this general rule there are exceptions. Money in the hands of an agent in this state for investment here is taxable in this jurisdiction. Hutchinson v. Board, 66 Iowa, 35, 23 N.W. 249. Certainly it can make no difference that it is in possession of the owner instead of an agent. These cattle were here to be fed, in order to increase their weight and value for market. In this case there was something more than a temporary stoppage of the cattle here. In principle, it was the same as the investment of money in this state, and we cannot see why they should not be taxed here.

Guides for Class Discussion

1. Compare the decision in this case with the one rendered by the court in *Commonwealth* v. *American Dredging Co., supra.*
2. Are you in agreement with the court's thinking? Give reasons.

23. "... *a state legislature may make tangible personal property taxable elsewhere than in the domicile of the owner; and, where it is made taxable in a state other than the one of the owner's domicile, it cannot be taxed in both states*" (p. 5).

COLBERT V. BOARD OF SUPERVISORS,
60 Miss. 142 (1882)
(Decided by the Supreme Court of Mississippi)

[When the board of supervisors of Leake County, Mississippi, increased the assessment against plaintiff, a resident of that county, by adding 100 bales of cotton which he had previously shipped to New Orleans, and which remained there unsold at the time of the assessment, he appealed to the court. The lower court sustained the action of the board of supervisors, but the court here reversed the decision of the lower court.]

CAMPBELL, C. J., delivered the opinion of the court.

The law provides for the taxation of choses in action, and prescribes no place where they shall be assessed (except as, to money on deposit, or loaned at interest in or out of this State), but they are taxable, where the owner resides, because they have no place distinct from him. This does not apply to bales of cotton, which have a *situs* distinct from the person of their owner. As to such [tangible] personal property, the law has prescribed that it shall be assessed, where it is in fact, and not by fiction. It is true, this provision of the statute relates to personal property in this

State; but it is also true that there is no provision for taxing personal property capable of having a locality, which is permanently out of this State, and has a *situs* in another State. The cotton of the appellant was not taxable in this State.

Judgment reversed, and judgment here for the appellant.

Guides for Class Discussion

1. Compare the decision in this case with the one in *Commonwealth v. American Dredging Co., supra;* and with *Scripps v. Board of Review, infra.*
2. Do you see any conflict in these three cases?

24. *"Intangible personal property, such as stocks, bonds, and mortgages are taxable at the domicile of the owner"* (p. 5).

SCRIPPS V. BOARD OF REVIEW,
183 Ill. 278, 55 N.E. 700 (1899)
(Decided by the Supreme Court of Illinois)

[In this case plaintiff, a resident of Illinois, objected when an attempt was made by county authorities in Illinois to levy and collect a tax on "credits held and possessed by him in the state of Iowa from residents of the state of Iowa." These credits were examples of intangible personal property. He contended that the credits were payable in Iowa and were, therefore, subject to the laws and jurisdictions of that state. Consequently, he argued they were not taxable in Illinois. The court held against him.]

PHILLIPS, J. . . .

The actual situs of personal property having an actual and tangible existence, under the legislation of this state, will determine the town or district in which it may be taxed. . . . The general rule is that personal property of a tangible character is to be assessed where situated, without reference to the domicile of the owner. Debts and choses in action are a species of intangible property that, for purposes of taxation, are generally held to be situated at the domicile of the owner. A debt owing to a person is evidenced by an account, note, bond, or other promise of the debtor, and is a mere chose in action, which goes with the person of the creditor, and can be properly assessed, under the great weight of authority, only in the county where the owner resides. A debt has no situs other than the domicile of the owner. It cannot be taxed to the debtor, for in such case it would not be a tax on property or wealth, but would be a tax on the converse, and a tax on poverty. The debtor may be in one state, and the creditor and security for the debt in another. . . . In City of Davenport v. Mississippi & M. R. Co., 12 Iowa, 539, the question arose before the supreme court of Iowa whether mortgages on property in that state held by nonresidents could be taxed under a law which provided that all property, real and personal, within the state, should be subject to taxation; and the court said: "Both in law and equity the mortgagee has only a chattel interest. It is true that the situs of the property mortgaged is within the jurisdiction of the state; but, the mortgage itself being personal property, a chose in action attaches to the person of the owner. It is agreed by the parties that the owners and holders of the mortgages are nonresidents of the state. If so, and the property of the mortgage attaches to the person of the owner, it follows that these mortgages are not property within the state; and, if not, they are not subject to taxation." . . . The weight of authority is that money loaned in another state or county, in the absence of a statute to the contrary, is taxable in the state or county where the owner or creditor resides, and not in that of the debtor, and that the debt follows the residence of the creditor, and has its situs there.

Guides for Class Discussion

1. Differentiate between this case and *In Re Washington County v. Estate of Jefferson, infra.* Can they be reconciled?
2. In the last sentence quoted, where the court announced the rule of law covering this case it used the words "in the absence of a statute to the contrary." Did the court thereby imply, at least, that the rule could be changed by statute?
3. What did the court say with regard to the situs of tangible personal property for tax purposes? Is this authoritative?

25. *"The state legislature may provide that intangible personal property shall be taxed where located and . . . [it] may attain a business situs in a state other than the owner's domicile and if so it is taxable there"* (p. 5).

In Re Washington County v. Estate of Jefferson,
35 Minn. 215, 28 N.W. 256 (1886)
(Decided by the Supreme Court of Minnesota)

[This was an action to determine the responsibility of the estate of one Jefferson, a resident of New York, for taxes levied in Minnesota on bonds and notes secured by mortgages of real estate in Washington County, Minnesota, and held by Jefferson. In ruling against the estate the court commented on the legality of a statute requiring the payment of taxes on intangible personal property in the state under whose protection the property pledged to guarantee the loan was situated.]

Gilfillan, C. J. . . .

. . . .

The main question in the case is, can credits due to a resident of another state, from a resident within this state, for moneys loaned and invested by, and which credits are managed and controlled by, an agent of the creditor, resident within this state, be taxed here, under the present statute?

. . . .

The designation in the present statute (section 1, *c.* 11, Gen. St. 1878) is also broad enough to include credits due nonresidents, but which have a *situs* here: "All real and personal property in this state, and all personal property of persons residing therein, . . . is subject to taxation." Unless the words in this clause "and personal" are to be held surplusage, the clause shows an intent to tax personal property in the state of persons residing elsewhere, as well as the personal property of residents; and we find nothing in the following sections of the chapter to indicate that those words do not have their full natural meaning. . . .

. . . .

It is to be taken, therefore, as to the intent of the statute, that credits, to whomsoever owing, are taxable here if they can be regarded as personal property *in this state;* that is, situated in this state. To justify the imposition of tax by any state, it must have jurisdiction over the person taxed, or over the property taxed. As Jefferson was not a resident of this state, there was no jurisdiction over him. But if the property on account o which these taxes were unpaid was within this state, the state had juris diction to impose them as it might impose a tax upon tangible persona property permanently situated here, and to enforce the taxes against th property. The authorities which we cite in support of the proposition tha the credits taxed had a *situs* here, fully sustain this.

For many purposes the domicile of the owner is deemed the *situs* c his personal property. This, however, is only a fiction, from motives c convenience, and is not of universal application, but yields to the actua *situs* of the property when justice requires that it should. It is not allowe to be controlling in matters of taxation. Thus corporeal personal propert is conceded to be taxable at the place where it is actually situated. credit which cannot be regarded as situated in a place merely because th debtor resides there, must usually be considered as having its *situs* wher it is owned,—at the domicile of the creditor. The creditor, however, ma give it a business *situs* elsewhere; as where he places it in the hands o an agent for collection or renewal, with a view to reloaning the mone and keeping it invested as a permanent business. . . .

. . . .

The allegation to pay taxes on property for the support of the govern ment arises from the fact that it is under the protection of the govern ment. Now, here was property within this state, not for a merely tem porary purpose, but as permanently as though the owner resided here It was employed here as a business by one who exercised over it the sam control and management as over his own property, except that he did i in the name of an absent principal. It was exclusively under the protec tion of the laws of this state. It had to rely on those laws for the forc and validity of the contracts on the loans, and the preservation an enforcement of the securities. The laws of New York never operated on it If credits can ever have an actual *situs* other than the domicile of th owner, can ever be regarded as property within any other state, and a under obligation to contribute to its support in consideration of bein under its protection, it must be so in this case. Judgment affirmed.

Guides for Class Discussion

1. Compare this decision with the one rendered in *Scripps* v *Board of Review, supra.*
2. What did the court say with respect to the owner's domicile a the *situs* of his personal property?
3. Would the court have held as it did had there been no statut involved? Give reasons.

Taxation for education

6. "*A state may tax the income earned within its borders by a resident of another state*" (p. 5).

SHAFFER V. CARTER,
252 U.S. 37, 40 S.Ct. 221 (1920)
(Decided by the Supreme Court of the United States)

[When Oklahoma enacted a state income tax law which provided for the levying, assessing, and collecting of such tax from all sources, including every business, trade, or profession carried on in the state by non-residents, plaintiff, a citizen of Illinois, was required to make a return in Oklahoma. This he did under protest. It was to question the legality of this tax that this action was brought.]

MR. JUSTICE PITNEY delivered the opinion of the court.

. . . .

Plaintiff, a nonresident of Oklahoma, being a citizen of Illinois and a resident of Chicago in that State, was at the time of the commencement of the suit and for several years theretofore (including the years 1915 and 1916) engaged in the oil business in Oklahoma, having purchased, owned, developed, and operated a number of oil and gas mining leases, and being the owner in fee of certain oil-producing land, in that State. From properties thus owned and operated during the year 1916 he received a net income exceeding $1,500,000, and of this he made, under protest, a return which showed that, at the rates fixed by the act, there was due to the State an income tax in excess of $76,000. The then State Auditor overruled the protest and assessed a tax in accordance with the return; the present Auditor has put it in due course of collection; and plaintiff resists its enforcement upon the ground that the act, in so far as it subjects the incomes of non-residents to the payment of such a tax, takes their property without due process of law and denies to them the equal protection of the laws, in contravention of § 1 of the Fourteenth Amendment; burdens interstate commerce, in contravention of the commerce clause of § 8 of Art. I of the Constitution; and discriminates against nonresidents in favor of residents, and thus deprives plaintiff and other nonresidents of the privileges and immunities of citizens and residents in the State of Oklahoma, in violation of § 2 of Art. IV. . . .

. . . .

The contention [is] that a State is without jurisdiction to impose a tax upon the income of nonresidents. . . .
This radical contention is easily answered by reference to fundamental principles. In our system of government the States have general dominion, and, saving as restricted by particular provisions of the Federal Constitu-

tion, complete dominion over all persons, property, and business transactions within their borders; they assume and perform the duty of preserving and protecting all such persons, property, and business, and, in consequence, have the power normally pertaining to governments to resort to all reasonable forms of taxation in order to defray the governmental expenses. Certainly they are not restricted to property taxation, nor to any particular form of excises. In well-ordered society, property has value chiefly for what it is capable of producing, and the activities of mankind are devoted largely to making recurrent gains from the use and development of property, from tillage, mining, manufacture, from the employment of human skill and labor, or from a combination of some of these; gains capable of being devoted to their own support, and the surplus accumulated as an increase of capital. That the State, from whose laws property and business and industry derive the protection and security without which production and gainful occupation would be impossible, is debarred from exacting a share of those gains in the form of income taxes for the support of the government, is a proposition so wholly inconsistent with fundamental principles as to be refuted by its mere statement. That it may tax the land but not the crop, the tree but not the fruit, the mine or well but not the product, the business but not the profit derived from it, is wholly inadmissible.

.   .   .   .

The rights of the several States to exercise the widest liberty with respect to the imposition of internal taxes always has been recognized in the decisions of this court. . . . That a State may tax callings and occupations as well as persons and property has long been recognized. . . .

And we deem it clear, upon principle as well as authority, that just as a State may impose general income taxes upon its own citizens and residents whose persons are subject to its control, it may, as a necessary consequence, levy a duty of like character, and not more onerous in its effect, upon incomes accruing to non-residents from their property or business within the State, or their occupations carried on therein; enforcing payment, so far as it can, by the exercise of a just control over persons and property within its borders. This is consonant with numerous decisions of this court sustaining state taxation of credits due to non-residents. . . .

That a State, consistently with the Federal Constitution, may not prohibit the citizens of other States from carrying on legitimate business within its borders like its own citizens, of course is granted; but it does not follow that the business of nonresidents may not be required to make a ratable contribution in taxes for the support of the government. On the contrary, the very fact that a citizen of one State has the right to hold property or carry on an occupation or business in another is a very reasonable ground for subjecting such non-resident, although not personally yet to the extent of his property held, or his occupation or business carried on therein, to a duty to pay taxes not more onerous in effect than those imposed under like circumstances upon citizens of the latter State. Section 2 of Art. IV of the Constitution entitles him to the privileges and immunities of a citizen, but no more; not to an entire immunity from taxation, nor to any preferential treatment as compared with resident citizens. It protects him against discriminatory taxation, but gives him no right to be favored by discrimination or exemption.

Guides for Class Discussion

1. Are you in agreement with the court's reasoning? Give reasons.
2. Compare the decision in this case with the one rendered by the court in *In Re Washington County* v. *Estate of Jefferson, supra.*

27. *"Where illegal taxes are paid voluntarily or merely under protest they cannot be recovered. . . ."* (p. 5).

SAN DIEGO LAND & TOWN CO. v.
LA PRESA SCHOOL DIST. IN SAN DIEGO COUNTY,
122 Cal. 98, 54 P. 528 (1898)
(Decided by the Supreme Court of California)

[This was an action to recover $525 paid by plaintiff in taxes under a mistake of fact. It was contended that the property in question was in reality located outside the district. This meant, of course, that the tax was illegal. The evidence indicated, however, that the payment was made voluntarily and with the full means of knowing the facts had they been investigated. The question was whether, under such circumstances, the plaintiff could recover the tax he had paid. The court held he could not.]

CHIPMAN, C. . . .

. . . . The authorities are generally agreed that a tax voluntarily paid cannot be recovered back. Mr. Cooley says: "Every man is supposed to know the law, and, if he voluntarily makes a payment which the law would not compel him to make, he cannot afterwards assign his ignorance of the law as the reason why the state should furnish him with remedies to recover it back. . . . The rule of law is a rule of sound policy also; it is a rule of quiet as well as of good faith, and precludes the courts being occupied in undoing the arrangements of parties which they have voluntarily made, and into which they have not been drawn by fraud or accident, or by any excusable ignorance of their legal rights and liabilities." Cooley, Tax'n, p. 809. . . . It is the legal duty, we think, of the owner of property to see that it is properly assessed; and ample provision is made for correcting mistakes in the roll or list. The manager of the company did not testify that he paid the tax under mistake of fact, but that when the tax was paid he believed the property was inside the district. Conceding, however, that plaintiff made a mistake of fact in paying when it was not liable, the mistake was caused by its own neglect of duty, and, the payment being voluntary, the law will furnish no relief.

In 1858 the legislature of this state passed an act imposing a stamp tax upon shipments of gold out of the state. Stamps were placed on sale with the county treasurers. In Brumagim v. Tillinghast, 18 Cal. 265, plaintiff sued the county treasurer of the city and county of San Francisco to recover back money paid in the purchase of these stamps. The act was held to be unconstitutional and void. Recovery depended upon the character of the payment—whether voluntary or under compulsion or coercion. It was held that "the rule is well settled that moneys voluntarily paid upon claim of right, with full knowledge of all the facts, cannot be recovered back merely because the party at the time of payment was ignorant of or mistook the law as to his liability. The illegality of the demand paid constitutes of itself no ground for relief. . . . It is the compulsion or coercion under which the party is supposed to act which gives him a right to relief. . . . If he voluntarily pay an illegal demand, knowing it to be illegal, he is entitled to no consideration; and if he voluntarily pay such demand in ignorance or misapprehension of the law respecting its validity, he is in no better position, for it would be against the highest policy to permit transactions to be opened upon grounds of this character." This case has been many times cited with approval. We can see no reason why the rule should be different, and we do not understand that it is different, where the mistake is one of fact, if the mistake is such that with ordinary diligence it could have been discovered. The law imputes knowledge to one who has the means of knowledge. The assessment was notice to plaintiff as to how its property was described. It had the means of knowledge, and was put upon inquiry as to the facts.

Guides for Class Discussion

1. Compare the decision in this case with the one rendered in *Harding v. Wiley, infra.*
2. Which case represents the better law?
3. On what ground did the court base its reasoning in this case?

28. ". . . *if illegal taxes are paid under duress they may be recovered*" (p. 5).

HARDING V. WILEY,
219 Ill. App. 1 (1920)
(Decided by the Appellate Court of Illinois, Second District)

[In this case, when a question existed regarding the legality of a tax, a taxpayer paid his taxes under protest. This was so noted on the margin of the tax books. Later, when a court ordered the ouster of the board of education, the taxpayer brought this action to recover the taxes he had previously paid. It should be noted that the tax collector to whom the taxes had been paid neither made nor threatened a distraint against the taxpayer. The question before the court was whether the plaintiff could recover his taxes. The lower court ruled he could not, and the higher court affirmed its decision.]

MR. JUSTICE HEARD delivered the opinion of the court.

. . . .

Appellant was one of the relators in the quo warranto proceedings mentioned . . . and had full knowledge of all the facts with reference to the purported school district and the tax levies.

In *Conkling* v. *City of Springfield*, 132 Ill. 420, a case in which the circumstances of payment were like those in the present case, the court said: "As a general rule, where a person is compelled, by duress, to pay an illegal tax for which he is not liable, he may recover it back. The rule on this subject is well stated by Shaw, C. J., in *Preston* v. *Boston*, 12 Pick. [Mass.] 13, as follows: 'A party who has paid voluntarily, under a claim of right, shall not afterwards recover back the money, although he protested at the time against his liability. . . . But it is otherwise when a party is compelled, by duress of his person or goods, to pay money for which he is not liable. It is not voluntary, but compulsory, and he may rescue himself from such duress by payment of the money, and afterwards, on proof of the fact, recover it back.' 'The warrant to collect . . . is in the nature of an execution. . . . When, therefore, a party not liable to taxation is called on, peremptorily, to pay upon such a warrant, and he can save himself and his property in no other way than by paying the illegal demand, he may give notice that he so pays it by duress, and not voluntarily, and by showing that he is not liable, recover it back as money had and received.' . . .

"It is manifest, on a moment's reflection, that the facts relied upon here do not bring the case within the rule announced in the cases cited. So far as the tax on real estate is concerned, the town collector had no authority, under the statute, to levy on personal property. If payment was refused, it was his duty to return the land delinquent to the county collector, and the county collector, in case payment was not made to him within the time prescribed by the statute, could only collect by obtaining judgment and selling the land. As to the personal property tax, the collector held a warrant which authorized him to levy on personal property, but before he was authorized to levy, section 155 of the Revenue Law [J. & A. ¶ 9374] required him to call on the persons [*sic*] taxed, at least once, at his place of residence or business, if in the town of the collector, and demand payment of the tax. This had not been done when the taxes were paid, and while the collector held a warrant, as he could make no levy at the time the taxes were paid it cannot be held that the payment was a compulsory one. Had the taxes been demanded by the collector, and after demand he had attempted to levy on personal property, and to avoid a levy and sale the plaintiff had paid under protest, then he might well insist that the payment was made by compulsion; but such is not this case."

We are of opinion that under the law of this State we must hold that the payments made by appellant were voluntarily made and not made under compulsion or duress and therefore cannot be recovered.

Guides for Class Discussion

1. Can this decision be reconciled with the one rendered in *San Diego Land and Town Co.* v. *La Presa School District in San Diego County, supra?*

2. Do you think this decision is equitable? Why or why not?

29. ". . . *funds derived from athletics or other extra-curricular activities must go into official accounts of the school treasurer and be subject to audit the same as other funds*" (p. 5).

Petition of Auditors of Hatfield Township School District,
161 Pa. Super. 388, 54 A. (2d) 833 (1947)
(Decided by the Superior Court of Pennsylvania)

[In this action the school district challenged the right of the statutory auditors to examine an account called "Hatfield Joint School Accounts," funds from which could be withdrawn only by

Elmer B. Laudenslager, the supervising principal. This account was created by resolution of the board of education, which provided that extra-curricular funds such as those derived from athletics, dramatics, the school paper, and the school annual, were to be deposited therein. Likewise, in the same bank there was a savings account which was also under the sole control of the supervising principal. This account was really composed of six accounts: Hatfield Joint School, Library, Farmcraft, Miscellaneous Department, Athletic Association, and Orange and Black (school publication). The court ruled that the moneys in these accounts must go into an official account of the district treasurer and be subject to audit.]

ARNOLD, Judge.

. . . .

In the so-called activity accounts various situations obtain. Of course if pupils of a class give money to a supervising principal to purchase for them class jewelry or similar things the school district has no official duty (although it may have a moral duty), for the supervising principal acts as agent of the pupils. This is the smaller end of the problem. At the other pole, a school district, acting under the express provisions of § 405 of the Code, 24 P.S. § 339, has athletic events. These activities produce large sums of money from paid admissions. Under the instant system these sums of money are not disbursed through the treasurer, nor through a resolution of the board, but are solely at the command of one individual, who has no statutory standing or duty. It is possible that some school district may neither *directly* nor *indirectly* furnish any money for the playing field or stadium; or for the coaching of the athletes, or for their uniforms or playing togs, or for the apparatus with which the sport is connected, or for the lighting of the field; although it is very doubtful whether such case exists. But it is certainly true that, if a school district operates and expends tax money for the acquisition, maintenance or lighting of the playing field, or for the payment of services of a coach, the admissions charged result from the use of public property and from the expenditure of tax monies and are the property of the school district, must go into the official account of the treasurer thereof, and are subject to audit.

. . . .

We have not attempted to discuss each situation that may present itself, but where monies or property are derived directly or indirectly through the use of school buildings, or from the expenditure of public funds of the district, the monies thus derived are public property, must be handled exactly as tax monies and be paid to the district treasurer.

We have some difficulty in understanding why it is desirable to have this system, which is alleged to be general in the state, and thus handle these funds separate and apart from the general funds of the district. It is said that it is a convenience, although of course convenience cannot override the legislative mandate that the funds must be handled by the treasurer. . . . Certain it is that the statute never contemplated that large sums of money thus coming in through the use of the school property and appropriations should pass into the hands of those who are not officials and have no public or official responsibility, who are not statutorily required to be bonded, and whose expenditures are not subject to public inspection and audit. Probably the real reason for the system lies in the fact that those in charge of our schools, having full confidence in their own integrity and educational skill, feel that there would be considerable difficulty in making members of the public understand the wisdom of the expenditures in question. With that position we have sympathy, but to give that plan, wise and honest as it may be, a legal status, requires a legislative enactment, for which even the best of intentions is no substitute.

Guides for Class Discussion

1. Are you in agreement with the decision as rendered by the court?
2. What line of reasoning motivated the court in arriving at its decision?

30. "*A taxpayer will not be permitted to enjoin the collection of a tax on the ground that the proceeds will be used for an illegal purpose*" (p. 5).

PEOPLE V. SCOTT,
300 Ill. 290, 133 N.E. 299 (1921)
(Decided by the Supreme Court of Illinois)

[Plaintiffs—appellants—objected to the school taxes levied in their school district in the year 1920. At the hearing the court "gave judgment for the taxes against the lands of appellants," and this appeal was taken. The main ground on which the legality of the taxes levied was questioned was that the school board intended to use the money raised for an illegal purpose. The court held this was not a sufficient reason for enjoining the collection of the taxes.]

Duncan, J. . . .

. . . .

It is . . . argued by appellants that the school board in question did not have in contemplation at the time of the levy the actual building of a school-house, but was only intending to accumulate money by the levy to build a school-house at some time in the future, without any definite ideas as to when it would build or as to how much the building would cost. This contention is not supported by the record. . . .

. . . .

As to the levy for educational purposes little else need be said. The record evidence does not show that it was so excessive as to be considered fraudulent as to appellants or the other taxpayers in the district. This levy was for only $8,000. . . . The consolidated board contemplated purchasing carriages to convey certain school children to the school, which appellants have estimated from the evidence in the record would cost not less than $3,000. Appellants contend, too, that these carriages could properly be paid for only out of the educational fund, and we are inclined to agree with them, although we are not deciding that question as it is not necessary. No contention is made that this expense is one that the board has no power to incur. Considering the levy at the time it was made, as we must, there is no basis in the record for the claim that the levy was intentionally excessive or so excessive as to be deemed fraudulent as to appellants. We must therefore sustain this levy as one that is legal and binding on the residents of the district.

It is contended by appellants that the board of education had intended to pay the expense of carrying the school children out of the building fund, and that such expense is not legally chargeable to the building fund. It was not incurred or paid out of either fund. The record does not support the conclusion that the levy for building purposes was to include this expense at the time the levy was made. The payment of this expense out of the building fund, or the intended payment thereof out of such fund, can only be considered as an intentional diversion of such fund for improper purposes. Such an intentional diversion of the fund cannot be obviated or reached by the objections in this case, as the remedy is in equity, and no specific objections were made.

Guides for Class Discussion

1. Differentiate between the decision rendered in this case and the one registered in *Pickett v. Russell, infra.*
2. On what basis did the court arrive at this decision?

31. "... *a taxpayer may enjoin the collection of an illegal tax*" (p. 5).

PICKETT V. RUSSELL,
42 Fla. 116, 28 So. 764 (1900)
(Decided by the Supreme Court of Florida)

[This was an action brought by an elector and taxpayer in Duval County, Florida, residing in the city of Jacksonville, to determine the legality of a tax assessed by a sub-school district.]

CARTER, J. . . .

. . . .

. . . The relief prayed is an injunction against the assessment and collection of a tax levied, but alleged to be unauthorized. The legislature can authorize this tax to be levied and collected only when a majority of the qualified electors of the school district that pay a tax on real or personal property shall vote in favor of such levy. Proceedings for the levy, assessment, and collection of the tax will cast a cloud over the title to the complainant's real estate sought to be subjected to the tax. Under these circumstances, equity has jurisdiction to enjoin the assessment and collection of the tax if illegal, and to inquire into the validity of the election, in so far as the authority to levy and collect the tax is derived therefrom. . . .

It is . . . contended that under section 8, art. 9, Const. 1885, which provides that "no person or corporation shall be relieved by any court from the payment of any tax that may be illegal, or illegally or irregularly assessed, until he or it shall have paid such portion of his or its taxes as may be legal, and legally and regularly assessed," the bill ought to have alleged that complainant had paid all taxes legally assessed against him for the year in which the levy of this special tax was made, and that without such allegation there is no equity in the bill. It does not appear that any other tax was in fact assessed against complainant's property during the year 1899, or at the time of filing the bill, though it is quite probable that the assessment roll for state and county taxes of that year was then being made up. We do not understand that the constitutional provision requires payment of taxes legally assessed as a prerequisite to beginning proceedings for relief against illegal taxes, but that such payment must be made before the applicant is relieved from the illegal tax, and such seems to have been the construction placed upon it in Town of Kissimmee City v. City of Cannon, 26 Fla. 3, 7 South. 523, and City of Tampa v. Mugge, 40 Fla. 326, 24 South. 489. If in fact any tax was due by complainant which it was his duty to pay before obtaining the relief sought by this bill, it does not appear upon the face of the bill, nor does it otherwise appear in the proceedings before us.

Guides for Class Discussion

1. Can this decision be reconciled with the one rendered by the Supreme Court of Illinois in *People* v. *Scott, supra?*
2. Do you think this decision is equitable? Why or why not?

32. "*A statute which provides for the collection of a state-wide tax and for its distribution to the various districts on such bases as seem wise in order to equalize educational opportunities is not unconstitutional on the ground that it violates the principle of uniformity, provided the mode of distribution is made to apply to all districts in the same class or category*" (p. 5).

SAWYER V. GILMORE,
109 Me. 169, 83 A. 673 (1912)
(Decided by the Supreme Court of Maine)

[This was an action to test the constitutionality of a statute that provided for the taxing of all property in the state at the rate of 1.50 mills for common-school purposes and the distribution of the receipts of the tax to the various cities, towns, and plantations according to a definite formula. Unorganized townships, although subject to the tax, were not included among its recipients. For this reason, the constitutionality of the statute was questioned on the ground it imposed an unequal tax burden on unorganized townships.]

CORNISH, J. This bill in equity is brought to enjoin the Treasurer of State and his successors in office from collecting a tax assessed under the provisions of chapter 177 of the Public Laws of 1909, entitled "An act relating to the common school fund and the means of providing for and distributing the same." . . .

. . . .

Objections . . . are raised to the manner of distribution, and the plaintiff contends that in considering the constitutionality of a statute creating revenue by taxation the method of distribution as well as of assessment should be scrutinized.

The first objection is that this act imposes an unequal burden of taxation upon the unorganized townships of the state, because, while the fund is created by the taxation of all the property in such townships as well as upon the property in the cities, towns, and plantations, no provision is made for the distribution of any part thereof to such townships, but it is all apportioned among the cities, towns, and plantations. The townships are omitted. In other words, while four subdivisions of the state are made to contribute to the fund, only three are permitted to share in the financial benefits.

This objection, however, is without legal foundation. The Legislature has the right under the Constitution to impose an equal rate of taxation upon all the property in the state, including the property in unorganized townships, for the purpose of distributing the proceeds thereof among the cities, towns, and plantations for common school purposes, and the mere fact that the tax is assessed upon the property in four municipal subdivisions and distributed among three is not in itself fatal.

. . . .

. . . The fundamental question is this: Is the purpose for which the tax is assessed a public purpose, not whether any portion of it may find its way back again to the pocket of the taxpayer or to the direct advantage of himself or family. Were the latter the test, the childless man would be exempt from the support of schools and the sane and well from the support of hospitals. In order that taxation may be equal and uniform in the constitutional sense, it is not necessary that the benefits arising therefrom should be enjoyed by all the people in equal degree, nor that each one of the people should participate in each particular benefit. Laws must be general in their character, and the benefits must affect different people differently. . . .

. . . .

But the plaintiff further attacks the method of distribution as unconstitutional because it is made, not according to the number of scholars . . . but one-third according to the number of scholars and two-thirds according to valuation, thus benefiting the cities, and richer towns more than the poorer.

But that result is not the test of constitutionality. Inequality of assessment is necessarily fatal, inequality of distribution is not, provided the purpose be the public welfare. The method of distributing the proceeds of such a tax rests in the wise discretion and sound judgment of the Legislature. If this discretion is unwisely exercised, the remedy is with the people, and not with the court. Such distribution might be according to population, or according to the number of scholars of school age, or according to school attendance, or according to valuation, or partly on one basis and partly on another. The Constitution prescribes no regulation in regard to this matter, and it is not for the court to say that one method should be adopted in preference to another. We are not to substitute our judgment for that of a co-ordinate branch of the government working within its constitutional limits.

Guides for Class Discussion

1. Explain what the court meant by saying "Inequality of assessment is necessarily fatal, inequality of distribution is not, provided the purpose be the public welfare."
2. Do you understand the court's position to be that the legislature can provide any method for distributing tax funds that it sees fit? Defend your answer.

33. *"Authority to finance the costs of education by the issuance of school bonds is an authority that is not usually implied . . ." (p. 6).*

HEWITT V. BOARD OF EDUCATION
OF NORMAL SCHOOL DISTRICT,
94 Ill. 528 (1880)
(Decided by the Supreme Court of Illinois)

[This was an action questioning the legality of a bond in the amount of $500, and two coupons of $25 each. It was contended that the board of education that issued the bond had no authority so to do. The evidence indicated that the bond was not issued to "pay for a school house site or to erect a building thereon." In other words, it was not issued for purposes mentioned in the statute, but for purposes not contemplated by the law; and the only authority which the board had for so doing was that which was implied.]

MR. CHIEF JUSTICE WALKER delivered the opinion of the Court:

. . . .

The fact, then, that the bond was not issued for an authorized purpose, undeniably rendered it void. Municipal corporations are not usually endowed with power to enter into traffic or general business, and are only created as auxiliaries to the government in carrying into effect some special governmental policy, or to aid in preserving the order and in promoting the well-being of the locality over which their authority extends. Where a corporation is created for business purposes, all persons may presume such bodies, when issuing their paper, are acting within the scope of their power. Not so with municipalities. Being created for governmental purposes, the borrowing of money, the purchase of property on time, and the giving of commercial paper, are not inherent, or even powers usually conferred; and unless endowed with such power in their charters, they have no authority to make and place on the market such paper, and persons dealing in it must see that the power exists. This has long been the rule of this court. . . . We might refer to other cases where it has been held that bonds issued without authority are void, even in the hands of purchasers before maturity and without actual notice.

A person taking bonds of a municipal corporation has access to the records of the body, and it is his duty to see that such instruments are issued in pursuance of authority, and when without power, they must be held void in whosesoever hands they are found. If, therefore, this bond was not issued to purchase a schoolhouse site, or for erecting a school building, as the Appellate Court seem to have found, the bond is void, as it was issued without power. . . .

Guides for Class Discussion

1. Compare the decision in this case with the one rendered by the court in *Ashuelot National Bank* v. *School District, infra.*
2. Do you think this decision, that required boards to have specific rather than implied authority in order to issue bonds, is equitable? Give reasons.

34. ". . . *authority to borrow money does not, as a rule, authorize a school board to issue bonds*" (p. 6).

Ashuelot National Bank v. School District,
56 F. 197 (1893)
(Decided by the Circuit Court of Appeals, Eighth Circuit)

[This action was brought to recover on certain negotiable instruments—bonds, with interest coupons attached—held by plaintiffs. The defendant district contended that the bonds in question were illegal because they were issued without authority of law. For that reason, they argued that they were void even in the hands of an innocent purchaser for value. Under one statute, the district had authority to borrow money to pay for school sites and to erect buildings and furnish them. Another statute provided " 'for the registration of precinct or township and school-district bonds.' " Plaintiff contended that under these statutes the board had the implied authority to issue the bonds in question. The court, however, held otherwise.]

THAYER, District Judge. . . .

.   .   .   .

These being the only laws in force in the state of Nebraska on the 21st day of November, 1874, under and by virtue of which the power to issue negotiable securities can be derived, the question arises whether they are adequate for that purpose. In the case of Merrill v. Monticello, 138 U.S. 673, 681, 11 Sup. Ct. Rep. 441, it was held that although a municipal corporation has an implied power to borrow money, and to give written evidence of the indebtedness in the form of a note or bond, yet that it has no authority, as an incident of such power, to issue a negotiable security. It was further held that the power to borrow money, and the power to give a negotiable bond which may circulate in the market freed from all equitable defenses, are essentially different powers, and that the latter power will not be implied from the former. In a later case (Brenham v. Bank, 144 U.S. 173, 12 Sup. Ct. Rep. 559) it was held that a city which had an express power, under its charter, "to borrow for general purposes not exceeding $15,000 on the credit of the city," had no authority, as an incident of such power, to issue negotiable securities. In accordance with that view, certain negotiable bonds, in the hands of an innocent purchaser, were declared to be void, although another provision of the charter of the city declared, that "bonds of the corporation of the city of Brenham shall not be subject to tax under this act," and although the latter clause could only have had reference to bonds issued in pursuance of the power to borrow money for general purposes on the credit of the city. In speaking of the scope of the decision in Brenham v. Bank, Mr. Justice Harlan, in the dissenting opinion, says:

"It seems to us that the court in the present case, announces for the first time that an express power in a municipal corporation to borrow money for corporate or general purposes does not, under any circumstances, carry with it, by implication, authority to execute a negotiable promissory note or bond for the money so borrowed. . . . A declaration by this court that such notes and bonds are void because of the absence of express legislative authority to execute negotiable instruments for the money borrowed will, we fear, produce incalculable mischief." . . .

It is unnecessary for us to assert that the decision last referred to goes to the full extent last indicated, of holding that a municipal corporation can only acquire authority to issue negotiable securities, by a statute which confers such power in express language, and that the power will not be implied under any circumstances. We think, however, that we may fairly affirm that the two authorities heretofore cited do establish the following propositions: First, that an express power conferred upon a municipal corporation to borrow money for corporate purposes does not in itself carry with it an authority to issue negotiable securities; second, that the latter power will never be implied, in favor of a municipal corporation, unless such implication is necessary to prevent some express corporate power from becoming utterly nugatory; and, third, that in every case where a doubt arises as to the right of a municipal corporation to execute negotiable securities the doubt should be resolved against the existence of any such right. The application of these principles to the case at bar satisfies us that the judgment of the circuit court was for the right party, and should not be disturbed.

Guides for Class Discussion

1. Compare the decision in this case with the one rendered by the court in *Hewitt* v. *The Board of Education of Normal School District, supra.*
2. Again, do you think this decision is equitable?

35. *"The legislature may prescribe the conditions under which school bonds may be issued, and failure to conform to the prescribed conditions will render the bonds illegal"* (p.6).

Dupont v. Mills,
39 Del. 42, 196 A. 168 (1937)
(Decided by the Supreme Court of Delaware)

[This was an action by plaintiffs against the board of school trustees of the Rehoboth School District of Sussex County to recover a sum of money which plaintiffs had deposited as evidence of good faith in bidding for school bonds issued by the defendant. The board had decided to issue bonds in the amount of $160,000, in 21 lasses, according to maturity dates ranging from September 15, 1938, to September 15, 1958. The plaintiffs' bid required that the bonds be legally issued. When the board attempted to deliver the bonds to the plaintiffs, plaintiffs refused them, on the ground that, among other things, "they were not legally issued, direct general obligations of the School District, in that . . . the Board was not authorized to issue bonds not redeemable prior to maturity . . ." The plaintiffs then demanded the return of their "good-faith money," and the board refused. It was stipulated that if the court found the bonds tendered were invalid for any reason advanced, judgment should be entered for plaintiffs; otherwise judgment should be entered for the defendant. The court ruled in favor of plaintiffs, on the ground that the bonds were illegal.]

LAYTON, Chief Justice, delivering the opinion of the majority of the Court:

The enabling act provides that any or all of the bonds issued under its authority may be redeemed at the option of the Board of School Trustees at par and accrued interest at any interest period after the expiration of five years from their date; and it provides, further, that if the Board shall elect to redeem any or all of the bonds, the redemption shall be in pursuance of a prescribed notice.

The bonds tendered the plaintiff by the defendant are, specifically, not redeemable prior to their respective maturity dates. Wherefore, the plaintiffs contend that they do not meet the conditions of their bid for them, in that they are not legally issued, direct obligations of the school district.

The precise question presented is whether the permissive language of section 6 of the act, gives absolute discretion and power to the Board to determine, at the time of issuance, the redeemable or non-redeemable character of the bonds, or, whether the language is descriptive of the bonds in the particular that they must be redeemable after the expiration of five years, the discretion then to be exercised as circumstances may warrant.

It will be agreed that the Legislature, under article 10 of the Constitution, has, subject to certain exceptions, plenary power over free public schools; and that, with respect to the building of a school house and the manner and method of defraying its cost, the defendant school district is subject to that power. It will not be denied that the Legislature had the power to prescribe the kind and character of the security to be issued by the school district to secure the money which it was authorized to borrow.

The general principle, as expressed in Dillon on Municipal Corporations, 4th Ed., vol. 1, 156, is that

"Powers are conferred upon municipal corporations for public purposes; and as their legislative powers cannot . . . be delegated, so they cannot without legislative authority, express or implied be bargained or bartered away. Such corporations may make authorized contracts, but they have no power, as a party, to make contracts or pass by-laws which shall cede away, control or embarrass their legislative or governmental powers, or which shall disable them from performing their public duties."

. . . .

The Board could not, at the time of issuance, make its election to redeem pursuant to the prescribed notice indicating the bonds to be called and the method and manner of calling them. The right of election to redeem refers, therefore, specifically to a time not less than five years from the date of the bonds. The language of the section, considered as a whole, clearly expresses the legislative purpose. Unless violence be done to plain language, and a vital part of the section ignored, its language cannot fairly be construed as conferring an absolute power and discretion in the Board to determine the redeemable quality of the bonds. The Legislature considered the question of the marketability of the bonds, and provided a certain life of five years. It considered the welfare of the taxpayers as affected by possible future conditions, and protected them against a non-callable debt. Much was left to the Board's discretion, but the right to issue non-redeemable bonds was not conferred. The provisions of the section, although permissive in form, are mandatory in the sense that a duty was imposed upon the Board to reserve the right to redeem the bonds after the expiration of five years.

The conclusion must be that the bonds tendered the plaintiffs were not such as were authorized by the act; and it follows that the plaintiffs were justified in refusing to accept and to pay for them.

Guides for Class Discussion

1. Are you in agreement with the court's reasoning? Give reasons.
2. See *Hewitt* v. *The Board of Education of Normal School District, supra;* and *Ashuelot National Bank* v. *School District, supra.* Do they shed any light on the question before the court here?

36. *"Where bonds are authorized for a particular purpose, the funds derived from their sale must be used for that purpose and no other"* (p. 6).

BYER v. RURAL HIGH SCHOOL DISTRICT,
169 Kan. 351, 219 P. (2d) 382 (1950)
(Decided by the Supreme Court of Kansas)

[This was an action to enjoin the issuance of school district bonds. Plaintiff alleged that defendant was about to issue bonds in the amount of $70,000 as the result of an election, and he further contended that the bonds were illegal because the notice was invalid, in that it did not inform the electors of the entire purpose for which the funds were to be used. The notice and the ballots indicated that the funds were to be used for remodeling, improving, and enlarging a school building, but did not clearly state that the improvements contemplated required the moving of the building from its present location to another site, at a cost of approximately $5,000. Plaintiff contended this was an illegal purpose, under the statute. Defendant apparently admitted that it contemplated moving the building in question.]

THIELE, Justice.

. . . .

. . . There can be no controversy but that the election notice and the ballot specified the question to be voted upon was, should the school district issue bonds in an amount not exceeding $70,000 "for the purpose of providing funds to pay the cost of enlarging, remodeling and improving the High School Building," nor is it arguable but that, standing alone, such statement of the question is unequivocal. But in view of the conceded fact that the moneys were not to be used for those purposes alone but that it was proposed by the school board that the building was to be moved from one site to another, the expense of moving to be paid out of bond proceeds, may it be said the question submitted was unequivocal?

. . . .

Inherent in the case is the question of the power of the school district to issue bonds, a part of the proceeds of which was to be used to pay for the removal of the school house from one site to another. In discussing this question we do not overlook appellees' contention that it was not properly before the court in an action to enjoin issuance of bonds, but would be properly raised in an action to enjoin wrongful appropriation of the bond proceeds. Whether that be correct need not be determined. The nature of the proceedings before us is such that a complete determination should be made of all issues. . . . The statute provides for "equipping, enlarging, remodeling, repairing and improving" the schoolhouse and "the purchase, repairing and installation of equipment therein." Certainly those words do not include removal of a schoolhouse from one site to another, and it may not be said there is any express authority. And when the details of the statutory language are considered, it may not be said it is clearly implied there is any such power. Were we in doubt as to whether the language conferred power on the school district to issue bonds to raise moneys to move the schoolhouse from one site to another, our conclusion would be the district was not given such power. We conclude, however, there is no doubt and that the district was without power under the statute relied on to issue bonds, the proceeds of which were to be used for the removal.

Guides for Class Discussion

1. Are you in agreement with the court's reasoning?
2. See *DuPont* v. *Mills, supra.* Does this case have any bearing on the case under consideration?

37. *"In case the voters of a school district authorize the sale of bonds in an amount greater than the law permits, the authorization is not therefore illegal, and the school board may issue bonds in the amount authorized by statute"* (p. 6).

SHOVER v. BUFORD,
17 Colo. 562, 208 P. 470 (1922)
(Decided by the Supreme Court of Colorado)

[This was an action by resident taxpayers to restrain a school board from issuing bonds in any amount. At an election the voters had approved the issuance of bonds in the amount of $20,000. This amount, however, was in excess of the debt limit. The maximum that could legally be issued was $14,160. The board's answer to the plaintiffs' contention was that it did not intend to issue bonds in excess of this amount. The question was whether it could issue bonds in any amount.]

CAMPBELL, J. . . .

. . . .

The parties themselves are in accord that the substantial question involved is whether the vote of the electors at the called meeting to instruct the school board to issue bonds in the sum of $20,000 for building a schoolhouse, which sum is in excess of the statutory limit, prevents the board from issuing bonds for the lesser sum of $14,160, which is within the limit?

. . . .

In Stockdale v. School District No. 2 of Wayland, 47 Mich. 226, 10 N.W. 349, in an opinion by Judge Cooley, it was held that a vote of the electors of a school district in favor of the issuance of bonds beyond the statutory limit nevertheless was valid to the extent that would have been admissible had the limited sum been proposed and voted, and cites McPherson v. Foster Bros., 43 Iowa, 48, 22 Am. Rep. 215. In the Iowa case there is an elaborate discussion by the court of this proposition. The court said that, where a school district may become indebted in a certain amount by bonds, and the electors of the district authorize a debt in excess of that amount, such authorization is void only as to the excess and valid as to the sum which it is within the power of the district to issue. . . .

In Meyer v. City and County, 150 Cal. 131, 88 Pac. 722, 10 L.R.A. (N.S.) 110, the decision was that, in the case of an overissue of bonds, they would all be valid, except those issued after the limit was reached.

In 19 R.C.L. 1021, § 313, the author says an overissue of bonds does not affect the validity of the entire issue authorized, but only those in excess of what was authorized, citing a number of cases, some of which have already been referred to.

Plaintiffs say there is a distinction between some of these cases which we have cited that involved the validity of bonds issued and disposed of, and where, as here, the issue is not yet made, and where the suit is to restrain the entire issue. We do not perceive any valid distinction in principle between the two classes of cases. It is fair to presume, when there is no evidence to the contrary, that electors of a school district, who vote in favor of an issue of bonds in the sum of $20,000, would vote for an issue of $14,160. There is force in the argument that the electors of district No. 82 had no opportunity to express themselves as to an issue of any bonds except one for $20,000, and that, if they had been called upon to vote for an issue of $14,160, they might have considered it inadequate for the construction of a schoolhouse which they wished to build and would have voted against the proposition for a sum which seemed to them inadequate. While appreciating the force of the argument, we are of the opinion that, by the weight of authority, and upon principle, the vote of the electors in this district was a sufficient authorization to the defendant school board to issue bonds in the maximum sum authorized by the statute, as applicable to a school district of this class, in the absence of evidence that the smaller sum would not have been voted.

Guides for Class Discussion

1. Are you in sympathy with this decision? Give reasons.
2. How could you answer the argument that, while the voters approved the issue of bonds in the maximum amount, they might not have approved the issuance of bonds in the amount permitted by law, on the ground that this was inadequate to build the type of school building they wished?
3. See *Covington* v. *McInnis, infra.*

38. *"It has been held that where a school board has statutory authority to call an election to determine whether bonds shall be issued, if the proposition is defeated at the election the board may call as many additional elections as it sees fit"* (p. 6).

McKINNEY v. BOARD OF TRUSTEES,
144 Ky. 85, 137 S.W. 839 (1911)
(Decided by the Court of Appeals of Kentucky)

[A statement of the facts will be found in the first paragraph of the material quoted.]

CARROLL, J. In October, 1910, an election was held in the Cadiz Graded School District to ascertain the wishes of the voters as to whether or not the trustees of the district should issue bonds not exceeding $12,000 for the purpose of repairing or erecting a school building. The tax was voted by more than the requisite majority, and its validity is assailed by appellant, a taxpayer of the district, upon the following grounds: First. That as an election was held in August, 1910, for the same purpose and the tax defeated, another election could not be held in October, 1910, submitting to the voters substantially the question that was submitted to them in August, 1910. In other words, the contention is that, where the tax is defeated, a second election cannot be held in the same year. . . .

. . . .

Section 148 of the Constitution provides in part that: "Not more than one election each year shall be held in this state or in any city, town, district, or county thereof, except as otherwise provided in this Constitution." But section 155 exempts school elections from the operation of the constitutional provisions in reference to elections, providing that: "The provisions of sections 145 and 154, inclusive, shall not apply to the election of school trustees and other common school district elections. Said elections shall be regulated by the General Assembly, except as otherwise provided in this Constitution." The statute does not prohibit the holding of more than one election like the one involved in this case in the same year, and in the absence of any statutory limitation upon the authority of the trustees to submit the question of creating an indebtedness more than once in the same year we think that when a tax has been defeated the trustees may again and as often as they think proper submit the same or a different question to the voters. As the manner in which elections like this shall be held was left to the legislative department, and it has not been seen proper to limit the number, we must assume that it was intended to leave this matter to the discretion of the trustees of established districts, and to the people of territory seeking to establish a new district.

Guides for Class Discussion

1. Are you in agreement with this decision? Is it equitable? Give reasons.
2. In case the election had been favorable to the bond issue, do you think the court would have permitted a second vote shortly thereafter to nullify the original vote? Why or why not?

39. *"Failure to issue bonds for several years after they have been authorized will not render them void"* (p. 6).

COVINGTON V. MCINNIS,
144 S.C. 391, 142 S.E. 650 (1928)
(Decided by the Supreme Court of South Carolina)

[This was an action to enjoin the issuance of school-district bonds. The purpose of the case was to have the proposed bonds declared illegal on several grounds, one of which was that, because the election authorizing them had been held several years previous to the time it was decided to issue them, it no longer was legal justification for their issuance.]

WATTS, C. J. . . .

. . . .

It is contended, first, by the petitioner that, as more than seven years has elapsed since the authority was given by the election to the trustees to issue the bonds and a part of said bonds having been issued and sold, after so long a lapse of time the trustees are now without authority to issue the remaining portion of said bonds or any part thereof.

This court has recognized the validity of bonds issued many years after the election. The voters in the election declared their willingness to have the school district issue $50,000 of bonds. At the time of the election on account of the 8 per cent. limitation of the Constitution the full amount of these bonds could not be issued, but this disability having been removed and in the opinion of the trustees it is necessary for the school district to come into funds to be used for the purposes for which the election was held, there can be no valid objection to the bonds being issued for that purpose. This court has recognized in the case of Robinson v. Askew et al., 129 S.C. 188, 123 S.E. 822, that bonds can be issued many years after the election authorizing it; in that case the issue being sold four years after the election. This has been recognized in other jurisdictions. Miller v. Carbon County School Dist. No. 3, 5 Wyo. 217, 39 P. 879; Sutherland v. Board of Education, 209 Ky. 351, 272 S.W. 887. The only limitation which should affect the right to issue bonds under these circumstances is where the purposes for which the bonds were originally voted have ceased to be necessary, or where the conditions have so changed that it would be inequitable to allow the bonds to be issued, and, unless one of these conditions clearly appears to the satisfaction of the court, the exercise of their discretion by the trustees should not be interfered with.

Guides for Class Discussion

1. Are you in agreement with the reasoning followed by the court in arriving at its conclusion?
2. Could this line of reasoning make for an inequitable situation?
3. What did the court say about the length of time that might elapse between the date of voting the bonds and their issuance?
4. See *Hebel* v. *School District, infra.*

40. *"A taxpayer may bring action to enjoin the issuance of illegal bonds"* (p. 6).

Morgan v. Board of Supervisors,
67 Ariz. 133, 192 P. (2d) 236 (1948)
(Decided by the Supreme Court of Arizona)

[The facts of this case will be found in the material quoted below.]

Udall, Justice.

This is an appeal by Milo Morgan (plaintiff-appellant) from a judgment dismissing his complaint for injunctive and other relief against the Maricopa County Board of Supervisors and the Board of Trustees of Washington School District No. 6. The defendants will be termed appellees.

At a regularly called election held in said district on May 14, 1947, the vote was 308 in favor of the issuance and sale of bonds in the sum of $164,000, and 187 "bonds no" votes were cast. Appellant, who was a qualified elector and a real property taxpayer residing in the district, brought this suit for himself and all others similarly situated, seeking to void the results of the bond election by restraining the issuance and sale of the bonds thus voted.

The assignments of error, which will be stated more in detail later, contend that the lower court disregarded the constitutional limit of bonded indebtedness for school purposes and also challenge its implied finding that the election was fairly conducted, particularly as to the exclusion from voting of ex-service men and widows who had claimed exemption from payment of taxes.

If the bonds in the instant case are issued and sold unquestionably the property rights of the appellant and other taxpayers similarly situated would be involved; hence, appellant had the right to bring an action seeking injunctive relief on the ground that the constitutional limitation of indebtedness was exceeded.

"The right of properly interested persons to have an illegal issuance, sale, or delivery of the bonds of a political subdivision enjoined is so well settled as to be beyond dispute, and, as a matter of fact, is tacitly recognized by the courts and various litigants as a mere matter of course in many hundreds of decisions. . . ." 43 Am.Jur., Public Securities & Obligations, section 335, page 538. See also 43 C.J.S., Injunctions, § 121.

Guides for Class Discussion

1. Compare the decision in this case with the one rendered by the court in *Pickett* v. *Russell, supra;* and in *People* v. *Scott, supra.*
2. Do you feel the court was justified in ruling that plaintiff had the authority to bring the action?

41. "*While earlier decisions generally held that where statutes authorizing the issuance of school bonds prescribed the procedures to be followed, these statutes were mandatory, and failure to follow the procedures rendered the bonds illegal, more recent decisions hold that a substantial compliance with such statutes is all that is required and minor irregularities, questioned after the election has been held, will not void the election*" (p. 6).

STATE v. ALLEN,
102 Ohio. App. 315, 143 N.E. (2d) 159 (1955)
(Decided by the Court of Appeals of Ohio, Ross County)

[This was an action to compel a school district clerk to "sign a $500,000 note authorized by the board of education in anticipation of a like amount of bonds voted by the electors of the school district." The clerk defended on the ground that the figure for the average annual levy to pay the principal and interest on the bonds was incorrectly stated as 3.5 mills per dollar of valuation, instead of 4.2 mills, in both the notice of the election and on the face of the ballot. The statute required the publication of the figure indicating the average number of mills required to liquidate the principal and interest in both the notice and the ballot. In requiring the clerk to sign the note, the court commented rather extensively on the effect of the board's failure to comply strictly with the statute relating to the issuance of bonds.]

COLLIER, Judge.

. . . .

Counsel have not cited any authority directly in point and we have been unable to find any decision in which this identical question has been determined. However, there are many reported cases in Ohio dealing with irregularities and omissions in similar proceedings. The earlier decisions held that the provisions of the Uniform Bond Law, Chapter 133, Revised Code, should be strictly construed. The more recent decisions hold that a substantial compliance with the statutory requirements is all that is necessary. In the case of State ex rel. Board of Education of Springfield [*sic*] Local School Dist., Summit County, v. Maxwell, 144 Ohio St., 565, 60 N.E. 2d 183, 185, Judge Zimmerman states the rule as follows:

"It has been generally held that defects, variances and irregularities in the several steps relating to the issuance of bonds should be material, harmful or both before the proceeding may be successfully attacked. . . . It has also been held that unsubstantial irregularities in the resolution of a political subdivision inaugurating an election on a bond issue which do not prejudice anyone will be disregarded, especially where the proposed bond issue as submitted was approved by considerably more than the requisite number of electors."

The bond issue in the instant case carried by a majority of 75.8 per cent of the electors. Under the rule above quoted the test is whether the voters were misled by the mistake in the auditor's figures. To determine this question it is proper to consider the degree of the error, the nature of the calculation and the closeness of the vote. . . . It is probable that the actual amount required to retire the bonds may vary from year to year to a greater degree than the error discovered in the auditor's calculation. A statute requiring a statement of costs in ballots used in an election with reference to a public improvement is to be given a practical construction. . . .

A vital consideration in the determination as to whether an election should be declared invalid is the reluctance to reach a decision which would result in the disfranchisement of the voters. In the instant case more than three-fourths of the voters were in favor of the bond issue.

In all the cases we have examined, where the courts of Ohio have held elections invalid, there was a complete omission of some vital and jurisdictional condition to be performed. In the instant case there was no departure from the regular procedure prescribed by statute and all the proceedings were in conformity with the statutes.

Guides for Class Discussion

1. Compare this decision with the decision of the court in *Baker v. Scranton Independent School District, infra.*
2. Do you think this decision is equitable? Give reasons.

42. *"Elections to authorize the issuance of school bonds must be called by the proper authorities or the bonds will be void"* (p. 6).

Barry v. Board of Education,
23 N.M. 465, 169 P. 314 (1917)
(Decided by the Supreme Court of New Mexico)

[In this case the legality of bonds was questioned on the ground that the election at which they were authorized was not called by the proper authorities. The court agreed with this contention and held the bonds invalid.]

Roberts, J. . . .

On the 17th day of November, 1917, the appellants filed suit in the district court of Curry county against the board of education of the city of Clovis and A. Z. Rogers, the contractor, and in their complaint they set forth the facts as above stated, and further alleged that said bonds were illegal and void because such elections had not been called and held by the proper authorities; that such elections had been called and notice thereof given and the officers for conducting such elections had been appointed by the board of education of the city of Clovis; whereas, under the law such elections could only be legally called, held, and conducted by the mayor and city council of the city of Clovis. . . . The district court held the bonds to be valid and legal obligations of the school district and denied the injunction, from which judgment of the district court this appeal is prosecuted.

The only attack upon the validity of the bonds in question is that the election was not called and notice thereof given by the proper authorities. In the case of Board of Education v. Citizens' Nat. Bank, 167 Pac. 715, this court construed the statutes relative to voting bonds by municipal school districts and held that such an election should be called, held, and conducted in the same manner as school officials are elected, in so far as such procedure is applicable, and said that the election should be called by the city council, notice thereof given by the mayor, and the returns made to and canvassed by the city clerk and mayor, all as provided for in the case of election of the municipal school district officers. In the instant case appellees concede that the proper procedure in this regard was not followed, but insist that it was an irregularity in calling and conducting and holding the election which did not invalidate the result of the election, no fraud being practiced. They are wrong, however, in this contention.

Guides for Class Discussion

1. Are you in agreement with this decision? Give reasons.
2. Differentiate between this decision and the one rendered in *Baker* v. *Scranton Independent School District, infra.* Can they be reconciled? How?

43. *"Statutory provisions governing the giving of notice of elections for the issuance of bonds should be strictly followed, but courts are reluctant to hold bond elections void for mere irregularities and will not do so unless it can be shown that the irregularities complained of could have affected the results of the election"* (p. 6).

BAKER v. SCRANTON INDEPENDENT SCHOOL DISTRICT,
287 S.W. (2d) 210 (Tex.) (1956)
(Decided by the Court of Civil Appeals of Texas, Eastland)

[This case was an election contest resulting from certain alleged irregularities, including the posting of notices.]

COLLINGS, Justice.

. . . .

Appellant first contends that it is established by uncontroverted evidence that the notices of election were not posted as required by law and that the court therefore erred in rendering judgment sustaining the validity of the election. We cannot agree with this contention. . . . These notices were posted within the district for the length of time provided by the statute. One notice was posted on a telephone pole on the right-of-way of a farm to market road at the Eastland-Callahan County Line. Another was posted on the school house door at Scranton where the district maintains its school. The school year began during the posting period. A third notice was posted on a telegraph pole at the intersection of the Scranton-Nimrod-Cisco Highway. The evidence indicates that these notices were posted in conspicuous places where notices of election in the community were usually posted, and in the best places available for publicizing an election. Such posting of the election notices was in compliance with the statute. Appellant's first point is overruled.

.   .   .   .

Although the evidence shows the existence of irregularities in holding the election and that illegal votes were cast appellant's contention that the election was void is not well taken. The irregularities and omissions complained of involved statutory provisions which are directory. The failure to comply with such provisions does not invalidate an election unless there is fraud or serious misconduct, and the irregularities changed or contributed to changing the result of the election. . . . There is no evidence of fraud or misconduct or that the irregularities complained of affected the result of the election. On the contrary the evidence indicates that the results would have been the same regardless of the irregularities and omissions.

.   .   .   .

Even if the posting of the notices had not been in compliance with the statute the election would not have been void under the facts of this case. It is shown that only six qualified voters failed to vote because of lack of knowledge of the election. Four of these testified that they would have voted against the tax and bonds and the other two stated that they were for the tax and bond issue. Their votes would not have changed the result of the election and the irregularity in posting, if it had existed, would not have rendered the election void. . . . The fact that some qualified voters knew of the election and did not vote does not affect its validity. . . .

When all illegal votes are withdrawn from the announced result of the election and not counted and all qualified voters who were against the bond issue but failed to vote because of lack of knowledge of the election are added there is no change in the declared result of the election. A majority of the qualified voters in the district who voted or would have voted if the claimed irregularities had not existed were in favor of the propositions submitted. It appears that the election was fairly held and the result correctly declared. The court did not err in refusing to hold the election void. The judgment of the trial court is affirmed.

Guides for Class Discussion

1. Do you think the court acted equitably? Give reasons.
2. See *DuPont* v. *Mills, supra.*

44. "*In case the voters of a school district are called upon to authorize the issuance of bonds, the proceeds of which are to be used for separate and distinct purposes, they must be given the opportunity to vote on each proposition separately; otherwise the election will be held void because it violates the general principle that double propositions cannot be submitted as one. Frequently the courts are asked to rule on whether a stated purpose of two or more parts constitutes a single proposition*" (p. 6).

School District v. Michigan Municipal Finance Commission,
339 Mich. 96, 62 N.W. (2d) 445 (1954)
(Decided by the Supreme Court of Michigan)

[This was an appeal from an order of the municipal finance commission refusing permission to plaintiff to issue bonds as authorized by a bond election. Specifically the commission took the position that the election was illegal because the ballot " 'contained at least two separate and independent propositions.' " It stated that the bonds were to be issued " 'for the purpose of purchasing a new school bus, purchasing an additional school site, and erecting and furnishing an addition to the school building in said District.' " While recognizing the legal principle that the statement of purpose must concern a single proposition, the court ordered the commission to authorize plaintiff to issue the bonds, as the statement of purpose was but a single proposition.]

REID, Justice.

. . . .

. . . Defendant does not question the adoption by plaintiff district of the proposition of transportation of pupils.

The only question in the case is whether the ballot . . . contains separate and independent propositions.

. . . .

It is to be noted that the board of education in submitting the ballot, uses the words "for the purpose of" as though the three matters of new bus, additional site and addition to the school building, are considered by the board as part of *one* purpose; the language used with the word "purpose" in the singular, so implies. We conclude that the board of education intended and considered the submitted bonding proposition as a comprehensive plan to provide for the increased educational needs of the district.

. . . .

There has been a very great change in the attitude of the public toward use of school buses in the last 20 years, reflected by the present very extensive use of school buses. There is also a change of the legislation of the State relative to the purchase and operation of school buses, including enactment of the statute, Stat. Ann. 1953 Cum. Supp. § 15.520, which expressly permits bonding for the purchase of a bus. With the great change of attitude on the part of the public, the purchase of a bus is a matter no longer necessary to be considered separate and apart from the purchase of school sites and erection of school buildings.

The purchase of an additional or new school bus is not out of line with the purchase of a new school site and making addition to the present school building. Providing additional school building facilities probably would be useless without full attendance of children. The new school bus should be considered as a necessary incident to increased school facilities. The good faith and propriety of the board's proposition are fairly indicated. The necessity was for the voters to finally decide. The ballot should be considered to embody a comprehensive plan to provide for the increased educational needs of the district. The proposition as submitted was appropriate for submission. The vote was a valid approval of the bond issue.

Guides for Class Discussion

1. Do you agree with this decision? Give reasons.
2. In light of this decision, name two purposes that might not be considered as constituting a single proposition.

45. "Where recitals in school bonds relating to matters of fact, and made by those having authority to make them, contain statements that all conditions for their legal issuance have been complied with, the recitals estop the district from denying the validity of the bonds even though the recitals may in fact be false" (pp. 6-7).

GIBBS V. SCHOOL DISTRICT,
88 Mich. 334, 50 N.W. 294 (1891)
(Decided by the Supreme Court of Michigan)

[This action was brought to recover the amount of a bond issued by defendant. The records of the school district failed to show any legal authority for the issuance of the bond. There was no denial of the execution of the bond, however. The defense relied upon the failure of the record to show any legal authority for the issuance of the bond. The statute authorized school boards to issue bonds in certain amounts, in specified instances, upon a vote of the school district. While the record of the board meeting at which the bond was issued was not clear, there was a recital in the bond evidencing that the statute had been met. The question before the court was whether this recital in the bond was sufficient to protect a *bona fide* purchaser.]

CHAMPLIN, C. J. . . .

. . . Purchasers of municipal bonds are bound to know the extent and limitations upon the authority of the corporation to issue the bonds. They are bound, in other words, to know the law under which the authority is exercised. Purchasers of such securities have a right to rely upon all facts asserted or appearing upon the face of the bonds made by any person or body authorized by law to pass upon and determine the facts. In purchasing this bond the purchaser was bound to know that school-districts have no authority to issue bonds except for the purposes specified in the statute, and that their authority is limited by the number of scholars between 5 and 20 years then residing in the district; that there must be a two-thirds vote of the qualified electors in favor of their issue. The purchaser is chargeable with knowledge of the prerequisites of a legal special meeting, and of the provisions for a board of inspectors and their duties, and of the requirement that the vote shall be by ballot. The recitals in this bond are made by the director and moderator, who compose a majority of the schoolboard. Neither the schoolboard nor the moderator and director are authorized to issue the bonds unless voted by the district at a lawful meeting; and, under section 5104, before the board can act, they have a function to perform, in its nature somewhat judicial, and that is as to their own authority to issue the bonds. The statute limits that authority to bonds voted by the school-district, and consequently the question whether the proceedings to vote such bonds are such as will authorize the board to issue them must be passed upon by the board. A purchaser of the bonds, therefore, need look no further back than the face of the bonds for the facts which show a compliance with the law. We think the assertion appearing upon the face of the bond is sufficient evidence to an innocent purchaser that the board ordered and directed the bond to be issued. The officers signing the bond are two of the three officers who constitute the board, and the director is the officer who the statute requires should make a record of the proceedings of all district meetings and the orders, resolutions, and other proceedings of the board. It matters not, therefore, that the records kept by the board do not show the order of the board to execute the bonds. The title of a *bona fide* holder of the bond cannot be defeated by a neglect to enter the order in cases where the face of the bond upon which he has a right to rely recites the fact that such order was made.

. . . The law under which these bonds were issued authorized the school board to issue them, and made that board the body to determine when such facts existed; and hence when the bonds were issued by their orders, that fact appearing upon the face of the bond, a *bona fide* holder is entitled to recover, and, as against him, the district is not allowed to defend upon the ground that the law was not complied with previous to their determination to issue the bonds. The law having placed that responsibility with the district board, the school-district, if defrauded, must seek their remedy against such board.

Guides for Class Discussion

1. Do you think the court's reasoning is sound? Give your reasons.
2. Compare the decision in this case with the one rendered by the court in *Livingston* v. *School District, infra.*

46. ". . . *in case a school bond contains a recital with respect to a matter of law it will not bind a school district if it is false; in such a case there can be no such thing as an innocent purchaser because everyone is bound to determine the law for himself*" (p. 7).

LIVINGSTON V. SCHOOL DISTRICT,
9 S.D. 345, 69 N.W. 15 (1896)
(Decided by the Supreme Court of South Dakota)

[This was an action upon a bond issued by the defendant school district pursuant to a special act of the territorial legislature approved in 1879. The statute provided that no bonds in excess of $2,000 should be issued, and that the bonds should be issued in denominations of no more than $500 and no less than $50. The bond in this case was in the amount of $1,400. It was alleged the district had issued no other bond, and the question was whether this one was void because it was in an amount in excess of $500.]

HANEY, J. . . .

No question of fact is involved; nothing but a question of law: What construction shall be given the statute? The bond does not comply therewith. Is the provision in respect to denomination a limitation upon the power conferred, or merely a direction as to the manner of its exercise? Upon the answer to this question depends the validity of the security in the hands of even a bona fide holder. It was held in North Dakota that where a statute authorized the issue of municipal bonds, payable in not less than 10 years from date, bonds issued thereunder, payable in 11 days less than 10 years from date, are void, even in the hands of a bona fide purchaser. People's Bank of St. Paul v. School Dist. No. 52, 57 N.W. 787. That decision rests upon sound reason and abundant authority. We can discover no difference in principle between it and the case at bar. "If," in the language of Mr. Justice Corliss, "the question is to depend upon the magnitude of the departure from the statutory requirement, it will be impossible to know where to draw the line." Assuming $1,400 were required to pay for defendant's schoolhouse, and, as alleged in the complaint, such house was furnished by the original payees, by whom the bond was taken without discount, it may be suggested that the district could not be affected by the fact that payment was made with a single bond of $1,400, when there should have been two of $500 each, and one of $400. Doubtless, in this particular instance the materiality of the difference is not apparent, but the wisdom of the requirement does not concern this court. There are cases in which the denomination of municipal securities is a matter of vital importance,—a matter peculiarly within the legislative discretion. Should the court disregard the plain provisions of this special statute, and substitute its own notions of public policy for those adopted by the legislature, a way would be open for the annulment of all restrictions upon the exercise of municipal powers.

There is much practical wisdom in the observation of Chief Justice Tripp in the case of Dartmouth Sav. Bank v. School Dists. Nos. 6 and 31, 6 Dak. 332, 43 N.W. 826. He says: "While courts are disposed to protect the rights of innocent purchasers, and to uphold commercial paper, the rights of a people will be much better protected, and the principles of commercial law sufficiently extended, by requiring all persons dealing with public officers and public corporations to inquire into their powers, and see that they are authorized to enter into the contract they assume to make." Defendant's officers and the original payees of the bond sued upon, either wantonly or through inexcusable carelessness, disregarded an express provision of law. Plaintiff purchased the bond with notice of such conduct on their part, and cannot complain if compelled to suffer the consequences. The district was clothed with power to issue bonds of a certain and clearly-defined description. It was not authorized to issue bonds of any other description. There was want of power to issue such a bond as the one sued upon. Therefore the bond is void.

Guides for Class Discussion

1. Are you in agreement with this decision? Give reasons.
2. Compare this case with *Gibbs* v. *School District, supra.*
3. Do you think the same principle of law should be applied to recitals with respect to matters of fact as to recitals with respect to matters of law? Why or why not?

47. *"The holder of an illegal bond, one that has been issued without authority or in violation of some constitutional or statutory provision, cannot recover on the bond against the district even though he may be an innocent purchaser"* (p. 7).

First National Bank of Decorah v. District Township of Doon,
86 Iowa 330, 53 N.W. 301 (1892)
(Decided by the Supreme Court of Iowa)

[This was an action to recover the amount alleged to be due on certain bonds issued by the defendant. Plaintiff claimed to have purchased the bonds in good faith for a valuable consideration, without any knowledge or notice of any matter affecting their validity. The defendant, on the other hand, claimed the bonds were fraudulent and void because they were issued without consideration, and because the judgment for the payment of which they purported to have been issued was paid and canceled before the date of issuance; and also because of a constitutional provision that provided that no political or municipal corporation could become indebted in any manner to an amount in the aggregate exceeding 5 per cent of the taxable property within such corporation. Plaintiff contended that the bonds were issued to satisfy a judgment and that the defendant was estopped from questioning their validity.

[The lower court found that the judgment on account of which the bonds were issued had been satisfied before they were issued; that they were issued fraudulently and in violation of the constitutional provision mentioned, and, as a result, held that they were void in the hands of the plaintiff. Defendant's record concerning the authorization for the issuance of bonds was not available, but it was shown that a diligent search for such a record had been made. The higher court held that "the circumstantial evidence is quite satisfactory, and fully justified the district court in finding that the judgment was paid in the year named, and that the attempt to revive it and the issuing of the bonds in suit were fraudulent." In arriving at its decision the court found it necessary to rule on the right of an innocent purchaser to collect on bonds issued illegally.]

Robinson, C. J. . . .

. . . .

... This court is committed to the doctrine that the purchaser of negotiable bonds issued by a municipal corporation is charged with notice that
the indebtedness of the corporation is in excess of the amount limited by
the constitution. In French v. Burlington, 42 Iowa, 617, it was said that
"he who contracts with a city, whereby an indebtedness is created, must,
at his peril, take notice of the financial standing and condition of the city,
and whether the proposed indebtedness is in excess of the constitutional
limitation." True, that case does not involve the rights of an innocent
purchaser of negotiable bonds, but it is authority for the conclusion that
bonds issued on a contract which created a debt in excess of the constitutional limitations would be invalid. In McPherson v. Foster, 43 Iowa, 59,
the validity of bonds issued by an independent district for the building
of a schoolhouse in excess of the amount permitted by the constitution
was considered, and they were held to be void in the hands of purchasers
without actual notice of the fact. In Mosher v. School Dist., 44 Iowa, 124,
it was said of bonds of a municipal corporation, issued in excess of the
constitutional limitation: "The bonds and coupons attached are void,
without regard to the good faith with which they are purchased, and the
want of notice of their invalidity by the holders." In Kane v. Independent
Dist., 47 N.W. Rep. 1076, this court, in approving a decree of the district
court, which set aside a judgment rendered on alleged indebtedness in
excess of the constitutional limitation, used language as follows: "A party
who becomes the creditor of a municipal corporation must, at his peril,
take notice of the fact that its indebtedness is in excess of the constitutional
limitation." See, also, Doon Tp. v. Cummins, 142 U.S. 366, 12 Sup. Ct.
Rep. 220, for a discussion as to constitutional limitations. The evidence
submitted fully justified the district court in finding that the bonds in suit
were issued contrary to the constitutional inhibition. The fact that defendant caused taxes to be levied, and the interest on the bonds to be paid
for a term of years, is immaterial. Having no power to issue the bonds,
its acts in levying taxes for their payment and paying interest were illegal,
and neither gave validity to the bonds nor estopped defendant to assert
their invalidity.

Guides for Class Discussion

1. Compare this decision with the one rendered by the court in
   Gibbs v. School District, supra; and with the one in *Livingston
   v. School District, supra.* Is there any conflict between them?
2. Do you think the rule laid down by the court in this case was
   equitable? Give reasons.

48. "In some states . . . it has been held that where illegal bonds have been sold and the proceeds applied to the purposes of the district, the holder of a bond may recover on quantum meruit" (p. 7).

LIVINGSTON V. SCHOOL DISTRICT,
11 S.D. 150, 76 N.W. 301 (1898)
(Decided by the Supreme Court of South Dakota)

[Following the earlier decision by this court in the same case (See Case No. 46) in which the court declared a certain bond unauthorized and void, plaintiff brought this action "to recover, as on a quantum meruit, the value of a school house in settlement for which said bond was issued, and which the defendant has ever since retained."]

FULLER, J. . . . For the purposes of this appeal it is conceded by the demurrer that, pursuant to contract, a school house worth $1,400 was erected and furnished by a predecessor of respondent's assignor, which appellant duly accepted, and has ever since retained for the continuous use of the district, and the exact question to be determined is whether, under such a state of facts, respondent is entitled to recover the reasonable value of the building of which appellant has thus received the full benefit. While the doctrine denying relief to all who contract with reference to a subject-matter malum in se is well recognized, the rule that, where a contract is merely malum prohibitum, courts will take notice of circumstances, and in the interest of common honesty grant such relief as justice and equity may require, rests as securely upon principle, and is equally sustained by authority. . . . It would violate the plainest rules of good faith to permit appellant, without any consideration, to retain everything of value received in exchange for a bond executed by itself in a denomination unauthorized; and, while respondent cannot recover upon the instrument, he is entitled to relief against it. . . . Although no enforceable right emanates from the bond, it was proper to allege the successive preliminary steps taken by the board in strict conformity with a special act authorizing the district to issue its bonds for the erection of a school house, so that the court may require performance on the part of appellant as nearly in accordance with the terms of the contract as the law and equity will permit.

Guides for Class Discussion

1. Compare the decision in this case with the one in *Appeal of Luburg, infra;* and *Board of Trustees* v. *Postel, infra.*

2. On which basis did the court arrive at its decision? Are you in agreement with it?

49. *"Generally, the courts permit the purchaser of an illegal bond to recover the money paid for it if it has not been so commingled with the other money of the district that it cannot be identified; and they will also permit the purchaser of an illegal bond to recover property bought with the proceeds from the sale of such a bond provided no other money of the district was used to purchase the property"* (p. 7).

BOARD OF TRUSTEES V. POSTEL,
121 Ky. 67, 88 S.W. 1065 (1905)
(Decided by the Court of Appeals of Kentucky)

[The facts of this case will be found in the following quoted material.]

HOBSON, C. J. In the year 1897 the trustees of the Fordsville graded common school district issued bonds to the amount of $4,000 on behalf of the district for the purpose of providing it with a lot, schoolhouse, and suitable furniture. The bonds were sold, and the trustees used the proceeds of the sale in buying a lot, building a schoolhouse, and furnishing it. But no vote of the legal voters of the district was taken before the issual of the bonds, and they were adjudged void. . . . The holders of the bonds, being in part the original purchasers and in part persons who had bought the bonds from them, instituted this action in equity asking that the lot, house and furniture which was purchased with the proceeds of the bonds be transferred to them; and, the court having adjudged them the relief sought, the school district appeals.

. . . .

. . . The money which the plaintiffs paid is distinctly traced into the schoolhouse, the lot, and furniture, and no other money went into them. This property can be reclaimed, without taking any other property with it or injuring any other person or interfering with his rights. . . .

No liability, direct or indirect, may be imposed upon the school district under the bonds in question. It is not liable on the bonds, nor can it be made liable by indirection in any way. But, if we ignore the bond transaction altogether, what have we? The district received $4,000 from the bondholders. The bonds being void, the district should have returned the money to the bondholders. If the bondholders had learned of the invalidity of the bonds while the district still had the $4,000 in its treasury which they had paid to it, manifestly a court of equity would have required the district to pay back their money to them. It was money obtained by a mutual mistake. While under the Constitution no liability would attach to the district for the money if it had lost it, or if it had spent it and the fund could not be identified and followed, where it may be followed and identified, there is no more reason why property which represents the fund should not be returned than there would be for not returning the money, if it had been placed in a bag and the district had the bag locked up in its safe. . . . A loss must not be placed upon the district; but, when justice may be done without inflicting any loss upon the district, equity will lay hold of the conscience of the parties and make them do what is just and right. . . .

. . . The true owner of a fund may in equity pursue it, where it is clearly identified, equally whether it has been transmuted by the holder into personalty or realty. Properly, under the statute, he should not be adjudged the land, but a sale of it to satisfy the claim. But in this case appellants are not prejudiced by the form of the judgment, as the property is not of value more than the fund. We see no reason why the right to follow a fund should not be applied against municipalities under the clause of the Constitution above quoted, just as it is against other persons obtaining the property of another under a void contract, where the fund may be identified and is separated from other property of the municipality. The present holders of the bonds stand by subrogation in the shoes of the original purchasers from whom they bought, and under the Code the action may be maintained in the name of the real party in interest.

Guides for Class Discussion

1. Compare the decision in this case with those in *Livingston* v. *School District, supra;* and *Appeal of Luburg, supra.*
2. Do you think the court's reasoning is sound?
3. Does this decision encourage or put a premium upon doing that which is illegal?

50. "*In determining whether the indebtedness limit of a school district has been exceeded, the courts commonly hold that the limitation is upon the net and not the gross debt—the gross debt includes all legal obligations of the district including bonds, contracts and interest accrued; the net debt is determined by subtracting from this gross debt, cash on hand or in a sinking fund, taxes levied but not yet collected, . . . and any other assets which may be applied to the payment of debts*" (pp. 7-8).

LOLLICH v. HOT SPRINGS INDEPENDENT SCHOOL DISTRICT,
47 S.D. 624, 201 N.W. 354 (1924)
(Decided by the Supreme Court of South Dakota)

[The facts of the case are to be found in the material quoted.]

POLLEY, J. On the 26th day of February, 1924, the board of education of Hot Springs independent school district No. 10, pursuant to a resolution theretofore duly adopted, held an election to determine the proposition of issuing and selling bonds of said school district in the sum of $86,800, for the purpose of building a high school building in said district. At such election the affirmative of said proposition carried by a large majority. The board thereupon proceeded to issue and offer said bonds for sale, when the plaintiff herein, a resident taxpayer of said school district, brought this action, for the purpose of enjoining the issue and sale of said bonds.

The ground upon which said injunction is asked is that the indebtedness of $86,800, to be created by the issuance of said bonds together with an existing indebtedness of $48,500, will exceed the constitutional limit of indebtedness of 5 per cent. of the assessed value of the assessable property in said school district. Section 7, art. 13, S. D. Const. The school district demurred to plaintiff's complaint. The trial court overruled said demurrer, and defendants, school district, board of education, and the president and secretary of said board appeal.

From the allegations in the complaint, the truth of which is admitted by the demurrer, it appears that the assessed value of the property in the district is $1,736,408. Five per cent. of this amount equals $86,820.40. The existing indebtedness of the district is $48,500, which with the amount of the proposed bond issue is $135,300. But the district has cash assets in its treasury of $40,197.08, and taxes levied and in process of collection amounting to $40,000. These two items amount to $80,197.08, and defendants contend they are entitled to have this amount deducted from $135,300, in order to determine the true indebtedness of the district, including the said bond issue.

The facts presented by this record are parallel to the facts in McCavick v. School District, 25 S.D. 449, 127 N.W. 476. In that case the assessed value of the property in the defendant school district was $145,975. Five per cent. of this amounted to $7,748.75. The incurred indebtedness was $9,589.05, but the district had net assets to the amount of $427.80, and $2,000 in taxes levied and in process of collection. These two amounts deducted from $9,589.05 left $7,161.70, or $587.50 less than the constitutional limit. This court held that the indebtedness was within the constitutional limit. In this case the two items of assets, $40,000 of taxes levied and in the process of collection, and $40,197.08, deducted from $135,300 leaves only $55,102.92 net indebtedness, and considerably less than the constitutional limit of $86,820.40. Following the rule announced by this court in McCavick v. School District, supra, and in Williamson v. Aldrich, 21 S.D. 13, 108 N.W. 1063, the defendant may issue and sell the said bonds in the amount of $86,000 without exceeding the constitutional limit of indebtedness and said bonds when issued and sold will constitute a valid indebtedness against said school district.

The order appealed from is reversed.

Guides for Class Discussion

1. Do you think taxes levied but not collected should be considered as assets of a district? Give reasons.
2. See *Mannsville Consolidated School District* v. *Williamson, infra* and *Prohm* v. *Non-High School District, infra.*

51. *"In determining whether the indebtedness limit of a school district has been exceeded, . . . some courts hold that delinquent taxes may be regarded as . . . assets [to be deducted from the gross indebtedness]"* (pp. 7-8).

RIDGELAND SCHOOL DISTRICT v. BIESMANN,
71 S.D. 82, 21 N.W. (2d) 324 (1946)
(Decided by the Supreme Court of South Dakota)

[This action was brought to determine the validity of a large number of the district's warrants, which it was contended were void because they were issued for obligations which had been incurred after the constitutional debt limit had been reached. One of the big questions before the court was that of determining what the constitutional debt limit was. In so doing, it found it necessary to rule on the question of whether delinquent taxes were to be considered as assets that should be deducted from the gross indebtedness in order to determine net indebtedness.]

BENSON, Circuit Judge.

  .   .   .   .

In arriving at the debt of a school district for the purpose of the constitutional prohibition it is agreed that bonds, unpaid warrants and interest on both should be totaled to arrive at the gross debt, from this should be deducted the cash on hand and at least the amount of the current tax levy. . . .

  .   .   .   .

It is respondent's contention that not only the current tax levy but also the delinquent taxes for at least five prior years should be deducted from the gross debt. . . .

  .   .   .   .

There is a sharp conflict between the decisions of the several states, some holding that uncollected taxes for years prior to the current year may be deducted from the gross debt. However, in Mansville [sic] Consolidated School District No. 7, Johnson [sic] County v. Williamson, 174 Okla. 18, 49 P.2d 749, 752, the court says:

"The better reasoned cases hold that only cash on hand and available assets and resources readily convertible into cash should be considered deductible assets and subtracted from the outstanding indebtedness. To us this seems the better rule. Delinquent taxes are not readily convertible into cash."

"School districts and other municipal and political divisions of the state should pursue a sound business policy in their fiscal management. To consider as assets delinquent taxes which are not only not readily convertible into cash but are improbable of collection violates that policy. . . ."

We would be inclined to agree with the Oklahoma court except that . . . the contrary doctrine is firmly entrenched in the law of this state.

In Lollich v. Hot Springs School District No. 10, supra, the court allowed the deduction of taxes levied and in process of collection amounting to $40,000. It is not clear from this court's opinion whether such taxes constituted the current levy or the levy for prior years. An examination of the record in that case, however, discloses that the $40,000 constituted taxes levied and uncollected for years prior to the then current levy. Thus the doctrine, pernicious though it is, has been established to cover not only current but delinquent taxes so that they may be deducted from the gross debt in determining that debt for constitutional purposes. . . .

Deducting such current and delinquent taxes from the gross debt in each year involved in this case brings the debt well within the constitutional limitation. It follows, therefore, that the judgment of the trial court must be affirmed.

Guides for Class Discussion

1. See *Lollich* v. *Hot Springs Independent School District, supra.*
2. Compare the decision in this case with the one in *Mannsville Consolidated School District* v. *Williamson, infra.* Which do you think represents the better law?

52. *"In determining whether the indebtedness limit of a school district has been exceeded, . . . some courts hold that delinquent taxes . . . cannot be . . . regarded [as assets to be deducted from the gross indebtedness]"* (pp. 7-8).

MANNSVILLE CONSOLIDATED SCHOOL DISTRICT v. WILLIAMSON,
174 Okla. 18, 49 P. (2d) 749 (1935)
(Decided by the Supreme Court of Oklahoma)

[This was an action to compel the Attorney General, an ex officio Bond Commissioner of the State of Oklahoma, to approve $12,000 of bonds issued by the plaintiff district. Defendant contended that the issue, together with other existing indebtedness of the district, exceeded the constitutional maximum for which the plaintiff might become indebted. In arriving at its decision, the court found it necessary to decide, among other things, whether delinquent taxes should be considered as assets of the district and therefore deducted from the over-all or gross indebtedness.]

GIBSON, Justice.

. . . .

An examination of the decisions of other states having similar constitutional provisions with reference to debt limitations discloses a sharp conflict between them. The better reasoned cases hold that only cash on hand and available assets and resources readily convertible into cash should be considered deductible assets and subtracted from the outstanding indebtedness. To us this seems the better rule. Delinquent taxes are not readily convertible into cash. Nor do our statutes under which the collection of delinquent taxes can be enforced insure the collection of such taxes in cash. Property sold to the county at the annual tax sales, for lack of individual purchasers, may be resold under our statute; but if at such sale it cannot be sold to individual purchasers, the county becomes the purchaser and owner in fee of the property sold for delinquent taxes, and the taxes are canceled. Such property does not become assets of the county, or of the school district in which the property may be located, that may be considered in determining the net indebtedness of such county or any municipal subdivision thereof. Nor are the proceeds of sale of such property, if and when sold by the county, allocable to the payment of the warrant indebtedness of the school district or other municipal subdivision of the county.

School districts and other municipal and political divisions of the state should pursue a sound business policy in their fiscal management. To consider as assets delinquent taxes which are not only not readily convertible into cash but are improbable of collection violates that policy, and in our opinion violates the laws of this state.

Guides for Class Discussion

1. Compare the decision in this case with the one rendered by the court in *Ridgeland School District* v. *Biesmann, supra.* Which represents the better law?
2. Do you think that the position taken by the court in this case makes for a sound business policy for the fiscal management of the school? Why or why not?
3. See *Lollich* v. *Hot Springs Independent School District, supra.*

53. "*Most courts hold that refunding bonds do not increase a school district's indebtedness; they merely change its form*" (p. 8).

PROHM V. NON-HIGH SCHOOL DISTRICT,
7 Ill. (2d) 421, 130 N.E. (2d) 917 (1955)
(Decided by the Supreme Court of Illinois)

[Plaintiff brought this action to enjoin the extension of a tax levy provided for by a refunding bond resolution. The plaintiff's land upon which the tax in question was to be levied had been detached from defendant district. At the time of the detachment, the territory within the defendant's boundaries, including plaintiff's property was "subject to taxation to pay the principal due upon certain outstanding legal bonds, both funding and refunding, of said district in the aggregate sum of $2,448,000, and interest thereon." About six months after plaintiff's land had been detached from defendant district the board of education refunded the outstanding bonds by the adoption of a refunding bond and tax levy resolution calling for the issuance of refunding bonds in the amount of $2,448,000 and the levy of taxes to pay the principal and interest thereon. It was to enjoin the tax levy authorized by this resolution that this action was brought.

[Defendant's action was taken under authority of a statute that made all the property included in a non-high school district at the time bonds were issued or tuition claims accrued liable for its share of such indebtedness. Plaintiff contended this law was unconstitutional because it violated a constitutional provision that provided for the levying of taxes by a municipal corporation " 'within the jurisdiction of the body composing it.' " (Section 9, Article XI). He reasoned that because his property was not a part of defendant district at the time the refunding resolution was passed by the board, it had no application to his property. Defendant argued that the enactment of the resolution did not create a new obligation but simply changed the nature of the obligation that already existed. With this the court was in complete agreement.]

DAVIS, Justice.

. . . .

The defendants contend that the refunding-bond resolution merely authorizes the issuance of refunding bonds and tax levies to pay the same in such a manner as to prevent future defaults in existing bonds and spreads the burden over the years more evenly; and that there is no change in the indebtedness, but merely a revision of the maturities and method of payment of the already existing bonded indebtedness.

The general statement that all post-detachment tax levies are unlawful is both inaccurate and misleading. Section 9 of article IX of the constitution does not extinguish the existing bonded indebtedness of the territory wherein plaintiff resides upon the detachment of said territory from Non-High School District No. 216; nor does it prevent the levy of taxes by the county clerk of Cook County, as provided for in the bond resolutions duly filed in said office, even though such levies are made for the payment of principal and interest on said bonds, due after the effective date of the detachment.

. . . .

This court has, on several occasions, held that detached territory remains liable for predetachment debts and subject to tax levy to pay said debts if a statute so provides at the time of such detachment. . . .

. . . .

The plaintiff was obligated to pay her share of the bonded indebtedness existing before the detachment of her property and this obligation was affected neither by subsequent detachment nor by the refunding of the bonded indebtedness. The new levy for the refunding bonds merely continues, in a new form, the prior levy for the funding and refunding bonds which were still a subsisting debt upon the detached territory, and the constitutional prohibition against taxation of territory beyond the boundaries of a municipality is not pertinent.

Guides for Class Discussion

1. Differentiate between "funding" and "refunding" bonds.
2. What line of reasoning motivated the court?
3. Compare this decision with the one rendered in *Hebel* v. *School District, infra.*

54. *"Some courts . . . hold that refunding bonds . . . increase the indebtedness of a school district"* (p. 8).

STATE v. ROSS,
43 Wash. 290, 86 P. 575 (1906)
(Decided by the Supreme Court of Washington)

[The facts of this case are narrated in the material which follows.]

FULLERTON, J. School district No. 93 of Snohomish county issued bonds in the sum of $1,500 for the purpose, as expressed in the original resolution authorizing their issuance, of paying "warrants issued for building and furnishing a schoolhouse for said district and other expenses in connection therewith." These bonds were tendered the state as an investment for the permanent school fund, and were accepted as such by the board having authority to invest that fund. Before the transfer could be completed the Attorney General on his own relation instituted this proceeding to restrain the board from proceeding further in the matter on the ground that the bond issue was illegal. In his petition the Attorney General recites that the school district at the time the bonds were issued had an existing indebtedness equal to the amount of the bonds, and that by issuing the bonds it had increased its indebtedness to such an extent that the same exceeded the amount for which it could lawfully become indebted under the constitutional limitation by more than $700; that the bonds issued were for that reason illegal and void, and not bonds of the character in which the board of state land commissioners could lawfully invest the permanent school fund. The trial court sustained the contention of the Attorney General, and this appeal is taken from the judgment entered prohibiting the purchase of the bonds.

The attorney for the appellant contends that, inasmuch as the resolution of the board of directors of the school district shows that the purpose of the district in issuing the bonds was to use the money derived from their sale in taking up and canceling its outstanding warrant indebtedness, the indebtedness of the district is not thereby increased, since the bonds were intended to merely change the form of the indebtedness; the chief purpose being to reduce the rate of interest. He frankly concedes that his position is directly contrary to that taken by this court in the case of State ex rel. Jones v. McGraw, 12 Wash. 541, 41 Pac. 893, but he argues that that case is opposed, not only to the great weight of authority, but to the better reason as well, and should be overruled. The case cited holds that bonds issued under circumstances such as were had in this case are invalid on the principle that the debt is necessarily increased while the exchange is being made, and whether or not it is permanently so depends on the application that is made of the money received from the sale of the bonds. If it is applied to extinguish the outstanding obligations, the debt is not permanently increased, while if it is applied to current expenses, or in some manner as not to decrease these outstanding obligations, the debt is so increased; and "it would be inconsistent alike with the words and with the object of the constitutional provision, framed to protect municipal corporations from being loaded with debt beyond a certain limit, to make their liability to be charged with debts beyond that limit depend solely upon the honesty of their officers." But while this may be a somewhat technical view of the matter, and may be opposed to the weight of authority upon the question, we think the reason given for the decision sufficiently substantial to warrant us in adhering to it.

Guides for Class Discussion

1. Compare this decision with the one rendered in *Prohm* v. *Non-High School District, supra*. Which represents the better law?
2. What line of reasoning motivated the court in arriving at the decision it did?

55. *"In determining whether the amount of bonded indebtedness is within the debt limit, it is generally held that it is the amount of such indebtedness that exists at the time the bonds are issued and not at the time they are voted that governs"* (p. 8).

Hebel v. School District,
131 Colo. 105, 279 P. (2d) 673 (1955)
(Decided by the Supreme Court of Colorado)

[After a bond election had approved the issuance of bonds "from time to time" in an amount not to exceed $10,000,000, this action was brought to test its legality. The total amount of the bonds approved would have created a debt in excess of the constitutional limit, but the board issued them at various times in amounts that kept the total indebtedness within the limits prescribed. Nevertheless plaintiffs contended the election was ineffective as it authorized the issuance of bonds in an amount that was excessive.]

HOLLAND, Justice.

.   .   .   .

The prayer of the petition was for the declaration of the rights, status and legal relationship between petitioners and the Board, and for a determination by the court as to the time when the limit of bonded indebtedness of the district should be computed, whether at the time of the election at which bonds are authorized or the time when the bonds were actually issued.

To this petition for declaratory judgment and injunction, defendant school district and defendant members of the board of education of said district filed a motion to dismiss on the ground that the petition failed to state a claim upon which relief could be granted. The trial court sustained this motion and plaintiffs elected to stand upon the petition. Whereupon a declaratory judgment was entered by the court, denying the claims of plaintiffs for relief and declaring that the lawful limit of the . . . bonded indebtedness is to be determined by the assessed valuation of the taxable property at the time of the issuance or delivery of the bonds and not at the time or date of the election at which time bonds were authorized.

.   .   .   .

It seems to be conceded that the bonds issued in the instant case were within the debt limit at the time of their issuance. . . . The fixing of the proposal of the amount is for a future indebtedness and not one as fixed or limited at the time of the calling of an election or of the date of the election. . . . The board, in arranging for an election and the time thereof, is not required to determine the date on which the bonds are to be issued. In the last analysis, the function of the board is to propose and suggest an amount; the electors determine whether the bonds shall be issued, and in the case before us, the electors from the ballot in their hands were informed that the bonds were to be issued from time to time within the then lawful limit. The arrangement and plan submitted to the electors was for future operation and it was proposed that an indebtedness was to be contracted and evidenced by bonds issued "from time to time." "Time to time" could only be at such times when the property valuations of the year before would keep the issue within the statutory limit. Of course, the authorization when once adopted by the electors is not to be considered as an authorization for all future time, but only for such time as is reasonable, necessary or prudent.

Guides for Class Discussion

1. Are you in agreement with this decision? Give reasons.
2. How would the court have held had an attempt been made to issue all the bonds at once?

SELECTED BIBLIOGRAPHY

1. Edwards, Newton. *The Courts and the Public Schools,* rev. ed. Chicago: University of Chicago Press, 1955.
2. Garber, Lee O. (Ed.) *Law and the School Business Manager.* Danville, Ill.: The Interstate Printers & Publishers, Inc., 1957.
3. Garber, Lee O. *Yearbook of School Law.* "School Finance." Danville, Ill.: The Interstate Printers & Publishers, Inc., annually since 1950.
4. Hamilton, Robert H. and Paul R. Mort. *The Law and Public Education,* rev. ed. Brooklyn: The Foundation Press, Inc., 1959.
5. Hamilton, Robert R. and E. Edmund Reutter, Jr. *Legal Aspects of School Board Operation.* New York: Bureau of Publications, Teachers College, Columbia University, 1958.
6. Reutter, E. Edmund, Jr. *Schools and the Law.* ("Legal Almanac Series," No. 17.) New York: Oceana Publications, Inc., 1960.